DOING CHRISTIAN ETHICS

FROM THE MARGINS

Doing Christian Ethics from the Margins

Third Edition

Miguel A. De La Torre

ORBIS BOOKS
Maryknoll, New York 10545

Founded in 1970, Orbis Books endeavors to publish works that enlighten the mind, nourish the spirit, and challenge the conscience. The publishing arm of the Maryknoll Fathers and Brothers, Orbis seeks to explore the global dimensions of the Christian faith and mission, to invite dialogue with diverse cultures and religious traditions, and to serve the cause of reconciliation and peace. The books published reflect the views of their authors and do not represent the official position of the Maryknoll Society. To learn more about Maryknoll and Orbis Books, please visit our website at www.orbis-books.com.

Manufactured in the United States of America

Library of Congress Cataloging-in-Publication Data

Names: De La Torre, Miguel A., author.
Title: Doing Christian ethics from the margins / Miguel A. De La Torre.
Description: Third edition. | Maryknoll, NY : Orbis Books, 2023. | Includes bibliographical references and index. | Summary: "Develops the hermeneutic circle of liberation theology for ethical action"— Provided by publisher.
Identifiers: LCCN 2023017742 (print) | LCCN 2023017743 (ebook) | ISBN 9781626985346 | ISBN 9781608339914 (epub)
Subjects: LCSH: Christian ethics—Textbooks. | Marginality, Social—Moral and ethical aspects—Textbooks.
Classification: LCC BJ1251 .D38 2023 (print) | LCC BJ1251 (ebook) | DDC 241—dc23/eng/20230614
LC record available at https://lccn.loc.gov/2023017742
LC ebook record available at https://lccn.loc.gov/2023017743

To my brother Ricky

Contents

Prefaces and Acknowledgments

Preface to the 2024 edition

People change. So do academicians. I am no different. Scholars holding the same views professed twenty years earlier probably have not grown, refusing to engage the challenges arising within their field. What I assumed to be relatively true (lowercase "t") twenty years ago now seems more ambiguous. Concepts I embraced with confidence back then now seem to me naïve, if not somewhat cringeworthy. I find I know less now than I did back then, I am less sure of my opinions, and I hold greater doubts. And surely, I am less hopeful about the future. This is not necessarily a bad thing. The hubris of my conclusions during my early academic career have given way to a more nuanced understanding of reality. In the rewritten conclusion to this edition, you will notice I bring my personal thoughts into greater conversation with this book, more so than in the two previous editions.

But one method has remained constant in my thoughts: the epistemological privilege of the marginalized. Their pain and their suffering continue to inform a perspective that I believe continues to hold a greater grasp of reality than those who are more privileged by power and profit. Because my ethical analysis remains rooted at the margins, my overall conclusion—even as my views shift and change—remains grounded in a certainty that they are closer to reality. This is not to argue that those on the margins are smarter or holier; it is a recognition that, to survive, they must be fluid in understanding the ethical perspectives of those claiming morality but nonetheless remain complicit with oppressive and repressive social structures.

The book you hold is the product of almost two decades of thoughts concerning the same issues. What I find amazing is that we continue to wrestle with these issues, at times making little progress. As I bring this third edition to its conclusion, the reader will benefit by seeing how an issue, first explored in 2004, has morphed over twenty years. Updating concepts by paying close attention to the now reveals a historical trajectory that was first explored shortly after the start of a new millennium. But also, if close attention is paid, the astute reader will also notice a change in the author.

Acknowledgments for the 2024 Edition

For almost twenty years, since obtaining my doctorate, I have been doing Christian ethics from the margins. Two decades of seeking to hear the testimonies of the disenfranchised, the dispossessed, and the disinherited have taught me that we live in a more economically oppressed world today than when I first began to conduct research. We also live in a more racist and more sexist world. If proof ever existed that the enlightened concept of history's progression was a myth accepted as true through blind faith, it is evident in the lives of those living on the margins of society. The wars we assumed were winding down in the last edition continued for a second decade. A newly minted father who joined the armed forces after 9/11 as an expression of patriotism was joined on the battlefield by their child. The postracial naiveté many believed arrived with the election of the first Black president gave way to a whitelash as hate groups proliferated. A global pandemic not seen since the 1918 Spanish Flu [*sic*] has brought the global economy to a standstill. As a nation, we fell into the worst economic crisis since the Great Depression, dwarfing the pain caused by the 2008 Great Recession. Unsurprisingly, US citizens of color were disproportionately dying from the virus when compared to their white counterparts and feeling the brunt of the economic devastation. We experienced four years of a presidential administration that exploited racist tropes to consolidate power, and when the 2020 election was lost, the president instigated an insurrection. His followers stormed the Capitol to undo the electoral vote of the people.

In the past decade, the world radically changed. These changes were so profound that the first two editions have become obsolete. As I write this new edition, I am cognizant of the danger of allowing the principalagent for many of these monumental shifts, Donald Trump, to suck up all the book's oxygen. Although it can be difficult to remember, he is but a symptom of generational institutionalized social structures—the sneeze of a cold, the pus of a wound. I kept the focus on the structures of oppression and not any singular person.

I am deeply grateful for the trust Orbis Books has placed in me to do this rewrite. I am also thankful for my research assistants, Rudy Reyes and Hesron Sihombing, who spent a year tracking documented sources so that my writing task could be easier to accomplish. A special thanks is also due to Leslie Diane Poston for proofreading the manuscript. The children whom I acknowledged in the first edition, who were recent college graduates in the second edition, are now young adults (one of which made me an *abuelo*), struggling to survive in an economy that has provided them with fewer opportunities than those considered baby boomers. And like always, a special thanks to my wife (who is now pursuing her own PhD) with whom we debate the ethical issues arising in the daily news each morning as we drink *café con leche* together.

Preface to the 2014 Edition

My students and I were sitting on a dirt-floor hut in a squatter village on the outskirts of Cuernavaca, Mexico. Joining me were mostly white, economically privileged students who sought to learn about God from the poor. Our "teacher" that day was an illiterate *mestiza* who was patiently answering our questions (with me serving as translator). We asked who God is to her. Who is Jesus Christ? Who is the Virgin Mary? Her answers, theologically speaking, were frightful. They were a mixture of superstition and popular Catholicism. It soon became clear she lacked orthodoxy—correct doctrine. Then her barefooted boy (about eleven years old) entered the one-room hut with a few pesos earned selling Chiclets to tourists. As she collected the money, she placed one peso aside. I asked her what that was for. She replied that it was for the poor. At that moment, the orthopraxis, correct action, of this poor woman taught my students (and me) more about the essence of Divinity than all of the academic books we had read. Witnessing the giving of the "widow's mite" was more effective than any lecture I could have possibly given.

When those who have so little *do* their faith by providing for those who have even less, those of us privileged by class should be profoundly humbled. It is the privileged who see the oppressed and do nothing that are the ones that do not know God. I may have had the educational training to tease apart the inconsistencies in this woman's beliefs, but she knew far more about God than I did. This is not a romanticization of the poor, for surely there is nothing romantic about poverty. Rather, it is a theological truth that I learned directly from this poor woman's actions.

When we all get to heaven, we will discover how wrong we all were. No group has a monopoly on truth. So in a sense, orthodoxy—correct belief—is not that important. What should take precedence is orthopraxis—correct action. For this reason, academics who do ethics from the margins are scholar-activists. Perceiving great theoretical thoughts about the Divine is less important than doing the works of love as called for by the Divine.

The poor of Cuernavaca, and elsewhere throughout the world, bring our privileged suppositions into conversation with those who many consider devoid of something to offer the intellectual dialogue. Only by being scholar-activists can my students and I contribute toward the struggle against oppression that has become institutionalized. The praxis of dealing with oppressive structures within dispossessed communities is more crucial than books published by the "experts," including the book you hold in your hands. No doubt, such a methodology will usually anger those accustomed to their power and privilege; still, doing ethics from the margins of society must be done if any one of us wishes to be faithful to what we claim, as Christians, to believe.

Since publishing this book a decade ago, my resolve that a closer understanding of the Divine can only be attained by listening carefully to those on the margins has only been strengthened. In all the books I have ever written, in all the classes I have ever taught, in all the lectures I have ever given, the wisdom expressed has never been something I produced while sitting in my ivy tower. Whether it be in the squatter villages of Cuernavaca, walking the migrant trails taken by the undocumented entering the United States, or working beside poor rural rice farmers in Indonesia—everything I hold true I learned from them. This book is a product of the margins.

Acknowledgments for the 2014 Edition

During an academic lecture, a colleague approached me and asked when I was planning to update my book *Doing Christian Ethics from the Margins*. Frankly, I really had not given it much thought until then. The book was being used in many ethics classes and was selling well, but it was very outdated. Since it was written, the wars in Afghanistan and Iraq had begun winding down. The Supreme Court made decisions in campaign financing and affirmative action. The country elected its first biracial president. The Great Recession of 2008 hit, devastating the middle class. Much has changed, except the formula that the many are sinking in greater want so that the few can continue to enjoy their excess. Yes, it was time to update the book.

Since the first edition a decade ago, I left (or better yet, was forced out of) Holland, Michigan, when I began to advocate for LGBTQ+ civil rights. Standing with the oppressed can at times be costly. The children whom I acknowledged in the first edition, Victoria and Vincent, are now college graduates starting out in a world with fewer opportunities available than in the past. For their sakes, and the sake of this new generation, this book attempts to ask why.

Finding the latest statistics and updated facts was not an easy task. It would never have occurred without the help of a small cadre of research assistants, specifically Patrick Bowen, Rebecca Chabot, and Sarah Neeley. A special thanks to Samuel (Slam) Trujillo, who was my assistant on this project for over a year. And yes, my wife, Deb, continues to be my moral compass as we discuss (debate?) a multitude of ethical issues.

Preface to the 2004 Edition

The (class)room is appropriately named, for it is indeed a room of class—a room where students learn the class they belong to and the power and privilege that comes with that class.[1] The fact that some students are able to pay sufficient money to attend particular rooms of class located on prestigious campuses indicates that they will have certain opportunities that are denied to those of lower economic classes, those who are more often than not students of color residing on the margins of society.

Our educational system is far from being objective or neutral, and students who attend classrooms, from community colleges to highly selective universities, can either be conditioned to accept the present system of social structures or seek liberation from it. All too often, the educational system serves to normalize these power structures as legitimate. The task of educators, specifically those who call themselves ethicists, is to cultivate students' ability to find their own voices by creating an environment in which individual and collective consciousness-raising can occur.

As an ethicist unapologetically grounded in a Latino/a social context, I create an environment within the (class)room that attempts to perceive the will of the Divine from within the social location of marginalized people—that is, those who are not usually able to participate in the (class)room where I teach. Such a process analyzes their reality, a reality tied to an ethical perspective that demands a sociopolitical response to oppression. In this way a relationship can develop between intellectuals aware of the structural crises faced by people of color and the disenfranchised in the United States.

Nevertheless, the danger facing liberative scholars is that they can become an intellectual elite disconnected from the everyday struggles of the marginalized and have little or no impact upon the churches in disenfranchised communities. Ethicists from the margins attempting to overcome this disconnect advocate connecting the work done by Christian ministers serving disenfranchised communities with the academic work done by faculty and students in our colleges and universities. These ministers and scholars attempt to learn from the disenfranchised while serving them as organic intellectuals (to borrow a term from Antonio Gramsci), that is, intellectuals grounded in the social reality of the marginalized, and acting in the consciousness-raising process of the faith community.

The pedagogy I employ in my (class)room, and will attempt to unfold in this book, seeks to open Christian ethics to the rich diversity

---

[1] I am indebted to one of my mentors, John Raines, who constantly reminded me of this fact during my doctoral studies.

found among those who are usually excluded—those who are multiracial and multicultural people. In my "room of class" I attempt to construct a collaborative ethics through studying and reflecting on the lives and circumstances of marginalized people. This is not to make students aware of some quaint or exotic perspective of those who are disenfranchised; rather, it is to help them realize that because the gospel message was first proclaimed in the colonized spaces of Judea, those who reside in these marginalized spaces—then and now—hold the key to properly interpreting this message. In this way the salvation of the usually eurocentric-dominant culture depends on hearing what is proclaimed by those from the margins.

This approach demands a response to injustice and oppression. By forcing my students to occupy an uncomfortable space, I can provide them with a unique outlook, with a view I believe enhances more traditional learning. I try to bring their lifetime of experiences and knowledge into conversation with people whose lives and experiences may be quite different from theirs, people who may often be thought of as having little to contribute to the educational process.

This pedagogy, however, is useless if it is restricted solely to the (class) room. The liberating ethical praxis I advocate is pertinent to the larger community as well. For example, the community in which my school is located, called Holland, was settled by the Dutch in the early 1800s. Located on Lake Michigan, Holland features wooden shoe factories, a windmill imported from the Netherlands, and an annual May festival called Tulip Time that attracts more than one hundred thousand visitors to celebrate Holland's Dutch heritage.

But Holland is also a town where all people are not Dutch. On the underside of Holland, we discover Hispanics who make up approximately 22.2 percent of the overall population. (If those who are undocumented were counted, the numbers would hover at 30 percent.) In addition, 3.5 percent of the population is Asian and 2.3 percent Black. Despite these demographics, those who live on the margins of Holland are seldom seen walking or shopping on Eighth Street, the main business center of the city. This is often true even if they live a few blocks away.

Holland is a town where many from the dominant culture may wish to live in a more just and equitable society, but they also find themselves trapped within social structures created long ago (and some more recently) to protect their privilege by masking racism and classism. Consequently, those who are oppressed by these structures, along with those who benefit, are in need of liberation, another word for salvation.

To bring about liberation as salvation, Christianity must become a way of life rather than just a doctrinal belief. If simple belief is all that is required for salvation, then complicity with structures that perpetuate oppression is inconsequential to the Christian life. Besides, do not the demons themselves believe Jesus Christ is Lord of all (Jas. 2:19)? The perspectives of Christian liberative ethicists are crucial to help establish a more just society. Faculty and students alike can contribute to the struggle against oppression that has often become institutionalized. For this reason, my role as an ethicist must include participation in both a faith community and the overall society. What I do—my praxis—is more crucial than any book I might write. Most Christian ethicists working from a liberation framework write or teach to give voice to the voiceless, to shout from the mountaintop that which is commonly heard among disenfranchised people, to put into words what the marginalized are feeling and doing. No doubt, such writing may anger or alienate those who view their power and privilege as birthrights; nonetheless, perspectives from the margins must be voiced to bring about repentance for those who participate in injustice through their privilege, and to bring about salvation for those who suffer from injustices.

As can be imagined, this type of pedagogy does not come easily in a conservative religious and political environment like Holland, Michigan. It might be wiser to simply conform to the dominant culture and remain silent in the face of racism, classism, sexism, and heterosexism. There is a tremendous temptation to turn my back on the oppression that surrounds me. But it seems my scholarship has been influenced by Don Quixote, and like Don Quixote, I feel the need to charge the windmills of Holland. But in a world that normalizes oppression—our world today—maybe some Don Quixotes can bring hope when there is none as they set out on a path that establishes a justice-based ethics by taking on the foes of power and privilege.

Acknowledgments for the 2004 Edition

Even Don Quixote had his Sancho. Likewise, this book is a reality because of the many who labored with me to bring it to fruition. It would be a travesty to take full credit for what appears on these pages. Many of the ideas and insights for this book took shape in a senior-level class I taught at Hope College by the same name, Doing Christian Ethics from the Margins. Although the class was composed of approximately twenty students (all Anglo students, save one) with most sharing in middle- and upper-class privilege, these students were committed to seeking justice. They seriously undertook the quite difficult task of reflecting upon ethical case studies by seeking the voices of those who are usually disenfranchised by prevailing social structures. I give my deep-felt thanks to these students. Specifically,

PREFACES AND ACKNOWLEDGMENTS

I wish to highlight three of them: Dustin Janes, Lauren Hinkle, and Phil Johnson. They worked with me for an additional semester as research assistants, spending countless hours gathering and organizing data.

Thanks to a McGregor Fund grant offered through Hope College, Phil Johnson was able to continue assisting me with this project through the summer months. I am also indebted to librarian Anthony Guardado at Hope College, who worked with us in locating hard-to-find sources. I also greatly appreciate the Religion Department at Hope College, whose faculty set up a colloquium to read early versions of this manuscript and provided valuable feedback. In addition, I am grateful to John Raines and Allan Verhey, who carefully read sections of the manuscript and provided much constructive criticism. Any success this book has is due to their wise counsel. I continue to be indebted to Jonathan Schakel for his faithfulness in proofreading my text, and to my editor Susan Perry, who was always ready to prod me toward excellence. As always, I owe eternal gratitude to my children, Vincent and Victoria, and my soul-mate Deborah, my moral compass who continues to be the source of my strength.

PART I

ETHICAL THEORY

Chapter 1

Doing Christian Ethics

Even white supremacists can be ethical and virtuous. Hate crimes have risen in 2020 to their highest level in more than a decade. According to the Federal Bureau of Investigation, a 32 percent increase in hate crimes occurred from 2019 to 2020 against all racial and ethnic groups with the most incidents occurring against African Americans (49 percent) and Asian Americans experiencing the highest increase of incidents (77 percent).[1] Making matters worse, hate crimes increased another 11 percent in 2021 from 2020, with African Americans remaining the most targeted group while Asian Americans witnessed a 339 percent increase.[2] Emboldened during the Trump administration, what were once considered "fringe" white supremacist groups took center stage during the armed January 2021 assault on the US Capitol. While most Christians were celebrating the Feast of the Epiphany, armed subversives wearing camouflage, carrying Confederate flags, and brandishing the symbols and colors of white nationalism in all its forms—neo-Nazis, Proud Boys, Ku Klux Klansmen, Oath Keepers, Three Percenters—stormed the Capitol. While it may be tempting to simply dismiss these hate groups as pure evil, the fact remains that they sung the hymn "How Great Is Our God" as they marched toward insurrection, waving "JESUS 2020" placards, flags brandishing the Christian fish symbol, and "In God we Trust" banners, along with posters and flags with the motto: "Jesus is My Savior, Trump is My President."[3]

In all fairness, hate groups such as these advocate motherhood, patriotism, the welfare of children, and apple pie. The Oath Keepers had a nondiscriminatory clause in their by-laws (Code of Conduct 2:1-8), declaring as their mission "to support and defend the Constitution against

---

[1] US Department of Justice, *2020 FBI Hate Crime Statistics*.

[2] Kimmy Yam, "Anti-Asian Hate Crimes Increase 339 Percent Nationwide Last Year, Report Says," NBC News, January 31, 2022.

[3] See Robert P. Jones, "Taking the White Christian Nationalist Symbols at the Capitol Riot Seriously," Religion News Service, January 7, 2021.

all enemies, foreign and domestic, so help [them] God (8.05)."[4] While the Oath Keepers militia group embrace patriotism, wrapping themselves in the flag, other hate groups embrace the cross. According to the Ku Klux Klan explanation of the fiery cross, prior to their official website being taken down,

> The Knights' Party is a political organization and believes we right-fully place our foundation upon the word of Jesus Christ. This we feel is what made America great.... It is only by basing govern-mental policy and laws upon the Christian faith that our nation and people will retain our cherished liberties and freedom. Our nation must repent of its sins and return to the laws of God and the precepts which made America Great.[5]

These groups exhort their members to live by a code of ethics that cele-brates and defends the values and virtues advocated by some of the world's great faith traditions. It would be somewhat reductionist to simply write off these groups as purely evil with no comprehension of good. In fact, as their websites indicate, they do have a set of ethics, a sense of proper behavior, and a self-imposed mandate to live an honorable life, hence proving Cicero's dictum that "there is a kind of honor even among thieves."

The problem with the value systems of militia groups and the KKK is that others, among them people of color, deeply disagree with their under-standing of morality. The issue then is not so much whether humans should follow some set of ethical precepts but, rather, whose ethical precepts. Moral relativism recognizes the variety of ethical beliefs existing between different racial and ethnic groups, economic classes, and gender identities. But if ethics is simply relative, where no one group's ethics is necessarily superior or inferior to another, then adhering to the ethics spouted by white supremacists should be as valid as any ethics emerging from the marginalized spaces of society, or any other spaces for that matter. It appears that a preferential option needs to be made for some set of ethical precepts. The question is: whose?

While supremacist groups may appear as extreme examples, other ethical perspectives expounded by Christians within US eurocentric culture also raise questions and concerns about the incongruence of what they

---

[4] The original quote was taken from https://usaoathkeepers.com/.

[5] While websites for the Ku Klux Klan have been widely taken down, this quote originated on one of the websites, kukluxklan.org, and was accessed in both 2004 and 2013. Currently, the Southern Poverty Law Center maintains a webpage on the Ku Klux Klan as an extremist ideology in their "Fighting Hate: Extremist Files."

conceive to be moral based on their social location and the day-to-day experiences of marginalized people. Regardless of the virtues claimed by the dominant culture, there still exist self-perpetuating mechanisms of oppression that continue to normalize and legitimize how subjugation manifests itself in the overall customs, language, traditions, values, and laws of the United States. Our political systems, our policing authorities, our judicial institutions, and our military forces conspire to maintain a status quo designed to secure and protect the power and wealth of the privileged few. In some cases, the ethics advanced by the dominant culture appears to rationalize these present power structures, hence protecting and masking the political and economic interests of those whom the structures privilege—in effect, an ethics driven by the self-interest of euroamericans.

If the religious leaders and scholars of the dominant culture continue to construct ethical perspectives from within their cultural space of wealth and power, the marginalized will need an alternative format by which to deliberate and, more importantly, to do ethics. Through critical social analysis, it is possible to uncover the connection between the prevailing ideologies (namely, the ethics of the dominant culture) that accept the present power arrangements as legitimate and normal, with the political, economic, and cultural components of the mechanisms of oppression that protect their power and wealth. Anchoring ethics on the everyday experience of the marginalized challenges the validity, or lack thereof, of prevailing ideologies that inform eurocentric ethics.

For example, the fact that, once upon a time in US history, the "peculiar" institution of slavery was biblically supported, religiously justified, spiritually legitimized, and ethically normalized raises serious questions concerning the objectivity of any code of ethics originating from the dominant white culture. At the very least, the marginalized are suspicious of how ethics is defined and constructed by those who benefit from what society deems to be Christian or moral—then, as well as today. Although hindsight can easily facilitate our understanding of how unchristian and unethical previous generations may have been, we are left wondering whether perspectives considered by some to be morally sound today future generations might define as unchristian and unethical. How will our descendants interpret today's incarceration of undocumented Latine children in camps like those located in Tornillo, Texas? Regardless as to how we conduct ethical analysis, one thing is clear: extremist groups like supremacist militias or the Klan are not, nor should they be, our focus. They would be an easy strawman to dismiss. Instead, our concentration rests with ethics advocated by traditionally Christian-based congregations found throughout the United States.

This book aims to explore how the disenfranchised struggle against societal mechanisms responsible for much of the misery they face, preventing them from living out the mission of Christ as recorded in the Gospel of John: "that they may have life, and have it abundantly" (10:10).[6] Christian liberative ethics becomes the process by which the mechanisms that dehumanize life, as well as cause death, are dismantled. All too often, ethics, as presented by the dominant culture, paternalistically explores Christian virtues without seriously considering the existence of most oppressed people. This text seeks the re-creation of proper relationships where all can live full and abundant lives, able to become all they have been called to be, free from the societal forces (racism, classism, sexism, and heterosexism) that foster dehumanizing conditions. Within such relationships exist the potential for healing, wholeness, and liberation.

Why Christian

One may ask why this book unapologetically centers ethical reflection upon the Christian perspective, relying mainly on Christian sacred texts (specifically the Hebrew Bible and the New Testament) and Christian theological concepts (specifically the liberationist motif advocated by many marginalized communities). Should ethical perspectives not incorporate a wider variety of responses, including those that are not necessarily Christian-based? Realizing the absence of a homogeneous cultural and religious center upon which to deduct moral thinking, does it not make sense to reflect the world's religious diversity when determining proper ethical responses?

If all theology is indeed contextual, then the focus of this book is the particular religious context of its author. This does not mean liberation or salvation can only be achieved through a Christian paradigm by those who are not Christian. It just means it does for those professing Christianity. The last thing we would want is to simply export Christian liberative concepts to other religious contexts as if they were some sort

---

[6] The reader should be aware that all scriptural quotes are translated by the author from the original Hebrew or Greek. Usually, biblical scholars discuss the authenticity of authorship, as well as the accuracy of events, stories, or statements appearing in the text; however, such an analytical endeavor is beyond the scope of this book. Instead, my use of Scripture attempts to read the text from the perspective of the faith community, a perspective that is probably different from that of privileged scholars within the security and safety of hallowed academic hallways. The biblical reading conducted in this text is from the marginalized domains of society, attempting to understand and apply the biblical message to the reality of disenfranchisement.

of commodity. Surely there is much to learn about liberative ethical deliberation from other major world religions like Islam, Judaism, Hinduism, or Buddhism, as well as overlooked earth-based religions from Africa, Australia, and the preconquest Americas, or even among those who reject the concept of God like atheists or humanists. As worthy as such an ethical exploration of comparative traditions may be, it is beyond the scope of this book.[7]

Ethics remains a reflection of the social location and theological beliefs (or disbeliefs) of a given people. We focus on the Christian perspective because this book is written by and for those who claim to be followers of Jesus Christ. Although ethics can be done devoid of Jesus Christ (as well as devoid of the influence of a supreme God-type deity), such ethics, although valid for those constructing it, is not necessarily Christian-based, even though agreement may be found in several areas of deliberation. Thus, it is crucial to realize that the "Christianity" upon which the ethical perspectives of this book are based is not necessarily Christianity as defined and understood by those privileged by the dominant culture.

If theological or philosophical thought is a product of a particular cultural context, then those born into or raised within the United States are a product of a society where white supremacy and class privilege have historically been interwoven with how whites, for centuries, see and organize the world around them and impose that worldview on the rest of society. How they see and interpret Christianity has become, in their own eyes, universally legitimate. A worldview with racist and classist underpinnings is constructed in which complicity with eurocentrism is deemed normal and fails to contemplate the racialization of how those wielding this view see and organize their world. Regardless of how alluring eurocentric Christianity might appear, or how normalized it is presented to those relegated to the margins, most of it remains unconsciously embedded within white supremacy and thus incongruent with any gospel message of liberation (De La Torre 2021). As such, the Christianity of the dominant culture must be rejected by the disenfranchised if they ever hope to achieve liberation.

The Christianity as defined by this book is forged from the underside, by those who exist on the margins of society. For those who claim Christianity while struggling within oppressive structures, the personhood of Jesus Christ as a source of strength becomes crucial. The life and sayings of Christ, as recognized by the disenfranchised faith community

---

[7] Those interested in exploring liberative ethical perspectives from the matrix of other faith traditions (or no tradition whatsoever) can see De La Torre, *The Hope of Liberation in World Religions* (Waco, TX: Baylor University Press, 2008).

who search the biblical text for guidance to life's ethical dilemmas, serve as a standard for morality. While eurocentric theology, and the ethics that flow from it, tends to understand the Christ event in the abstract, those on the margins instead recognize a Christ who incarnates themself among the world of today's dispossessed.

Theologian James Cone reminds us that it is from within the oppressed Black community (and I would add any oppressed Christian community) that Christ becomes a means to bring about liberation from oppressive structures (1999a [1979], 5). For this reason, Jesus Christ—as understood by the disenfranchised Christian faith community—becomes authoritative in how ethics develops among marginalized groups. For them, the incarnation—the Word taking flesh and dwelling among us—becomes the lens through which God's character is understood. Although Christ remains the ultimate revelation of God's character to humanity, the biblical text becomes the primary witness of this revelation and, as such, shapes Christian identity while informing moral actions. The ultimate values of Christ as witnessed in the biblical text become the standards by which individuals and, more crucially, social structures are judged. Regardless of how many ways the biblical text can be interpreted, certain recurring themes understood by the marginalized, specifically a call to justice and a call to love, can be recognized by all who call themselves Christians.

Why Ethics?

Neither the overall biblical text nor the pronouncements of Jesus are silent or abstruse concerning the type of actions or praxis expected of those who claim to be disciples of Christ. The prophets of old would answer in a very straightforward matter the ethical question of what God wants of God's people. God was not interested in church services devoid of praxis toward the marginalized. As the prophet Isaiah reminds us, "Do not bring me [your God] your worthless offerings, the incense is an abomination to me. I cannot endure new moon and Sabbath, the call to meetings and the evil assembly" (1:13). Instead, the prophets proclaimed justice for society's most vulnerable members as true worship, a testimony of one's love for God and neighbor.

Jesus sounds an eschatological admonishment on what is expected from his followers. In the Gospel of Matthew, Jesus warns, "Because lawlessness shall have been multiplied, and the love of many will grow cold, the one enduring to the end, this one will be saved" (24:12–13). In short, there can be no faith, in fact no salvation, without ethical praxis—not because such actions are the cause of salvation, but are, rather, their manifestation. To participate in ethical praxis is to seek justice. To ignore ethical praxis is to be complicit with oppressive structures. For those on the margins of society, the ultimate goal of any ethical praxis is to establish a more just society.

Yet justice has become a worn-out, hollow expression—an abstract and detached battle cry. Every political action initiated by the dominant culture, no matter how self-serving, no matter how hate-based, is construed as just. The maintenance of an economic system that produces poverty is heralded as being based on the justice principle of *suum cuique tribuere* (to each what is due). Sending military personnel into battle to protect "our" natural overseas resources is understood as securing our freedoms and way of life. Storming the Capitol to nullify the democratic results of an election is spun as patriotism. The most unjust acts are portrayed as just by those with the power and privilege to impose their worldview on the rest of society. This is what sociologist Emile Durkheim meant when he insisted that the beliefs and sentiments held in common by the inhabitants of the dominant culture become the moral norms codified in laws, customs, and traditions. Consequently, the primary function of society becomes the reaffirmation, protection, and perpetuation of this "collective or common conscience" (1933 [1893],79–82). If this is true, then those on the margins of society must ask if it is possible to formulate a universal principle of justice apart from the definitions imposed by the collective conscience of the dominant culture.

Two of the most foundational components of ethics are the concepts of justice and love, both rooted within the biblical narrative. Although these are separate concepts, for the liberationist they are forever connected. Biblical scholar Gerhard Von Rad expounds upon the importance of justice to ethical living:

> There is absolutely no concept in the Old Testament [*sic*] with so central a significance for all the relationships of human life as that of "tsedaqah." It is the standard not only for man's [*sic*] relationship to God, but also for his relationship to his fellows, reaching right down to the most petty wrangling—indeed, it is even the standard for man's [*sic*] relationship to the animals and to his natural environment. (1962, 370)

Justice, the English equivalent of *tsedaqah*, can never be reduced simply to some ideal to be achieved or a code of precepts to be followed. Rather, justice denotes how a real relationship between two parties (God and human, human and human, nature and human, or human and society) is properly conducted. The emphasis is not on some abstract concept of how society is to organize itself, but rather on loyalty within relationships, specifically those dealing with humans (371). Right relationship with God is possible only if people act justly toward each other.

Right relationships are prevented from securing an abundant life (here understood as intellectual, physical, and material development) when one party, to secure greater wealth and power, does so at the expense of the Other. Injustice thus becomes a perverted relationship that ignores coordinating the proper good or end of individuals with that of their communities. Such perverted relationships insist that its members should pursue their own self-interests, for only then will such self-serving relationships be capable of contributing to the overall common good.[8] Such thinking asserts that everyone has a moral obligation to follow self-interest so that justice can be actualized. Still, such an approach to relationships is fundamentally incongruent with how justice is defined in the biblical text, specifically Paul's admonition to put the needs of others before oneself (Eph. 5:21). The danger of not incorporating the relational aspects of the term "justice" can lead to the rejection of God, even while one professes to belong to God and to live a pious life. Liberation theologian Gustavo Gutiérrez reminds us, "To know Yahweh, which in biblical language is equivalent to saying to love Yahweh, is to establish just relationships among persons, it is to recognize the rights of the poor. The God of biblical revelation is known through interhuman justice. When justice does not exist, God is not known; God is absent" (1988 [1973], 110–11).

If justice is what Christians are called to do, it is done in obedience to love. As Cornel West constantly reminds us, "Justice is what love looks like in public" (2009, 232). Love can never be understood or defined as an emotional experience (although such feelings could, and usually do, become a symptom of the love praxis). Neither is it a response due to pity or a duty based on paternalism. Brazilian theologians Leonardo and Clodovis Boff remind us that "love is praxis, not theory" (1988 [1984], 4). Love is action, a verb that describes something done by one person to or toward another, an action taken regardless of how one feels, or as the author of 1 John 3:18 stated, "Let us not love in words, nor in mere talk, but in deed and in truth." Love is the deed of justice, or as the Medellín documents eloquently stated, "Love is the soul of justice. The Christianity which works for social justice should always cultivate peace and love in one's heart" (CELAM 1968, 71). For the Christian, this deed is done in spite of the Other deserving to be loved. Paul reminds us, "But God loved us by commanding Christ to die for us, even while we were still sinners" (Rom. 5:8). It is this same type of

---

[8] Adam Smith makes such an argument within the economic sphere (1976 [1776]).

love that binds the believer to the abundant life of the Other. Hence, to love in this fashion is to question, analyze, challenge, and dismantle the social structures responsible for preventing human flourishing, reaching the fullest potential of the abundant life promised by Christ.

Love becomes the unifying theme of the biblical text, specifically when expressed as a relational love for God and for one's neighbor. The false dichotomy existing between faith (love the Lord your God) and ethics (love your neighbor as yourself) is collapsed by Jesus, who demands manifestations of both by those wishing to be called disciples. The doing of love becomes the new commandment Christians are called to observe (Jn. 12:34–35). The Apostle Paul understood how paramount Christ's command was for all ethical actions committed by those calling themselves his followers. Hence, 1 Corinthians states, "If I can speak in the tongues of humans, even of angels, but I do not have love, I become like a sounding brass or clanging cymbal. And if I have prophecies, and know all mysteries, and all knowledge, and if I have all faith so as to move mountains, but I do not have love, I am nothing" (13:1–3).

The love that liberates can only be known and experienced from within relationships established upon acts of justice. Relationships with each other, and God, become a source for moral guidance, capable of debunking the social structures erected and subsequently normalized by the dominant culture. By first learning to love humans through just relationships, the ability to love God also becomes possible. For, as 1 John 4:20 reminds us, how can we love God whom we cannot see, unless we first learn to love humans whom we do see? Love toward the least among us, demonstrated through a relationship founded on justice, manifests love for God. Only by loving the disenfranchised, by seeing Jesus among the poor and weak, can one learn to love Jesus who claims to be the marginalized. To love the marginalized is to love Jesus, making fellowship with God possible as one enters just fellowship with the disenfranchised.

Ultimately, the basis for all ethical acts can be reduced to one verse from Galatians: "The whole Law is fulfilled in one word, Love your neighbor as yourself" (5:14). How do we love our neighbor? We can look to the biblical narrative, seeking concrete examples of love manifested as an act of God's work to create justice-based relationships. The very identity of those claiming to be Christian becomes defined by their relationship to their God and to their neighbor. To construct justice apart from a love relationship with others becomes a perversion designed to protect the privilege of those doing the construction. If, according to Luke 4:18, Jesus came to "proclaim liberation to the captives . . . [and] set those oppressed free," how then can the bondage of many be preferred simply because it protects the power, profits, and privilege of the few? For this reason, a preferential option for the poor characterizes a sincere commitment to justice, not because the poor are inherently more holy than the elite, but simply because they lack the elite's power, profits, and privilege. Consequently, we must now ask, why then from the margins?

Why from the Margins?

If the dominant culture continues to be the sole interpreter of moral reality, then its perspectives will continue to be the norm by which the rest of society is morally judged. The danger is that, to some extent, the dominant culture's ethics has historically been and, some of us would argue, continues to be, a moral theorizing geared to protect the self-interest of those who are and aspire to be privileged. Consequently, which ethical perspectives are chosen or discarded becomes a decision that establishes or reinforces power relationships. To choose one ethical precept over another justifies those who will eventually benefit from what is chosen. Once members of the dominant culture recognize the ethical precepts that support their lifestyle, claims of moral absolutism can be made. When members of the dominant culture legitimize the values that advance their power within the social structures as moral "truths," they ignore how the Christian ethics that they advocate in fact legitimizes power, specifically, who has it and how it is to be used. This form of eurocentric moral imperialism forces serious consideration of the question asked by Argentinean theologian José Míguez Bonino: "In this world of power, of economic relations and structures, a world that maintains its autonomy and will not yield to voluntaristic moral ideals imposed from the outside, a world in which power and freedom seem to pull in opposite directions—what can Christians say and do?" (1983, 21). For those who do ethics from the margins, the issue of power becomes paramount in the development of any ethical discourse. Foremost for those who are marginalized is the ethical response to the use, misuse, and abuse of power rather than issues of character, values, virtues, or moral principles.

Any ethics arising from Christianity that wishes to remain faithful to the gospel message must remain rooted in the praxis of liberation. Christian ethics should first struggle with the question of power and how to crucify power and the privilege that flows with it so that justice and love can instead reign. Yet, if those who are privileged by the present political, economic, and social structures refuse to acknowledge that being wealthy and white provides specific advantages over and against the disenfranchised, then how can they participate with integrity in any discourse that addresses injustice? For Christian ethics to be relevant, the faith community's struggles with oppression must be engaged, always with the goal of dismantling the mechanism responsible for creating the inhumanity faced within marginalized spaces.

Jesus can never belong to the oppressors of this world because he is one of the oppressed. The radicalness of the gospel message is that Jesus is in solidarity with the very least of humanity. Ironically, it is the least who represent the majority of the population. The last shall be first; the center shall be the periphery. In Matthew 25:31–46, Christ returns to earth to judge and decipher between those destined for the reign of heaven and those who are not. The blessed and the cursed are separated by what they did or did not do to the least among us. Specifically, did they or did they not feed the hungry, welcome the alien, clothe the naked, and visit those infirm or incarcerated? Is the ethical lifestyle of individuals in solidarity with the marginalized demonstrated in liberative acts that lead others toward an abundant life? So that there would be no confusion about God's preferential option, Jesus clearly states, "Truly I say to you, inasmuch as you did it to one of these, the least of my people, you did it to me."

The church of Jesus Christ is called to identify and stand in solidarity with the oppressed. The act of solidarity becomes the litmus test of ethical fidelity and the paradigm used to analyze and judge how social structures contribute to or efface the exploitation of the marginalized. To be apart from the marginalized community of faith is to exile oneself from the possibility of hearing and discerning the gospel message of salvation—a salvation from the ideologies that mask power, profit, and privilege along with the social structures responsible for their maintenance. Ideologies and social structures are shaped and formed by individuals who are in turn shaped and formed by these same ideologies and social structures. Like everyone else, Christians are born into a society where the dialectical relation between the person and the community informs their beliefs and their character—in short, their identity. For this reason, the sociohistorical context of any people profoundly contributes to the construction of their ethical system. When Christians, in accordance with their faith, attempt to develop ethical responses to the conflicts of human life, they participate in a dialogue between Christianity and what their community defines as Christian.[9]

---

[9] H. R. Niebuhr was correct in observing that Christian ethics are fused and confused with what the civil social order determines is best for the common good. However, Darryl Trimiew calls Niebuhr to task for his underlining principle to Christian social action. According to Niebuhr, "Responsibility affirms: God is acting in all actions upon you. So respond to all actions upon you as to respond to his

Unfortunately, those who control the instruments of social power claim a monopoly on truth to the detriment of the disenfranchised. Black ethicist and my academic mentor Katie Cannon succinctly captured confusion of the dominant culture's self-interest with the interest of the public when she wrote,

> The welfare of the state is now fully identified with the interests of the wealthy class. Everything else is subordinate to the prosperity of the wealthiest businesspeople and to the welfare of the commercial class as a whole.... Their control of taxation, judiciary, and the armed forces gives them free access to all political processes.... The interest of the ruling class becomes de facto the interest of the public. (1995, 150)

The common good becomes restricted to those who benefit from the privilege obtained within these same social structures. Yet seldom do those in power admit they are disproportionately rewarded by society. Concealing this truth makes any ethics emanating from that same dominant culture incomplete and heretical. Appeals to Christianity or reason will fail to affect the existing power structures, for the dominant culture uses both to defend their interests. Thus, the disenfranchised can only bring liberative change through empowerment.

The immoral hoarding of power, profit, and privilege by the dominant culture makes it difficult for those benefiting from the status quo to be able to propose, with any integrity, liberative ethical precepts. For this reason, Cone, as well as many other theologians of color, concludes there can exist no theology (and I would add ethics) based on the gospel message that does not arise from marginalized communities (1999a [1979], 5). Francisco Moreno Rejón, a Latin American ethicist, maintains that for ethics to be liberative, its origins must rise

---

action" (1963, 126). Niebuhr continues by claiming, "The will of God is what God does in all that nature and men [*sic*] do.... Will of God is present for Jesus in every event from the death of sparrows, the shining of sun and descent of rain, through the exercise of authority by ecclesiastical and political powers that abuse their authority, through treachery and desertion by disciples" (164–65). Trimiew finds Niebuhr's admonition troubling for marginalized communities because it encourages believers to interpret all actions, regardless as to how repressive such actions may be to the disenfranchised, as God's providence. Oppression becomes conformity to God's will. Thus God is chastising the marginalized for their sins. But how can any "responsible self," Trimiew wonders, claim the death and misery faced by those marginalized at the expense of the privileged is God's providence? (1993, xi, 8).

1. From the underside of history and the world: from among the losers of history, from within the invaded cultures, from dependent [peoples] without genuine autonomy and suffering the manifold limitations that all this implies. 2. From the outskirts of society, where the victims of all manner of oppression live, the ones who "don't count"—the ones whose faces reflect "the suffering features of Christ the Lord" (Puebla Final Document, no. 3). 3. From among the masses of an oppressed, believing people: it cannot be a matter of indifference to moral theology that the majority of Christians and humanity live in conditions of inhuman poverty. (1993, 215)

Only from the margins of power and privilege can a fuller and more comprehensive understanding of the prevailing social structures be ascertained—not because those on the margins are more astute, but rather because they know what it means to be a marginalized person attempting to survive within a social context designed to perpetually benefit the privileged few at their expense. Cone says it best when he writes, "Only those who do not know bondage existentially can speak of liberation 'objectively.' Only those who have not been in the 'valley of death' can sing the songs of Zion as if they are uninvolved" (1999b, 22).

Is there any hope then for those who benefit from the present oppressive structures? Before answering this question, it must be realized that those privileged by the current sociopolitical and economic structures are themselves oppressed. While they do not experience the full extent of intellectual, physical, and material deprivation felt in economically deprived areas, still, the oppressor lacks their full humanity. To oppress another is to oppress oneself. Because oppressive structures also prevent the master from obtaining an abundant life (specifically in the spiritual sense), those supposedly privileged by said structures are also in need of the gospel message of salvation and liberation. Those on the margins may have their humanity denied by oppressors, but oppressors lose their humanity by their complicity with oppressive structures.

Participation in ethical praxis designed to establish justice bestows dignity on the marginalized "non-persons" by accentuating their worth as receptacles of the *imago Dei*, the very image of God, but it also restores the humanity of the privileged who falsely construct their identity through the negation of the Other. The ethical task before both those who are oppressed and those who are privileged by the present institutionalized structures is not to invert roles or to share the space of privilege at the expense of some other group but, rather, to dismantle the very structures responsible for causing injustices along the lines of race, class, gender, sexual orientation, or any combination thereof, regardless of the attitudes bound to those structures. Only then can all within society, the marginalized as well as the privileged, achieve their full humanity and be enabled to live the abundant life offered by Christ in John 10:10.

How, then, can those who are privileged by the present social structures find their own liberation from those structures, a liberation that can lead to their salvation? They do so by nailing and crucifying their power, profit, and privilege to the cross so as to become nothing. According to the Apostle Paul's letter to the Philippians 2:6–8, "[Jesus Christ], who subsisting in the form of God thought it not robbery to be equal with God, but emptied himself, taking the form of a slave, in the likeness of humans, and being found in the fashion of a human, he humbled himself, becoming obedient until death, even the death of the cross." At the cross, Jesus becomes nothing in total solidarity with those made nothing by social structures.

Ethics begins with our own surrender, with our self-negation. Those who benefit from the power, profit, and privilege of social structures can encounter the Absolute only through their own self-negation by crucifying their whiteness, their cisgender maleness, their classism. The late-sixteenth-century mystic Juan de la Cruz (John of the Cross) captures this concept of self-negation in his ascent of Mount Carmel: "To reach satisfaction in all, desire its possession in nothing. To come to the knowledge of all, desire the knowledge of nothing. To come to possess all, desire the possession of nothing. To arrive at being all, desire to be nothing" (1987 [1618], 45). Jesus was fond of saying, "For whoever desires to save their life shall lose it, but whoever loses their life for my sake and the sake of the gospel, that one shall save it" (Mk. 8:35). True liberation takes place when the individual sees into their own nature and thus becomes Christ-like. This praxis liberates those trapped by their race, class, gender, and heterosexual privilege, so that they, in solidarity with the marginalized, can bring about a just society based on the gospel definition of justice.

Still, with which marginalized group will those from the dominant culture stand in solidarity? Does each group create its own ethical reflection, or do they work together to overturn oppressive structures affecting all marginalized people? Darryl Trimiew, a Black ethicist, has asked similar questions. He warned,

> The refusal of various liberation movements to concern themselves
> with the fates of others is the self-issued death warrant of these
> moral movements. This new universalism is daunting, as it will

require the cooperation of strangers, even strangers who may be competing for the very same scarce resources.... Yet the tendency of liberationists to concern themselves with parochial interests cannot be underestimated. In this country alone, liberation ethicists show little interest in working together on projects of solidarity in order to overthrow common oppressions. (2004, 108–9)

Artificial walls have been constructed within religious academic fields among the marginalized as a means of separating natural allies. All too often, religion scholars of color participate in self-segregation, constructing impressive cul-de-sacs from which to engage the dominant academic culture. No doubt, Black theology, Latine hermeneutics, Native American worldview, and Asian American Christian history provide unique and distinctive perspectives within different disciplines. Unfortunately, marginalized scholars of color construct separate cul-de-sacs that operate side by side with few paths venturing into adjoining driveways. And while solidarity occasionally occurs, if truth be known, it usually happens with minimal intellectual engagement.

The field of ethics can be one of those spaces where scholars of color move beyond their particular niche. Unlike biblical interpretation, theology, or other religious disciplines, ethics should not be conducted from only one marginalized perspective, for to do so may prove counterproductive. Nuances between different races and ethnicities exist and must be articulated in the overall conversation. Still, if the ultimate goal of ethics is to create a response—a transformative praxis that brings change to existing oppressive structures—then no one group contains the critical mass required to bring forth the desired just society. In fact, keeping marginalized groups separated ensures and protects the power, profit, and privilege of the dominant culture.

When a front-page article in the *New York Times* (January 22, 2003) proclaimed, "Hispanics Now Largest Minority, Census Shows," some Latines felt that they had finally come into their own, receiving long-overdue recognition. Yet an unspoken underlying message was being communicated to other marginalized groups, specifically African Americans: Latines are now the top dog, so you are going to have to compete against them for resources. As Justo González perceptively observed, justice can never be served by having marginalized groups compete with each other for the meager resources available to them. For example, within churches, seminaries, church agencies, and church colleges, a small portion of the budget, a few positions, and a couple of courses are reserved for the minoritized, who are encouraged to fight among themselves for their small slice of the pie

(1990, 36). These Christian institutions can now point at programs run, in spite of such limited resources, to herald their political correctness, all while continuing institutionalized oppressive structures that secure the dominant culture's privilege. In effect, marginalized groups are often prevented from working together to bring changes to these institutions.

This is not the first time the dominant culture has fostered division between marginalized groups to secure its power. In fact, this strategy is older than the nation. Thandeka, a professor of theology and culture, shows how Virginians in colonial America learned to better secure their power by forcing what could have been natural allies against their rule to compete against each other. The dominant culture succeeded in preventing allegiances from developing between two oppressed groups, the enslaved (Black people) and ex-indentured servants (poor white people), by endowing the latter with white privilege. Prior to 1670, little difference existed between poor white indentured servants, considered "the scruff and scum of England," and enslaved Black people, considered posses-sions.[10] As more of those being enslaved flooded the colonies, an economic shift developed from a white indentured servitude-based economy, where poor whites worked for a limited number of years, to a Black enslave-based economy where Africans, although costing twice as much as poor whites, worked, along with their progeny, for life. Fear of future rebellions and a changing economic base led the Virginia elite to pass legislation to create social divisions between Black people and poor white people to secure the elite's privileged place in the emerging nation (Thandeka 1999, 42–47). These laws effectively caused a division based on race between natural allies, a strategy that has continued to serve the privileged class well throughout this country's history.[11]

---

[10] Both the indentured servant and the enslaved person lived an underfed and underclothed existence in separate inadequate quarters, supervised by overseers who would whip them as a form of correction. Both groups would run away from the oppression, while others, specifically freemen (former indentured servants who were without property) formed alliances to rebel. The most intense challenge to the status quo came in the form of "Bacon's Rebellion" of 1676, which ended with the burning Jamestown to the ground. The last rebels to surrender were eighty enslaved Black people and twenty indentured white servants.

[11] In 1670, the Virginia Assembly forbade Africans and Native People from owning Christians (hereby understood as white) and non-Christians from Africa were to be enslaved for life; in 1680, any white Christian was permitted to whip any Black or enslaved person who dared lift a hand in opposition to a Christian; in 1682, conversion to Christianity would not alter lifelong slavery for Africans; in 1705, white indentured servants could not be whipped naked, only Black enslaved people,

Then, as now, the dominant culture's privilege is maintained because different marginalized groups fight with limited resources for Black justice, Latine justice, Indigenous justice, gender justice, Asian American justice, LGBTQI+ justice, and so on. Any intellectual resistance against injustice must include a concerted effort to eliminate the abuses of all oppressed groups. Although it is obvious that differences, particularly in cultural expressions, exist among numerous marginalized groups within the United States, a shared common history of disenfranchisement and the common problems of such a history create an opportunity to work together to dismantle oppressive structures affecting all who live on the periphery of power and privilege.

Ethics must be conducted from the overall margins of society more so than from any one particular marginalized perspective. Although equal access to the socioeconomic resources of our society is desirable, the marginalized must stand vigilant of the danger of simply surmounting the present existing structures causing oppression. Ethics is, and must remain, the dismantling of social mechanisms that benefit one group at the expense of another, regardless if the group privileged is white, Black, Brown, Asian, Indigenous, or any combination thereof. Not until separate marginalized groups begin to accompany each other toward justice—understood here as the dismantling of oppressive structures—can the dominant culture's hold upon resources be effectively challenged.

---

who could also be dismembered for being unruly; also in 1705, all property (horses, cattle, and hogs) was confiscated from the enslaved and sold by the church so that the proceeds could be distributed among poor whites (Morgan 1975, 329–33).

Chapter 2

The (De)Liberation of Ethics

My mother (may she rest in peace) was illiterate. She never had the opportunity to attend school and obtain an education. Growing up in the hills of Cuba, she spoke one language: Spanish. Upon arriving in the United States, she had difficulty communicating in English. But what my mother lacked in formal education she overcompensated for with street smarts. Needing employment, she, like so many other refugees, did whatever had to be done to procure a job. Failure meant her child would go hungry. "Do you know how to waitress tables?" she would be asked. "But of course, back in the old country I was the head waitress in one of the most famous and busiest restaurants in La Habana," she would respond, even though she had never carried a tray of dishes in her life. "But can you read English well?" the potential employer would ask. "But of course, I have a high school diploma from the old country." In reality, she simply memorized some important phrases found on most menus. She did get the job, and I, her son, got fed.

If I had been an ethicist back then and approached my mother questioning her character, her virtues, or her values, she would have simply laughed at me for my naiveté. If she demonstrated the virtue of honesty and confessed that she had no work experience, no education, and could barely speak the language, she would never have been hired. Yet the moral reasoning she employed enabled her to surmount societal structures fundamentally averse to her very existence. "Which is more ethical," I imagine her asking me, "doing what needs to be done to get the job, or letting the racial and sexist sins of others force us to live on the streets?" For her, houselessness was neither hyperbole nor a hypothetical case study; it was a reality we faced. She sought to meet the basic needs of her family, in other words to survive, while retaining her dignity. Because she was a woman and had been impoverished as a child (sexism and classism), she had no opportunity to obtain a formal education. Because she was a Latina in the United States living within a social structure hostile to her presence (but not her labor), few employment opportunities were available (racism). She simply did not have the luxury to wait for the "art of the possible" to feed her family.

Although my mother never read the theological works of historically marginalized women, like Delores Williams's *Sisters in the Wilderness* (1993), I have no doubt that the alternative ethical paradigm of Williams would have resonated with my Latina mother's experience. Just as the heroes of the faith, Abraham and Sarah, exploited and abused Hagar, their enslaved girl, so too was my mother exploited and abused by self-professing Christians who capitalized on her inability to resist structures designed to benefit them at her expense due to her marginalized status as a woman, specifically a poor Latina woman. Although God did not liberate Hagar from her oppression (no doubt a concern for those of us engaged in liberative ethics), she became empowered to survive and endure the institutionalized forces responsible for her marginalization. Williams balanced resistance to oppression (by whatever means possible—even escaping to the desert) and survival with a liberation that may be far into the future, if at all. A spring found in the desert, where none had existed before, enabled Hagar to survive, at least momentarily.

Likewise, my mother, who was without the requisite language skills or listed work experience, made "a way out of no way" by waitressing. My mother never read Williams's book, but, in the depth of her being, she understood Williams's message, for she was also a sister in the wilderness. Although illiterate, my mother understood what Black ethicist Katie Cannon claimed was the essence of Howard Thurman's theological ethics: "that the religion of Jesus is a 'technique of survival for the oppressed'" (188, 162). The hope of my mother was to rely on a God who always provided the means and resources to meet the harsh realities of life. She never wrote a thesis on this subject but, in her often-stated aphorism, "Dios aprieta pero no ahogar" (God squeezes but does not choke), she taught me the message of a survival ethics that relies on the God of Hagar, whom she named *El Roi*—"the God who sees me"—although it seems that this God who sees is, at times, blind.

How easy was it for the intellectual elite to dismiss my mother, along with the others who were disenfranchised, as unschooled and untrained in understanding the proper implementation of sound ethical principles? In their minds, her "opinions" are biased perceptions based on her circumstances, no matter how unfortunate her situation may be. Nevertheless, while she might have lacked the means to articulate her ethics properly to a learned audience, my mother and fellow Others constantly sit in the back of my mind as I wrestle with the ethical paradigms constructed in the prestigious halls of academia. Their moral reasoning is not the product of neatly categorized concepts found in theological textbooks, but rather produced by the messiness of struggling to meet basic needs within a social structure that successfully facilitates the failure of the marginalized. What, then, did or does eurocentric ethical theory, formulated from the secure space of privilege where employment is taken as a given, have to say to my mother? And more important, what can my illiterate mother teach those at the center of society about their own unexamined "biased opinions" of ethics as it relates to the everyday?

The Dilemma

In the name of Jesus Christ, crusades have been launched to extermi-nate so-called Muslim infidels; women seeking autonomy were burned as witches; Indigenous people refusing to bow their knees to the white God and European king were decimated; Africans were kidnapped, raped, and enslaved; and today the pauperization of two-thirds of the world's population is legitimized so a small minority of the planet can consider itself blessed by God. Yet the ethical pronouncements articulated within traditional Christian institutions such as churches, seminaries, Christian colleges, or Bible institutes tend to reinforce the ideologies of the dominant culture—ideologies that brought untold death and misery to humanity. If it is important for abusers to remain in power, then the moral precepts they create, the political states they fashion, and the religious orders they support must either explicitly or implicitly maintain, if not justify, the status quo. Even when ethical pronouncements are made that are critical of the power, profit, or privilege amassed by few at the expense of many, little if any praxis is enacted to dismantle the mechanisms responsible for maintaining the status quo. Usually cosmetic reforms are offered, with no serious consideration of the structural forms of injustices or social sin. As long as oppressive social structures persist, actions by individuals, no matter how well intended, are incapable of liberating those existing on the margins of society. Liberation occurs through radical structural change. Reform simply avoids questioning the basics of the dominant culture's life-style, a lifestyle that many professional ethicists share.

White male (and increasingly female) ethicists with the economic or race privilege that accompany endowed chairs or full professorships at prestigious academic institutions do not theorize in empty vacuums. Like the rest of the privileged dominant culture, they occupy a certain loca-tion—an environment or context—that influences, affects, and shapes their ethical deliberations: deliberations that tend to justify their social location while consciously or unconsciously disenfranchising those on their margins.

If we are to deal with issues of ethics, grounded in the reality of today's world, then we are forced to deal with the structural forces that form the "habitus" of those benefiting from the present social structures. If Christian ethics is constructed at the center of society and rooted in a particular culture that is understood from a position of power, profit, and privilege, then doing ethics from the margins becomes an attempt to transform how ethics itself is done. Some ethicists from the periphery or margins of the dominant culture believe that their voices, usually silent or ignored, are capable of radically changing the theology, the doctrine, the practices, the mission, and the teachings of Christian institutions, starting at the grassroots level. To participate in an ethical discourse from the margins is to engage the proactive practices preceding the liberation and salvation of the least among us.

(De)Liberating Liberation

Since the start of the twentieth century, ethicists of the dominant culture gradually moved away from discussing which praxis should be employed when facing an ethical dilemma and instead devoted more of their energies to issues that dealt with the nature of ethics, specifically questions concerning virtues and the good. The proclivity of the dominant culture to deliberate ethics by pursuing the abstract good usually concludes with ethics being (de)liberated. Praxis leading toward a more just social order was one of the first casualties of abstract ethical thought. Even though such abstract deliberations may be sympathetic to the plight of the oppressed, they still fall short by failing to alleviate the root causes of disenfranchisement and dispossession.

But for those doing ethics from the margins, the key concern is not to determine some abstract understanding of what is ethical; rather, in the face of dehumanizing, oppressive structures, the issue is to determine how people of faith adapt their actions to serve the least among us. Ethics becomes the process by which the marginalized enter a more human condition by overcoming oppressive or controlling societal mechanisms. For them, the starting point is not some ethical truth based on church doctrine, unexamined belief, or rational deliberation. Instead, the starting point is analyzing the situation faced by the disenfranchised of our world, our nation, and our workplaces and then reflecting with them theoretically and theologically to draw pastoral conclusions for actions to be taken.

Still, when ethical perspectives are voiced from the margins of society, all too often they are easily dismissed, especially if the articulators have not developed their methodology along the lines of acceptable eurocentric thought, usually viewed as the only appropriate form for participation in academic discourse. For some euroamerican ethicists, the praxis of liberation is reduced to a "theological symbol" designed to garner support from Christians for a particular social movement. But liberation is not just a symbol; it should mean a radical break with the status quo designed to maintain oppressive structures. Nonetheless, several ethicists of the dominant culture respond by accusing those doing ethics from a liberative perspective of "moving from theology to politics without passing through ethics." Such arguments dismiss the formation of ethics from the margins as a very limited understanding of ethics.[1]

While proficiency with the eurocentric ethical canon is the admission ticket to acceptability within academic discussions on ethics, those doing ethics at the margins of power, profit, and privilege concentrate on practical praxis—behavior and actions. It is not what is said that bears witness to the good news of the resurrection, but what is done to those still trapped in the forces of death. When abstract deliberations are applied to reality, the attempts, although admirable in their aspirations to create a more just society, most often fail to assist those who are marginalized. Such deliberations continue to reinforce the very social structures responsible for much of the oppression experienced by the disenfranchised. In large part, this is due to the present social structures being viewed and accepted as necessary to maintain a well-ordered society.

In *The City of God*, Augustine explains that the ultimate good is eternal life, while the ultimate evil is eternal death. The ultimate moral response for those living in the earthly city is a life lived in faith, awaiting the heavenly city to come (1960 [426], 19.4). Augustine goes so far as to suggest that, if we remain loyal to the heavenly city through faith, all other aspects of living a moral life will ensue. Nonetheless, shaken by Rome's political vulnerability and eventual sack in 410 CE by the Goths, Augustine looked to the civil structure to provide peace and order.[2] While salvation could be achieved only through the church, the state, although corrupt, was a necessary evil that maintained law and order. "Every use of temporal things is related to the enjoyment of earthly peace in the earthly city, while in the heav-

---

[1] For example, see the works of Gustafson, *Theology and Christian Ethics* (1974) and *Can Ethics Be Christian?* (1975). See also McCann and Strain, *Polity and Praxis* (1985, 146–52).

[2] Non-Christian writers such as Celsus and Porphyry blamed the deterioration of the Roman Empire on the rise of Christianity, which embraced such "weak" virtues as love. They claimed that Christianity was a seditious movement that undermined the traditional brute militarism that originally forged the empire. One of the reasons Augustine wrote *The City of God* was to refute such accusations.

enly city it is related to the enjoyment of everlasting peace" (Ibid.: 19.14). Acknowledging injustices and advocating their redress, Augustine insisted that correcting injustice should not occur if it endangers societal order and peace. This social order is arranged according to a hierarchy where husbands ruled over wives (sexism) and masters ruled over the enslaved (classism) so that peace could be maintained (19.14).

Martin Luther was greatly influenced by Augustinian thought. Luther maintained that the gospel is to be placed in heaven and the law on earth, erecting a barrier between the two. Humans are to obey the laws on earth, even when those laws dehumanize others. When peasants fought for the abolition of serfdom, Luther reminded them that earthly kingdoms can exist only if there is inequality, where some are free and others subservient. Repudiating the oppressed peasants' demand for their full humanity, Luther wrote to them:

> You assert that no one is to be the serf of anyone else, because Christ has made us all free.... Did not Abraham and other patriarchs and prophets have slaves? ... A slave can be a Christian, and have Christian freedom, in the same way that a prisoner or a sick man is a Christian, and yet be free. [Your claim] would make all men equal, and turn the spiritual kingdom of Christ into a worldly, external kingdom; and that is impossible. A worldly kingdom cannot exist without an inequality of persons, some being free, some imprisoned, some lords, some subjects. (1967 [1525], 46:39)

Luther went so far as to advise those in authority to "smite, slay, and stab, secretly or openly" the rebelling peasants, who like "mad dogs" must be killed (46:50). For Luther, political stability, even if maintained through the oppression of the marginalized, takes precedence over the humanity of the marginalized.

The influence of these patriarchs of Western Christianity continues to be felt today. Some ethicists of the dominant culture, such as James Gustafson, warn of the danger of "[upsetting] a necessary equilibrium in society" (1975, 119–20). Liberative praxis is fine, as long as society's equilibrium is maintained. Ethicist John Rawls insisted that the pursuit of justice be constrained within the limits of ensuring a well-ordered society, for only through such a society can a sense of justice be acquired (1971, 453–57). While those from the dominant culture strive to maintain society's equilibrium—an equilibrium that secures their place within the overall social order—those who remain marginalized hope to disrupt said equilibrium. They clearly see their needs subordinated to those of the "well-ordered" society (understood here as a society that continues to privilege one group). They also recognize those who benefit from the status quo will never voluntarily forfeit their privilege.

While we may all agree on the need for a well-ordered society, the question under dispute is who determines how and what form of a well-ordered society is to be maintained. For example, in his 1961 book concerning the sit-ins conducted by African Americans protesting segregation at lunch counters, ethicist Paul Ramsey heaped praise upon these protestors and their calls for more equitable race legislation. Yet he found the sit-ins to be contradictory to proper Christian social action because they disrupted a well-ordered society. For him, the sit-ins promoted "lawlessness" and violated the rights of others, specifically the orderly stewardship of private property (1961, xiv). While desiring to end the racist segregation of his time, he first insisted on the preservation of the existing well-ordered society:

> But in the Christian view, simple and not so simple injustice alone has never been a sufficient justification for revolutionary change. There is always also the question of order to be considered, and a need for restraints placed upon all and upon the injustice infecting even our claims for greater justice. The Christian stands, then, for the rule of law against every utopian liberalism, however high-minded. (48–49)

Raising the consciousness of the marginalized always endangers the secure space of those calling for "law and order" who envision their privilege as being threatened. All too often, in the name of "law and order," structures oppressive to marginalized groups are legitimized. For those on the underside of society's equilibrium, upsetting the dominant culture's serenity is the primary goal. As Martin Luther King Jr. reminded us, "We know through painful experience that freedom is never voluntarily given by the oppressor; it must be demanded by the oppressed" (1964, 80). Such demands will create disharmony within "well-ordered" societies.

There have always been eurocentric religious scholars who tolerate a social order, regardless of how unethical it may appear to be. The marginalized are expected to respect and honor those who are at the center not just for the good of society, but because this is how God ordained the social structure. With suspicion, those on the margins approach scholars like the sixteenth-century reformer John Calvin, who insisted that those who are marginalized, specifically the poor, should respect and honor those who are economically their superiors because God in God's wisdom bestowed the "elect" with special material gifts. In the political realm, Calvin called citizens to submit to governments, regardless of how tyrannical their rulers may have been because it is up to the Lord to avenge such despots, while it is up to the citizens to simply "obey and suffer" (1873 p1536], 4.20.31). Furthermore, Calvin stated that the "poor must yield to the rich; the common folk, to the nobles; the servants, to their masters; the unlearned, to the educated." Clearly Calvin, as with most of the eurocentric culture, ignored how the amassing of power, profit, and privilege is connected with the marginalization of the poor, the common folk, the servants, and the unlearned. For this reason, the marginalized, for their very liberation, must reject eurocentric Christianity, which insists on maintaining oppressive social structures for the sake of order and the white male God created in its image.

The Social Power of Ethics

Since the rise of modernity, specifically manifested in the eighteenth century as the Age of Enlightenment, ethicists have moved away from religious ethical systems founded on revelation, biblical hermeneutics, or church tradition. For the "modern" mind, there existed unambiguous universal truths about the very nature of reality and reliable methodologies for arriving at the answers to all the dilemmas humanity faces. All that was required was their discovery. The process of discovering these truths made God, to some extent, irrelevant. God was, in effect, replaced with a scientific process of secularization that found the answers to ethical dilemmas in humanistic or naturalistic moral deliberations. The Enlightenment asserted that an individual was capable, via one's own reasoning ability, of discovering absolute and universal moral laws. An instinctive moral compass found within human nature could guide the individual in determining to do good and in refraining from doing evil.[3] Other ethicists, employing a utilitarian approach, defined what is ethical by the principle that all actions can be numerically scaled; hence the action providing the greatest net benefits becomes the correct moral choice.[4] Yet, more often than not, such appeals to self-evident propositions become a justification for those in power to protect their self-interests.

---

[3] Ethicists like John Rawls suggest that an intuitive sense of justice will guide humans in making correct moral decisions (1971, 114–15).

[4] Most ethicists today would agree that, if a society is unjust to a minority portion of its population, even though greater utilitarian benefits are enjoyed by most of the population, then that society as a whole is acting unjustly.

As previously mentioned, ethical precepts do not develop in a social or cultural vacuum. Yet, ironically, the social context for the construction of ethics is usually ignored. What is termed "moral" is more often a product of the power residing within a person's social location than of a person's understanding of natural law or, for that matter, an "objective" reading of the Scriptures or the product of enlightened moral reasoning or logic. Nonetheless, the reasoning or logic of the center is often inappropriate for the margins. As Malcolm X reminded us,

> What is logical to the oppressor isn't logical to the oppressed. And what is reason to the oppressor isn't reason to the oppressed. The black people [and I would add all who are from the margins] in this country are beginning to realize that what sounds reasonable to those who exploit us doesn't sound reasonable to us. There just has to be a new system of reason and logic devised by us who are at the bottom. (1968, 133)

The reality from the margins of society is that those with power impose their constructs of morality upon the rest of the culture. Even though the privileged are quite adept at convincing themselves their acts are altruistic, those who are disenfranchised are seldom convinced. Virtues, no matter how desirable, can be imposed to ensure the subservience of the marginalized. Martin Luther King Jr. made a similar point when discussing the difference between just and unjust laws. In his letter from a Birmingham jail he wrote,

> Sometimes a law is just on its face and unjust in its application. For instance, I have been arrested on a charge of parading without a permit. Now, there is nothing wrong in having an ordinance which requires a permit for a parade. But such an ordinance becomes unjust when it is used to maintain segregation and to deny citizens the First-Amendment privilege of peaceful assembly. (1964, 83)

This is not to say that the law King refers to or certain virtues are unimportant; it is to insist that whatever becomes law, or is defined as virtue, is more often a product of power relationships than we are willing to admit.

Ethics from the margins insists that racism, sexism, heterosexism, and classism are the end products of the exercise of power. The power of the dominant culture, which creates Christian ethics, can no longer be explained simply as a group of institutions ensuring obedience, or as a mode of subjugation, or as a form of domination exerted by one group over another. Rather, power is used to normalize and legitimize what the dominant culture determines to be ethical; it does so by harnessing the existing forces to which it has access (Foucault 1988 [1982], 18). For this reason, power's hold upon people is based on its ability to produce. Power creates pleasure, constructs knowledge, and generates discourse. In this sense, power can be understood as something positive, producing reality and creating the subject's opinion of what is "truth" (Foucault 1984, 60–61). Whether consciously or unconsciously, Christians of the dominant culture, while truly wishing to remain faithful to their religious convictions, at times construct ethical perspectives to preserve their power, while defining their self-serving ethical response as Christian. In their minds, their perspectives are viewed as "truth," answering the question concerning what Jesus himself would do.

These perspectives are then taught as truth to those who suffer by how these very same ethical perspectives are employed within society. The illegitimate power to subjugate the race, gender, orientation, or class of others is legitimized and normalized by the dominant culture. French philosopher Michel Foucault explains how this process of normalization and legitimation takes place through his analogy of an insane asylum. Individuals committed were freed from their chains if they promised to restore themselves—in other words, if they imposed upon themselves their own "domestication." Those deemed mentally insane were treated as children who needed to learn how to respect the authority of their superiors. Foucault provides an example of a cure achieved through tea parties, because civilized people knew how to act during tea parties. Patients, to prove they were no longer mad, had to behave with the proper decorum befitting civilized persons—learning in effect to become an anonymous "normal" person. Because the patients were always observed, they learned how to watch themselves. In short, they learned how to police their own actions. With time, the patient internalized the acceptable behavior through self-discipline. The asylum became a religious domain without religion, where the mad were taught ethical uniformity. Although free, their chains could always be reinstated (Foucault 1965, 246–59).

Like the patients in the asylum, the marginalized suffer from their own "madness"—their refusal to conform to the ethical standards of the "civilized" dominant culture. In the minds of those with power, profit, and privilege, marginalization is self-imposed, a refusal on the part of the disenfranchised to assimilate to what is perceived as the common good. When they behave, when they submit to the law and order of the dominant culture, they are "free." Those who reject the dominant view are eyed and often handled with suspicion. Rejection of the dominant culture's superiority, and the morality it advocates, proves they have not yet been cured of their "madness." The danger of doing ethical reflection from the center of power, profit, and privilege is that any moral truth can be distorted or perverted when the perspectives of the marginalized are ignored.

Yet for these ignored voices to question the validity of how the dominant culture arrives at ethical precepts becomes an act of madness, or even sacrilege. As in Foucault's asylums, those who benefit from the then-present power structures get to legitimize their version of ethical truth for all, including the disenfranchised. The dominant culture operates within a framework constructed from the social location of privilege, and the resulting system of ethics functions to justify the norm. Even when such ethical deliberations assail poverty, the economic structures responsible for causing poverty—which are also responsible for securing the privilege of the dominant culture—are seldom analyzed.

Normalization of the dominant culture's ethical views is a product of their "habitus," a product of the social location of its members. Habitus can be understood as a system of internalized dispositions that mediates between social structures and practical activities, shaped by the former and regulating the latter (Brubaker 1985, 758). Those born into positions of privilege possess a socially constructed lifestyle that facilitates their ability to justify their privilege. This lifestyle, in a sense, unconsciously teaches them how to understand their economic and social success. Their identity is indebted to the community from which they come, which is primarily responsible for their so-called personal opinions. Their position within society, justified through customs, language, attitudes, dispositions, beliefs, traditions, values, and so on, existed prior to their birth and will continue to shape future generations after they are dead. As the "memory of the body," they bear the culture within them, assimilating from childhood the community's knowledge and experiences. From the moment of birth, these constructs were imposed on them, molding their childhood and guiding them through adulthood by decoding and adjusting to new situations. When their position within the privileged class is threatened, they protect their self-interest without realizing they are doing so. To protect their self-interest, they merely assert what they were born into in order to become what they are, an effort done with the lack of self-consciousness that marks their so-called nature (Bourdieu 1977 [1972]).

One's habitus so imprisons the mind it becomes difficult to move beyond a particular social location without making a major shift in how reality is conceived and understood. Consequently, few members of the dominant culture question the construction of their conscience. Accordingly, those who approach ethics from positions of power and privilege must remain vigilant during their moral deliberations, lest they confuse what is ethical with what is their habitus. Their only hope is to move beyond their social location by forming relationships of solidarity with the marginalized. According to José Míguez Bonino, a Latin American theologian, ethical reflection done from the margins becomes a resource by which the overall society can be transformed, so that human possibility can be maximized at a minimum human cost (1983, 107).

We are left questioning the role that social factors play in influencing how ethical reflection is constructed and conducted. Those of the dominant culture often find it difficult to accept that much of their moral understanding may in fact be a product of their privileged position rather than an ordained gift handed down to them by a Supreme Being. The morality that protects the status quo is often mystified through religious symbols and taboos ensuring that ethical precepts are regulated and enforced. By defining Christian ethics as commands proceeding from the Divine or as interpretations of Scripture—rather than formulated at the center of privilege—any arguments questioning privilege can be dismissed as a distortion of morality. It is not that the marginalized lack the academic rigor to do ethical reflection, nor do they simply bypass ethical reflection altogether. Rather, their approach to their oppressive situations produces a different way of doing ethics. The schism existing between privileged academic centers and the marginalized periphery that surrounds them is so wide that many Christian "principles" become abstract concepts lacking any application to disenfranchised lives.

Incarnation: Experiencing in the Flesh

"In the beginning was the Word, and the Word was with God, and the Word was God.... And the Word took on flesh and resided among us" (Jn. 1:1, 14). The God of the Gospel does not stand aloof from human experiences, but rather as enfleshed Godself in the concrete events of human history. Not only does incarnation demonstrate how to become Christ-like, but God, through the Christ event, "learns" how to be humanlike. God can understand the plight of today's crucified people, who hang on crosses dedicated to the idols of race, class, gender, and heterosexual superiority. The crucifixion of Christ is God's solidarity with the countless multitudes who continue to be crucified today. Jesus's death on the cross should never be reduced to a sacrifice called for to pacify some angry Deity offended by human sin. Ignored for centuries by Christian theology is that Jesus, in the fullness of his humanhood, was put to death, like so many today, by the civil and religious leaders who saw him as a threat to their power, profit, and privilege. There is nothing redemptive in the suffering of the just. The importance of the cross for the marginalized is that they have a God who understands their trials and tribulations because God in the flesh also suffered trials and tribulations. The good news is not so much that Jesus was crucified, but that Jesus rose from the dead—not to demonstrate God's power, but to assure the marginalized that crucifixion is not how the story ends.

This God who became human continues to enflesh Godself in the everyday lives and experiences of today's crucified people. A crucial element in ethical reflection is what Latines call *lo cotidiano*, the Spanish term for "the everyday." Latina theologian María Pilar Aquino, among others, avers the importance of *lo cotidiano* in the doing of theology. For Aquino, the salvific experience of God in the here and now is experienced by the marginalized in their "daily struggles for humanization, for a better quality of life and for greater social justice" (1999, 39). As such, I insist that *lo cotidiano* is the necessary source of all liberative ethical reflection. Ethics from the margins is contextual, where the everyday experience of the disenfranchised becomes the subject and source of ethical reflection. To do ethics from the margins is to reflect on autobiographical elements to avoid creating a lifeless ethical understanding.

"Story theology," a major theme among some Asian American theologians, attempts to challenge the West's hyperemphasis on grounding all theological thought in the rational. Similarly, the "third eye," according to Japanese Zen master Daisetz Suzuki, is an Asian attempt to become open to that which is unheard because of one's own ignorance. To perceive reality with a "third eye" allows Christianity to turn to the abundant Indigenous stories, legends, and folklore of the people, as well as the experiences of the marginalized. An autobiographically based narrative ethics resonates among the disenfranchised who find that the inclusion of their stories provides a needed "heart" to the Western emphasis on the rational (Yang 2004, 178). Additionally, the methodological inclusion of one's story in an ethical dilemma powerfully connects reality with theory. Such an inclusion challenges the predominant assumption that all ethical deliberations must occur apart from and independent of the interpreter's social location or identity. Rather than verifying what is truth as explicated by those who are traditionally viewed as authorities (such as clergy or scholars), or through sacred texts as historically interpreted by experts, the source of ethical deliberation begins with *lo cotidiano* as experienced and understood by those existing on the margins. The perspective of those who are considered nonpersons because of their race, class, orientation, or gender becomes the starting point for any ethical act, thus shattering the grip of those atop theological hierarchies, halting them from being the sole legitimate interpreters or arbiters of what is ethical.

Christian Ethics from the Center

We live in a world where social, political, and economic offenses are common. Only a privileged few can use institutionalized racism, classism, sexism, and heterosexism to insulate themselves from the ravages of maltreatment. If doing ethics from the margins provides liberation for both the oppressed and the oppressor, then to insist on doing ethics only from the center of power, profit, and privilege frustrates the hopes of not just the disenfranchised but also the privileged. Before we can begin to participate in a liberative ethics, we must explore how the ethics of the dominant culture masks the oppression of those who are disenfranchised. How is ethics constructed to encourage the dominant culture to remain complicit with institutionalized racism, classism, sexism, and heterosexism?

A Wretch Like Me

Are humans innately good or innately evil? If human nature is good, is society then responsible for human corruption? If so, ethics is reduced to education that reveals the error responsible for present injustices, given the assumption that good people will not knowingly participate in evil actions.[5] But if human nature is evil, then legal sanctions are needed to force humans to live morally.[6] Although such neat good-evil dichotomies concerning human nature simplify the complexity concerning the inherent essence of being human, however one answers such abstract philosophical questions, the fact remains that depravity exists. While depravity may be a reality, we should beware of the eurocentric fallacy of concluding we are simply evil vessels devoid of all good—as some would have us believe.[7]

---

[5] Eighteenth-century French philosopher Jean-Jacques Rousseau understood the original human as living in a state of innocent harmony with nature. Even though humans are presently wicked, they originally were naturally good in the state of nature. They were, in his view, a type of noble savage (1964 [1755]).

[6] Thomas Hobbes, the seventeenth-century English philosopher who formulated the doctrine of psychological egoism, argued that the state of nature is one "where every man is enemy to every man" so that human life in this state of nature is one that is "solitary, poor, nasty, brutish, and short" (1651, 96–97).

[7] Karl Barth understood that the depravity of humanity forbade any goodness

When aligned with colonial and imperialist thinking, the "sin" that exists among humans can contribute to relegating people of color to the level of nonpersons. Being nonpersons, their land can be stolen, their bodies raped, their labor exploited, and their humanity disregarded. Some from the dominant culture repent and attempt to live a humbler life. For them, there is an emphasis upon repentance from their depraved nature, as was the reported case of the slave captain who penned the words to "Amazing Grace." He wrote that grace exists "for such a wretch like me." For those who live a life of privilege due to advantages paid for by those who were made to believe in their nonpersonhood, such emotions of self-derogation may prove to be a healthy step toward a spiritual path of healing. The danger occurs when those with power impose upon the wretched of the earth the requirement that they be "saved" in similar fashion.

One size does not fit all. It was—and often continues to be—assumed that the salvation needed by those on the margins is the same yearned for by those from the dominant culture. An assumption is usually made that the sins of the dominant culture (as Reinhold Niebuhr held with the sin of pride) are also the sins of those on the margins of power. While those who formulated the theological concepts and ethical precepts—usually from locations of power, profit, and privilege—may have wrestled with the prideful sin of self-centeredness, the marginalized have instead suffered from a lack of self-identity. The images and thoughts of the dominant culture are usually at the center. Thus, the marginalized often interpret reality through the eyes of their oppressors rather than through their own disenfranchised eyes. Therefore, many from the centers of society preach self-denial, submission, and unworthiness to the marginalized, when the disenfranchised should instead be hearing about pride in self, liberation, human dignity, and worth.

There is no need to preach humility to those who are already humble. Humbled by the sins of the dominant culture, they do not need to be exhorted to become still more lowly—quite the contrary. Salvation for the marginalized is the transformation from nonperson to personhood. The liberating message of the gospel they need to hear is that they are worthy, precious, and due dignity because they are created in the very image of

---

from residing within individuals, making it impossible for them to be ethical, that is, determining the good. Only Christ can do this, and only by faith can the Christian rely on God's grace and participate in an authentic ethical deliberation. Apart from grace, humans lack the capacity to distinguish good from evil. For those lacking Christ in their lives, anything proposed as the good is simply a distortion (1928, 136–82).

God. Jesus understood that part of his salvific message was to humble the proud and lift the lowly. As it is written in the Magnificat, "[God] pulled down the powerful from their thrones and exalted the humble ones. God filled the hungry with good things, and the rich God sent away empty" (Lk. 1:52–53). The privileged are the ones who need to come to terms with their spiritual wretchedness. The wretched need to come to terms with their infinite value.

Grace, Not Works

Martin Luther, like Augustine before him, believed good works would flow from any individual who was freed from the bondage of sin through the justifying love of God. For Augustine, grace did not free the moral agent from his or her obligations to perform good works; in fact, conversion generated a new creature in Christ now capable of doing good because their life was dominated by God's grace. Still, experiencing the forgiveness of Christ took precedence over any need to know the good. And, although Luther fought against a misinterpretation of his doctrine of justification by faith that advocated a release from ethical obligations, the Reformation formula of *sola fide* (only faith) undermined the need to consider ethics crucial to the Christian identity. Contrary to what Augustine or Luther may have said or meant about the duty of Christians to do good works, the way that eurocentric Christians have interpreted *sola fide* has proven detrimental to the marginalized. It is wrong to reduce Christianity to an issue of grace, where one can profess Christ as Lord without seriously considering how justice affects and impacts the believer's life.

Sola fide as practiced by those who are privileged is harmful for those existing on the margins of privilege. Used in this manner, the doctrine of justification—which encompasses the forgiveness of sin, freedom from guilt, and reconciliation with God—fosters a sense of impunity among the powerful and privileged. It gives the impression that those who benefit from the present power structures can receive from Christ pardon for their sins without any need to convert from the practices and actions contributing to oppressive social structures. Relationships are thus limited to the vertical, without seriously considering the marginalized neighbor.

Sola fide can become the extreme counterpart to the danger of solely relying on works for justification. During Jesus's time, those who were religious created a set of rules that excused them from fulfilling their obligations to their faith. Through a strict adherence to tithing, they ignored issues of justice. Jesus condemned them by stating, "Woe to you scribes and Pharisees, hypocrites! Because you tithe on the mint, the dill, and the cumin, yet you have ignored the weightier matters of the law, like justice, mercy, and faith" (Mt. 23:23). On another occasion, Jesus condemned the hypocrisies of the religious scholars who "dedicated" their property to God to avoid the just praxis of caring for their aging parents (Mk. 7:11–13). Rather than being legalistic, as were some during the time of Jesus, many ethicists and theologians from the dominant culture today have gone to the other extreme. While unquestioning obedience to the law undermines the establishment of a justice-based relationship with the marginalized, so also does an unquestioning acceptance of grace effectively contribute to ignoring the needs and concerns of the disenfranchised.

Heaven-Bound

Ethical praxis that can lead to a more just society is, at times, ignored by emphasizing the hereafter rather than the here and now. If belief in Christ is all that is required for a blessed hereafter, those with the power to form theological discourse can present heaven to the wretched of the earth as a future place where they will be rewarded for their patient suffering. The present state of misery endured by the disenfranchised is justified as the consequence of some original sin. Their doleful existence on earth will be compensated by heavenly mansions and ruby-crested crowns of gold. Such escapist illusions only help to pacify the disenfranchised by encouraging them to shrug off their misery as God's will. If the hereafter becomes a narcotic (like Marx's reference to opium), it negates what is of value in the here and now.

Christian ethics, as formulated within the margins of society, rejects the notion that God somehow wills God's children to subsist under oppressive structures so that they can eventually live with everlasting riches. Any view of an afterlife—eschatology—that justifies present oppressive structures is satanic. "The reign of God is at hand," Jesus was fond of saying. God's reign is not in some far-off, distant place disconnected from the trials and tribulations here on earth. Rather, God's reign is a present-day social, political, public, and personal reality evident among God's people. While not negating some form of final reward in the hereafter, the gospel message is primarily for the here and now. Salvation, understood as liberation in its fullness, has as much to do with the present as with a final resting place. And even though praxis (or what Luther called "works") might be insufficient for some eurocentric theologians for obtaining the salvation that remains a gift according to God's grace, praxis is an act of obedience, an outward expression of an inward conversion.

Juan Luis Segundo, a Latin American liberation theologian, insists that genuine conversion provides for true reconciliation with God and among humans. Conversion requires a confession of the causes of estrangement (specifically those dealing with power, profit, and privilege) and an attempt to take action to eradicate these causes. If not, premature reconciliation will develop, masking unresolved structures of oppression. Although "conversion" is Christian terminology, Segundo uses it to indicate a change of attitude (1993, 51). If conversion does not establish justice-based relationships with God and fellow human beings, then salvation hasn't taken place. Any conversion devoid of actions for human liberation from structures of oppression is a façade that only normalizes present oppressions along gender, sexual orientation, race, and class lines and masks forms of repression. Any salvation based on Jesus Christ—whether socially, culturally, or legally imposed—should free believers from the bondage that reduces humans to disposable objects. In short, as a spiritual dimension, conversion heals. If not, old enmities and unresolved hatreds from present systems continue in any supposedly reconciled future.

If conversion is understood as a rupture with and a turning away from sin (sin caused by individual actions and sin caused by social institutions), then salvation can occur only through the raising of consciousness to a level that recognizes the personal and communal sins that prevent the start of a new life in Jesus. Conversion is a witness, a testimony to an unsaved world whose rejection of God, through the worship of the idol of self-interest, is manifested in oppressive relations according to sexual orientation, race, class, and gender. Conversion to Christ does not mean some recognition of an abstract concept of Jesus sitting on a throne in heaven, nor is it an ethereal emotional experience. Rather, conversion to Christ serves the oppressed flesh-and-blood neighbor who, as "the least of my people," is, in reality, Jesus in the here and now. Salvation through Christ is, at its essence, a relationship with God and with each other, a justice-based relationship whose very nature transforms all aspects of humanity so that everyone can have the abundant life to its fullest.

Unfortunately, in too many cases, the pursuit of salvation has been privatized. Peruvian theologian Gustavo Gutiérrez reminded us,

> Faith cannot be lived on the private plane of the "interior life." Faith is the very negation of retreat into oneself, of folding back upon oneself. Faith comes alive in the dynamism of the good news that reveals us as children of the Father and sisters and brothers of one another, and creates a community, a church, the visible sign to others of liberation in Christ. (1984 [1979], 67)

Too often, personal salvation has become spiritual escapism rather than justice-based transformation. Some conservative evangelicals are consumed with a passion to witness for life after death. But the real message hungered for by the vast majority of those living in oppression is life prior to death. Such a message must be communicated through action rather than just through words. Christian evangelism is thus understood as any action that leads toward the transformation of the individual, as well as the community, to the basic principles of justice lived and taught by Jesus Christ. The conversion resulting from such an evangelical venture does not lead toward a "once saved, always saved" understanding, but rather to a lifelong process of working out the liberation made possible by Christ, or as the Apostle Paul would suggest, "[the working out of] your salvation in fear and trembling" (Phil. 2:12).

Some people attempt to Christianize the social order to remedy social ills, believing that society's peccadilloes are caused by decisions made by non-Christians in positions of power. Yet saving a powerful individual so that a so-called Christian is making decisions in the public arena does not reform the social structure. As previously mentioned, most moral precepts reflect the cultural and philosophical milieu of a people, not of an individual. The conversion of decision-makers within the social structures often has little or no impact on how these social structures operate. Concentrating solely on personal piety, morality, or virtues without engaging the actual structures responsible for producing injustices will lead to discouraging results. A change of heart within individuals usually is insufficient to produce a more just social order. The social structures themselves require transformation and conversion. Without such transformation, reform may occur, but the marginalized will often still find themselves disenfranchised due to race, sexual orientation, class, or gender.

Salvation in its truest sense becomes liberation from sin—sins committed by the individual and, just as important, those committed against the individual through social institutions. Reducing salvation to personal choice, disconnected from the community, is foreign to the biblical text. Take the example of Moses in the Hebrew Bible or Paul in the New Testament. Both were willing to be cut off from God and face eternal damnation for the sake of the community's liberation. Moses pleaded to God to blot him from the book of life if it would save God's people (Ex. 32:32), while Paul was willing to be condemned and cut off from Christ if it would help his compatriots find salvation (Rom. 9:2). Both Moses and Paul refused to exchange their quest to transform society as an expression of their love for their neighbor for some privatized faith that assured them of individual immortality. They serve as models of a self-sacrificing faith that places the needs of the community before personal ethereal reward. They understood the depths of the words of Jesus when he said, "A person can have no greater love than to lay down one's life for one's friends" (Jn. 15:13). While for Christians belief in Christ is important, if not crucial, it remains insufficient. Jesus states, "If, then, you offer your gift on the altar, and there remember that your companion has something against you, leave your gift there before the altar, and go. First be reconciled to your companion, and then come offer your gift" (Mt. 5:23–24). The implication is that God is more concerned with loving and reconciling with those who have a grievance than with the would-be worshiper's personal relationship with God or their attempt to gain moral perfection through obedience to religious law, tradition, or custom.

Conversion for those of the dominant culture must move beyond simple belief. Rather, conversion should move toward a consciousness-raising experience linked to a specific praxis, a praxis that breaks with personal and social sin and leads the new believer to turn away from the old life of privilege and begin a new life in Christ manifested as solidarity with the same people with whom Jesus sought to identify himself: the outcasts. Consciousness-raising is, then, the process by which persons become cognizant of their existential being, leading toward a self-reflective, critical awareness of how a person benefits or is oppressed by the prevailing social structures. For both the privileged and disenfranchised, conversion as a consciousness-raising praxis leads to the transformation of the person and society so that the convert can encounter the "neighbor" in the fullness of the other's humanity. Regardless of the neighbor's belief or confession in Christ, that neighbor retains their worth before God.

Still, salvation can never be equated with a social system or agenda created by humans (such as socialism, capitalism, or neoliberalism); liberation is a theological enterprise with a social ethical agenda of establishing justice so that all human beings can live in what Martin Luther King Jr. called "the beloved community," where justice rolls down like living water and righteousness flows like an everlasting stream. For Christian ethics to take hold, radical, concrete changes are required in the public arena (as well as in the life of the believer) to bring salvation, understood as liberation, to both the marginalized and to those who benefit from their disenfranchisement. Such radical actions move the church from teaching ethics as a collection of moral precepts for private living to teaching ethics as political and social actions that reflect one's faith testimony. The basic criterion for doing ethics from the margins becomes the salvation and liberation of all—both the privileged and the disenfranchised who are oppressed by political, social, and cultural structures that overtly or covertly foster racism, classism, sexism, and heterosexism. This evangelistic action for liberation is the ultimate love praxis.

A Personal Relationship

The pervasiveness of individualism, specifically the John Wayne type of rugged individualism celebrated in the United States, relegates moral decisions to the private sphere, in a sense essentially consigning views on morality to the individual. This tends to weaken social bonds and hamper the development of a communal apparatus authorized to foster and implement ethical actions that can lead to a social order grounded on relationships. When morality is privatized, individual members of the dominant culture can shop for a set of values or virtues, like any other consumer good, that is appropriate to the particular individual at a given place and time. This is not to minimize the importance of the individual, but, because the self should never be considered apart from the communal, ethics must be fashioned to acknowledge the relationships established by the interrelatedness of the individual and the community, where actions committed by one profoundly affect all.

Psychologist Carol Gilligan, well known for her work in gender studies, has proposed that psychology has ignored and misunderstood women's moral commitments because the discipline has historically focused on observing the lives of men. She maintains that men usually approach morality from an individualistic perspective that deliberates on issues of rights in a way that is interconnected with the celebration of personal autonomy. On the other hand, she observes, women approach moral dilemmas from the context of relationships grounded in the ability to care (1982, 17). I claim that the approach to moral reasoning for women, as described by Gilligan, is similar to how ethics is conducted within disenfranchised communities. Lacking privilege and power, members of marginalized communities find themselves clinging to each other in order to survive oppressive structures. They are supported by these relationships of caring, which become crucial in understanding ethics from the margins. Ethical praxis from the margins arises from the relational links of communal morality and the injustices caused by social structures, whether manifested as traditions, customs, or laws. To divorce ethics from critical social analysis is to reduce ethics to an individualistic morality that is often of little use to those struggling to survive. Those doing ethics on the margins of society realize that unequal alignments of power within social structures (male over female, heterosexual over LGBTQI+, white over nonwhite, or wealthy over poor) are usually the root causes of injustice and the antithesis of the gospel message.

To counter this trend, Christian ethics as done from the margins becomes a *koinonia* ethics, a political calling for radical structural changes in how society is ordered. *Koinonia*, the New Testament Greek term used to describe the faith community, connotes relationships and fellowship, where all things are held in common. Material possessions (Acts 5) and experiences are both held in common. Paul writes, "If one member [of the *koinonia*] suffers, with it suffer all members, or if one member is glorified, with it, all members rejoice" (1 Cor. 12:26). *Koinonia* occurs when the community gathers to stand in solidarity, sharing the trials and joys of the human condition. Any ethics labeled "Christian" must reflect the response of *koinonia* to the dilemmas preventing Christians from fulfilling Christ's mission for all to experience "life abundantly."

Because it emphasizes praxis, ethics from the margins confronts political and social structures normalizing injustice. Consequently, an ethics done from the margins influences the political realm. One cannot read the story of liberation found in Exodus, the call for justice found in Amos, the stories of Jesus, or those of Paul's dealing with the imperial powers of Rome without concluding that these are not simply religious documents, but also calls to political action.

While Christian ethics from the margins is not a political ethics, it does influence change in the political sphere. *Koinonia* ethics is understood as being "of the political," rather than simply a *koinonia* political ethics. Clodovis Boff uses the preposition "of" to maintain a distance between the (political or social) object and its (theological or scientific) theory, "[keeping] what it unites at an appropriate distance" (1987, xxv). Consequently, the *koinonia* ethics from the margins often conflicts with the individualistic ethics of the dominant culture; the former recognizes the unity Jesus expressed between God and neighbor, while the latter emphasizes a personal relationship between Jesus and the individual.

To some extent, ethical responsibilities are often compartmentalized into two spheres: either as two cities as in Augustine, or two swords as in Martin Luther. These theological perspectives allow eurocentric Christians to formulate two types of ethics, one for the private life (the heavenly city) and a different, if not contradictory, ethics for the public life (the earthly city). But why such ethical dualism? A major error committed by ethicists of the dominant culture is to depend excessively upon the great reformers of the faith while failing to recognize their limitations in bringing about justice in light of the oppression faced by the marginalized of their time. Cone reminds us about great reformers who did little to make Christianity a religion of the marginalized. He wrote, "Though no one can be responsible for everything that is done in their name, one may be suspicious of the easy affinity among Calvinism, capitalism, and slave trading. John Wesley also said little about slaveholding and did even less" (1979, 34). In Calvin's case, this may partially be due to his following Luther's thinking in separating the private ethical sphere from the public. In the *Institutes*, Calvin wrote,

> We may call the one the spiritual, the other the civil kingdom. Now, these two, as we have divided them, are always viewed apart from each other. When the one is considered, we should call off our minds, and not allow them to think of the other. For there exists in man a kind of two worlds, over which different kings and different laws can preside. (1873 [1536], 3.19.15)

Some philosophers—Kant, for example—insist that ethics belongs to the private and inner realm of human existence. Any public ethic that exists is simply the spillover of the individual conscience.[8]

Within this compartmentalized tradition, a dichotomy emerges between the Christian as individual and the Christian as public servant. For example, while a Christian might be inclined to follow God's commandment prohibiting killing and, in fact, may desire to offer the enemy the other cheek in obedience to Christ, the Christian would still have to remain responsible to the duty of the office placed upon their shoulder. A soldier would have a duty to kill to preserve the overall social structure. Individual religious feelings must be put aside for the administration of duty. The duty of obedience by the individual is so binding, the citizen should be willing to suffer death rather than rebel. Duty ensures that the government can continue to keep a check on the wickedness brought forth by humans. What reformers like Luther and Calvin ignored was that, for the disenfranchised, it is the government—working to preserve the rights of the privileged—who usually perpetuates wickedness. In such cases, the duty of

---

[8] It is essential to note that during the Reformation, the Anabaptists rejected the distinction between the Christian as individual and the Christian as public servant. This refusal to create a dichotomy between a private and public ethics led their spiritual descendants (the Amish, the Mennonites, and the Quakers) to become pacifists. Their refusal to justify war as a moral option for Christians could only be accomplished through their rejection of compartmentalization.

the citizen may well be to reject the duality of responsibility established to maintain the status quo and actually rebel against it.[9]

Can a Christian committed to turning the other cheek go off to war and kill Muslims to ensure the flow of oil to the United States? Can Christians commanded to give their cloaks as well as their tunics to the persons in need be entitled to bring a lawsuit against anyone? Can a Christian commanded to walk an extra mile be content simply to leave the "colored" urban centers after five in the afternoon for the secluded white suburbs where their children can receive a superior education and they can rest easy at night due to beefed-up security? Compartmentalizing love and justice into two separate spheres of human existence allows a person to claim to be a Christian (hence full of love) while supporting public policies that perpetuate mechanisms of death for marginalized persons.

But how, then, can a judge mete out punishment during a court procedure? If no ethical dichotomy exists between the public and private sphere, can a judge who is committed to unconditional love punish a wrongdoer? Can a soldier ever fight in a war? Such questions, while valid, miss how the status quo is detrimental to the most marginalized. Take the example of the judge. When we consider that a majority of those in prison are people of color from mainly economically depressed and deprived areas, we can reach two possible conclusions: (1) people of color are engaged in crime as a negative consequence of their marginalization, where the lack of economic opportunities coupled with an inadequate education system contributes to wrong (legal and moral) decisions on their part, or (2) the judicial and legal system is skewed to convict people of color at a greater rate than whites. While the question concerning how a judge should deliberate may appear to be an issue of retributive justice,[10] in reality, at its very core, it is an issue of distributive justice.[11] Hence, the dominant culture, often refusing to deal with the causes responsible for crime and the procedures by which those accused of crimes are convicted, instead deliberates about how a judge can hand down punishment while remaining a faithful Christian.

---

[9] It should be noted that in the *Institutes* (4.20.29–32), Calvin, unlike Luther, did not see the magistrate as a substitute for divine rule and thus made allowance for the overthrow of tyranny if obedience to the ruler led one to disobey God. Karl Barth, on the other hand, exhorted Christians to obediently follow tyrants, for in so doing, they deprive the tyrant of power, for obedience is then freely given, not coerced.

[10] Retributive justice is concerned with determining a just punishment or penalty for those who commit illegal or immoral acts.

[11] Distributive justice concerns itself with the fair and equitable distribution of the benefits and burdens of society.

While the dominant culture asks, "How does one remain ethical in a corrupt society like this?" those who are marginalized ask, "How does one make a corrupt society like this just?" Because different questions are being asked, different answers are being formulated. And while the question of how a Christian judge can reconcile love with meting out punishment may be crucial for the powerful and privileged, it remains irrelevant for the marginalized because it refuses to deal with the causes of injustice. Questioning how a judicial system metes out justice becomes an important discourse for the marginalized only after they have some sense that justice exists for them. Disenfranchised spaces in this nation testify to the prevalence of systemic injustice in our society. Such injustice is maintained, in large part, by an ethical compartmentalization allowing those with power to continue benefiting from unjust social structures in the public sphere while claiming to be Christian in the private sphere.

Compartmentalizing Christian ethics into two cities or two swords, one spiritual and the other civil, places the former under the authority of the gospel message while it unbinds the latter from following the same set of precepts. The result is an ethical understanding, particularly prevalent within the United States, that is highly privatized with little commitment to transforming social injustices. A dichotomy in eurocentric thought develops between the private and public life when moral purity is sought for the private life but not for the public life. This may stem from the conviction that the public life is incapable of obtaining the purity that only the private life can obtain. Justice, while desirable for earth, is reserved for heaven, so the only hope offered the oppressed is a privatized spiritual liberation from their individual sins. Christians on the margins of power, profit, and privilege reject the dominant culture's interpretation that suggests the biblical intent is to liberate the soul, not necessarily the body.

Influential mid-twentieth-century ethicist Reinhold Niebuhr may illustrate the fallacy of Martin Luther's severance between the experience of grace and the possibility for justice that reduces liberation to nothing more than liberation from God's everlasting wrath toward human sin (1943, 193–94); however, he continued the spiritual compartmentalization of Augustine, Luther, Calvin, and Kant by relegating love to the private sphere and social justice to the public realm. His commitment to Christian realism led him to conclude that the ideal of love as the basis for public action is simply impractical and unable to deal with the complexity of modern life. Nations, multinational corporations, and other collective entities, unlike humans, are simply incapable of moral behavior.[12] In fact, he maintained

---

[12] Christian realism, rooted in the tradition of Niccolo Machiavelli, is usually

that certain inequalities are necessary for society to properly function. According to Reinhold Niebuhr,

> No complex society will be able to dispense with certain inequalities of privilege. Some of them are necessary for the proper performance of certain social functions; and others (though this is not so certain) may be needed to prompt energy and diligence in the performance of important functions.... No society has ever achieved peace without incorporating injustice into its harmony. (1960, 128–29)

The impracticality Niebuhr feared is specifically the type of radical commitment those from the margins demand of themselves as well as from those who benefit from the present social structures. This eurocentric aversion to unite the public and private spheres to participate in justice-based transformation of society was best articulated by one of the leading euroamerican ethical thinkers of the late twentieth century. "The current emphasis on justice and rights as the primary norms guiding the social witness of Christians is in fact a mistake," wrote Stanley Hauerwas (1991, 45). As he stated, "Christian social ethics is not first of all principles or policies for social action, but rather the story of God's calling of Israel and the life of Jesus" (1985, 181–82). For him, and many euroamerican ethicists and clergy, "The first task of Christian social ethics, therefore, is not to make the 'world' better or more just, but to help Christian people form their community consistent with their conviction that the story of Christ is a truthful account of our existence" (1981, 112).

Hauerwas, and white ethicists who follow his teachings, fails to advocate praxis or show antipathy toward establishing justice-based principles upon which to foster praxis. As I have written elsewhere: "Ethicists like Hauerwas who are not directly impacted by oppressive structures, nor are interested in solidarity with the dispossessed, have the luxury of pontificating

---

associated with the neo-orthodox movement of the 1930s and 1940s, which challenged the prevailing view that society was continuously evolving toward universal justice. The social optimism of the turn of the twentieth century held that the upward-moving enlightenment of humanity was about to break through into an era of worldwide peace and prosperity. Even the ethical movement known as the social gospel, as articulated by Walter Rauschenbusch, saw the social ills of the time as soon being cured and eliminated through education and spirituality. Instead, a great worldwide Depression and two world wars (the first optimistically called the "war to end all wars") culminated with death camps and the first use of the atomic bomb. Consequently, any remaining optimism from earlier in the century was dashed.

morality." To some degree, eurocentric ethics has become a matter of explaining what is ethical, not doing the ethical (De La Torre 2010, 25). To do ethics from the margins is to insist that, while the two realms may be distinct, they are in fact related. The ethics advocated for the private life is the same advocated for the public life. The maintenance of a false dichotomy has facilitated the justification of some of the worst atrocities within Christian history, from the Crusades to the Inquisition, to our very own "peculiar institution" of slavery.

Subjective vs. Objective

Any system of ethics reflects the activity of a given space. All of us bring our social location to how we fashion our ethical perspectives. We also bring our subjective understanding of God based on our experience and our upbringing. Systems of ethics often tend to provide more information about who we are than guidance as to what God wants. Eurocentric ethics is derived from theologies, themselves rooted in prior political commitments and thoughts. Even an "impartial" reading of a biblical text is understood by the reader trapped within a particular socioeconomic setting. All ideas are fastened to the social situation from which they arise. Naiveté is believing we could develop objective ethical propositions in a vacuum. Still, some eurocentric Christian moral agents assume they can arrive at an objective response to whatever dilemmas that exist. For example, ethicists such as Emil Brunner conclude that non-Christian ethical systems are unable to provide the whole answer to any ethical problem. Indeed, he says, only a Protestant understanding of Christianity can (1947, 41–43). John Rawls, on the other hand, accepts the possibility of developing a neutral framework of basic rights, believing society can objectively develop principles conforming to a concept of right (1971, 130–36). In the final analysis, the question remains: whose understanding of ethics becomes objective for everyone else?

Those doing ethics from privileged communities assume that "pure" reason or "proper" biblical hermeneutics are employed. These moral agents from the dominant culture assume their conclusions are objective; similarly, these same agents assume those conclusions coming from the periphery of society must be subjective because they are influenced by their believers' marginality. What moral agents from the dominant culture call "objective" is in fact highly subjective, a product of the moral reasoning conducted from their social location. They transmogrify their subjective moral views that justify their social location to the face of universal objectivity. What the moral agent concludes as a priori is a morality that resonates among those from the same background, possessing so-called economic and racial superiority. The ethical conclusions of marginalized groups are viable depending on how close they come to the eurocentric ideals or how many eurocentric ethicists they can fawningly quote.

Nevertheless, the work of theologians such as Cone helps define the meaning of ethical terms like "right" and "wrong" while showing why those belonging to the dominant culture—or any culture for that matter—are incapable of fashioning an objective ethical code of behavior. He wrote,

> All acts which impede the struggle of black self-determina-tion—black power—are anti-Christian, the work of Satan. The revolutionary context forces black theology to shun all abstract principles dealing with what is the "right" and "wrong" course of action. There is only one principle which guides the thinking and action of black theology: an unqualified commitment to the black community as that community seeks to define its existence in light of God's liberating work in the world.... The logic of liberation is always incomprehensible to slave masters. (1999a, 10)

What is true for the Black community is not limited to the Black community. Cone's words ring true for all marginalized groups. Here lies a major difference between systems of ethics advocated by the dominant culture and systems of ethics constructed from their margins.

By making a preferential option for the marginalized, ethicists of the dominant culture are prevented from achieving the objectivity for which they strive. Their "objectivity" is seen for what it is: the subjectivity of those who possess the power to make their view normative. A harmonious narrative based on some value-neutral analysis concerning the definition of justice simply does not exist. Injustice, oppression, and abuse are part of the human condition. Making a preferential option for the marginal-ized pushes against neat ideologies, ideologies that theoretically might help improve the situation of the marginalized yet fail to provide any holistic form of liberation. No ethics, and no theology for that matter, can be socially uncommitted. All ethics and all theologies are and will forever remain subjective—they are incapable of fully comprehending the infinity of the Divine.

Chapter 3

The Liberation of Ethics

Womanist ethicist Katie Cannon provided a rich definition for liberation ethics. She wrote,

> Liberation ethics is debunking, unmasking, and disentangling the ideologies, theologies, and systems of value operative in a particular society. "How" is it done? By analyzing the cultural, political, and economic presuppositions and by evaluating the legitimate myths that sanction the enforcement of such values. "Why" is it worth doing? So that we may become responsible decision makers who envision structural and systemic alternatives that embrace the well-being of us all. (2001, 14)

Choosing to do a liberative ethics from the margins is a proactive option made with, by, and for those who are disenfranchised. An option for the poor, for those on the margins, is made as an outward expression of an internal belief. Two Latin American liberation theologians, Clodovis Boff and George Pixley, reminded us, "Before being a duty . . . the option for the poor is a reality of faith, or theological truth. . . . Before being something that concerns the church, the option for the poor is something that concerns God. God is the first to opt for the poor, and it is only as a consequence of this that the church too has to opt for the poor" (1989, 109).

For those claiming to be Christians, no real dichotomy or separation can exist between ethics and social action if social action is understood as the praxis of ethics, the process by which privileged Christians are transformed into the image of Christ. Solidarity that comes from making an option for the poor is crucial not because Christ is with the marginalized but, rather, because Christ is the marginalized. In the words of the Apostle Paul, "Remember the grace of our Lord Jesus Christ who for [our] sake, although rich became poor, so that [we] might become rich through the poverty of that One" (2 Cor. 8:9). Who Christ is, is directly linked to what Christ does. Likewise, Christian ethics is directly linked to Christian praxis.

The Hermeneutical Circle for Ethics

God wills that all come into salvation—that is, liberation from sin. Here "sin" is understood as meaning more than simply individual peccadillos. Sin is social, the consequences of oppressive social structures. Ethics is the action by which liberation, also known as salvation, can be manifested. Any model or paradigm used to assist the faith community in developing ethical precepts must start with the experience of those most affected by the sin of oppression, those suffering most from the political and economic structures of society that undergird sin. Christian ethics should result in the transformation of such structures into a more just social order.

Liberation theologians have generally relied on a process called the "hermeneutical circle" as a guide for their reflection. Several ethicists from the margins have also adopted the hermeneutical circle as a paradigm by which to do ethics. Such a paradigm, motivated by a passion to establish justice-based relationships from which love can flow, begins with the lived experience of social situations faced by those minoritized and proceeds by working out a theory and course of action that have the potential of dismantling the mechanisms that cause oppression. It usually proceeds through different but closely related stages.[1] The hermeneutical circle begins with experiencing reality through radical solidarity with the oppressed, not with logic, biblical truth, or church teaching. Its purpose is to formulate a praxis—a system of Christian ethics—to change the reality faced by those living on the margins of society.

Step 1: Observing—An Analysis

To gaze upon an object is not an entirely innocent phenomenon involving the simple transmission of light waves. To "see" also encompasses a mode of thought that transforms the object being viewed into a concept for intellectual assimilation and possession. Think of the process of looking at a photograph of a loved one. Observing can be a very rich and emotional experience. We observe inanimate objects and persons, and we also observe their interactions as they exist together to form a society. Within a society people can be viewed both as subjects and objects. Those whom society

---

[1] The framework provided here is based on the model of seeing, judging, and acting employed by liberation theologians in Latin America who have been influenced by the Catholic Church's documents *Gaudium et Spes* (1965) and *Octogesima Adveniens* (1971). It is essential to keep in mind that this paradigm, like so many others, is a working model—not an absolute.

defines as "subjects" normally have far more power, including the power to legitimize and normalize what they see.

In "first world" countries, the dominant eurocentric culture defines reality for those on the periphery or margins. This is because seeing is political, a social construction that endows the person doing the observing with the power to provide meaning to an object. Probably the worst consequence to befall persons who are viewed as "objects" is that they see themselves through the eyes of their oppressors, as inferior and lacking power. This is antithetical to the gospel message and an affront to the social dignity of all human beings. When persons viewed as objects accept their oppressors' worldview as their own, they often feel compelled to behave and act according to the way in which they have been constructed by others. It would be naïve to view power as centralized in the hands of the elite of the dominant culture. Power is everywhere as it forms in and passes through a multitude of institutions. It is most effective when it is exercised through coercion that appears natural and neutral—a coercion based simply on the ability to observe.

The starting point for doing ethics, then, becomes the observing, which is done in most countries of the Global North by members of a white, male, eurocentric culture. Their understanding of morality and virtues has great weight for those who are disenfranchised. What can those who unjustly benefit from white cis-gendered, male privilege say about morality to those who suffer unjustly because of this privilege? Distrust of and experience with the ethics constructed by the dominant culture lead those on the margins to observe and discern the reality faced by marginalized people for themselves. Using the eyes of the marginalized, or observing from below, becomes the first step in arriving at any ethical response; it informs how God is understood, how Scripture is read, and how society is constructed. As the causes for oppression are unmasked through this analysis, consciousness of what is happening is raised, and the object, which has now become the subject, gains a deeper understanding of reality. To observe with one's own eyes becomes the first step toward decolonizing one's mind.

During the process of observing, it is also essential to consider seriously the historical situation that gave rise to the present situation. If we define history as the memory of a people, how do those on the margins recall their history apart from the imagery imposed upon them by those with power? All too often the "official" history is devoid of the voices of the disenfranchised. In the words of Frantz Fanon, a postcolonialist thinker and writer from Martinique, "The history which [the colonizer] writes is not the history of the country which he plunders but the history of his own nation in regard to all that she skims off, all that she violates and starves" (1963, 51). The history of marginalized people in the United States is written primarily by those who have the power to determine the official story. It is, in short, the history of the dominant power. Nation-building normally requires an epic tale of triumphant wars, heroic figures, and awe-inspiring achievements that elevate the dominant culture while disenfranchising the history of the defeated, or their "Other." Homi K. Bhabha, a postcolonial theorist, has termed this the "syntax of forgetting" (1994, 160–61). In the United States, the common narrative of nation-building not only disguises the complex political forces responsible for bringing forth that history, but, more important, it suppresses sexual differences, racial divisions, and class conflicts.

Any thorough understanding of an ethical dilemma must include the historical causes of the dilemma and a study of the ways in which the society maintains structures that caused the dilemma. Michel Foucault has pointed out that the domination of certain people by others creates values. Historical writings, in their turn, justify the values and social positions of those who write the history. This relationship of domination becomes fixed throughout history by means of procedures that confer and impose rights on one group and obligations on another. In this way, the dominant culture normalizes its power by engraving its memories on both people and institutions (1984, 83–85). The victors of US history inscribe their genealogies upon the national epic, emphasizing military victories, technological advances, and political achievements. These deeds become the official history.

Yet, the truth of the subject is not necessarily found in the history written by the subject. Psychoanalyst Jacques Lacan insisted that truth is found in the "locus of the Other" (1977, 286). Precisely for this reason, the dominant culture attempts constantly to obliterate the Other's locus. Or, as Frantz Fanon eloquently stated,

> Perhaps we have not sufficiently demonstrated that colonialism is not simply content to impose its rule upon the present and the future of a dominated country. Colonialism is not satisfied merely with holding a people in its grip and emptying the native's brain of all form and content. By a kind of perverted logic, it turns to the past of the oppressed people, and distorts, disfigures, and destroys it. (1963, 210)

To seek the voices of those who do not inhabit history is to critique those with power, profit, and privilege for substituting their memory for forgotten history. On the other hand, ignoring the voices of those neglected by history can be used to justify yesterday's sexual, racial, and economic domination, while normalizing today's continuation of that oppression; it also prevents hope for tomorrow's liberation.

The approach to ethics from the margins seeks to understand what justice is by exploring and understanding how justice was historically denied. If the mechanisms that produce death, such as hunger, nakedness, and houselessness, can be recognized historically as part of the lives of the marginalized, then the inverse—praxis or actions leading to life, and this means abundant life—should inform any system of ethics. For this reason, ethics done on the margins is and must remain a contextual ethics that seeks to see the liberating work of God through the eyes of those made poor, those marginalized, and those made to suffer because they belong to the "wrong" gender, race, sexual orientation, or economic class. We exchange the history constructed by the academy, the affluent, and the powerholders for one created from history's underside, whose ongoing struggle is to overcome oppression. We not only search for the God of history but claim that God takes sides with the faceless multitude suffering from oppression.

Step 2: Reflecting—Social Analysis

Social analysis is required before social structures can be transformed. Instead of turning to philosophical concepts or abstractions, an attempt is made, using the tools of sociology, anthropology, economics, and political theory, to ground ethics in analysis to best discern reality. By providing raw data, the social sciences provide a productive methodology to discern the structures of social phenomena and thus illuminate the reality faced by those marginalized by these structures. It should be noted that Christian ethicists can legitimately borrow analytical methods from other academic disciplines. Whatever tools of human thought are available should be used to illuminate the social location of the marginalized and to identify oppressive structures. To engage in the self-liberating praxis of naming one's own reality and to point out how political mechanisms maintain institutionalized oppressive structures is to point out sin—sin being understood as the product of existing social, political, and economic systems designed to secure the power, profit, and privilege of one group through domination of others.

Analysis of social systems is an integral component of ethical deliberation because it provides a necessary critique of how the present social structures justify racist, sexist, and classist norms. Ethics can never adequately respond to oppressive structures if it fails to fully understand how these structures are created and preserved through economic, social, and political forces. Ignoring social analysis prevents ethics from providing an informed and intelligent practical response to oppression.

In the way that biblical interpretation is never totally objective, social analysis is incapable of being fully neutral. Both biblical interpretation and social analysis—or any similar thought process—encompass the biases of the group undertaking the reading or analysis. For this reason, more weight, termed the "epistemological privilege," is given to the perspectives and interpretations emerging from marginalized spaces. This privilege accorded the disenfranchised is based on their ability to know how to live and survive in both the center and periphery of society, unlike the dominant cultures, which generally fail to understand the marginalized experience. Consequently, the primary source for doing ethics is the lived, everyday experience of marginalized people.

As important as social analysis may be, it cannot become the totality of an ethicist's reflection. For those who claim Christianity, ethical reflection is based on the life of Jesus and on Jesus's mission as illustrated in his pronouncement in John 10:10: "I came that they may have life and have it abundantly." Simply put, if the implementation of an ethical action prevents life from being lived abundantly by a segment of the population or worse, if it brings death, then it is antigospel. When ethics ignores how minoritized groups are denied access to opportunities, or reinforces the power, profit, and privilege amassed by one segment of the population, or when ethics is relegated to abstract discussions that seldom question how our social structures are constructed, then such ethics ceases to be Christian. Only ethical reflections that empower all elements of humanity, offering abundant life in the here and now instead of the hereafter, can be determined to be Christian. The claims of Jesus Christ's life-giving mission become the lens through which Christian ethical reflection is conducted. Such reflection leads to the praxis of liberation, a process of using reflection to develop actions that bring about the transformation—understood as both liberation and salvation—of all individuals and social structures.

Step 3: Meditating—A Theological and Biblical Analysis

Breathe. Take a breath. Seek connection to the spiritual. The mental exercise of meditating, for the Christian, may very well include prayer. For others, it may be a means of centering, a concentration upon one's value when considering the ethical dilemma at hand. Rush to action can lead to haste and not well-thought-out praxis rooted in one's beliefs or set of values. If we move directly from observing and reflecting to actions for liberation, ethics from the margins can be accused of simply being a reaction to a given situation. For this reason, meditating (prayer for those claiming Christianity) becomes a crucial step in the ethical paradigm as it ties theory based on observation with the faith community most affected by the given ethical dilemma. As Francisco Moreno Rejón, a moral theologian working in Latin America, reminded us, "A salient note in liberation theology and ethics is rooted in their effort to reconcile the requirements of a theoretical, academic order with a pastoral projection. Thus, we are dealing with a moral theology that, far from repeating timeless, ahistorical principles, presents itself as a reflection vigorously involved with the people's daily experience" (1993, 217).

As used here, prayer as meditation is not limited to an individual closed in a room to have a private conversation with God in hopes of gaining wisdom and guidance. While personal prayer is important or even central for some and thus not to be neglected, prayer is also understood to be communal, bringing together the different members of the spiritual body to share their joys and concerns. Meditation can be a communal process by which a disenfranchised faith community accompanies its members and stands in solidarity during its trials and tribulations. Ethics is also a communal activity. As such, within the faith communities (often called by the Greek word *koinonia*), particularly those established on the margins of power and privilege, God's ongoing activity within humanity finds its locus. God's presence is found within the faith community on the margins of privilege. Ethics, then, can never be reduced to a personal choice or an individual morality; it must instead remain a communal action guided by the relationships established in *koinonia*.

Pushing against eurocentric hyperindividualism, *koinonia* is based more on the relationships within the faith community than with precepts or principles. Solidarity and constant communication with the people of faith situated in marginalized communities afford a perspective that is lost on ethicists who confine their deliberations to theories found in academic books. Because morality is communal, ethics from the margins means listening critically to the stories of the marginalized and committing to work in solidarity with them in their struggle for full liberation, both spiritually and physically. Failure to incorporate the voices of the voiceless makes ethics useless for most of the world's humanity who struggle each day for the basic necessities of life: food, clothing, and shelter.

To meditate, to pray also includes a critical application of Holy Writ to the ethical situation faced by the marginalized. For those who are Christians, the biblical text is imperative, not as a rulebook but as a guide. Christians focus on the concept of justice as rooted in the life and acts of

Jesus Christ. The biblical text can guide how moral decisions are arrived at and implemented. The Bible is read as a book of life, providing keys to an abundant life now, not solely some eternal life later. As such, the Bible becomes a source of inspiration by which both Christian individuals and communities can undergo radical changes, otherwise known as conversion, from a life dominated by the sin perpetuated by oppressive social structures to a life in solidarity with "the least among us," those whom Christ chose to be among.

For Black biblical scholar Brian Blount, fusing the biblical narrative with the life situation of the marginalized produces a biblical witness uniquely capable of addressing their tragic circumstances. "In other words, they contextually construct their biblical story" (2001, 24). Doing ethics through prayer and meditation based upon biblical reflection becomes a process of interconnecting the reality faced on the margins of society with the Scriptures, fully aware of the contradictions existing between the biblical mandate for the fullness of the abundant life in Christ and how those from the center of society interpret sacred texts. All too often, the dominant culture views the Bible as God's "owner's manual," a book of moral precepts from which a "thou shalt not" list can be derived. Codifying the biblical text as a scriptural law book to be obeyed was an error made by more conservative and fundamentalist white Christians. Following specific precepts tends to excuse a person from living a life faithful to the call for justice as personified by Christ. Jesus did not provide a legalistic moral code for his disciples to follow. Even if he had, the world in which we live, with all its global complexities and technological advances, is vastly different from the social context in which Jesus found himself. Jesus had no need to speak of issues concerning affirmative action or the ethical dimensions of driving an SUV.

For the Bible to be taken seriously as a source of ethical guidance, we must examine the relationships that Jesus established. By examining the actions taken by Jesus toward others, a pattern emerges that can inform present-day praxes. Jesus articulated moral values that he contextualized within his social location, that of a Jew living in a basically agrarian economy in first-century Palestine, a colonized land that formed part of the Roman Empire. For liberation theologian Jon Sobrino, applying to present situations the values that Jesus proclaimed is informed by the recognition that Jesus's message of justice and love was brought to all people through his identification and solidarity with one particular group, the marginalized. In Palestine, as today, the marginalized lived in conflict with the privileged and powerful. In addition, Jesus battled against sin manifested as specific social injustices, a conflict that found its conclusion in his eurocentrism. The

Bible's authoritative role in the formation of Christian ethics is established if and when the principles lived and spoken by Jesus are contextualized for the present day. In this way, ethics can move away from abstract notions toward concrete praxes, that, when arising from marginalized communities, become valid (Sobrino 1978, 124–25, 138).

Nevertheless, there is not always a clear biblical mandate as to what action is moral. At times the biblical text even contradicts itself. For example, although the Sixth Commandment clearly states, "Thou shalt not commit adultery" (Ex. 20:14), the Leviticus code suggests that men can have multiple sex partners, even to the point of maintaining a harem (Lev. 18:18). Other laws simply cease to be applicable, as in the case of dietary regulations throughout the book of Leviticus. Still other pronouncements offend modern Christian sensitivities, specifically sections that reduce women and enslaved peoples to objects, as in the case of the Tenth Commandment, which prohibits the coveting of another man's possessions, specifically his ox, donkey, house, wife, and slave. Even though Christians on the margins look toward the Scriptures for the basis of ethical reflection, it is essential to remember that a certain amount of self-criticism should also be employed.

How does one's race, class, gender, and orientation influence how the text is interpreted? Even though the Bible remains, apart from Christ, the highest authority for most Christians, turning to the biblical text for guidance requires a critical analysis of the social context that gave rise to the text, a social context whose own milieu (such as patriarchy, for example) affected how the text was written. A social order that advanced patriarchal structures would likely not criticize the creation of harems or the sanction of bigamy. This kind of examination of a biblical text is termed the "hermeneutic of suspicion." A second type of danger exists when those in power use a biblical text to advance or justify their own ideologies; this is known as "proof-texting." For these reasons, the Bible is not read literally to determine how one group interprets a certain passage, but to learn the character of the God claimed to exist, and how that character manifests itself throughout history.

Step 4: Acting—Implementing Praxis

Even the most liberal-minded member of the dominant culture must recognize that, despite laudatory statements concerning the plight of those of other races, genders, and classes, the privilege of the dominant culture remains protected through social structures that normalize and legitimize the status quo, even if it is oppressive. Theorizing about justice, regardless of a person's best intentions, changes nothing. Matthew 7:12, also known as the Golden Rule, clearly states, "All things, whatsoever you desire others should do to you, you then should do to them." Simply stated, ethics from the margins is about doing rather than theorizing. While theory is not totally dispensed with, ethicists on the margins commit to grounding their praxis in the experience of the disenfranchised; ethical theory, then, becomes a reflection of that action, subordinated to the praxis.

While all may agree with the concept that poverty should be eliminated, specific acts beyond charity need to be taken to move this "utopian" concept toward a reality. All too often, concepts remain simply concepts and never become praxis. Because the basic needs of the marginalized are most often impeded by social structures established by the dominant culture, most praxis will concentrate on transforming the social institutions from being disabling to being enabling. This action can attempt to meet such basic human needs as feeding the hungry, clothing the naked, and visiting the imprisoned. On the other hand, such action can attempt to change the actual social structures responsible for causing hunger, nakedness, and imprisonment. In the end, both forms of action are needed; however, while those of the dominant culture are often willing to participate in the former through undertaking "charity work," seldom does the desire exist to participate in the latter because it threatens their privileged space.

As a result, eurocentric ethics, usually beginning with a "truth" discovered based on some teachings, revelation, sacred text, or rational analysis, lacks the ability to transform the overall power structures. When conducted from the margins, ethics attempts to work out truth and theory through reflection and action in solidarity with the oppressed. In this sense, praxis is not guided by theory. Ethics done from the margins is not deductive, that is, beginning with some universal truth and determining the appropriate response based on that truth. Those on the margins tend to be suspicious of such universal claims that have been used in the past to justify their oppression. The function of theory is an intellectual way of comprehending the reality experienced by the marginalized. It is not, nor should it be, construed as a truth by which a course of action is deduced.

Praxis becomes the Christians' pastoral response toward the structures responsible for heterosexism, racism, classism, and sexism. Although pastoral, the Christian response can also be highly political because, by its very nature, it challenges the overall political structure designed to benefit one group at the expense of others. Ethics can thus be understood as orthopraxis, which is the "doing" within a reality informed by theory and doctrine. Orthopraxis is opposed to orthodoxy, which means the arriving at the correct theory or doctrine. This doing of ethics attempts to bring the social order into harmony with the just society advocated by Christ's example, a community devoid of race, class, and gender oppression.

Still, given the multiplicity of possibilities, how do Christians decide what praxis should be used for the liberation of God's people? José Míguez Bonino provides us with an ethical thesis to inform the decision-making process. He wrote, "In carrying out needed structural changes we encounter an inevitable tension between the human cost of their realization and the human cost of their postponement. The basic ethical criterion is the maximizing of universal human possibilities and the minimizing of human costs" (1983, 107). Bonino's thesis, when coupled with the above-mentioned four steps of the hermeneutical circle for ethics, provides sufficient information for a moral agent to decide on an ethical process. Will it be the correct action? This is unknown until the final step, which reassesses the action taken. For now, the moral agent must take a "leap of faith" that their action is congruent with the liberative message of the gospel.

Step 5: Reassessing—New Ethical Perspectives

The praxis of liberation, at its core, can be understood as the process by which consciousness is raised. But praxis, in and of itself, is insufficient. At most, it informs ethicists about the validity of their interpretations of the oppression faced by a faith community. Further reflection is needed. Has the implementation of praxis brought a greater share of abundant life to the disenfranchised? If so, what additional praxis is required? If not, what should be done to replace the previous praxis with new and more effective action? The implementation of any additional praxis or a totally new praxis will depend on a reassessment of the situation.

Besides analyzing the effectiveness of the course of actions being taken, the process of reassessing also creates systems of ethics. As we have seen, eurocentric ethics is deductive, beginning with a "truth" and moving toward the application of that "truth," subordinating ethics to dogma. Doing ethics from the margins reverses this model. After praxis, as part of the reassessment, the individual returns to the source of their faith (i.e., the biblical text) with the ability to more clearly understand its stories and mandates. Through actions, the moral agent experiences the fullness of the dilemma, allowing them to better ascertain the proper moral response. As this response is formed, it is again tested by the hermeneutical circle. And the process continues through additional reassessment and further corrections, if necessary. In the end, it is praxis that forms doctrine, informs the interpretation of scripture, and shapes the system of ethics.

THE HERMENEUTICAL CIRCLE FOR ETHICS
THE HERMENEUTICAL CIRCLE FOR ETHICS

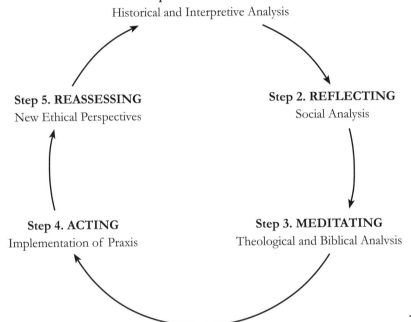

Step 1. OBSERVING
Historical and Interpretive Analysis

Step 5. REASSESSING
New Ethical Perspectives

Step 2. REFLECTING
Social Analysis

Step 4. ACTING
Implementation of Praxis

Step 3. MEDITATING
Theological and Biblical Analvsis

PART II

CASE STUDIES OF GLOBAL RELATIONSHIPS

Chapter 4

Introducing Global Relationships

Those of us who were alive some two decades ago remember the horror of September 11, 2001. More disturbing than the memory of watching the Twin Towers collapse on our television sets in real time is the fact that close to three thousand individuals created in the image of God perished. Some died because they were at work on time and others were heroes who rushed into collapsing buildings attempting to save lives. In their honor, the *New York Times* published short biographies of those who perished that fateful day.

While an impressive memorial was erected on Ground Zero to remember the names of those 3,000 who perished on that spot during the terrorist attacks, how many of us are aware that, according to UNICEF, more than four and a half times that number, 13,800 children, died each day of malnutrition-related symptoms and preventable diseases in 2020?[1] While these children perish, impoverished countries are spending three to five times as much to pay off foreign debt as they spend on basic services to alleviate the silent genocide of children. While many of those targeted by terrorists died quickly on 9/11, these children die slowly over time, often over years. Their pictures rarely appear in newspapers, and their deaths may not even be noted in any special or distinctive way. Nonetheless, they, too, are created in God's image. They, too, have worth and dignity. If we can agree that their deaths are an affront to God, then their deaths should also be an affront to our humanity.

---

[1] "Under-Five Mortality," *UNICEF Data*, December 2021. In addition, UNICEF estimates that between 2005 and 2020, more than 93,000 children were verified as being child soldiers, although the actual number of cases is believed to be much higher. "Children Recruited by Armed Forces or Armed Groups," *UNICEF*, 2021. Sadly, the United States is the only country in the world that has yet to ratify the United Nations' 1989 landmark treaty (U.N. Convention on the Rights of the Child) that attempts to deal with this atrocity, mainly due to objections from the Religious Right.

The death of the earth's wretched can be understood as the byproduct of institutional violence. The normative everyday experience of violence found throughout the Global South, affecting the world's most vulnerable members, is closely linked to the realities of socioeconomic injustice, ecological degradation, the militarization of society, uneven distribution of wealth, poor access to education and health, poverty, unemployment, racism, ethnic discrimination, gender inequality, and global economic policies that benefit a small portion of the world's population at the expense of the many. Violence moves beyond the personal dimension when its socioeconomic and political dimensions are considered. True, the act of flying a plane into a skyscraper is an act of immediate and bloody violence. The death of a child due to lack of food or sanitary conditions over a period of years may not be immediate nor bloody, but it is no less violent.

The institutional violence that these children experience can be understood as a violence created, supported, and rooted in institutions and powerful groups whose purpose is to maintain an unequal, unjust, and repressive sociopolitical order that blocks the human development of its citizens, especially those considered as inferior, abnormal, or a threat to the given global order. Institutional violence is more than the inadequate distribution of a country's or community's resources. It presupposes an organization, justification, and normalization of unjust socioeconomic relationships through legal and cultural frameworks that support the mechanisms of justice and establishes a coercive force to maintain an unjust established order. This form of violence is maintained through a repressive social structure that justifies its existence and incorporates its premises into the cultural, educational, and daily experiences of a given society. In this way, the system justifies the cycle of violence, protecting the structures and the social groups that most benefit from it.

The targeting of the World Trade Center in New York and the Pentagon in Washington, DC, was no coincidence. These structures served as symbolic headquarters of the world empire and the institutional violence it unconsciously (or consciously) supports. We still live in a world where, during 2020, 720 million to 811 million people (or about 10 percent of the global population) faced hunger (FAO et al. 2021, 8). Meanwhile, people in the United States spent more than $71 billion in 2020 trying to lose weight.[2] By 2020, of the almost 8 billion people inhabiting the earth, approximately 1.3 billion people in 107 countries (almost a quarter of their population) lived in multidimensional poverty, reflecting acute deprivation

---

[2] Allison Lau, "The Rise of Fad Diets," CNBC, January 11, 2021.

in health, education, and standard of living (United Nations Development Programme and the Oxford Poverty & Human Development Initiative 2020, 3). The World Bank estimates that, in 2020, an additional 115 million people, due to the consequences of the global COVID-19 pandemic, were pushed into extreme poverty while the accumulating effects of climate change are expected to push an additional 68 million to 132 million people into poverty by 2030 (Freije-Rodriguez and Woolcock 2020, 21).

The global policies that make an economically disproportionate world possible are also responsible for much of the world's poverty, hunger, destitution, and death. The gluttonous consumption of many first-world countries is not only morally indefensible, but also the root cause of much of the present instability in the world. This instability is a breeding ground for violence, fertilizing the mindset that originally birthed the 9/11 tragedy. Massive poverty is, without a doubt, the greatest threat to world peace and security. According to former secretary-general of the United Nations, Kofi Annan, "No one in this world can feel comfortable or safe while so many are suffering and deprived."[3] We have moved beyond the era when the Marines were used to secure the interests of US corporations, such as the United Fruit Company, throughout Latin America. Today, the greatest military force ever known to humanity, simply by its presence, creates a global hegemony that secures the expansion of the global market. If we can come to understand the depth of the misery of the world's marginalized as a byproduct of US affluence, created in part by its global economic policies of exclusion, we might begin to appreciate why "they" hate "us" and why our symbols of power became terrorist targets.

The Economic Might of the United States

The cultural influences of the Greek Empire, the imperial might of the Roman Empire, the religious supremacy of the Holy Roman Empire, and the global reach of the British Empire all pale in comparison with the cultural dominance, the military might, the capitalist zeal, and the global influence of the US Empire. The term "empire" can no longer be narrowly defined as the physical possession of foreign lands paying tribute. Today, "empire" is understood as a globalized economy that provides economic benefits to multinational corporations whose influences are secured through the military might of one superpower. Indeed,

---

[3] Tim Weiner, "More Entreaties in Monterrey for More Aid to the Poor," *New York Times*, March 22, 2002.

today's sun never sets on the dominating influence of the United States. At no other time in human history has one nation enjoyed such supremacy of power. While empires of old relied on brute force, the US Empire relies mainly on economic force, not to discount that it also has the largest fighting force known to humanity. Through its economic might, the United States dictates terms of trade with other nations, guaranteeing that benefits flow to the United States and the elite of countries that agree to its trade agreements.

Take corn, for example, a staple of life in many parts of the world. During the first decade of the new millennium, many poor nations experienced sharp spikes in food costs, especially corn. For example, Mexico experienced a 60 percent hike in the price of tortillas in 2007, sending tens of thousands into the streets to protest. The importance of corn to the Meso-American diet cannot be overstressed. Along with beans and squash, it has been the main source of nutrition and sustenance for centuries. The entire culture of the Americas revolved around its cultivation and consumption. For centuries—until recently—Mexican farmers cultivated corn the way their ancestors did, using a burro on a small plot of land and relying on the rain to irrigate their fields. A third of the crop would be reserved to feed the family; the rest would be sold at local markets. This simple formula kept the people fed during good and bad economic times.

But since the passage of the North Atlantic Free Trade Agreement (NAFTA), at least 1.7 million Mexican farmers lost their small plots of land, unable to compete with cheaper US-subsidized corn. Many Mexican farmers were forced to migrate to large border cities with high unemployment rates or risk the dangerous border crossing to the United States. Ironically, NAFTA was not a windfall for US farmers who don't grow corn. More than thirty-eight thousand US farms have gone out of business since NAFTA's passage, unable to compete with Mexican farmers who rely on large numbers of cheap farm workers to harvest crops other than corn. To survive, US farmers were forced to mechanize their farms and employ fewer people. It seems like the only winners of NAFTA were a handful of multinational corporations, especially those who had a hand in drafting NAFTA (De La Torre 2009, 39).

Originally, NAFTA set a fifteen-year period for gradually raising the amount of US corn that could enter Mexico without tariffs; however, Mexico willingly lifted the quotas in less than three years to assist its chicken and pork industries. According to Mexican NAFTA negotiators, the suspension of quotas directly benefited fellow negotiator Eduardo Bours, whose family owns Mexico's largest chicken producer. Although the lifting of quotas rewarded his family business, Mexico lost some $2 billion in tariffs while half a million farmers who grew corn abandoned their lands and moved to the cities in hope of finding a new livelihood.[4]

Because the United States provides subsidies to US farmers, underwriting the cost of their crops (especially corn), US farmers were able to sell their crops below international market price. According to the Environmental Working Group, of the $277.3 billion spent between 1995 (the start of NAFTA) through 2020 in subsidies to US farmers, the largest amount, $116.6 billion, went specifically to corn producers.[5] Meanwhile, the World Bank imposed structural adjustments on Mexico in 1991, eliminating all government price supports and subsidies for corn production. And while since 1994, the Mexican government has provided subsidies to farmers, more than half went to the richest 10 percent of the producers, excluding the target population victimized by NAFTA while disproportionately benefiting large-scale producers (Fox and Haight 2010, 7–8). When US subsidized corn is exported to countries like Mexico, local farmers who receive little to no subsidies from their government are unable to compete with the cheaper US subsidized corn (De La Torre 2009, 39).

The availability of cheaper corn was not a windfall for the Mexican people. The suspension of price control on tortillas and tortilla flour caused their prices to triple. During the first decade of NAFTA, corn-growing rural Mexican farmers witnessed corn prices plunge by as much as 70 percent while the cost of food, housing, and other essential services skyrocketed by as much as 247 percent since the start of NAFTA. Some products, like tortillas, saw prices increase by more than 483 percent from January 1994 to January 1999 (López 2007, 7–9, 41). Transnational traders like Cargill and Maseca, who can speculate on trade trends, further exacerbated the rising price of corn. With Mexican farmers squeezed out because of their inability to compete with US-subsidized corn, US-owned transnational traders were able to step in and monopolize the corn sector. They used their power within the market to manipulate movements on biofuel demand and thus artificially inflate the price of corn many times over.[6]

---

[4] See Tina Rosenberg, "The Free-Trade Fix," *New York Times Magazine*, August 18, 2002, and "Why Mexico's Small Corn Farmers Go Hungry," *New York Times*, March 3, 2003; see also Celia Dugger, "Report Finds Few Benefits for Mexico in NAFTA," *New York Times*, November 19, 2003.

[5] See the Environment Working Group's Farm Subsidy Database, where it has collected data on farm subsidies in multiple countries. For the United States, see the United States Farm Subsidy Breakdown, 1995–2021.

[6] Walden Bello, "The World Bank, the IMF, and the Multinationals: Manufacturing the World Food Crises," *The Nation*, June 8, 2008.

Studying the impact of NAFTA, the Carnegie Endowment for International Peace concluded that ten years of NAFTA has brought hardship to hundreds of thousands of subsistence farmers.[7] Not surprisingly, many of these farmers who have abandoned their lands have since made the journey north toward the United States, following their resources. According to Enrique Barrera Pérez, a farmer who works about five acres in Yucatán, "We cannot compete against this monster, the United States. It's not worth the trouble to plant. We don't have the subsidies. We don't have the machinery."[8] We can never understand the reason for the current US immigration crisis if we ignore the global economic policies of the United States and how it is driving those losing their livelihood to risk crossing the borders.

The United States is in no rush to change the present system of subsidies to US farmers. Agriculture is one of the few sectors of the economy where the United States runs a trade surplus. But what profits US businesses causes economic devastation for the rest of the world. Former World Bank president James D. Wolfensohn makes the connection between the $1 billion a day that wealthy nations "squander" on farm subsidies and their devastating impact on poor nations. To make matters worse, many wealthy nations place tariffs (at times exceeding 100 percent) on agricultural imports from two-thirds-world nations,[9] making any attempt of market accessibility into a "sham" (Wolfensohn 2001). This has led Ian Goldin, then the World Bank's vice president, to conclude that "reducing these subsidies and removing agricultural trade barriers is one of the most important things rich countries can do for millions of people to escape poverty all over the world." C. Fred Bergsten, director of the Institute for International Economics in Washington, was more blunt: "Our American subsidy system is a crime, it's a sin, but we'll talk a good game and get

---

[7] Ibid.; Celia Dugger, "Report Finds Few Benefits for Mexico in NAFTA," *New York Times*, November 19, 2003.

[8] "Mexican Farmers Protest End of Corn-Import Taxes," *New York Times*, February 1, 2008.

[9] The term *tiers monde* was coined by Alfred Sauvy in 1952 by analogy with the "third estate," a reference to the commoners of France prior to the French Revolution. The third estate stood in contrast to nobles and priests of the first and second estates, respectively. The term implies the exploitation of the third world, in the same way the third estate was exploited. Although a better term to describe the relationship between the first- and third-world nations might be "dominated" and "nondominated" nations, or sometimes "developed" and "undeveloped," I choose to refer to these countries as the two-thirds world, a term used by others who come from these areas. Two-thirds refers to approximately two-thirds of the land masses, resources, and humanity contained within these countries.

away with doing almost nothing until after the presidential election."[10] Every rural peasant forced to leave the land means another producer who is forced to migrate to the city, becoming, along with her or his family, one more consumer. This migration greatly contributes to the perpetual need for future food aid (George 1987, 8).

American Exceptionalism

"US exceptionalism" has become the justification used to rationalize foreign policies that would be condemned if other nation-states were to implement similar policies. Imagine another nation using drone strikes to kill "terrorists" on American soil, or another nation maintaining military bases within US territories. This American exceptionalism is the twenty-first-century reincarnation of the divine rights once professed by royalty, reserving for itself God-like powers over those subjugated to its will—powers over who gets to live and who gets to die, powers in the creation of truth, powers to punish sinners who threaten their rule, powers to demand devotion. The rhetoric of the United States being "the greatest country on earth," permits it to suspend ethical and moral imperatives used to keep other countries in check. It is the stuff of empires, claiming that normative global ethical rules and democratic virtues do not apply to those self-identifying as exceptional.

Claiming exceptionalism ensures that normative global ethical rules of order and conduct do not apply because exceptionalism implies being beyond good and evil, which is why an aversion exists among neoconservatives to be a part of international organizations like the World Court or the United Nations. We do not have to play by anyone else's rules because, the logic goes, "we are the shining city upon the hill" that is the light to and for the rest of the darkened world. The modern-day jingoistic proclamation of American exceptionalism, or as one usually hears in chants like, "We're number one," is but the latest manifestation of the previous generation's white supremacy—only this time, this white supremacy is also being adopted by people of color attempting assimilation. Americans once considered it a birthright, due to their whiteness, to have those who fell short of the white ideal labor and sacrifice for the benefits of all whites. Jim and Jane Crow, and slavery before it, maintained that whiteness provided certain benefits and privileges not available to nonwhites. Likewise, our present discourse concerning exceptionalism maintains the operation of American supremacy—benefiting and privileging "real" (read: mostly white) Americans. The world, and all its inhabitants, is at the service of the United States

---

[10] Elizabeth Becker, "Western Farmers Fear Third-World Challenge to Subsidies," *New York Times*, September 9, 2003.

because of our exceptionalism. Hence no one blinks at the fact that the major portion of the world's resources flows in the direction of the United States to support about 6 percent of the world's population.

US exceptionalism doesn't come in being number one. Ironically, the United States is ranked as occupying nearly last place when it comes to quality of life. Among the thirty-six countries with "advanced economies," the United States ranked thirty-third in infant mortality rates for 2019, with 5.8 deaths per 1,000 live births. The average among these thirty-six countries is 3.8 deaths (Schenck et al. 2019, 8). When it comes to health care, the United States ranks last on access to care, administrative efficiency, equity, and healthcare outcomes when compared to the top eleven global economies, despite spending far more of its gross domestic product on health care (Schneider et al. 2021, 2). Also, in 2018, before the pandemic, Americans were among those developed countries with the shortest life expectancy, ranking twenty-eighth at 78.6 years. The average life expectancy among the other thirty-six countries was 80.7 years (Schenck et al. 2019, 42). By 2021 the age dropped to 76.1 years, with the steepest numbers among Americans of color (Arias et al. 2021, 1).

Additionally, we are among the nations with the largest income inequality, ranking thirty-fourth, with only Turkey, Bulgaria, Mexico, Chile, Costa Rica, and South Africa having greater income inequalities among their citizens.[11] When it comes to education, 33 percent of eighth graders score at or above proficiency in math, with 34 percent scoring at or above proficiency in reading. By twelfth grade, only 22 percent have a command of grade-level content in science (Candal 2018, 4). Yet to point out that incongruences exist between our claims of exceptionalism and the economic realities faced by most Americans is to be accused of waging "class warfare." However we wish to examine quality of life in 2020, there was nothing exceptional about the United States, except how poor Americans' quality of life is when compared to other advanced economies.

Maintaining the concept that America is number one accomplishes two crucial tasks. First, it masks growing inequality as the elite few continue to enrich themselves at the expense of middle America through tax breaks, deregulation, and the elimination of social services—themes and issues discussed in greater detail in the next section of this book. Second, it allows the elite few to expand their wealth by imposing their "supply-side" economics on a global scale, to be discussed in this section in greater detail. "Exceptionalism" may provide the moral, ideological, and philosophical

---

[11] Organization for Economic Cooperation and Development, "Income Inequality," latest available data are from 2021.

justification for neoliberalism; nevertheless, the globalization of capital still requires strength to impose the will of the few upon the vast majority of the world's population. We need to be number one in at least one area: our military. This has been made a necessity if we wish to continue the flow of resources to our shores to benefit an elite few.

The Rise of Neoliberalism

The rise of the US Empire was neither an accident nor the result of luck. Near the close of World War II, the Bretton Woods Conference (1944) attempted to create an economic order that would rebuild Europe to prevent any further world wars. Free trade was perceived as the mechanism to bring stability to the global order. Although the original intentions may have been noble, in the end, the new economic order promoted the development of first-world banks and institutions (the World Bank and the International Monetary Fund [IMF] were both created at Bretton Woods) and transnational corporations. This new global economic order helped the United States and its Western European allies develop their economic wealth at the expense of the peripheral nations, which provided raw materials and cheap labor.

Underdevelopment of the periphery became a byproduct of development of the center. What was once accepted as colonialism, where world powers directly occupied the lands of others to extract their national resources and human labor, was replaced with a more modern form of global exploitation, often termed "neoliberalism." Underdevelopment will continue to persist so long as neoliberalism continues to privilege the nations that have placed themselves at the world's center. Therefore, any Christian ethical response to global injustices must start with an understanding of neoliberalism.

Neoliberalism is a relatively new economic term. It was coined in the late 1990s to describe the social and moral implications of the free trade policies of global capitalism since the collapse of the Eastern Bloc. Critics maintain that neoliberalism is responsible for the increasing disparity in global wealth and that it has created a parasitic relationship wherein the poor of the world sacrifice their humanity to serve the needs, wants, and desires of a privileged few. It provides the few with the right to determine what will be produced, who (which nation-state or group of individuals) will produce it, under what conditions production takes place, the price that will be paid for the finished product, what the profits will amount to, and who will benefit from the profits. Despite foreign aid programs designed by rich nations to assist so-called underdeveloped nations, more of the world's wealth, in the form of raw materials, natural resources, and cheap labor, is extracted through unfair trade agreements than the small portion returned to the exploited under the guise of humanitarianism or charity. The first world continues to appropriate the resources of weaker nations through the open market, causing internal scarcities in basic living needs required to maintain any type of humane living standard.

Ensuring stable political systems, regardless of how repressive they may be, is a prerequisite for the economic marketplace to function. Political stability, which is needed to ensure the steady and profitable flow of goods, supersedes the need for freedom and liberty. Thus, a history exists of US pressure to topple democratically elected governments and install tyrants who secured stability, as happened with the governments of Abenz in Guatemala, Allende in Chile, and Mossadegh in Iran. Ironically, supporters of neoliberalism's continuing expansion often confuse this economic structure with democratic virtues like liberty. Raising questions about ethics of the present economic structure can be construed as an attack on democracy itself (George 1999).

To some degree, neoliberalism can be understood as a religion, with the World Bank akin to its ecclesial institution. According to economic development experts Susan George and Fabrizio Sabelli, the World Bank is a "supernational, non-democratic institution [that] functions very much like the Church, in fact the medieval Church. It has a doctrine, a rigidly structured hierarchy preaching and imposing this doctrine [of neoliberalism] and a quasi-religious mode of self-justification" (1994, 5). According to Latin American theologians Clodovis Boff and George Pixley, "The theological status of [neoliberalism] today is precisely that of a vast idolatrous cult of the great god Capital, creator and father of so many lesser gods: money, the free market, and so on" (1989, 144). Like most religious beliefs, the economic pronouncements expounded by the World Bank or IMF can be neither validated nor invalidated but are usually accepted on faith. The ethics employed by these institutions is not based on concepts of morality, but rather on interpreted principles of economics and the power amassed by the institution. This point is best illustrated by a statement of Brian Griffiths, former vice chairman of Goldman Sachs International and member of the British House of Lords: "What should be the Christian response to poverty? First, to support global capitalism by encouraging the governments of developing countries to privatize state-owned industries, open up their economies to trade and investment and allow competitive markets to grow" (2003, 171).

For neoliberalism, market forces are guiding the deliberation of ethics, even when the market causes widespread hunger and poverty. Economist

Milton Friedman once wrote, "Indeed, a major aim of the liberal [market] is to leave the ethical problem for individuals to wrestle with. The 'really' important ethical problems are those that face an individual in a free society—what he [sic] should do with his freedom" (12). Any focus on individual and personal issues of faith and redemption poses problems for Christian ethicists, especially those working on and from the margins. The pursuit of gain for the few most often creates scarcity for the many. Liberation theologians such as Peruvian Gustavo Gutiérrez insist, "In the Bible, material poverty is a subhuman situation, the fruit of injustice and sin" (1984 [1979], 54). Here, then, is the crux of the conflict between neoliberalism and the gospel message of liberation: neoliberalism lacks a global ethical perspective because it reduces ethics to the sphere of individualism.

The dichotomy between communal and personal ethics—or between market forces and human development—allows Christians to accept the market as a "good." The market, then, determines the fate of humanity, and humans thus exist for the market. Maximization of wealth becomes a virtue in and of itself, as well as a reason for being, and competition separates the sheep from the goats. Economic "losers" result from a lack of personal ethics to manage their own lives properly. Failure to be employable indicates a collapse of moral duty to maximize one's potential in the labor marketplace. Transnational corporations also compete by eliminating competitors through mergers and acquisitions, which usually results in job losses. As technological advances reduce the need for manual labor, humans become dispensable, nonessential units that are rendered superfluous. Although raw materials remain in high demand, the populations of the two-thirds world are no longer needed (Hinkelammert 1995, 29–30).

Neoliberalism tends to encompass and dictate every aspect of human existence. Nothing can exist outside the market. Even nations are reduced to "companies" with which the transnationals form alliances. Every thing and body is reduced to a consumer good. If a nation is unable to compete in the global marketplace, then a process of financial prioritizing, known as "structural adjustments" or "austerity programs," takes place so that the nation can become a stronger player, usually at the expense of their populations, whose living conditions worsen.

The Structures of Neoliberalism

The World Bank and the IMF are key institutions (churches?) of neoliberalism. They impose conditions and structural adjustments (normally severe cuts in health, education, and social services) on member states starving for credit. A key component of structural adjustments is turning national enterprises over to private investors. The privatization of national economies shifts the emphasis from achieving social goals to profit-making. Workers most often face massive wage cuts and layoffs as private owners seek to improve their bottom line by cutting labor costs. The result of privatization in many underdeveloped countries entails a disappearance of social benefits and a direct reduction of the standard of living for workers. It is now the market that dictates how a society is to be ruled as global financial institutions set political policies that impact millions of lives.

The power of the World Bank and IMF to impose structural adjustments facilitates their ability to force nations to participate in the world economic order even if the terms of participation are unfavorable, especially to those who are disenfranchised (Hinkelammert 2001, 29). These structural adjustments invariably include devaluing the currency, correlating price structures to global markets, terminating import restrictions and exchange controls, imposing user fees on services (such as water, health care, and education), and reducing national sovereignty. The result is usually that the world's marginalized witness the weakening, if not the outright dismantling, of their economic safety net (protection for women and children in the workplace, social security benefits, labor unions), coupled with increased unemployment and pending ecological collapse. In a twisted form of logic, the increase of unemployment, which leads to deepening poverty and misery among the world's poor, is hailed as a plus. For the World Bank, unemployment means that "bloated" enterprises become lean units capable of competing in the open world market.

In the end, the state becomes the servant of the capitalist structures responsible for maintaining "law and order" by squelching any resistance to the status quo. Human freedom and liberty are redefined to mean freedom for the flow of capital and goods, access to a ready and flexible labor pool, and the dissolution of a state's rights to determine its own separate and contrary destiny. Whenever the United States engages in forever wars to fight for freedom, they are not referring to individual freedoms, but the "freedom" of economic markets to be open to US penetration. Those who question neoliberalism are not necessarily opposed to globalization, which has become a reality of modern life. Rather, they are against how globalization has come to be defined.

Capitalism has historically been based on making things (manufacturing) and growing things (agriculture) with the end goal of selling what was produced. To accomplish this goal, laborers were needed to toil in factories or harvest fields. To build factory buildings or buy heavy farming equipment, proprietors would engage in financial transactions as a means to an end by bringing their products to market. Neoliberalism, however, has moved beyond these traditional ways of making money. Instead, financial transactions, specifically international financial transactions, have become the means in and of themselves by which wealth is built without the need to produce anything tangible, which in turn creates employment. Consider the warning issued by the former French president Nicolas Sarkozy, a pro-laissez-faire conservative. He succinctly explained why the shift to creating wealth based on financial transactions is problematic:

> This crisis is not just a global crisis. This crisis is not a crisis in globalization. This crisis is a crisis of globalization.... Globalization took a wrong turning the moment we accepted unconditionally, unreservedly and without any limit the idea that the market was always right and that there could be no argument against it. Let us go back to the root of the problem: it was the imbalances in the world economy which fed the growth of global finance. Financial deregulation was introduced in order to be able to service more easily the deficits of those who were consuming too much with the surplus of those who were not consuming enough. The perpetuation and accrual of these imbalances was both the driving force and consequence of financial globalization.... Globalization of savings has given rise to a world where everything was given to financial capital, everything, and almost nothing to labor, one where the entrepreneur gave way to the speculator, where those who lived on unearned income took precedence over workers, where the use of leverage . . . was becoming unreasonably disproportionate, and all this created a form of capitalism in which it had become normal to play with money, preferably other people's money, to make easily and extremely rapidly, effortlessly and often without creating either prosperity or jobs, absolutely enormous sums of money.... The crisis we are experiencing is not a crisis of capitalism. It is a crisis of the distortion of capitalism.... Purely financial capitalism is a perversion which flouts the values of capitalism. (2010)

Huge transfers of wealth from the global middle class toward an elite global minority have radically changed the foundations of capitalism. Ironically, it appears that the continuous demise of entrepreneurship capitalism is caused by the rise of global neoliberal financial markets.

Using Case Studies in Ethics from the Margins

In closing, let us consider the words of former Brazilian archbishop Dom Hélder Câmara: "When I feed the hungry, they call me a saint; when I ask why they are hungry, they call me a Communist." Any ethical praxis geared to dismantling global injustices must begin here—by asking why people are hungry. We cannot begin to deal with the liberation of the world's marginalized unless we first deal with the root cause of all their misery and suffering: economic injustice. The next three chapters briefly explore some of the key consequences of neoliberalism—specifically, global poverty, war, and the environment.

Traditionally, the usual approach to teaching ethics is to emphasize theory: the student learns an ethical theory and then applies it to a hypothetical case study. The purpose of the case study is to determine objectively which ethical response is proper based on a multitude of possibilities. The focus is not on the dilemma outlined in the case study; rather, the methodology employed to arrive at the ethical response holds the spotlight. Such a case study might involve a car that loses control and crashes into a brick wall, immediately igniting in flames. You come upon the scene in hopes of aiding the sole person pinned within the wreck. You try to pry open the doors, but to no avail. The fire is rapidly spreading. Within minutes—if not seconds—the driver will be engulfed in flames. There is absolutely no means by which you would be able to open the doors to free the driver. It so happens that you are carrying a loaded pistol. Do you pull out your gun and administer "mercy killing," or do you take no action and watch the injured, yet conscious, driver burn to death?

Such case studies form a false dichotomy between ethical theory and practice. The purpose is not to determine what moral action should be taken when approaching burning cars but rather to answer the abstract question: is there ever a situation in which killing is justified? Regardless of how clever or creative such case studies may appear to be, they are useless to those residing on the margins of society because they fail to foster a concrete act to bring about change. While the question concerning a trapped person in a burning car may prove intriguing, the fact remains that most people will never come across such a situation. Such case studies reinforce a spectator-type ethics where debating theory, rather than transforming society, becomes the goal.

For those doing Christian ethics from the margins, relevant case studies must be contextualized in *lo cotidiano*, the everyday experience of marginalized people, the subject and source for all ethical reflection. Unfortunately, many ethicists of the dominant culture maintain that considering the interpreter's identity or social location interferes with the job of ascertaining a so-called objective rendering. The approach employed in this book, and particularly in the following case studies, challenges the assumption that ethical deliberation can be understood apart from what the interpreter brings to the analysis. The case studies and analysis in this book are unapologetically anchored in the experience of society's disenfranchised communities. Theologian Karl Barth once said that theology should be done with the Bible in one hand and the newspaper in the other. In reality, it is ethics that needs to be done with an open newspaper. By grounding case studies in the everyday, the margins are brought to the center.

The remaining chapters deal with ethical dilemmas from the perspective of the disenfranchised. They apply the hermeneutical circle for ethics described in chapter 3 to a particular social issue through the eyes of the marginalized. The reader is invited to analyze and reflect on the situation to determine what praxis may be appropriate. After the third step of meditating (theological and biblical analysis), each chapter presents several short case studies. The fourth (taking action) and fifth steps (reassessment) are missing so that the reader can ponder the case studies through the worldview of the marginalized.

Chapter 5

Global Poverty

Step 1: Observing

Since the collapse of the Soviet Union, the United States has emerged as the undisputed world power, both economically and militarily. The might of the US military facilitates the ever-expanding influence of transnational corporations whose single goal is to satisfy their stockholders through increased profits. One way to keep profit margins high is to pay low wages. Wages paid to workers, especially workers representing the global poor, are not determined by textbook economic theories of supply and demand, nor by the laborer's need to survive, but by the needs of the transnational corporation to increase profits. This happens throughout the world whenever humans are reduced to tools of production, the means by which corporations can profit at their expense. The disenfranchised become a commodity, an object, within an integrated global market; their sole purpose is to provide the world's powers with a reservoir of cheap labor. As theologian John Cobb observed, "Now that Marxism has been discredited, however, the capitalist countries no longer find it necessary to check the concentration of wealth in fewer hands. By moving from national economies to a single global economy, they can pit the workers of one country against the workers of all others" (1998, 36). The ever-present corporate goal of increasing profits creates a race to the bottom among transnational corporations as they seek the lowest possible wage to be paid. There was a time when business innovations (the automobile, the camera, the plane, the television, the computer) provided long-term domestic economic growth through millions of local jobs. Today, however, there is nothing anchoring an American business to the United States. A quick examination at one company illustrates this point.

Steve Jobs and Steve Wozniak, tinkering with electronic components in the garage of Jobs's parents, built the first Apple computer in 1976. It didn't take long for Apple to start manufacturing its new product, first at a building in San Francisco, then at a plant in Fremont, California. Bill Stamp was among the first employees at the Fremont plant, joining Apple in 1984. Soon, other assembly plants were opened, one of which opened in 1992 at Fountain, Colorado, near Colorado Springs. Stamp was offered an opportunity to transfer to the new plant, which he accepted. There he met his future wife, Christy, who was also an Apple employee. The Fountain plant was well run and profitable, becoming the company's largest manufacturing facility, producing about one million PowerBook and desktop computers a year. Rather than opening more plants within the United States, Apple instead moved its operations overseas, mainly to China. Just four years after its opening, in 1996 Apple closed the Fountain plant, creating a 40 percent regional loss of 15,000 manufacturing and information technology jobs that, at the time, were paying $55,000 to $80,000 plus benefits. The local economy lost an estimated $500 million (Barlett and Steele 2012, 84–86).

Stamp stayed working at the plant under its new owners, SCI Systems Inc., who had a three-year contract to continue producing Apple computers. But when the agreement was not renewed, SCI shifted its manufacturing offshore. Stamp tried his hand doing other work in lesser-paying jobs, but to no avail. He finally left Fountain in 2001. By 2008, when his newest job was shipped to Singapore, Stamp, then fifty years old with a lengthy résumé, was unable to get a job interview. The Stamps went through their saving accounts, retirement accounts, and at the end, lost their home. By 2011, after three years of unemployment, the Stamps found themselves renting a two-bedroom apartment and working at temporary jobs with no benefits. Meanwhile, almost all Apple products at the time—Macs, iPods, iPhones, iPads—were then made in China (88).

The problems Bill and Christy Stamp faced are manufactured in towns and cities throughout the United States. The high-paying Apple jobs that the Stamps lost are replaced with low-paying Apple retail jobs. Once upon a time, a high school graduate was able to obtain a factory job and live a comfortable middle-class lifestyle. Unfortunately, the factory job that used to be the backbone of America's prosperity has been disappearing. Today, many with college degrees are employed in retail jobs that only require a high school diploma. Unable to sustain themselves, many are forced to live with their parents or in group housing, trying to get by while carrying enormous student loan debt, unable to save enough to establish themselves. Meanwhile, older Americans are losing their security for their golden age as the concept of retirement is becoming an unattainable illusion. The loss of the so-called American Dream for US workers like the Stamps was not, however, a gain for the new Chinese employees working in high-tech sweatshops.

Moving its manufacturing jobs and some of its research facilities abroad, mainly to China, Apple hired the Taiwan-based electronics manufacturer

Foxconn to develop and assemble its products, conduct engineering research, and conduct logistics, sales, and after-sale services.[1] Today Foxconn, the largest electronics manufacturer in the world, operates in more than forty manufacturing complexes throughout nineteen Chinese provinces and in all four leading cities with provincial status: Beijing, Tianjin, Shanghai, and Chongqing. Its facilities can also be found scattered over twenty-eight other countries (Chan, Selden, and Ngai 2020, xii, 22).

Because Apple subcontracts all its manufacturing to companies like Foxconn, it can skirt fair labor standards, workplace safety regulations, and environmental standards. Workers in these Chinese plants are paid approximately $1.50 to $2.50 per hour, which represents about 2 percent of a $600 iPhone's sale value—around $12 (Russell and Toyler 2019, 453). Some who are assembling these phones are as young as fourteen years old.[2] Because more than 40 percent of the employees at Foxconn are agency workers, they are not eligible for sick pay or holiday pay. Furthermore, they can be laid off without wages during lulls in production, as was the case during the global COVID pandemic shutdown. Those working overtime were paid at the normal hourly rate instead of time-and-a-half.[3] These unscrupulous compensation practices enable Apple to capture almost 60 percent of an iPhone's value. Over a quarter of the workforce lives in crowded company barracks, ten- to twelve-story buildings outside Foxconn's gates. They sleep in tiny dorms that reek of rotting trash and sweat, six or eight to a room, for $25 per month with an additional internet fee of $3. It is common for three-room apartments to house twenty people.[4] Employees are unable to socialize because they work in different departments, on different shifts, and speak different languages (Chan, Selden, and Ngai 2020, 6-8).

Foxconn is by far China's largest employer, with 1.3 million workers assembling around 50 percent of the world's smartphones, computers, and other electric gadgets.[5] Because of Apple's dependency on these Chinese factories, they collude with the authoritarian regime to stay in the good graces of the government. For example, since 2017 Apple has moved its

---

[1] Apple is not the only company for whom Foxconn is a subcontractor. Others include Asus, Dell, Hewlett-Packard, IBM, Intel, Lenovo, Microsoft, Motorola, Nintendo, Nokia, Samsung, Sharp, Sony, and Panasonic. Foxconn plants are also responsible for making the Kindle, PlayStation, and Xbox.

[2] Harrison Jacobs, "Inside 'iPhone City,' the Massive Chinese Factory Town Where Half of the World's iPhones Are Produced," *Business Insider*, May 7, 2018.

[3] Jamie Condliffe, "Foxconn Is under Scrutiny for Workers Conditions. It's Not the First Time," *New York Times*, June 11, 2018.

[4] Condliffe, "Foxconn Is under Scrutiny"; Jacobs, "Inside 'iPhone City.'"

[5] Jacobs, "Inside 'iPhone City.'"

Chinese customers' data to China and onto state-run company computers lacking encryption technology, essentially handing over digital keys that unlock Chinese customers' information. Apple also proactively removed apps (approximately fifty-five thousand between 2012 and 2021) to placate Communist Party officials, like the app from Guo Wengul, who has posted critiques concerning corruption with the Communist Party.[6]

Subcontractors like Foxconn, in return, are willing to do whatever it takes to meet the high quotas set by Apple. They are infamous for subjecting workers to widespread beatings, in one case leading to a riot in 2012 (Chan, Selden, and Ngai 2020, 162–64). Some of these employees were forced to stand for so long that their legs swelled, making walking difficult. Workers are not allowed to speak to each other while working, nor are they able to leave their workstations. If they need to use the bathroom, they only have ten minutes, and will be reprimanded if they exceed the allotted time (56–57). Investigative research revealed a pattern of "low wages and benefits, compulsory overtime, lack of fundamental health and safety precautions, abusive treatment of teenage student interns, and managerial repression of workers' attempts to press demands for securing rights guaranteed by employment contracts and national labor laws" (xiv). Hazardous conditions within the plant caused by an ignored lack of proper ventilation led to two explosions within seven months of each other in 2010, killing four people and injuring seventy-seven others (101). The working conditions are so punishing that employees at times believe suicide is their only means of escape. By December 2010, eighteen workers were known to have attempted suicide at Foxconn facilities. Fourteen died, while four survived with crippling injuries (x). The situation has become so dire that large safety nets were attached to the building in hopes of catching possible jumpers (188).

These abusive situations exist and thrive because, as CEO Terry Gou infamously said, "To manage one million animals gives me a headache" (56). Those producing Apple products are perceived and treated as cattle. And yet, despite these horrendous working conditions, former CEO Steve Jobs once boasted that Apple "does one of the best jobs of any company . . . of understanding the working conditions in [their] supply chain."[7] One Apple executive, speaking on the condition of anonymity, revealed, "We've known about labor abuse in some factories for four years, and they're still

---

[6] "5 Ways Apple Has Compromised with the Chinese Government," *New York Times*, May 18, 2021.

[7] Charles Duhigg and David Barboza, "In China, Human Costs Are Built into an iPad," *New York Times*, January 25, 2012.

going on. Why? Because the system works for us. Suppliers would change everything tomorrow if Apple told them they didn't have another choice. If half of iPhones were malfunctioning, do you think Apple would let it go on for four years?"[8]

Apple is the most valuable company on Earth, becoming the first corporation in 2018 to record a market capitalization of $1 trillion. Three years later, in March 15, 2021, their market capitalization rose to $2.08 trillion, exceeding the GDP of all but seven countries or the total value of stocks on all but eleven out of the seventy-two worldwide exchanges.[9] At times, the company has more cash in its bank accounts than the US Treasury.[10] When Tim Cook became CEO after Steve Jobs's retirement, his cash salary was $900,000, plus Apple stock worth a staggering $376.2 million. At that time, Cook earned around $1 million each day, or about $42,000 an hour if he worked twenty-four hours a day—roughly an amount equal to the pay of more than five thousand US factory workers who still had Apple jobs, or approximately 60,919 years of employment at Foxconn. Cook further benefited when, within a year, the value of his stock increased to about $634 million.[11]

When President Obama asked Apple CEO Steve Jobs what it would take to make iPhones in the United States, Jobs bluntly responded, "Those jobs aren't coming back." Consider that a Foxconn employee at that time was paid $1.70 an hour to work forty hours a week assembling iPhones costing $800 each.[12] But, contrary to popular opinion, the reason these manufacturing jobs are not returning to the United States is not always because workers are paid substantially less overseas. Academic and manufacturing analysts estimate that, if American wages were paid instead, iPhone prices would only increase by about $65 per phone.[13] Why, then, are US jobs vanishing? Why won't those that went overseas return? What happened that led us to this economic predicament?

---

[8] Ibid.

[9] Mark Kolakowski, "At $2.08 Trillion, Apple Is Bigger Than These Things," *Investopedia*, March 17, 2021.

[10] Ben Popken, "Apple Is Now Worth $2 Trillion, Making It the Most Valuable Company in the World," *NBC Business News*, August 19, 2020.

[11] Natasha Singer, "C.E.O. Pay Gains May Have Slowed, But the Numbers Are Still Numbing," *New York Times*, April 8, 2012.

[12] Cissy Zhou, "iPhones Cost US$800; I Was Offered a Job at Foxconn to Assemble Them for US$1.7 per hour, 40 Hours per Week," *South China Morning Post*, March 1, 2019.

[13] Charles Duhigg and Keith Bradsher, "How the U.S. Lost Out on iPhone Work," *New York Times*, January 21, 2012.

In June 1979 the United States reached its zenith of manufacturing jobs. But years of low tariffs, unrestricted imports, and refusal to insist on reciprocal trade agreements with partnering countries—advocated and supported by Democrats and Republicans alike—eroded the economic backbone of the United States. Even though manufacturing wages are lower in the United States than in about a dozen economically developed nations, manufacturing jobs, after peaking at 19.5 million jobs in June 1979, dropped to 11.7 million by 2018.[14] In the first sixteen years of the millennium, around 20 percent of the nation's factories (eighty thousand establishments) closed their doors, most moving their operations overseas. These closures resulted in manufacturing job losses exceeding the jobs lost during the Great Depression of the 1930s.[15]

The last year that the United States posted a trade surplus was 1970 (Reinbold and Yi 2019, 1). Since that anemic $911 million surplus, the United States has posted an annual trade deficit. According to the US Census Bureau, the US trade deficit in 2020 stood at $915.8 billion (the largest on record).[16] When trade is in balance, that is, when imports and exports are about the same, good-paying jobs exist. But when there are more imports than exports—as has been the case for more than fifty years— the industries that provide good-paying jobs are undercut, resulting in vanishing jobs. Many manufacturing jobs, according to the US Department of Labor and the Bureau of Labor Statistics, have been primarily replaced by governmental jobs (increasing the size of the bureaucracy) and service jobs (including retail). Exporting manufacturing jobs overseas has led to an economic shift from high-paying to low-paying wages within the United States. When we consider that an average manufacturing job in January 2020 earned $30.57 an hour for a 40.4-hour workweek,[17] while the mean retail wage was $22.57 an hour for a 30.4-hour work-week[18] (a difference of $548.90 a week or $28,542.80 yearly), we can begin to appreciate the extent to which transnational corporations and the neoliberalism they practice in their quest for the cheapest labor are dismantling the US middle class.

---

[14] Adam Grundy, "Contributions of Key Economic Sector Recognized on Manufacturing Day," US Census Bureau, October 2, 2020.

[15] Alan S. Brown, "The State of American Manufacturing 2019," American Society of Mechanical Engineers, April 20, 2019.

[16] Robert E. Scott, "U.S. Trade Deficit Hits Record High in 2020," Economic Policy Institute, February 10, 2021.

[17] "Manufacturing: NAICS 31-33," US Bureau of Labor Statistics, accessed April 2022.

[18] "Retail Trade: NAICS 44-45," US Bureau of Labor Statistics, accessed April 2022.

According to the US Bureau of Economic Analysis, there were 14.4 million jobs outsourced overseas in 2018, accounting for 33.5 percent of the worldwide employment by US multinational corporations.[19] The loss of jobs was not and is not limited to manufacturing positions. Take the example of IBM, which has shifted service jobs, including software design jobs, to other countries. In 2003 IBM had 9,000 workers in India; by 2010, that number rose to 75,000, skyrocketing in 2017 to 130,000, or about a third of the total workforce. Since 2003 IBM has been eliminating some 8,000 US employees a year. And while IBM stopped disclosing exact numbers, it is estimated that they reduced employees in their US offices by 30,000 between 2007 and 2017, to about 100,000 workers. This means IBM has more employees in India than in the United States. Why pay more for US workers when Indian workers can get paid between one-fifth to one-half a US salary?[20] The total savings to a US company that shifts its job overseas can be as high as 50 percent, even when allowances are made for the extra cost of transportation, communication, and other expenses not needed if the production was done in the United States.[21]

Even the US government participates in the exportation of its bureau-cratic labor force, outsourcing its call centers overseas. Today's operators in Bombay, Bangalore, or Gurgaon are likely to handle calls from US welfare and food stamp recipients. Not only do they assist US citizens who have questions about their welfare benefits, they also prepare US tax returns, evaluate health insurance claims, handle airline reservations, transcribe doctors' medical notes, analyze financial data, and read CAT scans. These call center workers in India can earn approximately $2,766 a year (at 99.19 rupees or around $1.33 an hour), less money than is received by the unem-ployment recipients they are assisting who could at least earn $35,360 a year ($17 an hour) at an entry-level position if the call center was located in the United States.[22] Ironically, India's jobs (which were formally American) are themselves being outsourced. In 2011 the Philippines, with a population one-tenth that of India, surpassed the larger country's call center opera-tions. Now, an American is more likely to speak with a Filipino than an

[19] "Activities of U.S. Multinational Enterprises, 2018," Bureau of Economic Analysis, US Department of Commerce, August 21, 2020.

[20] Steve Lohr, "IMB Rides Global Focus on Services to Deliver a 12% Increase in Profits," *New York Times*, October 19, 2012; Vindu Goel, "IBM Now Has More Employees in India Than in the U.S.," *New York Times*, September 28, 2017.

[21] Louis Uchitelle, "A Missing Statistic: U.S. Jobs That Have Moved Overseas," *New York Times*, October 5, 2003.

[22] Adam Uzialko, "Homeshoring Brings Call Centers and Customers Closer," Business News Daily, March 7, 2022.

Indian when calling a service center, mainly because in India, which was colonized by the British, people speak British-style English while in the Philippines, colonized by the United States, people speak a more American-style English.[23]

Outsourcing jobs overseas received a boost during the Trump administration, which ran on an America First platform. According to the Institute on Taxation and Economic Policy, the 2017 tax law, which was passed with great fanfare, created incentives for American corporations to move jobs abroad, including a zero-tax rate for profits generated by offshore operations. Offshore profits are only taxable when they exceed 10 percent of the value of their offshore tangible assets—an extremely high profit margin to achieve. And if any US tax is due, the rate imposed is significantly lower than the tax rate imposed on domestic profits.[24] In 2018, after the tax bill passed, General Motors announced a major restructuring that included the closure of at least five factory plants, moving fourteen thousand jobs overseas.[25] One of the assembly plants scheduled to close was located in Lordstown, Ohio. Sherrod Brown, the US senator from Ohio, called Trump to solicit help. Senator Brown explained how his signature tax bill was responsible for the closing: "I said the first thing you can do is take away the provision in his tax bill that gives a company a 50 percent off coupon on their taxes. If you're producing in Lordstown, you pay a 21 percent tax rate, if you move to Mexico, you pay a 10 and a half percent tax rate." According to Brown, Trump did not know such a provision was in his bill. Brown continued, "[Trump] said he wasn't really aware of that."[26]

However, it would be erroneous to believe countries like India or Mexico have achieved a financial windfall from the importation of manufacturing jobs for US companies or its government. For example, Mexicans have sunk deeper into poverty, despite the opening of *maquiladoras* (assembly plants) along the international border with the United States. Mexican *campesinos*, many of whom used to live off the corn they grew, have surrendered to the fact that they can no longer compete with agricultural goods imported from the United States. Because the land

---

[23] Vikas Bajaj, "A New Capital of Call Centers," *New York Times*, November 25, 2011.

[24] Matthew Gardner and Steve Wamhoff, "Trump-GOP Tax Law Encourages Companies to Move Jobs Offshore—and New Tax Cuts Won't Change That," Institute on Taxation and Economic Policy, June 2, 2020.

[25] Angie Wang, Tom Krisher, and John Seewer, "Not Just Jobs Riding on Fate of GM Plant after Trump Promise," Associated Press, November 28, 2018.

[26] Chris Mills Rodrigo, "Sherrod Brown: Trump 'Said He Wants to Help' Keep GM Jobs in Ohio," *The Hill*, November 29, 2018.

could no longer support them, they abandoned their homesteads and moved to *colonias* (poor, sprawling slums of shacks patched together from pieces of metal, wood, and plastic) surrounding the *maquiladoras*. The 1994 North American Free Trade Agreement (NAFTA) scheme of moving goods freely across borders—free from tariffs or taxes—was supposed to be a bonanza for US exporters and provide high-paying jobs to US and Mexican workers.

Foreign workers searching for better jobs, however, were never intended to also freely cross borders, only their cheap labor as part of the goods they exported. Moving US factories, rather than people, across borders maintained high profit margins for companies by paying employees the lowest possible wages. This quest to pay the lowest wages meant industries relocated to the Global South. It is estimated that, in the first ten years since the implementation of NAFTA, approximately 780,000 jobs alone in US textile and apparel manufacturing were lost (Labor Council for Latin American Advancement and Public Citizen 2004, 5). Five years prior to NAFTA, the United States maintained a $168 million trade surplus with Mexico; five years after NAFTA, the surplus plunged to a $12.5 billion deficit (Barlett and Steele 2012, 55–56). The trade surplus with Mexico that was supposed to be a NAFTA outcome ballooned in 2019 to a goods trade deficit of $101.4 billion, a 29.5 percent increase ($22.8 billion) from 2018.[27] Still, as already stated, there was no windfall for Mexico. Many Mexican farmers were forced to abandon their lands, unable to compete against US-subsidized imported agricultural goods. Our trade policy pushed migrants out of Mexico and other Central American countries, while our hunger for cheap labor that native-born Americans don't want and refuse to perform pulled them toward the United States.

While numerous *maquiladoras* opened along the border since the implementation of NAFTA, Mexicans sank deeper into poverty. The poor of Mexico initially found salvation in the *maquiladoras*, but salvation proved illusionary. As Mexican workers demanded plant safety protocols, living wages, and a cleaner environment at these *maquiladoras*, corporations began looking elsewhere to relocate. Although first attracted to Mexico by low wages, low taxes, and little if any environmental regulations, some of these multinational corporations sought new territory to exploit. In the race to pay the lowest wages and adhere to the most lenient labor standards, other nations emerged as new leaders. For example, in 2000, the *maquila* city of Chihuahua, which specializes in producing automotive parts and

---

[27] "Mexico," Office of the US Trade Representative—Executive Office of the President.

electronics, led Mexico in employment. By the close of 2002, Chihuahua led in unemployment. Companies like General Electric, which over the years moved many jobs from the United States to Mexico, relocated those same jobs to China.

Yet China's entry into the global market has not translated into an economic boom for China's working class, as demonstrated by our earlier exploration of Foxconn. China, like Russia, had an economy completely controlled by an authoritarian state. Such a system supposedly guaranteed jobs for life and then retirement. But guaranteed jobs and retirement were the first casualties of privatization. Entire cities were built around huge mills, mines, and factories that provided a multitude of social benefits, from subsidized housing to hospitals and childcare. Privatization has brought an end to these guarantees and social benefits as plants closed, leaving retirees to go hungry and workers to face a bleak future (Jiang 2002, 23–25). In the final analysis, China may not remain the capitalists' paradise for long. Vietnam, Philippines, and Thailand are beginning to provide cheaper labor force options than China's. Ironically, while the average Mexican wage in 2003 was 188 percent higher than the average wage in China, by 2013, Mexican hourly wages dropped 19.6 percent lower. Lowered wages for Mexican workers are starting to bring manufacturing jobs back. This massive drop in Mexican wages has led to an increase in its US market share, growing at a faster pace than China's.[28]

Step 2: Reflecting

During the global pandemic (2020–2022), the top 1 percent of the world's wealthiest captured nearly twice the new generated wealth than the rest of the planet as their fortunes soared by $26 trillion. Ten years prior to the pandemic, they netted about half of all new wealth created. But during the two years of the pandemic, they netted two-thirds of all new globally created wealth. Global structures are designed so that the rich can get richer at the expense of the poor, who keep getting poorer. Making matters worse, during the pandemic, eleven countries cut taxes on the rich. Even the United States in 2021, when the White House and Congress were in the hands of the so-called liberal Democrats, efforts to raise taxes on the rich fell apart. Aggravating this reality is that some 1.7 billion workers live in countries where inflation outpaces their wages.[29]

---

[28] "Mexico Hourly Wages Now Lower Than China's—Study," Reuters, April 4, 2013.

[29] Tami Luhby, "The Top 1% Captured Nearly Twice as Much New Wealth as

A 2020 study conducted by Oxfam reveals a reality where the collective wealth of the world's 2,153 billionaires was, and remains, greater than that of the 4.6 billion people who constitute 60 percent of the planet's population.[30] This continuously growing income gap led James Gustave Speth, then–head administrator of the UN Development Programme, to conclude, "If present trends continue, the economic disparity between industrial nations and developing nations will assume proportions which are no longer merely unjust, but inhuman" (Moltmann 1998, 77). Consider the proverb that reminds us, "Those who oppress the poor curse their Maker, but those honoring God, favor [make a preferential option for] the needy" (Prov. 14:31).

The poor are those deprived of their basic necessities, the resources needed to live a life of dignity. They represents three distinct groups: (1) the socioeconomic poor, comprising those who exist outside the prevailing economic order (the unemployed, beggars, abandoned children, outcasts, sex workers) and the exploited (industrial workers paid substandard wages, rural workers, seasonal wage-earners, tenant farmers); (2) the sociocultural poor, consisting of Black and Indigenous peoples and women; and (3) the new poor of industrial societies, encompassing the physically and mentally disabled and neurodivergent abandoned to the streets of huge cities, along with the unemployed, the houseless, the depressed—often enduring suicidal ideation—the elderly dependent on insufficient state pensions, and the young addicted to drugs (Boff and Pixley 1989: 3–10). They are not necessarily lazy, backward, or underdeveloped, as so many want to believe. If so, then their only hope would rest on the generosity of the wealthy who might attempt succor by providing food, education, or loans. The poor are made poor by economic forces that cause the prosperity of one group or nation to be dependent on the poverty of another group or nations. These forces constitute a social phenomenon that enriches the few through the impoverishment of the many.

Treating workers as objects reduces their societal value to how they contribute to corporate profitability. Seldom are they defined by their humanity. Human rights become the process of removing obstacles hindering their engagement in trade and commerce rather than achieving human flourishing or self-fulfillment. For such reasons, neoliberalism is incapable of incorporating the basics tenets of Christianity or any other faith except the religion of capitalism. How does one reconcile the biblical

---

the Rest of the World over Last Two Years," CNN, January 16, 2023.

[30] Oxfam International, "World's Billionaires Have More Wealth Than 4.6 Billion People," press release, January 20, 2020.

mandate to forgive debts with the insistence that foreign debts be paid off at the expense of people meeting basic human needs? Ironically, toward the end of the 1970s in Latin America, as growing foreign debt was negatively impacting the lives of most people, some Catholic and Protestant clergy changed the words of the Lord's Prayer from "Forgive us our debts" to "Forgive us our offenses." Fears existed that Christians, pauperized by the policies of the World Bank and IMF, might take the Lord's Prayer literally, and actually demand that their debts be forgiven so that they could afford their daily bread. Churches succumbed to economic pressures when they neutered the potency of the biblical message (Hinkelammert 1995, 333–34).

Step 3: Meditating

A prominent feature of Christian worship is the concept of sacrifice, which is rooted in the Jewish faith. Among the many reasons mentioned by the Hebrew Bible for offering a sacrifice (such as tribute, cleansing, thanksgiving, supplication, ordination, or peace), most crucial for Christians were the sin and guilt offerings. Spilling the blood of an unblemished animal for the atonement of sin became the basis for understanding the crucifixion of Christ.[31] For many euroamerican Christians, the death on the cross of Jesus, "the lamb of God who takes away the sins of the world" (Jn. 1:29), becomes the ultimate sacrifice that served to reconcile God with sinners. The death of a sinless Jesus, as substitute for a sinful humanity that deserves God's punishment, restores fellowship between God and humans. Suffering and death become salvific. In other words, Jesus paid through his death so that others might live. But this concept is not limited to the Christ event. For some to live in abundance today, others must die.

Theologian Mark Lewis Taylor explained that the "nascent capitalism of modernity is a sacrificial economy worshiping money as its fetish, and sacrificing the subjective corporeality of the [marginalized]. So necessary is the sacrifice that it is rationalized as legitimate" (2001, 52).

The center of power can participate in all the riches life has to offer because those on the periphery die producing those riches. The death of those perceived to be inferior can be viewed as a sacrifice offered to the gods of neoliberalism so that a few can enjoy their abundance. Like Christ,

---

[31] For Jews, sin offerings were not given for the atonement of sin. Sins committed against others were handled with an appropriate punishment or restitution formula, while deliberate sins against God were beyond redemption (Num. 15:30–31).

the marginalized of the earth die so that those with power and privilege can have life abundantly.

Those suffering on the margins of society epitomize what liberation theologians call God's "crucified people," for they bear in a very real way the brunt of the sins of today's oppressive social and economic structures. As a crucified people they provide an essential perspective on salvation. Theologians coming from the margins of power insist that God intentionally and regularly chooses the oppressed of history, making them the principal means of salvation. They maintain that this is done in the same fashion that God chose the "suffering servant," the crucified Christ, to bring salvation to the world (Sobrino 1993, 259–60). God has always chosen the disenfranchised as agents of God's new creation. It was not to the court of Pharaoh that God's will was made known; instead, God chose the Hebrew enslaved to reveal God's movement in history. It was not Rome, the most powerful city of the known world, where God chose to perform the miracle of the incarnation, nor was it Jerusalem, the center of Yahweh worship; it was impoverished Galilee where God chose to proclaim the gospel message for the first time. Nazareth, Jesus's hometown, was so insignificant to the religious life of Judaism that the Hebrew Bible never mentions it. This theme of solidarity between the crucified Christ and the victims of oppression permeates scripture.

Still, liberative ethicists insist that nothing is salvific about suffering itself, for it tends to reinforce domination. Ethicists like Delores Williams find the image of Christ as surrogate victim too painful to incorporate into Black women's experience, who, during and after slavery, were forced and coerced into a similar role (1991, 8–13). Other Black feminist theologians and womanist thinkers such as Stephanie Mitchem have reminded us,

> Suffering in itself is not salvific. It is redemptive only in that it may lead to critical rethinking of meaning or purpose, as might any life crisis. Such reexamination is part of the process of human maturation. However, suffering is a distinctive starting place for thinking about salvation as it brings into sharp focus human experience in relation to God. (2002, 109)

Forgetting that the cross is a symbol of evil allows for the easy romanticization of those who are marginalized as some sort of hyper-Christians for the "cross" they are forced to bear. Such views tend to offer honor to those suffering, encouraging a form of quietism where suffering is stoically borne instead of encouraging praxis that can lead to the end of suffering. Take, for example, ethicist Stanly Hauerwas's argument that proves detrimental to disenfranchised communities. He reminds the marginalized that salvation is, in fact, "a life that freely suffers, that freely serves, because such suffering and service is the hallmark of the Kingdom established by Jesus" (1986, 69–70). All who know disenfranchisement should be concerned when privileged euroamericans tell them why their suffering, usually caused by euroamericans in the first place, makes them better saved Christians!

If salvation (liberation) exists in the life and resurrection of Jesus Christ, not just his death, then his crucifixion can be seen for what it was—the unjust repression of a just man by the dominant culture of his time. The crucifixion becomes an act of solidarity with those relegated to exist on the underside of our present economic structure. Ethicists from the margins maintain that the importance of the crucifixion lies in Christ's solidarity with the oppressed, Christ's understanding of how those who are oppressed suffer, reassurance for the disenfranchised that Christ understands their sufferings, and that, because of the resurrection, final victory might exist. All too often, romanticizing the crucified people leads to disturbing biblical interpretations that reinforce oppressive structures rather than seeking liberation from said structures. This especially occurs when the Bible's text is read from a position of power and privilege, even to the point of making the condition of those oppressed a model for the victims of racism, classism, and sexism.

In Mark 12:41–44 (see also Luke 21:1–4), we are told the story of a poor widow who gives all that she has to the Temple. The story of the widow's mite is generally idealized (especially during tithe-pledging season) by the dominant culture as an example of Christian behavior for those who are poor. The poor are expected, if they wish to be considered faithful, to give to the church—even if it means they go without. But missing from this interpretation is how the widow's self-sacrifice relates to the self-indulgence of the religious leaders who profit from her religious commitment. Reading the story with economic privilege ignores how the normative interpretation maintains societal power relationships detrimental to the poor. Yet to read the story of the widow's mite from the perspective of the poor, we would discover that Mark's account of the widow's offering is immediately preceded by Jesus's outrage toward the religious leaders who devour the possessions of widows. Mark states, "And [Jesus] said to them, … [the religious leaders are] devouring the houses of the widows under the pretense of praying at length" (12:38–40)." In Luke's account, Jesus immediately concludes the story of the widow's offering with his prediction of the Temple's destruction, stating, "These things you will see, days will come when one stone [of the Temple] will not be left on another" (21:5–6). If we read Mark and Luke together, we discover that Jesus is not praising the widow's offering as a paragon to be emulated by the poor. Instead, Jesus is denouncing a religious social structure that cons the widow out of what little she has. It is bad enough the biblical text is misinterpreted to mask the sin of the religious leaders who fleece the poor; what becomes worse is when the poor begin to interpret the text in such a way that they maintain the structures designed to oppress them.

Step 4: Case Studies

1. For decades, Foxconn profited from underage workers, hazardous working conditions, overcrowded living areas, suicides, long hours, and little pay. And yet, in anticipation of launching the iPhone 13, Foxconn was confident in meeting its goal of recruiting an additional two hundred thousand assembly-line workers.[32] Each day, busloads of potential employees showed up at the factory's gate of its flagship campus in Zhengzhou, eager to obtain one of these supposedly horrid jobs. If working at Foxconn is so terrible, why is there such a demand to work there? A young Chinese man studying in the United States provided a possible explanation:

> My aunt worked several years in what Americans call "sweat shops." It was hard work. . . . Do you know what my aunt did before she worked in one of these factories? She was a prostitute. Circumstances of birth are unfortunately random, and she was born in a very rural region. Most jobs . . . were held by men. Women and young girls, because of lack of education and economic opportunities, had to find other "employment." The idea of working in a "sweat shop" compared to that old lifestyle is an improvement, in my opinion. I know that my aunt would rather be "exploited" by an evil capitalist boss for a couple of dollars than have her body be exploited by several men for pennies. . . . Anyway, now my aunt has been living in New York for one year after saving up money for a plane ticket and visa, and she is wonderfully happy to have escaped Asia and reunited with our family. None of this would be possible if it wasn't for that "sweat shop."[33]

---

[32] Jane Zhang, "As the iPhone 13 Launch Nears, Apple Supplier Foxconn Rushes to Hire 200,000 More Workers," *South China Morning Post*, August 26, 2021.

[33] David Pogue, "What Cameras Inside Foxconn Found," *New York Times*, February 23, 2012.

- Are companies like Foxconn the salvation of the ultra-poor? Would closing these factories create greater misery among workers who come from rural areas? Would demanding higher wages mean the hiring of fewer workers seeking an escape route?

- Do we consider the workers' conditions at Foxconn to be horrible because we are comparing them to US work standards? Are the conditions at Foxconn better than the alternatives? Are the working conditions at Foxconn any better or worse than they are for other global subcontractors? In the messiness of life, is one form of exploitation better than another?

- How should we respond to the young Chinese man studying in the United States? To his aunt? Do they represent the views of all Foxconn workers? How do we proceed in determining what is just? Should the focus be on shutting down sweatshops? Reforming them? Is this more an issue of sexism and how women's bodies are globally commoditized? If so, how then should we proceed?

- Due to bad publicity, Foxconn has raised wages, shortened work hours, and provided chairs with backs at workstations. Are these changes cosmetic or structural? What else should be done? Is shaming corporations the best strategy to bring justice-based change? Are these reforms a commitment to justice or to the workers, or do such actions simply fix or merely address an image problem?

2. Lisa Rahman, at age nineteen, worked at the Shah Makhdum garment factory in Dhaka, Bangladesh, assembling Winnie-the-Pooh shirts. She was paid an equivalent of five cents to assemble Pooh shirts that the Walt Disney Company retailed at $17.99. In 2002, when workers united to publicly complain about poor working conditions, Disney canceled all future work orders, leaving garment workers like her with few options.[34] Garment workers took to the streets in August 2012 protesting wage cuts on already pitifully low wages, considered to be the world's lowest. They were brutally suppressed by the police and paramilitary officers. Labor leaders disappeared or turned up tortured and dead.

Suppression is justified when we consider that this poor nation, once irrelevant in the global economy, is now the second-largest apparel producer after China, employing 4 million workers in some four thousand factories, accounting for almost $38.8 billion in apparel sales for the

---

[34] Gary Gentile, "Group Slams Disney for Sweatshop Conditions in Bangladesh," Associated Press State & Local Wire, October 7, 2002.

2020–2021 financial year.[35] On April 2013, one of the factories making Disney garments[36] in Rana Plaza collapsed, killing more than four hundred Bangladeshi workers, mostly women and girls (globally, 80 percent of garment workers, or about 2.5 million people, are female). Even though large cracks appeared in the building beforehand, the lure of profit kept the owners and administrators of factories operating the facility. Rather than dealing with the consequences of the factory collapse, Disney chose to cut Bangladesh from its supply chain. After all, at the time, less than 1 percent of the factories in Bangladesh were used by Disney's contractors.[37] In 2021, eight years later, Disney resumed outsourcing garment production to Bangladesh.

• The collapse of the factory was mainly due to the negligence of the building's engineers, factory owner, and government inspectors. Do companies like Disney share in that responsibility? Why or why not? Does Disney have any responsibility toward these workers? Should Disney abide by worker demands? Which is more important for a corporation responsible to its stockholders: the basic rights of the workers or Disney's profit margin? Is Disney ultimately responsible for its refusal to pay more for the garments and demanding seamstresses to receive a more just wage?

• Is it ethical to own stock in a company such as Disney or mutual funds (even in the form of a retirement fund) when the profits earned stem from impoverishment of the world's most vulnerable people? Considering that most garment-factory owners serve in the local parliament or operate news sources, how impactful would any action be taken against global corporations?

• Is it ethical to profit from stock dividends paid out by companies, such as Apple, whose race to the bottom is responsible for creating dangerous working conditions in China and unemployed workers in the United States? Why or why not? Should multinational corporations have any obligations toward any particular nation-state—for example, the United States? If so, what type of obligations? What ethical responsibilities, if any, do dividend earners have in how transnational corporations operate? Does a moral connection exist between the person forced into poverty to increase dividend earnings on stocks and the person receiving those dividends?

---

[35] Ruma Paul, "Bangladesh Exports up 15% as Global Demand for Garments Rebounds," Reuters, July 6, 2021.

[36] Besides Disney, garment labels have connected this particular factory with Benetton, Children's Place, Calvin Klein, Tommy Hilfiger, and Cato Fashions.

[37] Susan Berfield, "For Retailers, Getting Out of Bangladesh Isn't So Easy," Businessweek, May 2, 2013.

• What responsibility, if any, do companies whose garments are cheaply made in substandard and dangerous factories have to the women and girls killed when the factories catch on fire or collapse? Do consumers have any responsibility when they purchase garments or merchandise made at the cost of blood? If a boycott against such garments and merchandise is advocated, would the workers suffer more if they lost their jobs for lack of consumer demand? These factory jobs have been a source of liberation for rural women who aren't even given a surname at birth. Some of these women have found a level of agency never experienced, making the garment industry a source of empowerment. Take, for example, Shahida Khatun, who dropped out of school at age twelve to work in the garment factory hoping to lift her family out of poverty. A decade later, the $30 a month she makes provides regular meals for her and her child, even occasional luxuries like chicken and milk.[38] Can companies like Disney, along with local factory owners, be seen as liberators?

• When the COVID pandemic led to cancelled orders and layoffs, Shahida Khatun was among those who lost her job. Within months, global gains accumulated by the world's poor over the last two decades were wiped away. Khatun, along with half a billion people (8 percent of the world's population) slid into destitution in 2020 according to the World Bank, the first time since 1998 when global poverty rates rose.[39] What responsibility do companies like Disney have to garment workers like Khatun who makes $30 a month as opposed to CEO Bob Chapek who in 2021 made $2.7 million a month—more than double his 2020 compensation?[40] What does it mean that some profited off the pandemic while others lost everything? Is anything owed to Khatun? Does responsibility for Khatun lie with the factory owners? With herself? Ashraf Ali also lost his garment job in Bangladesh. He considered suicide because he could not feed his family. And while severance pay could have provided some relief, it was not disbursed. Due to the pandemic, he, along with an estimated 160,000 other fired garment workers from some 213 factories throughout eighteen countries, were legally entitled to severance but were not paid, a combined total of $171.5 million.[41] Should companies like Disney place pressure on these factories to not engage in wage theft?

---

[38] Maria Abi-Habib, "Billions Slide Down Ladder That Took Decades to Climb," *New York Times*, May 1, 2020.

[39] Ibid.

[40] Robbie Whelan, "Disney Chief Bob Chapek's Pay More Than Doubled Last Year as Pandemic Strains Eased," *Wall Street Journal*, January 20, 2022.

[41] Elizabeth Paton, "Garment Workers Worldwide Still Awaiting Severance Pay," *New York Times*, April 7, 2021.

3. Nelly Kwamboka of Kenya wailed, cursed, and collapsed in anguish at the foot of the bed where her young son had just died of malaria. Next to her, three other children were battling for their lives.[42] If malaria doesn't kill a child, it often marks the beginning of a lifetime of illness and poverty. As malaria breeds poverty, poverty breeds malaria. If a child under five has malaria episodes five to ten times throughout the year, and needs the anti-malarial drug (Coartem) to treat each episode, the numbers are daunting. It is priced at about $11.24, which comes to a cost of about $112 a year (Dalaba et al. 2018, 2), almost a tenth of Kenya's minimum yearly wage of approximately $1,400, or about a fourth of the yearly income for those living in poverty at $400 a year. Now multiply the cost of medicine by four or five children, and having a child with a severe but treatable condition becomes unaffordable for many Kenyans, leaving no money for anything else—housing, food, or clothing.

Bill Gates, the former CEO of Microsoft, was listed by *Forbes* in 2021 as the fourth-richest individual living in the world, with an estimated worth of $130.7 billion, more than twice his 2011 worth of $59 billion.[43] His worth is greater than the gross national product of several countries. In 1999 Gates started the Bill & Melinda Gates Foundation with $32.8 billion in assets. In its first four years, the foundation distributed $6.2 billion, of which more than half ($3.2 billion) was earmarked for improving health in two-thirds-world nations.[44] During the 2018 Malaria Summit in London, Gates pledged to donate $1 billion by 2023 to eradicate malaria.[45] By 2022 the foundation was providing $2.5 billion to globally fight AIDS, tuberculosis, and malaria.[46] Thanks in part to the Gates Foundation, malaria deaths have been decreasing—from 896,000 in 2000 to 562,000 in 2015 and to 558,000 in 2019 (although a 12 percent increase over 2019 occurred due to disruption of services during the COVID pandemic).[47] Some people have criticized Gates for participating in a public relations campaign to polish or transform his image as a ruthless monopolist. Others are quick to point out

---

[42] "Kenya: A Predictable and Preventable Killer," *Africa News*, August 11, 2002.

[43] "Profile Bill Gates," *Forbes*, April 24, 2022.

[44] Stephanie Strom, "Gates Billions Reshape Health of World's Poor," *New York Times*, July 13, 2003.

[45] Nataha Bach, "Bill Gates Is Pouring Another $1 Billion into the Fight against Malaria," *Fortune*, April 18, 2018.

[46] Global Fund, "Private Sector: Bill & Melinda Gates Foundation," accessed April 22, 2022.

[47] World Health Organization, "Malaria," accessed April 22, 2022.

that the IRS rewards philanthropy by allowing tax deductions for donated funds. Yet the generosity of the foundation has contributed to rising vaccination rates in some of the poorest countries of the world.

• Are the criticisms of Gates justified? For the Kwambokas of the world, does it matter why he is donating money if its outcome is saving lives?

• Fourteenth-century Dominican nun Catherine of Siena prayed, "How can these wretched evil people share their possessions with the poor when they are already stealing from them?" (1980 [1388], 75). Is Gates being generous with money obtained through Microsoft's control of computer operating systems? In other words, is he simply being generous with other people's monies?

Chapter 6

War and Peace

Step 1: Observing

Many of the wars in which the United States participated started with a lie. The 1846 Mexican-American War began due to President James Polk's assertion that US troops came under fire in Texas; in reality, he deliberately had those troops cross disputed borders to provoke the Mexicans. The Spanish-American War started as a response to the lie that the Spanish blew up the USS *Maine* in Habana Harbor in 1898, but the Spaniards were not responsible; the explosion was caused by the ship's coal-burning boiler. Entry into the First World War was based on the sinking of the *Lusitania*, which, supposedly, carried no munitions for Allied forces; it did. The Vietnam War began in 1964 because of a lie that two US Navy destroyers came under a Vietnamese torpedo attack in the Gulf of Tonkin; no such attack took place. It was probably false radar returns. The 2003 invasion of Iraq was based on concerns that Saddam Hussein had weapons of mass destruction and was trying to obtain uranium from Africa; both assertions were lies.

From the start of the Cold War until 2001, there were 248 armed conflicts in 153 locations around the world. Of those, the United States initiated 201 of the overseas military operations. If we add military engagement with Afghanistan and Iraq, which commenced after 2001, then the total up to 2020 would be 203 (Garita 2016, 173). We engage in war because it is profitable. To mask profits, a lie must be perpetuated. In effect, war is a racket.

Major General Smedley D. Butler, USMC, was the most decorated Marine in US history at the time of his death. He fought for the United States in the Philippines, China, Central America, the Caribbean, and France during World War I. He was also a critic of US military adventurism, what we today would call empire building. He wrote, "War is just a racket," in the antiwar classic that goes by that title.

A racket is best described, I believe, as something that is not what it seems to the majority of people. Only a small inside group knows what it is about. It is conducted for the benefit of the very few at the expense of the masses. . . . [Basically] the flag follows the dollar and the soldiers follow the flag. . . . I spent most of my time being a high-class muscle-man for Big Business, for Wall Street and for the Bankers. In short, I was a racketeer, a gangster for capitalism. . . . I helped make Mexico, especially Tampico, safe for American oil interests in 1914. I helped make Haiti and Cuba a decent place for the National City Bank boys to collect revenues in. I helped in the raping of half a dozen Central American republics for the benefits of Wall Street. The record of racketeering is long. I helped purify Nicaragua for the international banking house of Brown Brothers in 1909–1912. I brought light to the Dominican Republic for American sugar interests in 1916. In China I helped to see to it that Standard Oil went its way unmolested. . . . Looking back on it, I feel that I could have given Al Capone a few hints. (1935)

According to Major General Butler, the most powerful military force the world has ever known existed for one reason: to make sure most of the world's resources flowed to our shores. If the United States were to be invaded, then yes, a right exists to defend oneself. But if we look at most of the military conflicts since the Second World War, the United States was the aggressor, the one doing the invading in the name of protecting and securing neoliberalism.

War, in most cases, remains an attempt by one nation to dominate another through superior military power, usually to procure or protect property rights, which can include resources and labor. To this end, the United States, the prime expansionist power since 1945, ensures its peace and security through the freedom of the open market. Peace is crucial to achieving and maintaining prosperity for the dominant culture. To protect this *Pax Americana*, a superior military force must be maintained to make certain that a nation with only 6 percent of the world's population can continue to benefit from 50 percent of the world's resources. When President George W. Bush announced his National Security Strategy in September 2002, he committed the United States to lead other nations toward "the single sustainable model for national success," meaning the model of the open market through free trade, or, we might say, the preservation of neoliberalism through economic or military force. The expansion and preservation of a new economic world order could at times require a regime change in nations that refuse to succumb to neoliberalism.

The wake of the 9/11 terrorist attacks ushered in a new doctrine under the Bush administration that embraced American exceptionalism. When engaging nations that are hostile to US supremacy, the United States maintains the right to start a war through a pre-emptive strike on any nation that *might* pose a possible future danger. Although at first somewhat leery of exceptionalism, the more liberal Obama administration nevertheless embraced Bush's doctrine, proclaiming, "I believe in American exceptionalism with every fiber of my being," praising among others, "the cowboys and ranch hands who had opened the West."[1] While Trump decried American exceptionalism before becoming president, he campaigned for his second term proposing teaching it in schools.[2] Even Biden's rhetoric of "America is back" is a sturdy reassertion of American exceptionalism and the leadership role it is called to play.[3] Each president may have sought to nuance American exceptionalism differently; still, all would reserve for themselves the right to engage in military action against any hypothetical threat before any and all other avenues for conflict resolution (such as the United Nations) have been exhausted. "First strike" to bring about "regime change" replaces the "containment"[4] and "deterrent"[5] strategies of the latter part of the last century. This new doctrine is but a repackaging of the US foreign policy toward Latin America carried out during the early twentieth century by folks like Major General Butler—a policy that reserved the right to determine what constituted a threat to US interests and security in "our" hemisphere, and then to act unilaterally.

Under President Theodore Roosevelt, the nexus of the first-strike and regime-change doctrines developed. At that time, "gunboat diplomacy," as it was known, resulted during the last century in every country bordering the Caribbean and several countries in South America being invaded by US forces, or covertly subverted by the CIA. Regime change was pursued when these countries chose to follow their own destinies in ways seen as unfavorable or unprofitable to the United States.[6] In some cases, brutal

---

[1] Greg Jaffe, "Obama's New Patriotism," *Washington Post*, June 3, 2015.

[2] Nicole Gaudiano, "Trump Wants to Teach 'American Exceptionalism,' an Idea He Once Disavowed," *Politico*, August 24, 2020.

[3] Tom Nichols, "President's Message to China and Russia: America Is Back, Trump Is Gone, the Free Ride Is Over," *USA Today*, April 29, 2021.

[4] The policy of coexisting with the threat of the Soviet Union while preventing the expansion of communism.

[5] The policy of building US defenses to assure a devastating response if attacked, thus keeping the Soviet Union from acting aggressively.

[6] During the twentieth century, US military incursions (*italicized*) or covert/indirect operations (**bold**) occurred in the following countries to bring about regime

dictatorships and military juntas were installed after the United States deposed democratically elected presidents, as was the case of Guatemala in 1954. Millions of peasants, students, church leaders, and intellectuals were abducted, tortured, or killed while opposing the US-backed and -installed government.

What does it mean to focus any discussion concerning issues of war on those who occupy the margins of society—the peasants, students, church leaders, and intellectuals? We can be assured that the discourse would take on a quite different tone. The argument moves from a just war debate fostered by ethicists from the dominant culture to a discussion of racism and classism at the margins from those who recognize that military violence usually stimulates and is stimulated by white supremacy and supposed eurocentric superiority. From the global margins, explorations on war become aware of the re-creation of the other's history (racism) and the spoils of war (classism). These concerns played themselves out during the post-9/11 wars, which are explored in greater detail below. For violence to occur, history must be re-created, usually to the disadvantage of those who will become the victims of war. The nation initiating the military conflict reconstructs itself as the defender of virtue and appears to have no ulterior motive. Think of Russia's 2022 invasion of Ukraine. According to Russia, the nation initiated the conflict to save ethnic Russians who are facing genocide by a Nazi regime—a regime, interestingly enough, led by a Jewish president whose family members perished in the Holocaust.

Starting an allegedly virtuous war under false pretense is not limited to authoritarian regimes. Take, for example, the comments made by Colin Powell, then–US secretary of state, during a September 8, 2002, interview. He made a case for the moral right to attack: "Our record and our history is not one of going out looking for conflict, it is not one of undertaking pre-emptive acts for the purpose of seizing another person's territory, or to impose our will on someone else. Our history and our tradition is always one of defending our interest."[7] Conveniently forgotten by Powell was the 1846 US invasion of Mexico to take half of the country's land—land that became our Southwest, now comprising six states. The justification of this massive land acquisition was based on a theology that conceived

---

change or protect the status quo: Cuba, *1906*, *1912*, *1917*, *1933*, **1960**, **1961**; Costa Rica, **1948**; Dominican Republic, **1904**, *1916–1924*, **1930**, **1963**, *1965*; El Salvador, **1932**, **1944**, **1960**, **1980**, **1984**; Granada, *1983*; Guatemala, **1921**, **1954**, *1960*, **1963**, **1966**; Haiti, **1915**, *1994*; Honduras, *1905*, *1907*, **1911**, **1943**, **1980**; Mexico, *1905*, *1914*, *1917*; Nicaragua, **1909**, *1910*, *1912*, *1926*, **1934**, **1981**, **1983**, **1984**; Panama, *1908*, *1918*, *1925*, **1941**, **1981**, *1989*.

[7] "Interview with Colin L. Powell," *New York Times*, September 8, 2002.

the dominant euroamerican culture as chosen by God. This concept of "Manifest Destiny" taught that God had intended euroamericans to acquire the entire continent. Our history disregards the expansionist war against Mexico. Absent from the rhetoric was the actual motive for the Mexican invasion: acquisition of land and its resources, specifically the gold of California, the silver of Nevada, the copper of Arizona and New Mexico, the oil of Texas, the gold and silver of Colorado, and all the natural harbors needed for commerce along the American western coast. These riches became the financial seed money that launched the expansion of the US economy, eventually making it a global leader.

Powell's call for invasion at the United Nations was not the first time the United States initiated regime change in Iraq. In 1963 the CIA collaborated with the relatively small anticommunist Baath Party to overthrow Abel Karim Kassem. Once in power, the Baath Party unleashed a bloodbath, murdering leftist sympathizers named on CIA-provided lists of suspected communists. The "house cleaning" allowed oil corporations like Mobil, Bechtel, and British Petroleum to conduct business with Baghdad for the first time. By 1968 infighting among Baath leaders threatened business interests, so Saddam Hussein seized power with CIA backing. Although the United States knew Saddam Hussein supported terrorists, killed his own people, and was attempting to build nuclear weapons, Donald Rumsfeld (as President Ronald Reagan's special envoy to the Middle East) traveled in 1983 to meet Hussein in hopes of establishing warmer relations. Later, as President George W. Bush's secretary of defense, Rumsfeld would execute the war against Hussein.

Iraq was seen as strategic to US attempts to thwart Iran's growing influence in the crucial oil-producing states along the Persian Gulf. During the Iran-Iraq War (1980–1988), the United States provided Hussein with satellite photography of the battleground. The US Commerce Department reports that during the early 1980s the United States provided Iraq with numerous shipments of "bacteria/fungi/protozoa" that could be used to create biological weapons (such as anthrax), along with 1.5 million atropine injections to be used against the effects of chemical weapons. When Hussein used chemical weapons against the Kurdish rebels in 1988, the Reagan administration responded by blaming Iran, only later relenting when mounting evidence pointed to Iraq.[8] Until the eve of the 1991 Gulf War, the United States had been providing Iraq with billions of dollars

---

[8] See Christopher Dickey and Evan Thomas, "How Saddam Happened," *Newsweek*, September 23, 2002; Patrick E. Tyler, "Officers Say United States Aided Iraq in War Despite Use of Gas," *New York Times*, August 18, 2002.

in financing and millions of dollars in equipment to build Iraq's missiles, conventional bombs, and nuclear, chemical, and biological weapons—all to stem the influence of Iran.[9] Most damning was the proposed mid-1990 sale of "skull furnaces" that was approved by the United States Department of Commerce, for the purpose of producing nuclear weapons components (Hartung 1994, 222, 232).[10]

Before the post-9/11 military conflict began in Iraq, a narrative of the country possessing weapons of mass destruction (WMD) was created, casting Iraq as a clear and present danger to the United States. But since the overthrow of Hussein, no stockpiles of WMD were found; consequently, a radical shift in the narrative was needed. Starting in September 2003, Bush's speeches on Iraq transitioned from the threat posed by Hussein to promoting democracy (Feith 2008, 475–77). The failure to find WMD meant that the original narrative to initiate war was at best wrong, at worst a lie—hence the need to re-create the past by developing a new narrative that focused on fostering democracy. No one was fooled by this sleight of hand. Consider Bush's 2022 Freudian slip. Attempting to criticize Russian president Vladimir Putin's war on Ukraine, Bush referred to the "decision of one man to launch a wholly unjustified and brutal invasion of *Iraq*." After quickly correcting himself, saying he meant to say Ukraine, he added—to the laughter of the Dallas audience at his presidential library—"Iraq, too, anyway."[11]

In addition to this need to re-create the past was the desire to profit from the present. "To the victors of war go the spoils." In the case of Iraq, the spoils included a proven reserve of 112 billion barrels of crude oil, the largest in the world outside Saudi Arabia. The first major contract for the reconstruction of Iraq, worth $680 million, was awarded to Bechtel, which faced only token competition. Bechtel's chief executive served on

---

[9] Iraq, after being removed in 1983 from the list of terrorist-supporting nations, became the largest recipient of the US Department of Agriculture's Commodity Credit Corporation (CCC) credits, acquiring 20 percent of all guarantees granted between 1984 and 1989. By 1989, the first President Bush signed National Security Directive 26, calling for "improved economic and political ties with Iraq." This improved relationship meant an approval of $1 billion in CCC credits. When the Gulf War broke out shortly afterward, Hussein reneged on a total of $2 billion in CCC loans, leaving US taxpayers to foot the bill (Hartung 1994, 238, 241).

[10] The sale was called off after Stephen Bryen of the *Philadelphia Inquirer* wrote about the transaction, bringing pressure upon the first Bush administration to cancel the agreement two weeks before Iraq invaded Kuwait.

[11] Bryan Pietsch, "George W. Bush Called Iraq War 'Unjustified and Brutal.' He meant Ukraine," *Washington Post*, May 19, 2022.

the US Commander in Chief's Export Council, and a Bechtel director, George Shultz, served as the first secretary of state in the first Bush administration, raising serious issues of impropriety. More questionable were contracts estimated to have reached $60 billion that were initially awarded with no public bids or discussion—and sometimes secretly to politically connected firms like Halliburton, directed by former vice president Dick Cheney, who served as Halliburton CEO from 1995 until 2000. While Cheney was defense secretary (1989–1993) under George H. W. Bush, he asked then-Halliburton subsidiary Brown & Root to conduct a study of the cost effectiveness of outsourcing military operations to private contractors. Based on the study produced, the Pentagon hired Brown & Root to implement the outsourcing plan, only for Cheney to then go to Halliburton, the parent company, as its new CEO in 1995.

Kellogg Brown & Root (KBR)[12] was among the first contractors that prospered from the Iraq War and occupation, awarded $33 billion to support military bases.[13] The work conducted by KBR was so shoddy that it endangered US soldiers. For example, the family of Green Beret staff sergeant Ryan Maseth was informed by an army criminal investigator that their son's death on January 2, 2008, was a case of negligent homicide by KBR. Maseth was electrocuted while taking a shower at his base in Baghdad. An underground water pump short-circuited, causing electricity to travel through to the water. Maseth was found on the shower floor after suffering a heart attack. His parents believed that his death could have been prevented if KBR contracted qualified electricians and plumbers to work at the barracks rather than pursued profits by employing unqualified personnel.[14] KBR did not challenge the merits of the couple's claims, instead arguing that, while it had the maintenance contract for the building, the army decided not to make the building electrically safe. US District Judge Nora Barry Fischer ruled in July 2012 that KBR could not be held liable because military commanders, and not the contractor, made the decisions on where to house soldiers and whether buildings with substandard electrical systems were suitable.[15] Shortly after the ruling, KBR's attorney

---

[12] Brown & Root, through mergers, was renamed Kellogg Brown & Root. Although Halliburton continued to own KBR during the height of the Iraq War, it sold the company in 2007.

[13] Rod Nordland, "Iraq, Rebuilding Its Economy, Shuns United States Firms," *New York Times*, November 13, 2009.

[14] Peter Spiegel, "Army Investigator Cited 'Negligent Homicide' by KBR," *Los Angeles Times*, January 23, 2009.

[15] Joe Mandak, "Judge Nixes Suit in Soldier's Iraq Electrocution," Associated Press, July 16, 2012.

Robert Matthews filed a motion that a federal judge should dismiss fifty-five pending lawsuits by military personnel and veterans, arguing that KBR should be exempt from litigation because it deserved the same immunity granted government entities and personnel.[16] The message was clear: corporate profits trump the lives of military personnel.

More recently, veterans have filed a lawsuit alleging that KBR and other companies dumped tires, batteries, medical waste, and other materials into burn pits—areas where items are disposed of via incineration. The suit claims that the smoke and fumes from some 230 burn pits in Iraq and Afghanistan have caused health issues to more than eight hundred veterans (the Department of Defense estimates 3.5 million service personnel have been exposed to these pits—including President Biden's deceased son, Beau, who died from an aggressive cancerous brain tumor). The appeal was rejected. The veterans lost the legal case, and the conservative US Supreme Court rejected the veterans' appeal in 2019.[17] Fortunately, by August 2022, President Biden signed into law a bill that made millions of veterans eligible for expanded healthcare access and disability benefits for those who were exposed to burn pits.[18]

Attempting to obtain immunity from prosecution for wrongdoings for companies like KBR contributes to a continuous slide toward privatizing future wars. Even during 2007, when the US military presence in Iraq surged to 160,000 soldiers, the number of US-paid private contractors exceeded US combat troops, as more than 180,000 pairs of boots were on the ground, with the largest employer of contractors being KBR. While these contractors are supposed to support the combat troops, they were employees who could actually jeopardize the mission, as in 2004 when drivers refused to take food rations to forces in a combat zone. Just as troubling were and are those contractors working for heavily armed private security companies, such as Blackwater, Triple Canopy, and Erinys, who at times found themselves engaged in firefights with insurgents (twenty-one security firms were responsible for deploying 10,800 armed personnel). As Peter Singer, a Brookings Institution scholar, quipped, "This is not the

---

[16] Patricia Kime, "KBR Seeks Dismissal of Lawsuits over Burn Pits," *Air Force Times*, July 16, 2012.

[17] Todd South, "Supreme Court Rejects Appeal from Veterans in Burn Pit Lawsuit against KBR, Halliburton," *Military Times*, January 14, 2019; Edward Helmore, "Toxic Burn Pits Put the Health of US Veterans at Risk. Can a New Law Help?," *The Guardian*, March 13, 2022.

[18] Leo Hane III and Jonathan Lehrfeld, "Biden Signs Burn Pit Exposure Health Bill into Law," *Military Times*, August 10, 2022.

coalition of the willing. It's the coalition of the billing."[19] The Iraq War became the first outsourced war that relied heavily on corporations (specifically the company previously run by Vice President Dick Cheney) at a substantial profit, paid for with US tax dollars.

Besides building and maintaining military bases, KBR was given control of the entire Iraqi oil operation, including distribution. Such acts violate international law. The World Trade Organization forbids discrimination against companies of WTO member nations in the awarding of contracts. Ironically, Halliburton conducted business with Iraq (as well as with two other members of the so-called axis of evil, Iran and North Korea) during Cheney's term as the head of the corporation. In addition to being fined $3.8 million in 1995 for reexporting US goods through a foreign subsidiary to Libya in clear violation of US sanctions, Halliburton has been accused of overcharging the US government for work conducted during the 1990s, resulting in a $2 million settlement to ward off criminal prosecution for price gouging.[20] In 2009 the US government agreed to pay nearly $1 million to Bunnatine Greenhouse, a former top Army Corps of Engineers contracting official, who charged she was demoted when she objected to a $7 billion no-bid contract granted to Halliburton to repair Iraq oil fields, thus bringing to a close a six-year legal battle.[21] She charged that Halliburton was awarded contracts without following rules designed to ensure competition and fair prices to the government. In one case she witnessed, Halliburton representatives were allowed to sit in as army officials discussed the terms of the contract that the company was to receive.[22]

---

[19] T. Christian Miller, "Contractors Outnumber Troops in Iraq," *Los Angeles Times*, July 4, 2007.

[20] Bob Herbert, "Dancing with the Devil," *New York Times*, May 22, 2003; Michael Kinsley, "To the Victors Go the Spoils," *New York Times*, April 20, 2003; Neela Banerjee, "2 in House Question Halliburton's Iraq Fuel Prices," *New York Times*, October 16, 2003; Don Van Natta Jr., "High Payments to Halliburton for Fuel in Iraq," *New York Times*, December 10, 2003; Douglas Jehl, "Evidence Is Cited of Overcharging in Iraq Contract," *New York Times*, December 12, 2003; Joel Brinkley and Eric Schmitt, "Halliburton Will Repay United States Excess Charges for Troops' Meals," *New York Times*, February 3, 2004.

[21] Erik Eckholm, "Army Corps Agrees to Pay Whistle-Blower in Iraq Case," *New York Times*, July 29, 2011.

[22] Erik Eckholm, "A Top United States Contracting Official for the Army Calls for an Inquiry in the Halliburton Case," *New York Times*, October 25, 2004. The awarding of no-bid contracts is not limited to times of war. KBR received a questionable $500 million contract from the Defense Department after Hurricane Katrina to do major repairs at navy facilities along the Gulf Coast. See Philip

To make matters worse, KBR has been accused of defrauding the US government by billing everything from meals it did not serve to inflated gas prices to bill duplication and excessive administrative costs. Even though the Pentagon's own auditors identified more than $250 million in unjustified or excessive charges, the army decided to reimburse KBR for nearly all the distributed items on its $2.41 billion no-bid contract. Henry A. Waxman (D-CA), ranking minority member of the House Committee on Government Reform, probably said it best: "Halliburton gouged the taxpayer, government auditors caught the company red-handed, yet the Pentagon ignored the auditors and paid Halliburton hundreds of millions of dollars and a huge bonus."[23] In 2014 the US government, under the False Claims Act and the Anti-Kickback Act, sued KBR, La Nouvelle, and First Kuwaiti. The complaint alleged that KBR employees filed false claims and took kickbacks from La Nouvelle and First Kuwaiti in 2003 and 2004 in connection with the award and oversight of subcontracts. Specifically, KBR submitted claims for reimbursement for costs it incurred under the subcontracts that allegedly were inflated or excessive, or for goods and services that were grossly deficient or not provided. The case was dismissed, citing lack of jurisdiction over foreign agencies.[24]

The lesson learned is that, when it comes to receiving billion-dollar military contracts, who you know goes a long way. Executives or political action committees of the seventy companies to receive lucrative government contracts for billions of dollars in reconstruction work in either Iraq or Afghanistan contributed at least $500,000 to the 2000 Bush-Cheney election campaign. Nine of the ten biggest contract recipients (Bechtel and Halliburton topped the list) employed senior governmental officials or had close ties to government agencies and Congress.[25] As already mentioned, most of the contracts awarded were conducted secretively, without competitive bidding, and without a single agency supervising the contracting process for the government. War, commoditized within the neoliberal paradigm, has indeed become a profitable venture.

Shenon, "Official Vows Investigation of No-Bid Relief Contracts," *New York Times,* September 14, 2005.

[23] James Glanz, "Army to Pay Halliburton Unit Most Costs Disputed by Audit," *New York Times,* February 27, 2006.

[24] *United States ex rel. Conyers v. Kellogg Brown & Root, Inc.*

[25] Edmund L. Andrews and Elizabeth Becker, "Bush Got $500,000 from Companies That Got Contracts, Study Finds," *New York Times,* October 31, 2003; Douglas Jehl, "Insiders' New Firm Consults on Iraq," *New York Times,* September 30, 2003.

President Dwight D. Eisenhower warned the American public in 1961 of this danger, coining the phrase "military-industrial complex." Eisenhower raised the concern that the defense industry's quest for profit, coupled with a close working relationship with politicians, would pervert US foreign policy while causing stagnation in the domestic economy. The results of the forever wars in Iraq and Afghanistan triggered a war in Syria, the rise of the deadly and brutal Islamic State, a genocide geared toward Christians and Yazidi, a stronger Iranian government, and a humiliating withdrawal from Afghanistan. These unintended consequences came with a hefty price tag. By 2022, as a line item, US military expenditures reached an estimated $754 billion, representing 10.5 percent of the federal budget, accounting for the second-largest expense category after Social Security and contributing to our $30 trillion debt.[26] The US military budget represents approximately 39 percent of the world's total military spending, a figure almost equal to the next eleven countries combined.[27] Additionally, most of the weapons used throughout the world are made in the United States. According to the US Department of State, authorized arms exports (both commercial and government-managed) totaled $175.08 billion in sales. Overseas government-to-government military sales represented $66.3 billion,[28] or around 37 percent of the overall arms market from 2016 to 2020. These figures do not include the cost of two decades of training and equipment totaling $83 billion that were left behind when the United States evacuated Afghanistan, leaving the Taliban military and police force well stocked for years to come.[29] While the United States provided weapons to ninety-six governments, 47 percent of all sales were designated to the Middle East.[30] The United States is the major global exporter of lethal

---

[26] Kimberly Amadeo, "United States Military Budget, Its Components, Challenges, and Growth," The Balance, February 24, 2022.

[27] China ($252 billion), India ($72.9 billion), Russia ($61.7 billion), UK ($59.2 billion), Saudi Arabia ($57.7 billion), Germany ($52.8 billion), France ($52.7 billion), Japan ($49.1 billion), South Korea ($45.7 billion), Italy ($28.9 billion), and Australia ($27.5 billion). Total: $761 billion. See Peter G. Peterson Foundation, "United States Defense Spending Compared to Other Countries," July 9, 2021.

[28] Bureau of Political-Military Affairs Fact Sheet, "United States Arms Transfers Increased by 2.8 Percent in FY 2020 to 175.08 Billion," US Department of State, January 20, 2021.

[29] Thomas Gibbons-Neff, "In Afghanistan, an Unceremonious End, and a Shrouded Beginning," *New York Times*, August 30, 2021.

[30] Pieter Wezeman, Alexandra Kulmova, and Siemon T. Wezeman, *Trends in International Arms Transfers* (Solna, Sweden: Stockholm International Peace Research Institute, 2021), 2–3.

weapons, selling the mechanisms by which so many of the world's marginalized die.

Representative Marjorie Taylor Greene (R-GA) probably said it best in a tweet criticizing war-profiteers: "War and rumors of war is incredibly profitable and convenient."[31] The main beneficiaries of war are the top hundred defense contractors, which produce the necessary hardware to conduct war at a tune of $398 billion (in 2017). The United States is home to five[32] of the top ten global military contractors, accounting for 57 percent of total arms sales (Wezeman and Fleurant 2019, 223–24). It should be noted that the day before Representative Greene sent her tweet, she and fellow members of Congress purchased stocks in US defense companies prior to the Russian invasion of Ukraine. Although difficult to track, at least fifty-one members of Congress or their family members own between $2.3 and $5.8 million worth of stocks in the top thirty defense contractors in the world.[33] In 2020, at least fifteen congressional leaders who hold powerful positions on both sides of the chambers and aisle, responsible for setting and controlling US military policies because of the committees on which they serve, have a combined $1 million in financial ties to prominent defense contractors.[34]

What may be profitable for corporations and politicians was extremely costly to the average person caught in these grinding wars. With the enactment of the 2021–2022 fiscal budget, a total of $5.8 trillion was spent to cover the post-9/11 military operations, base security, foreign aid, embassy costs, and veterans' health care ($2.313 trillion for Afghanistan and $2.058 trillion for Iraq). Although military activities have ceased, the United States still has an obligation to care for veterans of these forever wars for several decades at an additional minimum cost of $2.2 trillion, bringing the total cost of the post-9/11 wars to $8 trillion. This comes to about $8,094 per taxpayer (Crawford 2021, 1–3).

Just as costly is the measure in human lives. This twenty-plus-year war cost 929,000 lives due to direct violence (many times more died indirectly),

---

[31] Rep. Marjorie Tayler Greene @RepMTG, Twitter, February 23, 2022.

[32] Lockheed Martin with $44.9 billion in arms sales in 2021; Boeing, $26.9 billion; Raytheon, $23.9 billion; Northrop Grumman, $22.4 billion; and General Dynamics, $19.5 billion.

[33] Donald Shaw and David Moore, "The Members of Congress Who Profit from War," *American Prospect*, January 17, 2020.

[34] Warren Rojas, Camila DeChalus, Kimberly Leonard, and David Levinthal, "At Least 15 Lawmakers Who Shape US Defense Policy Have Investments in Military Contractors," *Business Insider*, December 13, 2021.

of whom more than 387,000 were civilians.[35] We know that 7,057 US soldiers lost their lives, and we know over four times more—30,177—committed suicide (Suitt 2021, 1); we do not know how many are suffering from PTSD. Those who survive war are left with psychological scars. One way to deal with this phenomenon is to medicate combat personnel. Between 2005 and 2011, there was a 682 percent increase in the number of psychoactive drugs (antipsychotics, mood stabilizers, sedatives, and stimulants) prescribed to active US troops. Compare this with a 22 percent increase among the civilian population during the same period. These prescriptions were handed out in ways not approved by the Food and Drug Administration, nor did such distribution meet the usual psychiatric standards of practice.[36] We literally drugged soldiers so that they could conduct war.

As bloody as war can be, advanced technology led the United States into a new phase of eliminating potential threats to the nation without the apparent need of committing boots on the ground. War can now be delivered to the enemy from the sky via the semisecretive drone program, raising some disturbing ethical questions. Take the example of Anwar al-Awlaki and Samir Khan, two American citizens. On the morning of September 30, 2011, the two Americans were headed toward their trucks at a remote desert patch called Jawf Province in Yemen. From a secret CIA airstrip in Saudi Arabia, a group of US drones, operated from thousands of miles away, took off and headed toward their targets. Shortly afterward, for the first time since the American Civil War, the US government deliberately killed American citizens as wartime enemies without a trial. Another drone mistakenly killed al-Awlaki's sixteen-year-old American-born son, Abdulrahman, who ventured into the desert in search of his father.[37] Between 2002 and 2020, US drone strikes in Afghanistan, Pakistan, Somalia, and Yemen killed between 10,000 and 17,000 people, 800 to 1,750 of whom are thought to have been "collateral damage"—a euphemism meaning innocent civilians, including children.[38]

---

[35] Watson Institute International & Public Affairs, Brown University, "Summary of Findings," Cost of Wars, accessed April 27, 2022.

[36] Richard A. Friedman, "Wars on Drugs," *New York Times*, April 6, 2013.

[37] At least one more American, Jude Kenan Mohammad, was killed by a drone strike on a compound in South Waziristan, Pakistan, on November 16, 2011. See Scott Shane and Eric Schmitt, "One Drone Victim's Trail from Raleigh to Pakistan," *New York Times*, May 22, 2013.

[38] Sarah Kreps, Paul Lushenko, and Shyam Raman, "Biden Can Reduce Civilian Casualties during US Drone Strikes. Here's How," Brookings Institution, January 19, 2022.

The use of drones is efficient and cost-effective, allowing the United States to engage in far-flung global wars. But should we equate the ethical with efficiency or cost-effectiveness? It is true that Anwar al-Awlaki was suspected of being an operative for Al Qaeda—even though his father, Nasser al-Awlaki, argues to the contrary, pointing out that no US court ever reviewed the US government's claims nor examined any evidence of criminal wrongdoing.[39] Still Khan, according to US officials, was not a significant enough threat to warrant targeted assassination,[40] and Abdulrahman's only crime was being Anwar's son. American citizens' constitutional rights were denied; they were sentenced to death without any charges levied, trials conducted, or judicial process followed. US technology has advanced to such a degree that enemies can now be surgically eliminated. Such strikes routinely rain fire from the skies. While, theoretically, targeting "terrorists" is the goal, the fact remains that the distinction between a terrorist whose intent is to do bodily harm and a sympathizer who visited a training camp is an important one.

Former president Obama noted that "this technology really began to take off at the beginning of my presidency." And—while he went on to stress—by spinning reality—his efforts about a year and a half into the program to reign in the overusage of this technology, he ignores how, after the suicide attack on an Afghanistan outpost in 2009 that killed multiple CIA officers, the agency—known for a history of secretive assassinations—vowed to avenge the deaths. Their vengeance, with Obama's consent and complicity, led to 2010 being the bloodiest year of drone strikes in Pakistan.[41] "Turns out I'm really good at killing people," Obama boasted to aides. "Didn't know that was gonna be a strong suit of mine."[42] Throughout his eight years in office, 1,878 strikes took place. Trump loosened the rules put in place by his predecessor that sought to reign in the indiscriminative usage of drones. During Trump's first two years, 2,243 strikes were conducted.[43] Biden reinstated most of the rules loosened by Trump, and despite the very public drone strike debacle during the closing

---

[39] Nasser al-Awlaki, "The Drone That Killed My Grandson," *New York Times*, July 18, 2013.

[40] Shane and Schmitt, "One Drone Victim's Trail from Raleigh to Pakistan."

[41] Conor Friedersdorf, "Obama's Weak Defense of His Record on Drone Killings," *The Atlantic*, December 23, 2016.

[42] Micah Zenko, "Obama's Final Drone Strike Data," Council on Foreign Relations, January 20, 2017.

[43] "Trump Revokes Obama Rule on Reporting Drone Strike Deaths," BBC, March 7, 2019.

days of the Afghanistan military pull-out, Biden has nearly ended the usage of drones, ordering fewer than 18 strikes in 2021.[44]

While the employment of drones has been significantly curtailed, their usage has not been repudiated, thus creating the possibility for future ethical dilemmas. What happens when other countries develop similar technology? For example, on December 4, 2011, around 140 miles inside Iran from its border with Afghanistan, a drone that was supposedly off course (or simply doing covert surveillance) fell into Iranian hands. On April 22, 2012, a BBC story had General Amir Ali Hajizadeh boasting that the Iranians had broken its encryption codes and reverse-engineered the aircraft to make their own copy. Although Iranians have yet to fly their own drones, thus far proving the boast empty, what if they were to share the drone's schematics with China? Will the Chinese government eventually develop its own drones? What happens when China has drones and decides to also target those they define as terrorists—like the Dalai Lama? The Chinese foreign ministry has accused the Dalai Lama of "terrorism in disguise" for supporting Tibetans who have set themselves on fire in protest against Beijing's rule. Our exceptionalism, which allows unilateral killing of those we call terrorists anywhere in the world without some form of global consensus, has created a precedent for other nations to follow suit.

Two post-9/11 wars that lasted over two decades and an amorphous never-ending war on terror have transformed the United States. The wealth of the nation has been ransomed on the altar of Mars, or in President Eisenhower's own words,

> Every gun that is made, every warship launched, every rocket fired signifies, in the final sense, a theft from those who hunger and are not fed, those who are cold and are not clothed. This world in arms is not spending money alone. It is spending the sweat of its laborers, the genius of its scientists, the hopes of its children. The cost of one modern heavy bomber is this: a modern brick school in more than 30 cities. It is two electric power plants, each serving a town of 60,000 population. It is two fine, fully equipped hospitals. It is some 50 miles of concrete highway. We pay for a single fighter plane with a half million bushels of wheat. We pay for a single destroyer with new homes that could have housed more than 8,000 people. This, I repeat, is the best way of life to be found

---

[44] Ryan Cooper, "Biden Nearly Ended the Drone War, and Nobody Noticed," *The Week*, December 1, 2021.

on the road the world has been taking. This is not a way of life at all, in any true sense. Under the cloud of threatening war, it is humanity hanging from a cross of iron. (1953)

Step 2: Reflecting

Most societies create systems designed to define what is good and what is evil. Such binary structures also define what constitutes legal and illegal, acceptable and unacceptable, criminal and noncriminal. What one society determines to be proper may be viewed with horror by another. Political assassinations, restriction of free expression, or brute intimidation could be construed as necessary evils for the advancement of a sacred cause. While all persons within that society might agree on the ultimate end, not all would necessarily subscribe or acquiesce to such tactics to achieve said goal. The question then emerges: how do such violent tactics become an acceptable procedure within the eyes of the society at large?

French philosopher Michel Foucault maintained that it can be done only by reducing what is deemed good to "normal" and what is deemed evil to "abnormal" or pathological (1965, 73). By extension, when engaged in a just war, warlike activities such as killing, bombing, and censorship are deemed acceptable to ensure the final victory of good. Terror, then, is understood as the legitimate use of violence to enforce justice. Terror, the spilling of blood, and other acts of war become "normal," regardless of how distasteful they may be. In fact, they become an inevitable moral imperative. The "enemies of freedom and democracy" (read: those opposed to the neoliberalism of today's eurocentric worldview) are a threat to "truth" and, as such, must be silenced. Many unjust attempts at power can be concealed in a holy war that rallies the people around the concepts of freedom, democracy, and justice.

War is inevitable because the United States continues its pursuit of global economic and military dominance, choosing to maintain international structures that make war possible and profitable. Still, can any war be considered "just"? Just war theory, a medieval concept embedded in international law, was first formulated by Augustine in the early fifth century (and expanded by Thomas Aquinas in the thirteenth) to provide guidelines for "Christian" rulers of empire to determine when the presence of evil and injustice justified the use of violence to stamp it out.[45] Under certain

---

[45] Traditional just war theory is based on six *jus ad bellum* principles that are concerned with establishing the moral justification for engaging in violence (1) just cause, (2) legitimate authority to declare hostilities, (3) just intention, (4) reasonable chance of success, (5) proper announcement of beginning hostilities, and (6) that the

circumstances, it was believed that God condoned wars (e.g., crusades) conducted to destroy evil (understood as Islam) and rectify injustices.[46] But can just war guidelines impartially help people decide if the use of military force within a given conflict is just? Or is the determination to conduct a war simply an amalgam of the subjective views of those applying the just war theory?

Take, for example, the early debate in 2003 over possible US entry into a war with Iraq. The majority of religious leaders and denominations, using the principles of just war theory, conclusively determined prior to hostilities that a US preemptive attack on Iraq did not meet the criteria for a just war.[47] One hundred Christian scholars of ethical theory issued the following statement: "As Christian ethicists, we share a common moral presumption against a preemptive war on Iraq by the United States."[48] Likewise, the US Conference of Catholic Bishops issued a statement on November 13, 2002, urging President Bush not to engage in a preemptive attack on Iraq. Nonetheless, a few ethicists believed that the conflict in Iraq met the demands of Christianity's just war doctrine, most notably, Jean Bethke Elshtain and Michael Novak.[49] While it would not be appropriate to question the sincerity of these ethicists in arriving at their conclusions, it is reasonable to explore if just war theory can conclusively indicate the correct ethical path. Why were two different conclusions reached after

---

means used be proportional to the desired objective. In addition, two *jus in bello* principles apply for how violence is to be morally conducted: (1) determining legitimate targets and (2) how much force is morally appropriate.

[46] Pope Gregory VII (1073–1085) assured combatants engaged in "holy" war that they would be forgiven from the consequences of their sins.

[47] The notable exception was Richard Land, then president of the Ethics and Religious Liberty Commission of the Southern Baptist Convention. The Convention supported the war in Iraq. Its decision was greatly influenced by its unwavering support for Israel.

[48] Shaun Casey, a just war ethicist, and Stanley Hauerwas, a pacifist, prepared the statement and circulated it among ethicists of different theological and political leanings. This author was one of the signatories.

[49] Novak, a Roman Catholic philosopher, argued that the conflict with Iraq was not a "preventative war," but the "lawful conclusion" of the 1991 Gulf War that attempted to enforce the disarmament terms Iraq accepted at the close of that conflict. Elshtain, a Protestant social ethics professor, argued that Christians have a moral duty to defend the innocent. Those brutalized by Hussein's regime and the neighboring countries threatened by the regime constituted the innocent, which required US military involvement. See Richard N. Ostling, "Against Widespread Clergy Protest, Some Lay Christians Justify War against Iraq," Associated Press, February 26, 2003.

following the same precepts of just war theory? One significant observation is that, even though ethicists employed the same just war theory, they still arrived at different conclusions, partly because they approached the dilemma from divergent social locations. All held a certain prior bias that prevented them from being completely objective. Objectivity, after all, is the subjectivity of the dominant culture with the power to make their subjectivity objective for everyone else.

Even if some sort of objectivity could have been achieved by those employing the just war theory, history has demonstrated that clerics are often used by politicians or governments to manipulate their believers into supporting war. This is evident when reviewing "war sermons" mainly issued prior to hostilities by white evangelicals. Charles Marsh, religion professor at the University of Virginia, shows how supporters of the Iraq War, like Pat Robertson, host of the *700 Club*, referred to the upcoming military conflict as "a righteous cause out of the Bible." Jerry Falwell of Moral Majority fame wrote an essay titled "God Is Pro-War." Tim LaHaye, coauthor of the popular *Left Behind* book series, saw Iraq as "a focal point of end-time events." Franklin Graham, evangelist Billy Graham's son, saw the war as an opportunity for proselytizing Muslims. Not surprisingly, 87 percent of all white US evangelicals supported President Bush's decision to invade Iraq.[50] Why, when it came to Iraq, was white evangelical Christianity standing on the wrong side of history? We are left wondering if white evangelical Christianity has become so interconnected to empire that it is now more likely to advocate violence required to maintain empire rather than peace as preached by the Prince of Peace.

The discussion of violence cannot be limited to war. Torture is also a form of violence. President Bush, in 2005, strongly defended US "enhanced interrogation practices" for detainees while insisting, "We do not torture."[51] Shortly after Obama assumed the presidency, he also declared, "America doesn't torture."[52] While a presidential candidate, Trump rather unequivocally embraced torture, noting, "Don't tell me it doesn't work—torture works. Half these guys [say]: 'Torture doesn't work.' Believe me, it works." At another event, he went on to say, "Only a stupid person would say it doesn't work.... [And] if it doesn't work, they deserve

---

[50] Charles Marsh, "Wayward Christian Soldiers," *New York Times*, January 20, 2006.

[51] Richard Benedetto, "Bush Defends Interrogation Practices: 'We Do Not Torture,'" *USA Today*, November 7, 2005.

[52] Barack Obama interview, "Obama on Economic Crises, Transition," *60 Minutes*, CBS, aired February 8, 2009.

it anyways, for what they're doing."[53] The 2014 bipartisan US Senate Select Committee on Intelligence released a 712-page review of interrogation and detention programs employed in the aftermath of 9/11. With more than thirty-five thousand footnotes and based on some 6 million pages of CIA documents, the report concluded that the United States did torture. The report went on to note that the use of enhanced interrogation techniques was not "effective," these techniques were "brutal and far worse" than what the CIA represented, and confinement conditions were "harsher" than what the CIA represented (Feinstein 2014, xi–xiii).

A popular torture technique employed by the United States is waterboarding, a forced suffocation caused by the inhalation of water. Waterboarding has been used by the United States for over a century to obtain information from prisoners. Ironically, after the Second World War, Yukio Asano, a military officer with the Japanese Imperial Army, was sentenced to fifteen years of hard labor for administrating a form of waterboarding on US civilians. Yet, in 2012, the US attorney general determined that CIA agents were not to be liable when their use of enhanced interrogation techniques like waterboarding led to the death of prisoners.[54] Ironically, waterboarding is a punishable offense when the technique is used *against* Americans but an acceptable interrogation procedure when used *by* Americans. Yet contrary to Trumpish claims, the use of torture has failed to provide useful information.

The US Senate Select Committee report found that so-called enhanced interrogation techniques were not a central component in finding Bin Laden (Feinstein 2014, 129). The committee's report documents one of the CIA's worst-kept secrets; following the 9/11 terrorist attacks, the agency established and maintained overseas prisons (known as "black sites") where coercive methods of interrogation were employed. Commenting on the report, Senator John McCain, himself tortured while a prisoner of war in North Vietnam, said, "What I have learned [from the report] confirms for me what I have always believed and insisted to be true—that the cruel, inhuman and degrading treatment of prisoners is not only wrong in principle and a stain on our country's conscience, but also an ineffective and unreliable means of gathering intelligence."[55] Torture's ineffectiveness is best

---

[53] Jenna Johnson, "Trump Says 'Torture Works,' Backs Waterboarding and 'Much Worse,'" *Washington Post*, February 17, 2016.

[54] Scott Shane, "No Charges Filed in Two Deaths Involving CIA," *New York Times*, August 31, 2012.

[55] Scott Shane, "Senate Panel Approves Findings Critical of Detainee Interrogations," *New York Times*, December 13, 2012.

demonstrated by the case of Ibn al-Sheikh al-Libi, a Libyan national arrested in Pakistan several months after 9/11. The CIA took custody of him in 2002 and transferred him, via the navy ship USS *Bataan*, to Egypt, where he was tortured. To avoid torture and receive better treatment, he fabricated information—specifically, that Iraq provided chemical and biological weapons training to Al Qaeda. This information was used by Secretary of State Colin Powell during his 2003 UN speech to justify starting a war against Iraq. By 2004, after the US invasion of Iraq, when it became obvious there were no weapons of mass destruction, al-Libi recanted. He eventually was transferred to Abu Salim prison in Tripoli, Libya, to serve a life sentence; in 2009 he was found dead in his cell (Singh 2013, 41).

The European Court of Human Rights condemned the CIA's extraordinary rendition programs, understood as the transfer of detainees without legal process to the custody of a foreign government for detention and interrogation. The court's condemnation was due to the case of a German car salesman named Khaled El-Masri, who, mistaken for a terrorist suspect, was kidnapped from Macedonia in 2003, held for four months, and brutally interrogated at the CIA Afghan-run prison known as the "Salt Pit." El-Masri, an innocent man, was severely beaten, sodomized, shackled, and hooded at the hands of the CIA and in the presence of Macedonian authorities.[56] In December 2012 the court ruled against Macedonia, finding that El-Masri's treatment by the CIA amounted to torture. The court could not rule against the United States because it lacked jurisdiction. The tone for handling potential enemies of the United States was set by Vice President Dick Cheney, shortly after 9/11:

> We also have to work through, sort of the dark side, if you will. We've got to spend time in the shadows in the intelligence world. A lot of what needs to be done here will have to be done quietly, without any discussion, using sources and methods that are available to our intelligence agencies, if we're going to be successful. That's the world these folks operate in, and so it's going to be vital for us to use any means at our disposal, basically, to achieve our objective.[57]

Rather than noting the moral complexities of employing torture at the time, Christian leaders like James Dobson, founder of Focus on the Family; Albert Mohler, president of Southern Baptist Theological Seminary;

---

[56] Angela Charlton, "European Court Condemns CIA in Landmark Ruling," Associated Press, December 14, 2012.

[57] Dick Cheney, *Meet the Press*, NBC News, September 16, 2001.

and Daniel R. Heimback, ethics professor at Southeastern Baptist Seminary supported the use of torture from the start (Towery 2008, 19). This is not the first time that Christian leaders have justified the use of torture. For example, in *The City of God,* Augustine, the original author of just war theory, condones torturing the innocent to obtain information (1960 [426], 6.19.6).

Early in the war, by 2004, the American Red Cross charged the US military with intentionally using psychological and physical coercion tantamount to torture at the US naval base in Guantánamo (Gitmo).[58] Detainees were sleep deprived for up to 180 hours, kept standing or placed in stress positions within small confinement boxes. At times their hands were shackled so high above their heads they were forced to remain on their tiptoes. Often, they were left to urinate or defecate on themselves. They were waterboarded while strapped nude to a gurney, slapped, and slammed against walls. Some were given forced enemas; others were placed in ice baths. Some men were kept nude, female interrogators sexually humiliated others, while others were still threatened with harm being visited upon their children, or they were threatened with promises of their mothers being sexually abused (Feinstein 2014, xii–xiii, 101, 490).[59]

Generally, there are two types of torture. The first encompasses psychological techniques to disorient and wear down the prisoner—such as sleep deprivation, exposure to extreme temperatures, withholding medical treatment, or sitting in painful and uncomfortable positions for long periods of time. The second type of torture includes physical violence. Although the first, "soft torture," was employed on prisoners held at Gitmo, military and government officials denied the use of "hard torture" until the Abu Ghraib prison photos became public. Members of the Army's elite 82nd Airborne Division confessed that fellow soldiers routinely beat and abused prisoners at Abu Ghraib to gather intelligence on the insurgency and to amuse themselves. Limbs, according to one sergeant, were usually broken; in at least one case, a prisoner's leg was broken with a metal baseball bat.[60]

When the Abu Ghraib atrocities became public, the US government reassured the public that these abuses were an aberration conducted by a few rogue soldiers who had sullied the name of all Americans. Abu Ghraib,

---

[58] Neil A. Lewis, "Red Cross Finds Detainee Abuse in Guantánamo," *New York Times,* November 30, 2004.

[59] Carol Rosenberg, "Captive of CIA Sketched Agony of His Torture," *New York Times,* December 5, 2019.

[60] Eric Smith, "3 in 82nd Airborne Say Beating Iraqi Prisoners Was Routine," *New York Times,* September 24, 2005.

however, was part of a systemic process of abuse. Take the examples of Task Force 6-26, the shadowy American military unit that operated another prison, Camp Nama. The camp, complete with a torture chamber known as the "Black Room," was secretly housed at Baghdad International Airport. Prisoners were repeatedly beaten with rifle butts and used for target practice in a game played by guards called jailer paintball. Under the mantra "No Blood, No Foul" (that is, if they don't bleed, they can't prosecute), prisoners were routinely tortured to obtain information about insurgents. Stories of prisoners punched in the spine until they fell unconscious, kicked in the stomach until they vomited, stripped naked and doused with ice water in refrigerated rooms, or deprived of sleep via rap music played at deafening decibel levels were all too common. Camp Nama was usually the first stop before prisoners were transferred to Abu Ghraib.[61]

Some enemy combatants never made it to US detention facilities, instead being originally transferred to black sites that served as off-site torture prisons operated by foreign governments that were not averse to employing physical torture to gain information that could be passed along to the United States—thus relieving the United States of any responsibility of adhering to the Geneva Convention (Feinstein 2014, xx, 97–99, 370–71, 541).[62] Ironically, while Syria was condemned by the international community for torturing its people and prolonging a brutal and bloody civil war in 2012, the United States had no qualms in handing over its prisoners to Syrian torturers to gather information. These transfers were a clear violation of US laws and the 1984 international convention that bans such transfers. We are left wondering if violence can *ever* be harnessed for good or declared just? Violence is not a political tool that can be picked up and used, and then put down later, never to be used again. Engaging in violence forever changes a person and a society. Generally, those engaged in violence and the hate it unleashes become unfit for the process of creating a new, just social order. While those from the dominant culture struggle with the ethics of employing violence, those on the margins recognize that violence is already a reality. Internationally, violence continues to be employed to secure financial markets and monetary gain. For example, Russia's invasion of Ukraine is considered a savage act, depriving Ukrainians of their right to self-determination. However, when the United States has overthrown governments, some of which were democratically elected,

---

[61] Eric Schmitt and Carolyn Marshall, "In Secret Unit 'Black Room,' A Grim Portrait of United States Abuse," *New York Times*, March 19, 2006.

[62] Douglas Jehl, "Inmates Were Reported Kept off Books to Speed Transfer," *New York Times*, October 9, 2004.

it has been labeled an act of defending liberty and democracy, even when the result was the installation of a brutal, undemocratic, unpopular regime. For US citizens, the primary difference between the actions of Russia and the United States is that the aggressive international acts of the latter were cloaked in moral rhetoric, sometimes justified using just war theory.

Aggressive violent acts can also entail lopsided trade agreements in which, as purchasers of the world's resources and labor, the United States sets deflated prices or engages in war when what is considered the US birthright to those resources is jeopardized by other nation-states. If "our" oil supplies are threatened, the United States has no qualms sending military forces to protect their continuous flow, all while claiming to engage in a crusade to uproot Islamic terrorism. Whoever happens to be sitting in the Oval Office, regardless of party affiliation, their job is to protect the interests of corporate America abroad. Therefore, in terms of US global economic policies, it really doesn't matter if the people elect a Black man or a woman, or conclude that all the change really needed is another white man. Our democratic system has reduced our electoral choice to candidates from two pro-empire parties who will show no significant difference in their commitments to protecting the rights of multinational companies to procure the majority of the world's resources while expanding globally.

Can any war then be just, especially if war represents a triumph over love? Are all wars morally reprehensible, but pardonable? Can the conditions for a just war ever be obtained? Regardless of moral discussions that take place within the dominant culture, one fact remains constant: those on the periphery of power are seldom consulted, even though they are disproportionately on the receiving end of the violence of war.

Today, it also seems that, while pacifism is an ethical option, absolute pacifism may be unattainable. There are differences between killing someone as an offensive strategy, defending oneself from violence inflicted by an oppressor, or protecting the most vulnerable from certain death at the hands of an oppressor. If forced to engage in violence, is it better to recognize it for the evil it is and rely on God's grace for forgiveness than to try to reason through usage of the gospel message to justify warlike actions by using just war-type theory?

Can nonviolence ever succeed as a strategy in the international arena? At the close of the First World War, the Versailles Peace Treaty sought revenge from Germany, creating an atmosphere that eventually led to World War II. But, by the close of the Second World War, the lesson had been learned. Rather than punish Germany and Japan for the violence they unleashed, the United States embraced their enemies by rebuilding their nations. The result was strong allies that continue to stand the test of time.

Yet at the close of the first Gulf War, the United States imposed an embargo on Iraq that brought death to thousands of Iraqis, mostly children. How, then, can we convince an Iraqi mother and her starving child of the moral superiority of US democracy? How can we convince her not to hate us? The *imago Dei* of the enemy must be recognized at all levels of conflict, for the enemy is also created in the image of God and thus has dignity and worth. This is as true for the Afghan or Iraqi populations as it is for people in the United States. Unfortunately, less value is given to those who are marginalized within an empire. As noted earlier, those who live on the margins of society are never consulted in the decision-making process about going to war. To go or not is determined in the halls of power, with an eye toward the geopolitical gains of such an encounter. Native Americans living on a reservation, African Americans relegated to the urban ghetto, or the Latines living on this country's borderlands are not calling for more missiles or aircraft carriers, or the latest fighter jet. Ethical debates concerning what makes a war just may have validity among ethicists of the dominant culture, but for the masses that live under the strain of racism and classism, such debates become irrelevant.

Although some multinational corporations such as Bechtel and Halliburton stand to benefit financially from war, others—specifically those who are economically disenfranchised—suffer during the preparation for war. Increases in military spending are directly related to increases in the national poverty rate. Increased military spending during peacetime has a direct relationship to increased unemployment, which is clearly linked to increased poverty.[63] High military spending in advanced industrial economies diverts capital to non-growth-producing sectors, crowding out investments, reducing productivity, and increasing unemployment (Henderson 1998, 503–20). Complicating the economic impact of the wars in Iraq and Afghanistan is that for the first time in US history, the United States engaged in a war without committing to pay for it upfront through taxes. The increase in defense spending, financed through deficit spending, creates an inflationary impact on the economy that disproportionately harms the poor, contributing to an increase in income inequality. In short, while war financially benefits the nation's elite class, the preparation for war further devastates the poor.

Perhaps a move away from the traditional understanding of security is needed, one that does not rely on the mechanisms of war. But violence might very well be the modus operandi of the United States. When we

---

[63] Note, however, that increased military spending during wartime has the reverse effect, decreasing poverty.

examine the domestic front, we realize that the United States is the only nation in the world where civilian guns outnumber people (120 to 100), a testament to what is relied upon for personal security. Yet the United States maintains the highest firearm homicide rate among nations with advanced economies, eighteen times the rate of other countries—and with only 4 percent of the global population, it accounts for 44 percent of global suicides by firearms. Additionally, while no other country with an advanced economy experienced more than eight mass shootings over a twenty-two-year period,[64] the United States recorded 611 in just one recent year—2020.[65] A nation's security is not obtained through more weapons, but by a just economy that closes the income gap, by a healthcare program that ensures that one does not die from a preventable disease, by an education system that prepares the next generation to lead, by a racial and ethnic diversity that is not on the edge of explosive violence, and by an open and affirming culture that does not privilege cisgender males.

Step 3: Meditating

Among Christians, one of the most powerful biblical stories is the exodus, where God enters history and guides God's chosen people toward the promised land. The trek of the former enslaved toward liberation resonates with many who today are dispossessed. Unfortunately, we usually ignore that this promised land was already occupied by the Canaanites, who first had to be slaughtered before God's chosen could take possession. The Hebrews, according to the book of Joshua, "enforced the ban on everything in [Jericho]: men and women; young and old; ox, sheep, and donkey, massacring all of them" (6:21). While most marginalized Christians read themselves into the story of the oppressed enslaved marching forward, many First Nations people see themselves as the modern-day Canaanites. When God's chosen people entered the land of Canaan, they found other people living there. How do you claim a land when it is already occupied? According to the text, God commands that everybody be put to death. The spears of God's people were thrust through babies. The swords of God's people lopped off the heads of children. Pregnant women were disemboweled. Families were decimated before each other's eyes. A gory bloodbath took place.

---

[64] Kara Fox, Krystina Shveda, Natalie Croker, and Marco Chacon, "How United States Gun Culture Stacks Up with the World," CNN, November 26, 2021.

[65] Gun Violence Archive, 2021; https://www.gunviolencearchive.org/.

Today we call God's command a war crime, genocide, and crimes against humanity. The Christian is left with disturbing questions. Does the book of Joshua depict a nonbiblical God? Some might argue that the Canaanites worshipped false gods and did despicable things. But do we then have a right to kill everybody who does not recognize "our" God? Should we then invade and decimate all so-called nonbelievers who in our eyes do what we define to be despicable things? The Hebrews' (read: European) dream of religious freedom and liberation became the Canaanites' (read: Native American) nightmare of subjugation and genocide. Like the Canaanites before them, Indigenous people were viewed as a people who could not be trusted, a snare to the righteous, and a culture that required decimation.

Robert Allen Warrior provides a rereading of the exodus story from the Canaanite perspective, questioning if it is an appropriate biblical model for understanding his people's struggle for dignity. He calls for a Christian reflection that places the Canaanites at the center of theological thought and that considers the violence and injustice they experienced that is rarely mentioned in critical works concerning the exodus (1989). Scholars like Vine Deloria Jr. are quick to remind us that the conquest of Native American land by "God's chosen people" ended their liberation, which was (and is) understood as communal and personal harmony and balance. Hence, any discussion of liberation and freedom among Indigenous people must be understood as liberation and freedom from European Christian invasion and its consequences. These consequences are witnessed today when we consider that Native Americans are the poorest of the poor in a "Christianized" North America, a poverty maintained by structures that politically, socially, psychologically, and economically oppress them. Liberation among Indigenous people, according to scholars like Deloria, begins with a firm "no" to Jesus Christ and Christianity, the source of Native American bondage. "There is no way," according to Deloria, "to combine white values and Indian behavior into a workable program or intelligible subject of discussion" (1969, 10). Can any student of history blame them for saying no?

Christians who take the biblical text seriously, and what that text says about war, must recognize that in some cases God commands blood-soaked war, even against Israel, while at other times God forbids war, even to protect Israel. In the Hebrew Bible, the violence caused by war is condoned some of the time and condemned at other times. Within the New Testament, Jesus abhors violence, yet he warns of the violence that will be committed against those who follow him to the cross. All too often, the commitment of the believer to follow Jesus's example leads to violence. However, violence should never be accepted as a necessary evil, nor rejected as antithetical to Jesus (he clearly used violence to cleanse the Temple and prophesied the violence of the Day of Judgment). Violence seems to be a reality that often arises from challenges to the dominant culture's grip on power. Such violence can be immediate or drawn out, as in the case of institutional violence, such as the economic forces that foster reservations, ghettos, and barrios. Governments act violently when they maintain social structures that inflict prolonged harm or injury upon a segment of the population, and that segment is usually disenfranchised due to race or economic standing.

The choice is whether to participate in the use of violence or to advocate nonviolent resistance to oppressive structures. As Gustavo Gutiérrez reminds us, it is important to distinguish between "the unjust violence of the oppressors (who maintain this despicable system) with the just violence of the oppressed (who feel obligated to use it to achieve their liberation)" (1988 [1973], 64). Not only does Gutiérrez distinguish between the two types of violence, but he also questions the prevailing double standards that exist. He writes, "We cannot say that the violence is all right when the oppressor uses it to maintain or preserve 'order,' but wrong when the oppressed use it to overthrow this same 'order'" (1984 [1979], 28). To remain silent or to do nothing in the face of violence is to participate in it through complicity. At times, in the face of the violence being committed against the marginalized, some purposely remain silent or speak their disapproval in muted voices, lest they jeopardize their privileged space. How, then, should the disenfranchised react to the constant institutional violence they face?

When asked if counterviolence is ever an option for Christians, Gutiérrez, along with other liberation theologians, reminds us that violence already exists in the hands of the oppressor. Thus, the question is not if Christians should utilize violence, but rather, do Christians have a right to defend themselves from preexisting or ongoing violence? For example, biblical scholar George Pixley maintains that the massacre of Egypt's first-born sons can be understood as a terrorist act, an act inspired by God (1987, 80). He goes on to note Moses's violent act of killing an Egyptian, a member of the dominant culture, for striking a Hebrew slave, a member of a marginalized group (Ex. 2:11–22). This act appeared justified even though a future commandment received by Moses would state, "Thou shall not kill." Pixley suggests that certain exceptions to the Fifth Commandment exist, such as capital punishment or the killing of enemies in times of war. Pixley also implies that the preferential option for the oppressed may lead to the act of taking life. Moses's killing of the Egyptian could be seen as a defensive act to protect the life of the marginalized. And it appears as if God (the ultimate defender of the oppressed) accepts Moses in later years, justifying his earlier use of violence for the sake of defending the oppressed (1987, 8–9).

During the period of chattel slavery in the United States, many rebellions against slavery were violent and bloody, most notably the 1831 revolt in Southampton, Virginia, led by Nat Turner. As a preacher, Turner believed that God directed him to live out his faith through actions that could lead to the liberation of the enslaved. Biblical authority for such action was seen in the exodus story of liberation from the tyranny of Pharaoh. The enslaved had a moral obligation to obtain liberation by whatever means possible. Interpreting Scripture in this way has led liberation ethicists to support violence (even revolution) when employed to protect the humanity of the marginalized. If the oppression of the marginalized is maintained through institutionalized violence—that is, through social structures designed to privilege the few at the expense of the many—then any hope of finding salvation or liberation from the status quo will inevitably confront those same social structures. History has demonstrated that denouncing unjust social structures is simply not enough, for those accustomed to power and privilege will never willingly abdicate what they consider to be a birthright. Some ethicists from the margins maintain that violence, when employed by the marginalized to overcome their own oppression, is, in reality, self-defense and can never be confused with the continuing violence employed by those in power.

Accordingly, some advocate a quest for liberation "by any means possible." They argue that to wash one's hands of violence is to allow the continued violence experienced by the marginalized. While all violence is evil, not all decisions to use violence are unethical. *Agape* (unconditional love) for the very least among us might lead a person, in an unselfish act, to stand in solidarity with the oppressed in the latter's battle for self-preservation. Protecting a "nonperson" might invite a violent confrontation as the oppressor, who, feeling backed into a corner, may fight tooth and nail to maintain the status quo that privileges them. Persons making a preferential option to love the oppressed may very well find themselves harming the oppressor. Unfortunately, the call for nonviolence usually comes from those who wish to maintain the unjust status quo. Writing during the height of racial unrest and the Vietnam War, James Cone made an astute observation:

> It is interesting that so many advocates of nonviolence as the only possible Christian response of black people to white domination are also the most ardent defenders of the right of the police to put down black rebellion through violence. Another interesting

corollary is their defense of America's right to defend violently the government of South Vietnam against the North. Somehow, I am unable to follow the reasoning. (1969, 138–39)

For Cone, African Americans, along with other "unwanted minorities," were placed in a situation in which only one option was made available to them, "deciding whose violence [will be] supported—that of the oppressors or the oppressed.... Either we side with the oppressed . . . in a dehumanized society, or we stand with the President or whoever is defending the white establishment for General Motors and US Steel" (1975, 219). No middle ground is available.

The early Christian community (pre-Constantine) maintained an absolute prohibition on violence, even to the point of refusing to fight the Romans when Jerusalem was burned and sacked in 70 CE. Warfare was understood to be a denial of Jesus's message to love one's enemies and a rejection of the life he asked his disciples to follow. For the early church, while Jesus Christ may not have been a zealot, he was a revolutionary, leading a rebellion to be won through his love. Not until 380 CE, when Christianity became the state religion and took on political power under Constantine, was it necessary to develop concepts for just war to maintain the empire.

For Martin Luther King Jr., the use of nonviolence aimed to create a relationship with the oppressors in the hopes that they too could be redeemed by God's grace. He rejected Niebuhr's understanding of pacifism as an unrealistic submission to evil power, insisting instead that it is better to be the recipient of violence than the inflictor (1958, 98).[66] King did not advocate passivity; rather he called for an active confrontation with injustice. Nonviolence was the embodiment of the Christian ideal of *agape*, an unconditional love that confronts the aggressor so that they also can live under the shadow of *agape*. Pragmatically, King insisted that the use of violence by the marginalized only encourages the oppressor (who controls the tools of torture) to unleash even greater violence, leading to a never-ending spiral of hatred. He maintained that violence only provokes greater retribution, and those without arms will find themselves at a greater disadvantage. Rather than continuing the cycle of violence, King looked toward the radical love advocated by Christ as the solution to oppression. He wrote, "Returning hate for hate multiplies hate, adding deeper darkness

---

[66] There are basically two types of pacifists. The "absolute" pacifist renounces violence under every circumstance, and the "contextual" pacifist looks for acts of nonviolent resistance, reserving the option that under exceptional circumstances, violence may be a necessary alternative.

to a night already devoid of stars. Darkness cannot drive out darkness; only light can do that. Hate cannot drive out hate; only love can do that. Hate multiplies hate, violence multiples violence, and toughness multiplies toughness in a descending spiral of destruction" (1963, 37). For social activist César Chávez, those involved in something constructive tend to refrain from violence, while those not committed to the rebuilding of a more just order tend to advocate the more destructive path of violence. Chávez insisted that nonviolence requires greater courage and militancy. He once said, "I am not a nonviolent man. I am a violent man who is trying to be nonviolent" (Dalton 2003, 120).

Step 4: Case Studies

1. Camilo Mejia, a permanent US resident, joined the armed forces when he was nineteen. With the rank of staff sergeant, Mejia served for five months in Iraq. During his tour of duty, he was assigned to guard prisoners at a detention facility, where he witnessed the employment of psychological torture in violation of the Geneva Convention. He was also assigned to instigate gunfights with insurgents to win battle medals. He and others were ambushed, and innocent civilians were hit in the ensuing firefight. He admits, "Being an occupier changes you. You become an agent for brutalizing a country." After a leave of absence, he refused to report for duty, becoming among the first to desert. "This is an oil-driven war, and I don't think any soldier signs up to fight for oil," said Mejia.[67] He was court-martialed and spent nine months in prison for refusing to return to duty.

Mejia's experiences were expressed some sixty years ago by Martin Luther King Jr., who proclaimed that the United States was the "greatest purveyor of violence in the world today" (1967). Since 1776, there have only been seventeen calendar years in which the United States was not been engaged in a military conflict. With the troop pullout from Afghanistan, President Biden declared at the United Nations that "for the first time in 20 years, the United States is not at war. We've turned the page." He, however, ignored that, the day before his speech, a US drone strike incinerated a car driving on a remote road in northwestern Syria, or that, three weeks earlier, an airstrike was launched in Somalia against Shabab militants.[68] Wars and killings, despite his proclamation, continue.

---

[67] Erik Schelzig, "Soldier: 'I Have Not Committed a Crime,'" *Grand Rapids Press*, March 16, 2004; Margaret Fosmoe, "Anti-war Veteran Talks at IUSB," *South Bend Tribune*, March 17, 2009.

[68] Mark Mazzetti, "Biden Declared the War Over. But Wars Go On," *New York Times*, September 22, 2021.

• Did Camilo Mejia have the right to renounce his military oath? Did he have an obligation to complete his military duty? Can soldiers choose in what wars they will participate? Why or why not?

• Non-US residents who serve in the military have been deported following honorable discharge from the military. Their deportation is at times due to crimes they committed, like domestic violence, bar brawling, or resisting arrest.[69] Should they be deported? Should they have been made US citizens while serving? What considerations are due their undocumented immediate family if they have been killed in action? Was Mejia's decision not to fight, even at the cost of possible deportation, morally correct for him?

• Was Martin Luther King Jr. correct in his characterization of the United States? Why or why not? Of the 104 military conflicts in which the United States participated since the 1980s, which, if any, can be considered a "just war"?[70] Who was the aggressor? Did the recent wars in Iraq and Afghanistan meet the principles of just war theory?

---

[69] Nancy Lofholm, "Veterans to Protest Deportations at President Obama's Buckley Air Base Visit in Colorado," *Denver Post*, January 26, 2012.

[70] Between 1980 and 2020 the United States dispatched military personal on at least 104 occasions. Some of those major conflicts were:
• Libya conflict, 1981
• War in Lebanon, 1982–1983
• Nicaragua: the covert Contra Wars, 1982–1990
• Invasion of Grenada: Operation Urgent Fury, 1983
• United States–Libya conflict, 1986
• Iran: Operation Earnest Will or the Tanker War, 1987–1988
• Invasion of Panama: Operation Just Cause, 1989
• Iraq: the Gulf War or Operation Desert Storm, 1991
• Iraq: the No-Fly Zone War, 1991–2003
• Intervention in Somalia, 1992–1994
• Yugoslav Wars, Operation Deliberate Force, 1992–1999
• Haiti: Operation Uphold Democracy, 1994
• Afghanistan and Sudan bombings: the bin Laden War, 1998
• Iraq, Desert Fox Campaign, 1998
• Serbia, Kosovo War, 1999
• Afghanistan, Operation Enduring Freedom, 2001
• Iraq, Operation Iraqi Freedom, 2003
• Intervention in Haiti civil conflict, 2004
• Intervention in Somalia Civil War, 2006–2009
• Intervention in Libyan Civil War, 2011

2. In August 2008 Russia launched a full-scale land, air, and sea invasion of Georgia, which lasted five days, under the pretense of protecting ethnic Russians in South Ossetia and Abkhazia from genocide. Although the United States and other Western powers condemned Russia's aggression, nothing—besides rhetoric—occurred. The approach was to not escalate the situation and provoke a military confrontation with Russia over strategically insignificant territories. Georgia ended up losing territorial control over parts of Abkhazia and South Ossetian as Russians established military bases and expelling ethnic Georgians. Russian international relations were largely unharmed when hostilities ceased. Failure of the Western powers to act emboldened Vladimir Putin.

One of the consequences of the Georgian invasion was the establishment of what came to be known as the Medvedev Doctrine, which reserves the right for Russia to invade any country where ethnic Russians live to protect their lives and dignity—creating a legal excuse to invade former republics of the Soviet Union. The Medvedev Doctrine came into play in 2014 with the Russian invasion and annexation of Crimea. Again, the United States and European Union condemned Russia, this time suspending Russia from the G8 group and imposing sanctions. During the Trump administration, a concerted effort was made by the then-president to normalize relationships with Russia. Facing little military pushback for invading Georgia and Crimea, Russia invaded Ukraine in 2022. This time, the Ukrainians fought back, and the Western powers did more than simply condemn, spending billions of dollars in aid and military hardware. As of this writing, the Russo-Ukrainian war continues.

• Did the failure of the United States and European powers to militarily challenge Russia during the 2008 invasion only embolden Putin to invade Crimea and Ukraine in later years? Is this an example where violence can prevent future wars? Russia has argued that they are doing nothing that the United States has not done in Latin America. Are they right? If so, why is it wrong for Russia to invade a sovereign nation and not the United States?

• In both Georgia and Ukraine, Russia invaded on the pretense of preventing genocide of ethnic Russians in those countries, yet Russia has been accused of war crimes, specifically bombing civilian-populated areas and fleeing refugees. What obligations do the United States and other self-proclaimed democracies have to nations that are victims of aggression? As of this writing, Ukraine has asked the United States for either a no-fly zone or airpower to stop the indiscriminate bombings, but they were refused, fearing widening a war with Russia. Is this the right strategy? Does an obligation exist to defend the lives of civilians from an aggressive foreign power? What if that power is the United States?

• In 2014, the corrupt Ukrainian president Viktor Yanukovych fled to Russia in the wake of what came to be known as the Revolution of Dignity, ushering reform-minded activists like President Volodymyr Zelensky into power. In 2016 a ledger found in Yanukovych's former headquarters was made public; it listed secret payments totaling $12.7 million to Paul Manafort, a political consultant and former presidential campaign manager for Donald Trump.[71] Making the ledger public led to accusations by the Trump administration that the Zelensky presidency was corrupt, leading to the withdrawal of desperately needed US military aid until they could do Trump a "favor" and fabricate dirt on his political opponent Joe Biden. Meanwhile, Trump exerted pressure on Zelensky to make peace with Putin and Russia. How much is the United States responsible for the eventual invasion of Ukraine? Was the United States on the wrong side of history, pardoning those advising pro-Russian forces while withholding aid from those attempting to build a bulwark against a future invader?

3. Maher Arar, a naturalized Canadian citizen, changed planes at Kennedy International Airport on September 26, 2002, during his return trip home. He was seized by US authorities, held in solitary confinement for two weeks, deprived of sleep and food, denied contact with a lawyer or his family, then handed over to Syrian authorities to be interrogated under torture (beaten with a metal cable) and held for ten months because he was suspected of being a member of Al Qaeda. The Syrian authorities cleared Arar of having any terrorist connections. Arar was just one of the estimated 100 to 150 people seized by intelligence officials in a post-9/11 world and transferred to other countries that practice torture. His ordeal seems to be based on nothing more than eating shawarma at a restaurant with a man who may or may not have known another man who may have had an Al Qaeda connection.

In 2005 Arar brought a civil suit against the United States, but a three-judge panel dismissed Arar's civil rights suit in 2008. Arar appealed, but in 2009 his appeal was dismissed by the Second Circuit Court of Appeals based on national security claims made by the Bush administration and extended by the Obama administration. In 2010 the Supreme Court refused to consider Arar's case based on President Obama's solicitor general Elena

---

[71] Manafort was eventually convicted on eight counts of tax and bank fraud and was pardoned by Trump in 2020.

Kagan (now on the Supreme Court bench) using overwrought secrecy claims. Nevertheless, in 2007 Canada apologized to Arar and paid $9.8 million in compensation.[72]

• Is it ethical to participate in physical torture to safeguard national security? What about psychological torture?

• Is it ethical for the United States to obtain vital information obtained through physical torture conducted by other countries? Why or why not?

• Is outsourcing torture a betrayal of American values? Is the violation of human rights justified to bring human rights to former oppressive regimes like that of Iraq or Afghanistan?

• Are the acts of torture justifiable if they lead to valuable information? Is torture to obtain information that can lead to fewer US casualties a necessary evil of war? Is the punishment being meted out to those who participated in the acts of torture necessary or sufficient?

---

[72] Scott Shane, "The Costs of Outsourcing Interrogation: A Canadian Muslim's Long Ordeal in Syria," *New York Times*, May 29, 2005; Nina Bernstein, "United States Defends Detentions at Airport," *New York Times*, October 10, 2005.

Chapter 7

Environment

Step 1: Observing

How prophetic are the words of the award-winning poet and author Alice Walker? "Earth itself has become the n*gger of the world." She goes on to elaborate:

> It is perceived, ironically, as other, as alien, evil, and threatening by those who are finding they cannot draw a healthful breath without its cooperation. While the Earth is poisoned, everything it supports is poisoned. While the earth is enslaved, none of us is free. While the Earth is a "n*gger," it has no choice but to think of us all as Wasichus. While it is "treated like dirt," so are we. (1981, 147)

The earth is poisoned, and we often ignore our complicity with said poisoning. Although a conservative Christian and largely evangelical segment of the US population dismisses anthropogenic climate change as a hoax, the evidence for global warming is unequivocal. Furthermore, human actions that embody and reinforce dominant cultural values of colonialism and exceptionalism are primarily for the occurrence and acceleration of climate change. Earth's degradation does not impact all of Earth's inhabitants equitably, equally, or even similarly. We may repeat the rhetoric that we are all in this together, but the reality is that communities of color and the poor face greater environmental degradation than do the Wasichus—the Lakota term for Western Europeans.

Apart from 2016, and that's only because it was the year of a "super" El Niño, 2020 was the hottest since record-keeping began in 1895. Not surprisingly, 2020 was characterized by a busy Atlantic hurricane season (thirty storms were named, while twelve made landfall), the worst drought in decades in southern Africa (specifically Zambia and Zimbabwe), a mostly ice-free Bering Sea (by the 2030s, the Arctic Ocean could experience ice-free summers), a rise in sea level (as much as nineteen inches by 2050, flooding as many as 300 million people in coastal areas and wiping out US coastal cities), and some of the largest and most destructive wildfires on record in Australia, Pantanal, Siberia, and the western United States. As temperatures hit 125° Fahrenheit in Baghdad in July and 100° north of the Arctic Circle, a new record was set for the amount of carbon dioxide released into the atmosphere. These conditions are not an exception. The 2010s were the hottest decade on record (with the second half hotter than the first half). The 2019 global surface temperature averaged 1.8° Fahrenheit higher than the middle of the last century. The 2020s are poised to break that record. According to United Nations secretary-general António Guterres, "Climate-related natural disasters are becoming more frequent, more deadly, more destructive, with growing human and financial costs."[1] The planet is literally on fire! We have already reached a tipping point of irreversible climate change.

While increasing temperatures and other climatic events are already causing tremendous suffering around the planet, those who are poor or marginalized are more vulnerable to extreme heat and dangerous weather. The world's wretched may not be able to afford the luxury of air conditioning, let alone depend on reliable electricity. They may be forced to work under a blistering sun for daily sustenance. Droughts can wither crops, ushering famine from which little protection exists. For example, the 1.8° increase in Guatemala's temperature since 1960 reduced rainfall needed for corn and bean crops, their staple foods. Yields of corn and beans are expected, due to climate change, to decrease 14 percent by 2050. Even though the Central American country plays a minor role in contributing to greenhouse gases, annually emitting only 1.1 tons per person (compared to the United States at 16.5 tons), Guatemalans disproportionately suffer the brunt of ecological degradation, leaving few with any alternatives, except traveling north toward the United States as environmental refugees.[2]

Communities of color in the United States face similar ecological hazards as those in the Global South. Heat waves are the most lethal

---

[1] Chris Mooney, Andrew Freedmann, and John Muyskens, "2020 Rivals Hottest Year on Record, Pushing Earth Closer to a Critical Climate Threshold," *Washington Post*, January 14, 2021; Henry Fountain, "2019 Was Hot. The 2010s Were Even Hotter," *New York Times*, January 16, 2020; Henry Fountain, "A World Speeding 'Dangerously Close' to a Tipping Point," *New York Times*, December 5, 2019; Jim Dobson, "Shocking New Maps Show How Sea Level Rise Will Destroy Coastal Cities by 2050," *Forbes*, October 30, 2019.

[2] Somini Sengupta, "As Earth Heats Up, Inequity Boils Over," *New York Times*, August 8, 2020.

weather-related disaster,[3] yet their risks are not evenly distributed. A study conducted in eleven states by the National Oceanic and Atmospheric Administration found that, within the same city, temperatures in some neighborhoods (specifically poor neighborhoods of color) can be up to 20° hotter than others, following patterns of historical redlining practices (associated with federal mortgage appraisal policy). The study showed that 94 percent of formerly redlined areas—which mostly remained low-income communities of color—are exposed to higher temperatures when compared to affluent white neighborhoods.[4]

Besides heat waves, there has been an increase in hurricanes, floods, and wildfires imperiling hundreds of toxic US sites. When Hurricane Harvey bore down on Houston, the San Jacinto River jumped its banks, flooding the historically Black town of Barrett and four hazardous-waste Superfund sites, filling the community with deadly toxins. The Environmental Protection Agency (EPA) later estimated that the potent human carcinogens in the river sediment exceeded by twenty-three hundred times the agency's standard for needing cleanup. Barrett is not the exception. According to experts and EPA records, more than 700 of the 945 Superfund sites are vulnerable to climate change. Rather than cleaning or clearing these sites, the EPA, since the 1990s, has been capping these zones with soil, clay, and even concrete.

During the Trump administration, the appointee running the Superfund program was Peter C. Wright, the former corporate counsel for Dow Chemical, who, in his former job, was responsible for minimizing the company's liability to clean up Superfund sites (like French Limited) for which the company was responsible by polluting the site in the first place. Foxes in charge of protecting the henhouse seek to dismantle the henhouse—best illustrated by the 26 percent cut to the EPA's 2021 budget, of which $106 million was stripped from Superfund cleanup programs.[5] The EPA was not the only agency impacted by the Trump administration's centerpiece agenda of dismantling federal climate policies. During Trump's four years in office, over one hundred environmental rules relegating clean air, water, wildlife, and toxic chemicals were reversed.[6] Forty-one scientists, many appointed

---

[3] National Oceanic and Atmospheric Administration, "Severe Weather Awareness—Heat Waves," accessed May 7, 2022.

[4] National Oceanic and Atmospheric Administration, "NOAA and Communities to Map Heat Inequities in 11 States," accessed May 7, 2022.

[5] David Hasemyer and Lisa Olsen, "Climate Change Poses a Growing Threat to Hundreds of Hazardous Waste Superfund Sites," NBC News, September 24, 2020.

[6] Nadja Popovich, Albeck-Ripka, and Kendra Pierre-Louis, "The Trump

by Trump to serve on the EPA's Scientific Advisory Board, signed a letter warning that these regulatory changes flew in the face of science, untethered from scientific data and evidence.[7] Twenty key officials of his administration in charge of environmental policy hailed from careers in the oil, gas, coal, chemical, or agriculture industries; three from state governments that spent years resisting environmental regulations; and at least four with ties to the Koch brothers, who spent millions to defeat clean energy measures.[8] President Trump, a climate change denier, rattled off a grab bag of "alternative facts" that were unmoored from reality and portrayed his administration's record as exhibiting "America's environmental leadership."[9]

To ignore science damns the poor. While the richest 10 percent of the world's population is responsible for half of global carbon emissions, the poorest 50 percent are responsible for just 10 percent.[10] The twenty richest countries are responsible for three-quarters of the world's emissions.[11] In response to the overwhelming evidence concerning global warming, upon which climate scientists agree, these richest nations spend billions to limit their own risks to climate change, specifically rising sea levels and drought. Yet those located farthest from the equator—specifically the industrial North, which is responsible for most global warming—will be least affected. Without facing immediate effects, many of these nations lack the necessary urgency to address the climate crisis. Lacking urgency or a belief that global warming is a hoax might explain the Trump administration's pattern of dismantling environmental regulatory safeguards, leading to significant increases in greenhouse gas emissions and thousands of deaths each year, primarily among communities of color who were mainly exposed to poor air quality.[12]

Administration Is Reversing Nearly 100 Environmental Rules. Here's the Full List," *New York Times*, October 15, 2020.

[7] Coral Davenport and Lisa Friedman, "E.P.A. Policies Scorn Science, Panel Reports," *New York Times*, January 1, 2020.

[8] Lisa Friedman and Claire O'Neill, "Who Controls Trump's Environmental Policy?," *New York Times*, January 24, 2020.

[9] Katie Rogers and Coral Davenport, "In Speech, Trump Portrays U.S. as a Leader on the Environment," *New York Times*, July 9, 2019.

[10] Pedro Conceição, *Human Development Report 2020: The Next Frontier— Human Development and the Anthropocene* (New York: United Nations Development Programme, 2020), 121.

[11] Somini Sengupta, "U.N. Report Says Rise in Emissions Is Still Alarming," *New York Times*, November 27, 2019.

[12] Popovich, Albeck-Ripka, and Pierre-Louis, "Trump Administration Rolled Back More Than 100 Environmental Rules."

To make matters worse, in 2022, the Supreme Court struck down an EPA plan to reduce carbon emissions from power plants, making it harder for the agency—as well as other regulatory agencies (such as the Occupational Safety and Health Administration or the Centers for Disease Control and Prevention)—to enforce similar types of regulations. The Biden administration might have sought to reinstate environmental protection through executive orders upon taking office, rejoining the Paris climate change agreement, and cancelling the controversial Keystone XL pipeline agreement, but the Supreme Court ruling made it difficult, if not impossible, for the United States to achieve its goal of significantly reducing greenhouse gases by 2030. In the shadow of *West Virginia v. EPA*, trading partners may rightly wonder if passage of the Inflation Reduction Act of 2022, which contained language to address and nullify the majority Supreme Court decision, was sufficient, or if this moment is but a political reprieve before another climate-change denier takes the reins of government.[13] Only time will tell, but time is no longer a surplus commodity.

The consequences of ecological degradation facing many throughout the Global South are also faced by those living on the margins within the industrialized North—specifically Black, Indigenous, and people of color (BIPOC) communities in the United States. In the summer, when temperatures are high and air pollution is more common, pregnant African American women have a greater likelihood of giving birth to children who are premature, underweight, or stillborn when compared to the population at large (Bekkar et al. 2020, 4). During the severe 2021 winter storms in Texas, rolling blackouts left some 4 million residents without electricity. Low-income communities of color faced the first power outages—forced to endure freezing temperatures which led to burst pipes—and were among the last to see power restored. In these areas, economic recovery after the disrupted delivery of water and electricity was restored was more difficult to achieve.[14] To make matters worse, just like in the summer, the proximity of minoritized communities to toxic industrial sites whose own air monitoring stations were down due to lack of power contributed to greater exposure to pollution.[15] The experiences of communities in Texas are a

---

[13] Lisa Friedman, "Question Looms on Biden's Climate Efforts: Is America's Word Good," *New York Times*, April 20, 2021.

[14] Alexa Ura and Juan Pablo Garnham, "Already Hit Hard by Pandemic, Black and Hispanic Communities Suffer the Blows of an Unforgiving Winter Storm," *Texas Tribune*, February 19, 2021.

[15] James Dobbins and Hiroko Tabuchi, "Minority Neighborhoods Were among the First to Face Rolling Blackouts," *New York Times*, February 17, 2021.

small portion of the year-round and disproportionate share of the negative consequences caused by global warming and air pollution that US communities of color bear.

The disproportionate burden borne by minority communities within the United States reflects broader trends in international policy related to climate change and its impacts on human communities. People who live in the United States, on average, generate almost three times more carbon dioxide (15.5 metric tons) per year than the global average (4.6 metric tons). As the World Bank's chief economist and vice president for development economics from 1990 until 1993, Lawrence H. Summers supervised international development discussions regarding the health and economic burdens of pollution and industry. Summers later served as undersecretary of the US Treasury Department during the Clinton administration—eventually serving as his secretary of the Treasury from 1999 until 2001. Afterward he served as the president of Harvard University from 2001 to 2006, and then as director of the White House National Economic Council under President Obama in 2009. Not some right-wing climate denier, Summers demonstrates the systematic extent of discriminatory economic policies and their impact on the environmental health and relationships of marginalized communities.

While working at the World Bank in the early 1990s, Summers made a name for himself as the bank's "high priest," responsible for supervising all economic publications, including the pacesetting *World Development Report*. Commenting on the topic of "dirty industries," the theme discussed in one of the publications he oversaw, he wrote a memo to six highly placed colleagues. This private memo was eventually leaked to the press. In it, he wrote,

> Just between you and me, shouldn't the World Bank be encouraging more migration of the dirty industries to LDCs (Less Developed Countries)? . . . The measure of the costs of health impairing pollution depends on the foregone earnings from increased morbidity and mortality. From this point of view a given amount of health impairing pollution should be done in the country with the lowest cost, which will be the country with the lowest wages. I think the economic logic behind dumping a load of toxic waste in the lowest wage country is impeccable and we should face up to that. . . . I've always thought that underpopulated countries in Africa are vastly underpolluted, their air quality is probably vastly inefficiently low compared to Los Angeles or Mexico City. (George and Sabelli 1994, 98–100)

In other words, if "a load of toxic waste" is dumped in a rich country, it would cause the infirmity and death of high-wage earners with standard or longer life expectancies. According to Summers's own publication, $20,000 per year of potential earnings for a forty-year-old with an estimated twenty-five more years of productivity can contribute $500,000 to the global economy. By contrast, if the "load of toxic waste" is dumped in a poor country with a GNP of $360 and average life expectancy of fifty-five years, the contribution of a worker to the global economy could be figured at a measly $5,400 (George and Sabelli 1994, 98–100).

Such an approach reduces humans to their economic value; people of eurocentric origins nearly always possess economic privilege that is considered worth more than the disenfranchised themselves. The sacredness of profits replaces the sacredness of life. Limiting the risk of the industrialized North is directly linked to increasing the risk of the Global South. Death-causing pollutants, therefore, should be "dumped" in poor countries, perpetuating the old patterns of colonialism and imperialism. This link between the domination of the earth and the domination of the disenfranchised has been termed "environmental racism."

As transnational corporations race to pay the lowest wage, they also compete to identify locations with few or no regulations governing pollution or safe working environments. The implementation of Summers's worldview, for example, is evident in Savar, Bangladesh, where a toxic stench rises off the polluted rivers, streams, and canals in which garment factories directly dump their wastewater. Textile dyeing is the second-largest polluter of water globally, responsible for one-fifth of all industrial water pollution and a tenth of all carbon emissions.[16]

With the exception of China, Bangladesh is the largest manufacturing hub in the world, exporting some $34 billion worth of garments in 2019 (Koopman et al. 2020, 101). These factories, which provide clothes for Western department stores like Walmart, J. C. Penney, and H&M, have contributed to the ecological devastation of the area. A recently built effluent treatment plant responsible for purifying the water supply is not yet fully functional. Many rice paddies are inundated with toxic wastewater, fish stocks are decimated, coconut trees no longer produce coconuts, and smaller waterways are filled with sand and garbage to sell off as land for further housing or factory development. The river is being killed, the soil poisoned, and the entire environment destroyed.[17] The situation is so bad

---

[16] Helen Reagan, "Asian Rivers Are Turning Black. And Our Colorful Closets Are to Blame," CNN, September 28, 2020.

[17] Julhas Alam and Martha Mendoza, "Toxic Tanneries Forced to Move Pollute

that the children of garment workers who attend Genda Government Primary School are often dizzy and lightheaded, and retch during class, making them unable to concentrate on their studies. These students know what colors are in fashion every time they look at the canal that runs by their school because the flowing water is at times red-turned-purple, gray, or blue, depending on the dyes used by the factories upstream. To make matters worse, Bangladesh is acutely vulnerable to global climate change. Millions could be displaced, and crop yields can significantly drop with the onslaught of changing weather patterns and rising sea levels.[18]

In addition to manufacturing for consumption, other countries have become the United States' dumping ground for its hazardous waste material. The United States exports as many as one in five lead-acid car batteries to Mexican recycling plants that fail to meet US environmental standards for workers and public health safety measures. Not one plant has costly pollution control or worker protection systems in place. Over the past decade, the number of old car batteries shipped to Mexico has increased by more than 400 percent. Mexico's less stringent limits for lead pollution, coupled with its less vigorous enforcement, makes the US neighbor an ideal locale to dispose of lead batteries. Eléctrica Automotriz Omega, located in Monterrey, converts spent car batteries (containing twenty pounds of lead per battery) into lead ingots to be reused in new batteries. Unfortunately, the United States fails to follow common procedures among developed nations that treat lead batteries as hazardous waste, which has led to a rise in lead poisoning, a byproduct of the battery recycling process when attention is not given to worker and public safety. Elevated levels of lead poisoning, which have turned up in the blood of the company's employees (who earn around $13 for a twelve-hour shift) and found in nearby lots where livestock is raised and children play, is linked to kidney damage and high blood pressure. Among children, lead poisoning leads to stunted developmental growth and behavioral problems.[19]

The United States has successfully learned how to export its environmental pollution to the detriment of other countries' inhabitants—not just car batteries, but also electronic waste, or e-waste, like used laptops, television sets, and iPhones. According to the United Nations, approximately

New Bangladesh Site," Associated Press, July 6, 2018; Jim Yardley, "Bangladesh Pollution, Told in Colors and Smells," *New York Times*, July 15, 2013.

[18] Alam and Mendoza, "Toxic Tanneries Forced to Move Pollute New Bangladesh Site"; Yardley, "Bangladesh Pollution."

[19] Joshua Partlow and Joby Warrick, "A Dangerous Export: America's Car-Battery Waste Is Making Mexican Communities Sick," *Washington Post*, February 26, 2016.

50 million tons of electronic waste are globally produced each year. In Koh Khanuh, Thailand, at the e-waste industry company New Sky Metal, for $10 a day, women crouched with hammers, their faces wrapped with rags to protect from toxic fumes, pull apart tons of the discarded modern technology in search of salvageable metals like gold, silver, or copper. Incinerated e-waste pumps dioxins into the air, infiltrating the food supply, causing cancer and developmental problems for those within the area of the factory. In Thailand, small companies are not subject to pollution monitoring. Even though Thai officials publicly claimed in 2019 that e-waste imports were banned, fourteen companies were given licenses that same year to process electronic waste. When the people affected protested, they were met with violence; a village chief who spoke out against the dumping of toxic waste in 2013 ended up being shot four times in broad daylight. The official from the local Department of Industrial Works, who ordered the kill, was acquitted.[20]

Obviously, the United States is not alone in derogating the environment for a profit. An increase in environmental pollution is also seen in the growing energy needs and rapid industrialization of countries like China. For example, Asian demand for coal contributed to global coal usage nearly doubling from 1980 to 2010, and China's demand alone accounted for 73 percent of Asia's coal consumption and almost half of the global coal consumption by 2010 (US Energy Information Administration 2011, 1–2). Although coal consumption declined from 2013 through 2017, the need to stimulate industrial growth due to economic challenges has seen a rise in consumption—a rise only interrupted with the initial COVID-19 global shutdown. During the first six months of 2020, China granted more construction permits for coal-fired power plants than in each year of 2018 and 2019.[21] While China's government is, philosophically, moving toward energy efficiency and antipollution measures (as a global leader in clean air technologies), its 2019 primary energy consumption was 58 percent coal, down from 59 percent in 2018, and 20 percent petroleum, about two-thirds of the incremental global oil consumption of 2019 (US Energy Information Administration 2020, 1–3). These numbers mean that China's annual carbon dioxide emission represents 28 percent of the global total, or is equivalent to the next three biggest emitters combined—the United States, the European Union, and India (Friedlingstein 2020, 3300). China may

---

[20] Hannah Beech and Ryn Jirenuwat, "As Thailand Recycles Your Laptop, Its Residents Pay the Price," *New York Times*, December 8, 2019.

[21] Steven Lee Myers, "China's Pledge to Be Carbon Neutral by 2060: What It Means," *New York Times*, September 23, 2020.

be ambitiously pledging to reach net carbon neutrality by 2060, but that can only happen after a 2030 peak in carbon dioxide emissions.[22] As the world's largest annual emitter of carbon dioxide, China threatens international efforts to curb global warming, regardless of the country's optimistic commitment to clean air technology.

While China can boast that the numbers of firms whose contribution to pollution was responsible for occupational health risks dropped to 12 million per a 2018 study, its numbers of workers (200 million, or 22 percent of the entire Chinese workforce) exposed to such hazards remains unchanged. Ninety percent of all work-related occupational risks is due to pneumoconiosis (black lung disease), caused by breathing coal or silicon dust. The disease is chronic and incurable.[23] Workers are not the only ones impacted by air pollution. In 2015, an estimated 4.2 million deaths, mainly from East Asia and South Asia, were attributed to air pollution.[24]

In Africa alone, children's deaths from air pollution rose from 164,000 in 1990 to 258,000 by 2017, a 60 percent increase. For many who survive death, they still face chronic infections and illnesses, including negative impacts to brain development (Rees, Wickham, and Choi 2019, 4). Some major culprits of African ecological degradation are big oil and chemical companies, which are making the continent, starting with Kenya, their dumping grounds for plastics by pressuring the United States to in turn pressure African nations to reverse their bans on plastic waste imports. Since China closed its ports to plastic waste in 2018, exports to Africa quadrupled in 2019 from the previous year.

In addition to particulate-matter pollution, increased emissions of carbon dioxide into the environment pollute the air as the means of countering this damage via oxygen-producing vegetation continues to be decimated. According to a 2018 study, approximately 12.4 million acres of forest—equivalent to five Yellowstone National Parks—are cut down each year to make room for industrial agriculture. Thirty percent of the planet's ice-free land mass is dedicated to livestock grazing. The need for grazing land is so acute that it is the main cause of global deforestation, especially in Latin America. Seventy percent of all agricultural land—30 percent of the planet's land surface—is designated for livestock production (Mateo-Sagasta, Marjani, and Turral

---

[22] Chris Buckley, "The Rock Standing in the Way of China's Climate Ambitions: Coal," *New York Times*, March 16, 2021.

[23] "Improving Occupational Health in China," *The Lancet* 394 (August 10, 2019): 443.

[24] Nadja Popovich, Blacki Migliozzi, and Anjail Singhvi, "What It Means to Breathe the World's Most Polluted Air," *New York Times*, December 16, 2019.

2017, 9). Cattle are the most carbon-intensive contributor to agricultural emission, responsible for a full 62 percent of it. Additionally, beef production requires twice as much land per gram than pork or chicken and twenty times as much land as an equivalent amount of bean-based protein.[25] According to the Yale School of Forestry and Environmental Studies, the cattle industry is responsible for 80 percent of the earth's recent rainforest deforestation.[26] In 2020, 10 million acres of primary tropical forest (about the size of Switzerland) were lost.[27] The next year, 2021, 9.3 million more acres of tropical forest was lost, resulting in 2.5 billion metric tons of carbon dioxide emission, or about two and a half times the amount emitted by all US passenger cars and light trucks.[28]

In addition to increasing land use for industrial livestock production, industrial agriculture further jeopardizes freshwater supply around the planet. In the United States, some 2.2 million people do not have access to running water. Globally, 4 billion people (about two-thirds of the human race) experience severe water scarcity at least one month out of the year. By 2030, a 40 percent gap will exist between global water supply and demand, according to the World Economic Forum.[29] Meanwhile, an estimated 100,000 liters of water are required to produce a kilogram of grain-fed beef, due mainly to producing the feedcrop. By contrast, a kilogram of soybean production uses 2,000 liters of water, rice requires 1,912 liters of water, wheat uses 900 liters of water, and potatoes only need 500 liters of water (Pimentel and Pimentel 2003, 662). And, while it is true that the earth is literally covered in water – occupying 70 percent of the globe – less than 1 percent is fresh water. According to the World Bank, half of the world's available fresh water is consumed by humans, of which 70 percent is diverted to agriculture. By 2050, a planet of 10 billion humans will require a 70 percent increase in agricultural production, with a 25 to 40 percent water reallocation.[30]

---

[25] Sarah Kaplan, "Are My Hamburgers Hurting the Planet?," *Washington Post*, November 18, 2019.

[26] Clifford Krauss, David Yaffe-Bellany, and Mariana Simões, "Why Amazon Fires Keep Raging 10 Years after a Deal to End Them," *New York Times*, October 10, 2019.

[27] Henry Fountain, "Tropical Forest Destruction Accelerated in 2020," *New York Times*, March 31, 2020.

[28] Henry Fountain, "9.3 Million Acres of Old Tropical Forests Lost," *New York Times*, April 29, 2022.

[29] Ayanna Runcie, "Demand for Water Is Rapidly Increasing as Supply Dwindles," CBS News, April 22, 2021.

[30] The World Bank, "Water in Agriculture," May 8, 2020.

In addition to the amount of land and water that is allocated to sustain the US meat-based diet, livestock production is also considered to be responsible for most of the water pollution, due mainly from animal waste runoff; chemical contaminations from tanneries, pesticides, and fertilizer runoff from feed crop; and the emergence of antibiotic resistance, causing global ecological damage, specifically in the Global South (Steinfield et al. 2006, xxi). Every year, 5 million people from the Global South die from water-borne diseases. According to a 2019 UNICEF study, 85,700 children under the age of fifteen die yearly from diarrhea linked to unsafe water, sanitation, and hygiene facilities, compared to 30,900 who die from military conflict.[31] The World Health Organization reports that approximately 2 billion out of the 7.7 billion people who inhabit the Earth use a drinking water source contaminated with feces. By 2025, half of the world's population will be living in water-stressed areas.[32]

The ecological global damage caused by the United States does not solely impact those living beyond our borders. To be a person of color in America, according to a 2021 study, means breathing in more polluted air containing high levels of ambient fine particulate air pollution ($PM_{2.5}$) than white people (Tessum et al. 2021, 1). $PM_{2.5}$, the largest environmental cause of human mortality and responsible for up to 200,000 excess US deaths a year, are solid or liquid particles suspended in the air while measuring smaller than 2.5 micrometers, too small to be seen with the naked eye. They evade the body's defenses, able to deeply penetrate the lungs and enter the bloodstream. Within the United States, communities of color are more exposed to higher levels of $PM_{2.5}$ than whites.[33] Even short-term exposure to $PM_{2.5}$ along with ozone (caused by industrial and vehicular emissions) has been associated with mortality, cardiovascular and respiratory-related hospitalization, and exacerbation of asthma, emphysema, and bronchitis (Yip et al. 2011, 28–32). Black and Latine people in the United States are more likely to live in neighborhoods with pollution of all kinds than whites who are primarily causing said pollution. Black people are exposed to about 56 percent more $PM_{2.5}$ pollution than is caused by their consumption while Latines are exposed at the slightly higher rate of 63 percent. Whites, on the other hand, experience 17 percent less pollution than is caused by their consumption (Tessum et al. 2019, 6002–3).

---

[31] United Nations Children's Fund, "More Children Killed by Unsafe Water Than Bullets, Says UNICEF Chief," March 21, 2019.

[32] World Health Organization, "Drinking Water," fact sheet, June 14, 2019.

[33] Popovich, Migliozzi, and Singhvi, "What It Means to Breathe the World's Most Polluted Air."

According to a study that examined 84,969 US public schools, only 728 achieved safe scores from air neurotoxicant exposure. Students attending public schools labeled "high risk" for air pollution are more likely to be Black, Latine, or Asian/Pacific Islander. They are significantly less likely to be white (Grineski and Collins 2018, 580–85).

Race and ethnicity, according to a growing body of empirical evidence, continues to be the most significant variable in determining the location of commercial, industrial, and military hazardous waste sites. Consider the environmental racism faced by three predominate North Carolina counties comprised predominantly of Black, Native, and Latine communities. These counties were already home to most of the state's industrial hog operations. From 2012 through 2019, 30 million turkeys and chickens were added to the equation, increasing their numbers by 36 percent, to 113 million (compared to a 17 percent increase for the rest of the state). Fowl agriculture produces 1 million tons of waste each year, added to the 4.4 billion gallons of liquefied waste annually produced by the hogs. Unlined pits of liquid manure and urine become the primary waste treatment, fouling air quality and, through runoff after rain, polluting the water supply.[34]

Furthermore, race and ethnicity are the most significant predicators in forecasting where the nation's commercial hazardous waste facilities are located. For example, African Americans are 75 percent more likely than other Americans to live in areas near facilities that produce hazardous waste (Fleischman and Franklin 2017, 6). Black people, regardless of their income levels, are subjected to higher levels of air pollution than whites, breathing 1.5 times more sooty pollution emitted from burning fossil fuel. Exposure to polluted air, as we know, is associated with lung disease, heart disease, premature death, and now COVID-19.[35] Womanist ethicist Emilie Townes has said that the endured effects of toxic waste on the lives of people of color who, due to poverty, are relegated to live on ecologically hazardous lands, are akin to a contemporary version of lynching a whole people (1995, 55).

Environmental racism is not limited to the location of hazardous waste sites. Violators of pollution laws received less stringent punishments when those violations occurred in nonwhite neighborhoods than when they occurred in white neighborhoods; fines were often 500 percent

---

[34] Sarah Graddy, Ellen Simon, and Soren Rundquist, "Exposing Fields of Filth: Factory Farms Disproportionately Threaten Black, Latino and Native American North Carolinians," Environmental Working Group, interactive map, 2020.

[35] Linda Villarosa, "Pollution Is Killing Black Americans. This Community Fought Back," New York Times, July 28, 2020.

higher in white communities than in communities of color. When violations occurred in minoritized communities the government was slower to act, taking as much 20 percent more time to respond, than when violations occurred in white communities (Acevedo-Garcia et al. 2008, 27–28). And even when a lawsuit was brought before the Eastern District Federal Court of Virginia about the placement of landfills in predominantly Black King and Queen Counties (*RISE v. Kay*), the judge, while acknowledging the historical trend of disproportionately placing landfills in African American areas, still ruled that the case failed to prove discrimination (Bullard 1993, 28).

Environmental racism also takes a heavy toll on children of color. It should therefore not be surprising that, in 2018, according to the Centers for Disease Control and Prevention (CDC), Puerto Ricans (15 percent), Native people (12 percent), and Black people (11 percent) had the highest rates of asthma, more so than whites (8 percent). Asthma rates were significantly higher (11 percent) among families whose incomes were below the poverty threshold as compared to those above the threshold. Puerto Ricans and Blacks with asthma have three times higher mortality rates than whites (Carver and Jaffee 2020, 8, 30). It is no coincidence that the United States' predominantly Puerto Rican and Black neighborhoods have the highest percentage of documented cases of asthma in the United States. An abundance of the worst triggers of asthma are found in these same neighborhoods. For example, in central Harlem and the South Bronx specifically, major causes are insect (cockroach) droppings, mold, mildew, diesel exhaust, and cigarette smoke. And yet, during a Senate hearing on the EPA budget in 2012, Jeff Sessions (R-AL), who would go on to be Trump's attorney general, claimed that air pollution victims were "unidentified and imaginary."[36]

The US military, whose carbon footprint is usually overlooked, is a major contributor to climate change, a polluter that causes more ecological damage than a hundred countries combined.[37] In addition to its relentless contribution to global warming, this expanding footprint is a major threat to the environment where people of color in the United States reside. Of the 651 nuclear weapons or devices exploded on the US mainland by the military, all test sites occurred on Native American territories (Seager 1993, 63). Most of these detonations occurred on the lands of the Shoshone nation (LaDuke 1993, 99). Uranium, used for atomic weapons, is mined mostly in Navajo territory. Worldwide, 70 percent of all uranium resources

---

[36] Dominique Browning, "The Racial Politics of Asthma," *Time*, March 29, 2012.

[37] Benjamin Neimark, Oliver Belcher, and Patrick Bigger, "The U.S. Military Is a Bigger Polluter Than More Than 100 Countries Combined," Quartz, June 28, 2019.

are located on Indigenous lands. Even though most US uranium mines are presently abandoned, they can still emit high levels of radioactive gases. One of the ingredients of the solid waste from uranium mining is radium 226, which remains radioactive for at least sixteen thousand years (99, 102). It is reported that Navajo teenagers have a rate of organ cancer seventeen times the national average (Hamilton 1993, 71).

Finally, since stress is known to be a major cause of illnesses, the environment and occupational assignments delegated to people of color contribute to disproportionately lowering their life expectancies. This phenomenon was made evident early on during the US response to the COVID-19 pandemic. Rather than considering the intersection between race/ethnicity, pollution, and the spread of the virus, medical doctor and Ohio state senator Stephen Huffman instead wondered, "Could it just be that African Americans or the colored population do not wash their hands as well as other groups or wear a mask or do not socially distance themselves? Could that be the explanation of why the higher incidence?"[38] Latines—as "the colored population"—did not disproportionately die from the coronavirus at higher rates because they are simply dirtier, as the good doctor suggests; they died because of where they lived. Environmental racism meant Latines faced greater exposure to the virus.

The residents of Globeville—a predominately poor, Latine Denver, Colorado, neighborhood—experienced higher hospitalization rates (2.9 per 1,000) than those living in the predominately white Denver neighborhood of Country Club (0.3 per 1,000), located six miles due south. Denver Latines were twice as likely than their white counterparts to be hospitalized for the SARS-CoV-2 virus that caused the COVID-19 pandemic. The culprit was not that Latines are dirtier. The air they breathe is dirtier than that inhaled in white neighborhoods. The Globeville zip code (80216) is one of the most polluted zip codes in the United States.[39]

Not surprisingly, air quality monitoring conducted over five years prior to the pandemic indicated Globeville frequently exceeded EPA's air quality safety limits.[40] Because a correlation exists between air pollution and the susceptibility of contracting COVID-19, where people of color live due to institutionalized racism and economic deprivation increases

---

[38] Trip Gabriel, "Ohio Lawmaker Asks Racist Question about Black People and Hand-Washing," *New York Times*, June 11, 2020.

[39] Kevin Beaty, "Denver's Got the Most Polluted ZIP Code in the Country? Not So Fast," *Denverite*, February 26, 2018.

[40] Katie Weis, "Denver Hispanics Neighborhoods with Higher COVID-19 Hospitalization Rates Also Have Higher Air Pollution Levels Than White Neighborhoods," CBS Denver, August 6, 2020.

their probability of contracting the virus. As an April 2020 Harvard study demonstrated, a small increase in long-term exposure to air pollution led to a major increase in COVID-19 death rates (Xiao et al. 2020, 1).

Globeville is the norm, not the exception. In the United States, the greatest indicator of daily exposure to greater levels of pollution is one's zip code. Communities of color—regardless of residents' average or median income level—are exposed to higher levels of pollution than white neighborhoods (Liu et al. 2021, 1–2). A 2022 study found that segregationist and discriminatory redlining practices dating from the 1930s are responsible for urban communities of color having higher levels of harmful air pollution almost a century later (Lane et al. 2022, 345). In the final analysis, Summers enunciated the neoliberal position on this issue when he said, "Promoting development is the best way to protect the environment" (George and Sabelli 1994, 170). Those from the margins of society who experience "a load of toxic waste" dumped upon them in the name of development might have a different opinion.

Step 2: Reflecting

Generally speaking, eurocentric theology has concerned itself with the relationship between the Deity and humans, as well as with relationships among humans. The emphasis remains, among many Protestants, on a "personal" relationship with Jesus. The prominent eurocentric thread within Christianity, as practiced by the powerful and privileged, has created a faith with little connection to or understanding of a collective or communal spirituality linked to the land. Nor has much attention been given to the relationship between humans and creaturekind.[41] Instead, the industrialization of agriculture has led to a disregard of animal welfare, which constitutes a major proportion of creaturekind. Few are concerned with how food arrives to their supermarkets. Industrialization has replaced husbandry, leading to the breaking of the human-animal social contract as concerns for animal well-being make way for cost-effectiveness. While, at one time, a farmer would have spent more time or money than an ill animal was worth, attention to corporate profit today discourages spending more on caring for animals than their book value. Yet we know that ignoring

---

[41] I am influenced by Carter Heyward, who uses the term "creaturekind" to refer to all God has created that is other than human, meaning animals, plants, and minerals. While the term encompasses humans, Heyward struggles for language that avoids defining all God created that is not human as "other-than-human." See Heyward 2004, 18, 20.

the conditions in which animals we consume as food must endure leads to ecological concerns.

Today, if anyone truly wishes to reduce their carbon footprint, probably the greatest contribution one could make is to eat less meat. Nevertheless, a Western meat-based diet that is mainly affordable to a global minority living in industrial nations is accepted as some type of human right, regardless of how this diet is negatively impacting the global ecology, as well as an individual's health. According to the Food and Agriculture Organization of the United Nations, the US livestock sector is one of the top two or three most significant contributors to the most serious environmental problems faced at every level of society, from local to global—impacting climate change, degradation of the earth, air pollution, water pollution, water shortage, and loss of biodiversity. Food production and distribution account for one-third of all human-caused global warming. The fossil fuel required by the US agricultural sector greatly contributes to greenhouse gas emissions. Roughly 123 million barrels of oil are consumed during the production of synthetic fertilizers and pesticides (Steinfeld et al. 2006, 86–87). Add to this figure the transportation cost of supplying the average American meal, which travels some fifteen hundred miles to our plates.

Also contributing to the greenhouse gas problem are the animals themselves, along with their waste. The methane released by cows and pigs, while less prevalent in the air than carbon dioxide, is 23 times more potent than carbon dioxide as a heat-trapping gas, making livestock responsible for 18 percent of the world's greenhouse gas emissions; compare that to transportation, which is only responsible for 13 percent (xxi). The sheer number of livestock in crowded facilities means it is impossible to properly process the manure generated. A dairy farm with 2,500 cows produces as much waste as a city of 411,000 individuals, but unlike the city, no sewage treatment plant exists to mitigate its impact (Haines and Staley 2004, 7). Properly processing animal waste becomes a logistical impossibility. Animal waste is sprayed onto the land, creating cesspools that pollute groundwater, streams, and rivers, leading to health problems among workers and nearby neighbors. When we consider that two-thirds of all human infectious diseases are zoonotic, we should not be surprised that respiratory illnesses, cardiovascular problems, and prenatal and neonatal health concerns are on the rise wherever livestock-based environmental contamination occurs (Rollin 2008, 15). Yet we ignore the ecological damage caused by the eating habits of industrialized nations because, for the most part, the environment has been seen as a means of satisfying the wants and desires of those human beings.

Human beings of the Global North, viewing themselves as the center of the created order, have historically perceived the environment as an unlimited storehouse of raw materials provided by God for human convenience. The resources of the Earth have often been sacrificed in the quest for economic growth and meeting human desires. Still, all that has life is sacred before the Creator of life, making it difficult to limit spiritual worthiness and well-being to human beings.

Native Americans remind us that, within the circle of creation, all are equal in value to the Creator. George "Tink" Tinker expressed this view when he wrote, "A chief is not valued above the people; nor are two-legged valued above the animal nations, the birds, or even trees and rocks" (1994, 126). Human beings' relationships to creation become a matter of life and death, balancing one's needs and place within the world with preserving the world for one's descendants who will live "seven generations from now." While one takes from the plenty of creation, something must always be returned to maintain balance (Kidwell, Noley, and Tinker 2001, 33).

Others, such as Indian scholar Aruna Gnanadason, totally reject the dualism intrinsic in Western theological thought, which sees an opposition between the spirit and flesh, men and women, or mind and body. She, instead, avers a cosmology that affirms the interdependence and harmony of all life forms (1996, 77). Instead of a binary opposition, many Asian theologians like Kwok Pui-lan emphasize the balance of "heaven and earth, yang and yin, sun and moon, and father and mother" where they are "complementally, mutually reinforcing and interplaying with one other" (2000, 90). Others, like this author, would argue that what eurocentric thought reduces to commodities (land, water, rocks, air) to be used and exploited for gain are in fact living entities containing spirit who deserve respect and agency (De La Torre 2021, 12).

The Earth's resources, as we are slowly learning, are not everlasting. Proper stewardship requires creating a harmonious relationship with nature, as with other human beings. Poor care of the environment creates pollution, lowers life expectancy, and is a major source of many illnesses and diseases for those living close by, who are predominately poor and of color. The exploitation of the Earth's resources, and the exploitation of the Earth's marginalized, are interconnected, making it difficult, if not impossible, to speak of one without mentioning the other. Brazilian theologian Leonardo Boff has given voice to the cry of the oppressed, connecting it with the very cry of the Earth. He insists that the logic and justification that lead the powerful and privileged to exploit and subjugate the world's marginalized are the same logic and justification that plunder the Earth's wealth and lead to its devastation (1997, xi).

Some women ethicists such as Karen Warren advocate ecofeminism, an environmental theology that seeks to overcome the hierarchy and dualism imposed upon nature. She claims ecofeminism is based on four central claims: (1) there are important connections between the oppression of women and the oppression of nature; (2) there is a need to understand the nature of these connections to understand the oppression of women and oppression of nature; (3) feminist theory and practice must include an ecological perspective; and (4) solutions to ecological problems must include a feminist perspective (1987, 4–5). The interconnectedness between women and nature has always existed. Wilderness or virgin land awaits insemination with man's seed of progress and civilization, for nature as feminine (Mother Nature) has always required its domination and domestication or, in the words of Vandana Shiva, "a woman to be raped" (1996, 69).

While ecofeminism unmasks the interconnectedness between the oppression of women and the oppression of nature, unfortunately white feminists often fail to fully develop or recognize the need to expand this paradigm to encompass marginalized groups of color. Eurocentric women who have the privilege of not living in toxic, infested neighborhoods fail at times to consider how race and ethnicity, more so than gender, remain the main indicators of who lives in ecologically hazardous areas and who does not. Womanist Karen Baker-Fletcher made a similar observation when she wrote,

> There is a tendency among middle-class eco-feminist and mainstream eco-theologians to enjoy the privilege of extensive international travel which informs their spirituality. Such a privilege enables them to have the luxury of providing a global analysis. In contrast, there are many within the U.S. environmental justice movement who would find it a luxury to leave their own neighborhoods. This is the cause of a credibility gap between theologians in the academy and the grassroots from which liberation spirituality emerges. (2004, 125–26)

When those racially and ethnically marginalized compare the environmental quality of life of where they live with that of the larger white society, the link that exists between polluted sites and disenfranchisement becomes all too obvious. Few white environmentalists seriously consider this link. Consequently, they fail to understand a major reason why pollution occurs disproportionately in certain areas. The failure of the environmental justice movement to come to terms with the inherent racism that relegates those on the margins to the greatest ecological health risks prevents fostering a truly planetary, holistic approach to the environment. Environmentalists benefiting from white and class privilege cannot continue to isolate ecological concerns from environmental racism. Continuing to mask environmental racism limits, if not frustrates, any attempt or hope for the liberation of humans and creaturekind alike.

Step 3: Meditating

If the creation story describes humanity's appointment as stewards of the earth's resources, then as caretakers, human beings are called to protect, preserve, and safeguard those resources so all can benefit and enjoy its fruits. Creation as gift means everything that draws breath has a basic right to its products and no group has the right to hoard its resources. Hoarding the earth's resources upsets the delicate balance between life and the resources needed to sustain life. Yet, ironically, Christianity has to some degree encouraged the destruction of God's creation. The first creation story ends with God saying, "to [human beings], be fruitful and multiply, and fill the earth, and subdue it, and have dominion over the fish of the sea, over the birds of the heavens, and over the beasts creeping on the land" (Gen. 1:28). Biblical passages such as these justified human domination of nature. Historically, we have come to read this verse as permission to use, misuse, and abuse creation, like how the ancient rulers reduced their subjects to commodities. "Man," like the ancient king, is ordained to rule over all. This understanding of humans (specifically males) occupying the pinnacle of creation has been echoed throughout Christian history. Even Pope John Paul II reinforced this concept when he wrote, "Everything in creation is ordered to man and everything is made subject to him" (1995, 61).

Western Christianity's understanding of stewardship and domination as subjugating nature has contributed to the present ecological challenges facing humanity. The belief that the destiny of human beings is to reside with God in heaven while Earth is but a place of sojourn until we reach our heavenly destiny has encouraged—at the very least—neglect of our environment. The greatest Christian threat to the environment comes from those who hold a view of the future or the end of time (an "eschatological" view) like the one made popular by LaHaye and Jenkins's twelve-book *Left Behind* series (published between 1995 and 2003). These stories focus on the tribulations faced by those unfortunate souls "left behind" during the "last days" of Armageddon (Judgment Day), when they must face the Antichrist. Although the books are fictional, the authors insist they are based on the correct and only valid literal interpretation of biblical prophecy. These Christians welcome the destruction of the earth, for it indicates Jesus's "Second Coming," when he raptures (takes away from the earth) those destined to be saved.

If the world ends in a conflagration and such an end is close at hand, then why worry about the environment? James G. Watt, secretary of the Interior during the Reagan administration and the cabinet member officially responsible for protecting the environment, best articulated this "premillennial" view. He explained his responsibility "is to follow the Scriptures which call upon us to occupy the land until Jesus returns."[42] In short, Jesus is coming soon to rescue the faithful from an Earth destined to total destruction. Any attempt to preserve or safeguard the Earth is a waste of time.

It seems, though, that refusal to recognize the damage being committed against the environment constitutes the ultimate form of oppression, for it brings destruction to life (including human life) on this planet. If liberation is to come to Earth's marginalized, then it must also come to the Earth. The Earth needs to be "saved" from anthropogenic destruction for individuals to obtain liberation. If nature is wasted, depleted, or destroyed, then individuals will not be able to control their destinies. Such a sin cannot be easily atoned for, for we cannot resurrect extinct species.

Scripture articulates that the Earth belongs to God. The psalmist boldly proclaims, "The earth is the Lord's, and the fullness of the world and those who live in it" (Ps. 24:1). The God who takes notice of the least of creation, the falling sparrow, is concerned with all of creation. "Man" is not called to dominate the Earth; rather, human beings are called to be stewards of the Earth's resources, ensuring each person has sufficient resources to meet their needs. Baker-Fletcher insists that the incarnation, God becoming flesh, is the act of Divinity joining the dust of the earth, the very dust from which human beings were created, to reconcile the broken relationship between God and creation (1998, 19). The abundant life promised by Christ cannot be accomplished within a depleted Earth. Survival is a key requirement for any form of abundant living.

Most Indigenous religions from Africa and the Americas maintain a sacred respect for creation, a respect that has been lost to and historically abused by many Western Christian groups. Earth-centered religions, rooted in the abode of ancestors, are unlike Western religions that emphasize a heavenly place or stress the placement of the stars and planets to determine the course of human events. For example, in the religion of the Yoruba

---

[42] Bill Prochnau, "The Watt Controversy," *Washington Post*, June 30, 1981.

people of West Africa as practiced by Caribbean Black people, whites, and biracial Latines, the earth is believed to provide all that is needed to live a full and abundant life. Like the oceans that can support and sustain all life existing within its waters, so too is the land able to support and sustain all life existing upon it. This abundance becomes evident as human beings learn to live in harmony with nature. Shortages occur when humans attempt to impose their own will upon the fair and natural distribution of nature's resources according to the needs of the people.

Step 4: Case Studies

1. Global warming contributes to the spread of infectious diseases and an increase in the means of its transmission (e.g., mosquitoes and ticks). The 2020 COVID-19 pandemic may have been exacerbated by climate change, and while the pandemic was a human tragedy, it nonetheless brought temporary relief to the planet. As a global lockdown took hold and humans were ordered to shelter in place, the planet experienced a reprieve. Within weeks, smog that hung over major global cities lifted as global carbon emissions fell. The polluted Grand Canal of Venice, fouled by boat traffic, ran clear.[43] And yet it was insufficient to slow down the threat of continuing heat waves, floods, and extreme storms. Worse, with the relaxing of pandemic lockdowns by that summer, global greenhouse gas emissions rebounded after a steep decline.[44]

• The rise of telecommute and work-from-home alternatives in a post-COVID-19 world may be beneficial for the global environment, but is it enough? Is traveling to the other side of the world for a destination wedding ethical? Is the focus on personal carbon footprint (e.g., aviation global emission accounts for approximately 2.5 percent of all global emission) distracting from major polluters like industrial manufacturing? Should the loosening of environmental regulations for oil, gas, coal, chemical, or agriculture industries be seen as a crime against humanity?

• Are alternatives like driving electric cars helpful? Mining lithium for the car batteries has negative impacts on the environment and the areas where they are mined. In 2020, only 65 percent of the entire global lithium carbonate that would be needed by 2030 had been mined. Furthermore,

---

[43] Meehan Crist, "What the Pandemic Means for Climate Change," *New York Times*, March 29, 2020.

[44] Brad Plumer and Nadja Popovich, "Fossil Fuel Emissions Come Roaring Back as the World Opens Up," *New York Times*, June 18, 2020.

unlike combustible engines, lithium batteries end up in landfills, where they are prone to leaks, yet electric cars produce 60 to 68 percent fewer emissions than other vehicles.[45]

2. Nguyen Van Quy, who suffers from cancer, has had two children born with birth defects. Nguyen Thi Phi has suffered through four miscarriages. Duong Quynh Hoa suffers from breast cancer and carries high levels of dioxin in her blood system. These three women worked in areas sprayed with Agent Orange at the height of the Vietnam War. They blame their physical disorders on the US military.[46] During the war, the US military dumped around 25 million gallons of assorted noxious chemicals, herbicides, and defoliants in Southeast Asia. Dioxin (TCDD), a major teratogenic (birth-deforming) contaminant, attaches itself to human and animal fat cells, and persists for decades in bodies as well as the food chain. A total of 622,043 individuals have been negatively affected by the chemicals to which they were exposed, including 169,693 of their children and 4,505 of their grandchildren who suffer from high rates of deformities and mental disabilities.[47] Vietnamese scientists claim that 5 out of 100 children are born with some form of mental or physical abnormality, representing a fourfold increase since the start of the war. The Vietnamese claims are consistent with studies conducted by the US National Institutes of Health, which found Agent Orange's chemical compounds caused birth defects in laboratory animals.[48]

• During the war, actions were taken to protect the lives of US soldiers. The use of Agent Orange defoliated the heavy jungles, exposing enemy troops, hence saving US military lives. Also, some five hundred thousand acres of cropland were destroyed, disrupting enemy troops' food supplies. Does war justify the use of toxic chemicals to protect US troops? Why or why not? Is preserving the lives of US soldiers of greater value than the lives of future generations of Vietnamese civilians? Why or why not?

• Two of the primary producers of Agent Orange were Dow Chemical Company and Monsanto. What responsibility, if any, do these companies or the US government have toward the people of Vietnam?

---

[45] Matt McFarland, "America's Electric Cars Need Lithium So Badly It May Wipe Out This Species," CNN, May 10, 2021.

[46] Tini Tran, "Vietnam's Agent Orange Victims File Suit," Associated Press, February 4, 2004.

[47] "More Than 620,000 Vietnamese Victims of War Herbicides," Associated Press, October 23, 2002.

[48] Jason Grotto, "Agent Orange: Birth Defects Plague Vietnam; U.S. Slow to Help," *Chicago Tribune*, December 8, 2009.

• On January 30, 2004, Quy, Phi, and Hoa filed a civil lawsuit at the US District Court in Brooklyn, New York, against ten American chemical companies that produced the defoliant, claiming these companies committed war crimes for supplying Agent Orange to the military. The suit sought billions of dollars in damages. On March 10, 2005, Judge Jack Weinstein dismissed the suit.[49] And on June 18, 2007, the Second Circuit Court of Appeals upheld Weinstein's ruling and dismissed the case. The Supreme Court, on March 2, 2009, refused to reconsider the Court of Appeals' ruling. In 2021 a French-Vietnamese woman and victim brought a new suit against fourteen chemical giants before a French court. The case is pending as of this writing.[50] Is Judge Weinstein correct in siding with the chemical companies that argued that supplying the defoliant did not amount to a war crime? Are these multinational companies liable? Do Quy, Phi, and Hoa have any legal or moral rights to bring suits against such corporations? Against the US government? Why or why not?

3. Canadian atmospheric scientist Katharine Hayhoe tweeted, "The six stages of climate denial are: it's not real. It's not us. It's not that bad. It's too expensive to fix. Aha, here's a great solution (that actually does nothing). And – oh no! Now it's too late. You really should have warned us earlier."[51] To do nothing will exacerbate existing US inequalities based on race, ethnicity, and income. Economist Solomon Hsiang notes that climate change "may result in the largest transfer of wealth from the poor to the rich in the country's history."[52] Globally, because poorer countries are in tropical regions, they will suffer the worst consequences. Heat waves will make it difficult, if not impossible, to be outside and will negatively impact elderly communities. Droughts will make food production more difficult. Wildfires will perpetuate. Melting glaciers will inundate coastal cities. Thanks to denialism, it is too late to stop global warning from intensifying over the next thirty years due to a 2° Fahrenheit increase in temperature since the nineteenth century.[53] Still, the most harrowing consequences can be decelerated. Yet denialism and kowtowing to the interests of the oil, gas,

---

[49] William Glaberson, "Agent Orange Case for Millions of Vietnamese Is Dismissed," *New York Times*, March 10, 2005.

[50] Nguyen Phan Que Mai, "Neglected Victims of Agent Orange," *New York Times*, May 2, 2021.

[51] Katharine Hayhoe, Twitter, from @KHayhoe, March 25, 2020.

[52] Oliver Milman, "Climate Change Set to Worsen Inequality in US If Greenhouse Gases Aren't Reduced," *The Guardian*, June 29, 2017.

[53] Brad Plumer and Henry Fountain, "A Hotter Future Is Now Inevitable, A U.N. Report Says," *New York Times*, August 9, 2021.

coal, chemical, and agriculture industries were so effective that they helped hamstring the ability of the Biden administration and the Democratic-controlled Congress to pass their original $1.7 trillion "Build Back Better" bill. The bill earmarked $555 billion for renewable energy, a crucial step to meet Biden's goal of cutting greenhouse emissions by 50 percent compared to 2005 levels by 2030. In its stead, the Inflation Reduction Act of 2022 incorporated some of the Build Back Better Act's climate change proposals, specifically $391 billion in spending for energy and climate change.

• What responsibility do US citizens have when voting for politicians who disregard global environmental agreements (e.g., the Paris Agreement)? Should economic policies that are beneficial to the few outweigh the environmental impact said policies might have? Does this generation have a responsibility to vote while thinking of the next generations, or should we focus on short-term profits? What exactly is the Green New Deal, and why is it so vilified?

• The sole holdout who doomed the Build Back Better bill was Senator Joe Manchin (D-WV). He owns a coal business started by his family, Enersystems, which has made him millions of dollars. And even though he has a blind trust, most of the income generated from his business is not under the supervision of that trust.[54] In addition, from 2017 through 2022, the oil and gas industries have contributed $923,377 to Manchin's reelection efforts.[55] He finally backed a watered-down version, the Inflation Reduction Act, which went into law in August 2022. But his backing came at a price. The doomed Mountain Valley Pipeline, a 304-mile gas pipeline that cut through the Appalachian Mountains—opposed by environmental activists, mired in delays, struggling with budget overruns, and fighting lawsuits—is back on track with government support and expedited approvals. Not surprisingly, natural gas pipeline companies increased their contributions to Machin from $20,000 in 2020 to $331,000 for the year.[56] Are his financial ties to the coal industry problematic? Are contributions to his campaigns a form of bribes?

• The environmental future is bleak. The issue is no longer how we might prevent climate change. That ship has sailed. Climate change is here,

---

[54] Michael Kranish and Anna Phillips, "Manchin Cites a Blind Trust to Justify Climate Votes. But Much Income from His Family's Coal Company Isn't Covered," *Washington Post*, December 13, 2021.

[55] "Joe Manchin," Open Secrets.org, 2022.

[56] Hiroko Tabuchi, "A Pipeline Project Seemed Doomed, until Manchin Stepped In," *New York Times*, August 8, 2022.

and it is nonreversible within the foreseeable future. For the next generation, life on planet Earth will be more unpleasant for those with economic means, deadly for those without. The issue before us is this: How do we make the consequences of climate change less horrific? How do we begin the generational work to begin healing the planet? What would a new worldview, a new spirituality, look like that sees the Earth not as something to be conquered and domesticated, but as a coequal partner with its own rights and spirituality?

PART III

CASE STUDIES OF NATIONAL RELATIONSHIPS

Chapter 8

Introduction to
National Relationships

When patriotism ("my country, right or wrong") replaces justice, a people are in danger of idolatry. Because the United States can be a strong force for good in the world, it must be confronted and challenged when it fails to live up to its rhetoric and potential. Unfortunately, this nation's quest for economic and military dominance in the world has usually led down a path that not only creates poverty abroad but also contributes to a widening domestic wealth gap. Fiscal resources lavished abroad to maintain supremacy in the neoliberal economic order are not available to spend at home to improve the lives and well-being of its citizens. And when funds are available, they are funneled to the richest and whitest Americans through unregulated business practices and regressive tax policies. Every empire in history has faced diametrically opposed choices: to wield awesome power abroad by strengthening and increasing its military capabilities, or to improve the living standards of residents at home. They choose between guns or butter.

The United States has the lowest minimum wage (as a percentage of the median wage) among advanced industrialized countries. In 2022 the United States remained the only country in the Americas and the only country among advanced industrialized nations without a national paid parental leave benefit, and, with the exception of Japan and Canada, the only industrialized nation without universal paid vacations. Additionally, we are the only industrialized nation, with the exception of South Korea, without any federal law requiring sick leave. During the height of the Great Depression, the US Senate overwhelmingly voted to establish a thirty-hour workweek. The measure failed in the House. Nevertheless, five years later, in 1938, the Fair Labor Standards Act passed, granting the statutory forty-hour workweek. Ironically, most Americans are working longer hours to make less money. During the 1960s, when compared to their counterparts in Japan and Europe, Americans spent less time on the job. By 2000, Americans were working longer hours than their overseas counterparts. By 2013, around 40 percent of men in professional jobs worked fifty-plus hours a week, as do a quarter of the men in middle-income occupations. Low-income workers are usually forced to have two jobs just to make ends meet.[1] According to the US Bureau of Labor Statistics, vast numbers of Americans in 2019 worked more than forty hours a week,[2] making the 1938 Fair Labor Standards Act a quaint relic of the past.

A 2019 study conducted by the Brookings Institution discovered that 44 percent of US workers (some 53 million people) between the ages of eighteen and sixty-four are employed in low-wage jobs that pay a median annual wage of only $17,950. Most are in their prime working years, earning a median hourly wage of $10.22 (Ross and Bateman 2019, 9). And while news concerning a reduction in unemployment may sound like an economic recovery, most of the new jobs being created are these types of low-paying jobs. Almost half of all workers have jobs that fail to create or sustain economic security. Not surprisingly, 43 percent of US households in 2020 are effectively poor, unable to afford a budget that includes the bare necessities of life: housing, food, health care, childcare, and transportation. Households of color—60 percent of Black households, 57 percent of Native American households, and 56 percent of Latine households—are disproportionately living in poverty (United Way ALICE Project 2020, 5, 19). The economic divide between euroamericans and people of color is as wide—if not wider—in 2020 as it was in 1968, changing little over the decades.[3] The United States has become a very wealthy poor country.

We may chant that we are number one, but the United States slipped from nineteenth on the Social Progress Index in 2011 to twenty-eight in 2020. Out of 163 countries, only three countries are worse off in 2020 than 2011: the United States, Brazil, and Hungary. We may rank first in the quality of our universities, yet we rank ninety-first in access to quality basic education. One-fifth of fifteen-year-olds are unable to read at a level expected of a ten-year-old. We may lead the world in medical technology,

---

[1] Stephanie Coontz, "Why Gender Equality Stalled," *New York Times*, February 17, 2012.

[2] US Bureau of Labor Statistics, "Average Hours per Day Spent in Selected Activities on Days Worked by Employment Status and Sex," 2021.

[3] Heather Long and Andrew Van Dam, "The Black-White Economic Divide Is as Wide as It Was in 1968," *Washington Post*, June 4, 2020.

yet we rank ninety-seventh in access to quality health care.[4] We may be number one when it comes to military strength (guns), but we are at the bottom of industrialized countries when it comes to the welfare of our citizens (butter). We obscure this truth with patriotic rhetoric of being number one despite the facts.

Take, for example, the indicator of earnings. Median income grew slowly in the United States between 2002 and 2008 (slower than in any other economic expansion), only to fall sharply with the 2008 Great Recession. Upper-income families were the only economic tier that was able to build on their wealth between 2001 and 2016, adding 33 percent at the median. Middle-income families, meanwhile, saw their median net worth shrink by 20 percent while lower-income families experienced a 45 percent loss. By 2020, the fifty richest Americans held almost as much wealth as half of the US population. While the fifty wealthiest Americans are worth almost $2 trillion, the poorest 50 percent (165 million people) of Americans hold $2.08 trillion in assets, or approximately 1.9 percent of all household wealth. Consider that the top 1 percent hold a combined net worth of $34.2 trillion and own 50 percent of the equity in corporations and mutual funds. And of course, 83.9 percent of the nation's wealth is disproportionately held by euroamericans, leaving a measly 16.1 percent to communities of color.[5]

The wealth required to maintain military domination creates domestic economic stagnation because financial investment in the armed forces is less effective in producing long-term economic growth than investing in industries geared to meet consumers' needs and desires. In other words, the money spent on "guns" leaves less for "butter," creating a drain on investment capital and raw materials, as well as on the scientists and engineers who would otherwise be engaged in commercial, export-oriented growth. The launch of the never-ending wars on terror, along with a redistribution of wealth through tax cuts to the wealthiest Americans during the George W. Bush and Trump administrations, have negatively impacted the economy, facilitating a financial downward spiral for the middle class.

---

[4] Nicholas Kristof, "We're No. 28! And Dropping!," *New York Times*, September 10, 2020.

[5] Ben Steverman and Alexandre Tanzi, "The 50 Richest Americans Are Worth as Much as the Poorest 165 Million," *Bloomberg*, October 8, 2020.

The Cost of Empire

Empire building costs money. According to the Watson Institute for International and Public Affairs, the cost for the so-called global war on terror exceeded $5.8 trillion—$2.313 trillion for Afghanistan and $2.058 trillion for Iraq (Crawford 2021, 1–3). These numbers will continue to soar as obligated long-term care is provided to wounded US veterans. Because what occurs in the domestic sphere impacts the foreign sphere, and vice versa, ethics transcends national borders. White supremacy and class exploitation at home are usually linked to aggressive military attacks throughout the two-thirds world as neoliberalism is established. The global struggle for survival is the same struggle faced by those who live on the margins within the empire. A correlation does exist between how the United States treats the marginalized throughout the Global South and how marginalized people within US borders are treated. According to Albert Camus, winner of the 1957 Nobel Prize for Literature, the worth of any society is measured by how it treats its marginalized people.

If true, what is the worth of the United States? The cost of a postwar Iraq, coupled with the George W. Bush and Trump administrations' tax cuts for the wealthy, sapped trillions from the nation's revenue, making it difficult—if not impossible—for those sinking deeper into poverty to ever recover. Can such an ethical system be called Christian? Pope John Paul II referred to such capitalism as "savage." Yet resources exist to end poverty in the United States. What seems absent is the will to do so. Could it be because those in control of economic policy benefit from maintaining these economic inequities? In the end, does refusing to hear the cry of the poor result in the loss of a nation's humanity, or even worse, its soul?

While a perfectly just society cannot be achieved here on earth, throughout human history, some cultures have proven to be more humane than others. These successes can help track our progress toward a more ethical moral order. Unfortunately, success within the United States continues to be measured by degrees of financial independence. At any twenty-year high school reunion, those who become doctors or lawyers and have six-figure incomes are deemed more successful than those who work as hourly laborers or in other nonprofessional positions. It is no surprise, then, that poverty is often viewed as an individual problem; a consequence of laziness, lack of intelligence, or self-motivation; or maybe just plain bad luck. The best and the brightest succeed, while the less than capable—through a social process of natural selection—are removed from the responsibility to govern. To protect and secure national tranquility, the "best and the brightest" attempt to keep the others at bay: the less worthy and the marginalized, who are usually people of color. Since the early years of this republic, this process has become institutionalized as part of the very fabric of national life, working to ensure power and privilege for the few.

From time to time, this attitude clearly manifests itself in the public sphere. The 2012 presidential election provided such an example. Republican candidate Mitt Romney was secretly recorded during a private fundraiser in Boca Raton, Florida, saying,

> There are 47 percent of the people who will vote for [Obama] no matter what. All right, there are 47 percent who are with him, who are dependent upon government, who believe that they are victims, who believe the government has a responsibility to care for them, who believe that they are entitled to health care, to food, to housing, to you-name-it. That that's an entitlement. And the government should give it to them. And they will vote for this president no matter what. . . . These are people who pay no income tax. Forty-seven percent of Americans pay no income tax. So our message of low taxes doesn't connect. . . . My job is not to worry about those people. I'll never convince them that they should take personal responsibility and care for their lives.[6]

Romney's comments seem to border on class warfare. Yet whenever the poor question the disparity of wealth in this nation, "class warfare" becomes a term used by politicians and political pundits to discredit them. To raise concerns about the ever-growing economic gap is to risk accusation of fomenting social unrest—or worse, being labeled a socialist. When billionaire capitalist Warren Buffett pondered in a *New York Times* op-ed column why he pays a lower tax rate than his secretary,[7] Fox News pundit Eric Bolling called him a socialist.[8] But after hearing candidate Romney's message to major donors, we are left wondering if indeed class warfare is already being waged by politicians protecting the superrich? If so, then it is obvious that they are winning!

---

[6] Rick Ungar, "Romney Fail: Caught on Video Revealing Extraordinary Contempt for 47 Percent of Americans," *Forbes*, September 17, 2012.

[7] Warren E. Buffett, "Stop Coddling the Super Rich," *New York Times*, August 14, 2011.

[8] Eric Bolling, Fox Business Network, August 15, 2011.

From the margins of society, voices have arisen to challenge the fairness of the perspective that the nation's poor are freeloaders looking for government handouts. Martin Luther King Jr. said it best: "Any religion that professes to be concerned about the souls of men [*sic*] and is not concerned about the slums that damn them, the economic conditions that strangle them and the social conditions that cripple them is a spiritually moribund religion awaiting burial" (1986: 38). The white nationalist Christianity that defends our current economic structures should perish. Let the dead bury the dead! The ethics of those privileged by present social structures will be explored in greater detail in this section of the book by examining poverty within the United States, how that poverty is maintained through the political system, and how death plagues those who are marginalized due to healthcare issues and the judicial system.

Chapter 9

National Poverty

Step 1: Observing

A bit of history is needed to understand poverty and the growing disparity between the poor and the wealthy within the United States. During the nineteenth century, when the emerging nation began to distribute its most precious resource through the Homestead Act—land stolen from Indigenous people—Black people were excluded from this land distribution, preventing them from establishing what became the nation's primary means to build generational wealth. During the Great Depression of the 1930s, the United States initiated programs that funneled large amounts of federal dollars into welfare initiatives to lift people mired in poverty. Known as the New Deal, legislation was passed to create a safety net to protect society's most vulnerable members, particularly the elderly. The New Deal sought to establish a social security pension for the elderly, a national minimum wage, and unemployment insurance; however, President Roosevelt could only get the legislation through Congress if he capitulated to the racism of southern Democrats who demanded that nonwhites—specifically Blacks— be excluded from these New Deal entitlements. Farm workers and servers, who were predominately of color, were also exempt.

As successful as the New Deal was in taming the Great Depression,[1] from its inception, nonwhites were excluded from federal programs designed to lift a nation out of poverty. Later that century, veterans of color, who risked their lives defending democratic principles during the Second World War, found themselves excluded from federal loan support programs and the G.I. Bill responsible for establishing a robust middle class during the 1950s.

---

[1] The success of the New Deal could be measured by the return of wage levels to their pre-Depression era and the reduction of unemployment from almost 25 percent to nearly zero on the eve of the Second World War. By 1949, only one-fifth of families were in the lowest earning quintile.

Despite exclusion based on institutionalized racism and ethnic discrimination, the 1950s witnessed a drop of those living in poverty—from 32 percent at the start of the decade to 22 percent by decade's end. Meanwhile, median family income was 43 percent higher in 1959 than in 1950. If we ignore sexism and racism for the moment, most families could, with one income, buy a house and car, take a vacation, and provide college education for their children. Two-income families were, for the most part, financially unnecessary to achieve these middle-class milestones. During the 1960s, with the War on Poverty and the civil rights movement, the income gap (difference between what the richest and poorest Americans earn) continued to narrow as unemployment dropped to a low 4.4 percent and income rose by 38 percent over 1959. Even the unemployment rates of Black men dropped twice as fast as that of white men. Increased employment opportunities for African Americans contributed to the poverty level falling by 50 percent, closing the 1960s at 12 percent (Cooper 1998, 347–49).

By the 1970s, multiple factors began to reverse this trend and rewiden the income gap. The energy crisis following the Arab-Israeli War brought income growth to a halt. By the close of the 1970s, median family income remained at 1973 levels while unemployment continued to rise, reaching 7.5 percent by 1980. With economic policies put in place after Ronald Reagan was elected in 1980, the income gap widened dramatically, and the middle class shrank. These new economic policies radically changed the distribution of wealth in this country. During the 1980s, the top 10 percent of the population increased their family income by 16 percent, the top 5 percent increased theirs by 23 percent, while the top 1 percent increased their income by 50 percent. Meanwhile, the bottom 80 percent lost income, with the bottom 10 percent down 15 percent, from $4,113 to $3,504 annually. At the beginning of Reagan's administration, the income of the top 1 percent was 65 times greater than that of the bottom 10 percent. By the end of the Reagan administration, the income of the top 1 percent was 115 times greater than that of the bottom 10 percent (Phillips 1990, 12–17).

The unweaving of New Deal safety nets was motivated by whites' resentment toward nonwhites receiving any type of governmental benefits, as best communicated by Reagan's coded narrative of a "welfare queen" driving a Cadillac or "young bucks" using food stamps to purchase "T-bone steaks." New Deal economic policies were replaced by a supply-side philosophy that consisted of cutting, if not eliminating, social services and benefits for the poor while providing tax breaks for the wealthy. The hope was that economic benefits given to the wealthy would "trickle down" to the less fortunate due to job creation. So-called Reaganomics pushed unemployment to almost 10 percent, median family income dropped to 6 percent below pre-1973 levels, and poverty rose from 11.1 to 14.4 percent. The bottom quintile of the American population received 4.7 percent of all income, a full percentage point below their 1973 level. From 1947 through 1979, real income had risen for all segments of society. Since the 1980s Reagan Revolution, income has risen only for the most affluent families (Cooper 1998, 338–54).

Throughout the 1990s, during the so-called economic boom of the Clinton years, only the top quintile increased its share of the nation's income.[2] From 1979 to 2000 the Congressional Budget Office (CBO) reported that the gap between rich and poor more than doubled as the United States experienced the greatest growth of wage inequality in the Western world (Wilson 1999, 27). Contributing to the widening income gap was the 1996 Welfare Reform Act, signed by President Clinton.[3] These radical economic changes within the United States have led to the smallest and fastest-shrinking middle class among all industrialized nations.[4] By 1999, at the close of the century, the top 1 percent of taxpayers each averaged $862,700 after taxes, more than triple what they had in 1979. Meanwhile, the bottom 40 percent was at $21,118 each, up by 13 percent from their 1979 inflation-adjusted average of $18,695. And while median household income reached its peak that year at $53,252, nevertheless, the year 2000 resulted in the greatest economic disparity since 1979, when the Budget Office began collecting such data.

The National Bureau of Economic Research, a nonpartisan, nonprofit research group, claimed that, by the close of the millennium, the top 1 percent enjoyed the largest share of before-tax income for any year since

---

[2] David Leonhardt, "In a Wealthy Country, Who Are the Truly Rich?," *New York Times*, January 12, 2003.

[3] Although initial reports indicated that hundreds of thousands of former welfare recipients moved off the rolls into jobs, providing a substantial raise in income, studies indicate a more disturbing trend. By 2003, seven years after the passage of the Welfare Reform Act, state and urban policy researchers demonstrated how a significant number of those left the welfare rolls were unemployed and had sunk to deeper levels of poverty. The Urban Institute in Washington, DC, estimates that one in seven families who left welfare from 2000 through 2002 had no work, spousal support, or government assistance—up from one in ten in 1999. Wade F. Horn, the assistant secretary of Families and Children within the Department of Health and Human Services, agreed with these figures. See Leslie Kaufman, "Millions Have Left Welfare, But Are They Better Off? Yes, No, and Maybe," *New York Times*, October 20, 2003.

[4] Keith Bradisher, "Widest Gap in Incomes? Research Points to the U.S.," *New York Times*, October 27, 1995.

1929.[5] For the next decade, all incomes except those of the ultra-rich steadily dropped. The top 1 percent garnered 65 percent of the entire nation's growth between 2002 and 2007.[6] According to the Federal Reserve, by 2010, real median household income dropped by 7.1 percent to $49,445 (DeNavas-Walt, Proctor, and Smith 2011, 5), literally wiping out almost two decades of accumulated prosperity.[7] The poverty rate in 2010 was 15.1 percent, the highest poverty rate since 1993, with 46.2 million people (the largest number in fifty-two years) living in poverty. The first decade of the millennium saw the median family income drop more substantially than it has during any era since the Great Depression.[8]

The 2008 Great Recession cemented, rather than reversed, the nation's wealth and income inequalities. According to the US Labor Department, in 2007, 1.7 million workers earned the minimum wage. By 2012, that number surged to 3.6 million. By 2012, during the first full year of so-called recovery from the Great Recession, 93 percent of income gains went to the top 1 percent while the remaining 7 percent was split among the other 99 percent of the US population. Those belonging to the top 1 percent of taxpayers made at least $352,000 in income. By 2022, a decade later, that number rose to $597,815 per year—a 58.9 percent increase. Compare this to the federal minimum wage in 2012, which was $7.25 an hour, the same amount in 2022. As executive pay soared, the median weekly earning of a full-time worker only saw a 1 percent increase in pay, from $747 to $756—but when we consider this so-called raise in constant dollars, wages actually fell by a little more than 2 percent.[9] During his 2013 State of the Union, President Obama mentioned raising the minimum wage from $7.25 to $9 and indexing it to inflation; this plan would have lifted hundreds of thousands of families above the poverty level. But when bills to this effect were introduced by Democrats, the Republican-controlled House of Representatives voted them down.[10] And yet, while income hit a fifty-year low, corporate profits continued to climb.

---

[5] Lynnley Browning, "U.S. Income Gap Widening, Study Says," *New York Times*, September 25, 2003.

[6] Steven Greenhouse, "Productivity Climbs, but Wages Stagnate," *New York Times*, January 13, 2013.

[7] Binyamin Appelbaum, "For U.S. Families, Net Worth Falls to 1990s Levels," *New York Times*, June 12, 2012.

[8] David Leonhardt, "Living Standards in the Shadows as Election Issue," *New York Times*, October 12, 2012.

[9] Natasha Singer, "C.E.O. Pay Gains Have Slowed, but the Numbers Are Still Numbing," *New York Times*, April 8, 2012.

[10] Annie Lowrey, "Six Faces of the Minimum Wage," *New York Times*, June 16, 2013.

The 2020 pandemic, and the inflation that took hold in its aftermath during 2022, promises to exacerbate income inequalities. A study questioning 9,494 respondents conducted by the Urban Institute over the summer of 2022 discovered that, even though food insecurity fell to its lowest levels over the past two decades, one in five adults experienced food insecurity during the previous thirty days. Among those employed (called with the oxymoronic phrase the "working poor"), 17.3 percent experienced food insecurity.[11] To make matters worse, food assistance programs like the Supplemental Nutrition Assistance Program (SNAP), which expanded benefits during the COVID-19 pandemic, came to an end in February 2023.[12] The program worked, reducing poverty by 9.6 percent and child poverty by 14 percent, keeping 4.2 million people out of poverty during the fourth quarter of 2021 (Wheaton and Kwon 2022, 2). Those most negatively impacted will, no doubt, be Black and Latine communities. We already know that the pandemic was economically devastating to these communities, who experienced higher infection and death rates, greater loss of jobs, and more failed businesses.

Decades of exclusionary economic policies are not limited to negatively impacting communities of color. True, those most affected by racist targeting are economically wounded. But studies reveal that the staggering cost of discriminatory policies is paid for by the entire country—including euroamericans. Besides an enormous creative loss as the talents of people of color are dismissed, an economic loss exists. According to a study conducted by economic analysts at Citigroup, if the four key racial gaps (wages, education, housing, and investment) between whites and Blacks would have been closed at the start of the new millennium, the 2020 US economy could have been $16 trillion stronger. If instead these gaps were closed in 2020, $5 trillion could have been added to US GDP by 2025. Additionally, more than 6 million jobs per year could have been added and $13 trillion in cumulative revenue gained if Black-owned business had equitable access to credit (Peterson and Mann 2020, 3, 7, 18, 36). But the United States seems to prefer holding on to the hatred undergirding racism and ethnic discrimination rather than engaging in the self-interested desire of benefiting from overall economic prosperity.

Nobel Laureate Joseph E. Stiglitz, former chief economist for the World Bank, fears the vicious cycle in which the United States currently

---

[11] Urban Institute, "Changes in Household Food Security among Adults Ages 18 to 64, March/April 2020 to June/July 2022," dataset from 2022.

[12] Michael Sainato, "The US Food Assistance Program Offered Expanded Benefits during the COVID Emergency, but They Ended Last Month," *The Guardian*, March 17, 2023.

finds itself: "Increasing inequality means a weaker economy, which means increasing inequality, which means a weaker economy. That economic inequality feeds into political economy, so the ability to stabilize the economy gets weaker."[13] Organizations that are not necessarily friendly to the global poor, like the International Monetary Fund (IMF), understand that income inequalities damage the ability of a country to experience long-term growth. Economists interpret this widening gap to mean slower job creation and lower levels of economic growth, mainly because wealth inequalities prevent most of the population from taking advantage of economic opportunities. "Growth becomes more fragile," according to Jonathan D. Ostry of the IMF, in countries like the United States that have high levels of income inequality.[14] Even our very democracy is threatened as the few (i.e., the Koch brothers) pour riches into political campaigns to elect candidates that will protect and secure the financial interests of a small elite class.

Step 2: Reflecting

Latin American liberation theologian Franz Hinkelammert insists that "the existence of the poor attests to the existence of a Godless society, whether one explicitly believes in God or not" (1986, 27). Nevertheless, most people within the United States hold the assumption that anyone can succeed if they just work hard enough—that anybody can grow up to become the president is the myth we install in our little boys (sexism starts young). The only thing that might hold them back is their own lack of initiative. The "Protestant work ethic," a term popularized by sociologist Max Weber, undergirds American society and preaches an equality of opportunities. Hard work in one's career is the calling to which God summons each of us. Every person is rewarded by God with material blessings, while those who fail to work hard are punished with poverty for their laziness.

Despite this assumption, it generally seems that, no matter how hard the poor work, they often continue to slip into deeper poverty. The growing disparity of wealth between the poor and the rich leads us to question if it is a "work ethic" issue or perhaps a "work ideology" issue that allows the wealthy and privileged to rationalize classism. Is wealth really a reward for hard work, and poverty a punishment for laziness? Or is there another

---

[13] Annie Lowrey, "Income Inequality Seen Blocking Economic Growth," *New York Times*, October 17, 2012.

[14] Stephanie Coontz, "Why Gender Equality Stalled," *New York Times*, February 17, 2012.

explanation for the accumulation of even greater wealth by those at the top of the economic ladder? Expanding poverty directly affects the well-being of our society: it leads to a rise in crime, drug and alcohol addiction, family disintegration, child abuse, mental illness, and environmental abuse. Instead of dealing with the causes of poverty and seeking a more equitable distribution of resources, those economically privileged seldom make the connection between their riches and the poverty of others. More often, they view their wealth as something earned, a blessing from God, or a combination of both. Just listen to the prayers of the well-off that mostly focus on thanking a deity for the possessions they have: a house, food, a job, a car. They tend to seek to insulate themselves from the consequences of their riches, moving to gated communities and sending their children to elite private schools.

Despite shielding themselves from the effects of poverty, even the rich make less when the poor are scantily paid. Henry Ford, the automobile manufacturer, understood this economic truth. In 1914 the Ford Motor Company paid an unprecedented five dollars a day to its employees. Ford believed that low wages weaken the market, causing the economy to become sluggish. Paying five dollars a day allowed his employees to make enough money to buy the product they were producing, the Model T. Well-paid workers create greater consumer demand for goods. Economists call this formula for economic expansion "the virtuous circle of growth." Thanks to capitalists like Ford, a middle class was created throughout the first three-quarters of the last century, before "the virtuous circle of growth" was philosophically replaced with "trickle-down" economics. While CEO salaries increase and record profits are posted, workers are pressured to accept wage freezes (if not cuts), work part-time or within a gig economy, or work with fewer employee benefits, such as health care.

Ethicists from the margins argue that communities that desire a just economic society must place the humanity of its members before economic development (code language for increasing corporate profits). Development today usually means short-term profit and often at the expense of the marginalized. Yet true development, economic as well as sociopolitical, takes place when society's treatment of its most vulnerable members enables them to pass from a less human existence to a more human condition. Circumstances faced by the poor are caused by oppressive structures that lead to the exploitation of workers, creating material want. The ethical quest for more humane conditions requires a set of social actions (praxis) designed to overcome extreme poverty, raise consciousness of classism, foster dignity for all people, develop an equitable distribution of the earth's resources, and secure peace.

Regardless of how we choose to define this more human condition, it remains threatened by increasing poverty. The so-called work ethic is debunked when the poor work, many full-time, simply to survive, when there are few if any options for work, and when the work is unrewarding and unfulfilling. Two adults working full-time at the federal legal minimum hourly wage of $7.25 in 2022 earn a before-tax yearly income of $30,160, which is insufficient to meet Maslow's bare necessities for survival: food, water, clothing, sleep, and shelter. According to the government, the official poverty level for a family of four in 2022 was $27,750 (US Department of Health and Human Services 2022, 3316). Although it appears that this family of four is making $2,410 above the poverty line, these figures are grossly misleading.[15] A full-time employee being paid the current minimum wage is unable to afford a fair-market two-bedroom rental anywhere in the United States.[16] A family with two working parents and two young children needs $79,244 a year, or about $18.76 an hour per worker, to cover life's bare necessities. If the job does not provide health care, then the amount needed is $83,544, or about $19.78 an hour (Suh, Clark, and Hayes 2018, 2). These numbers are averages. What is needed to survive varies by state. In Arkansas, a family of four needs $60,816 with benefits or $60,480 without, as opposed to those living in Washington, DC, where $124,320 is needed with benefits and $135,744 without (6). Although 33 percent of working adults (ages nineteen to sixty-four) in the United States lack economic security, most are of color. When sorted by race and ethnicity, euroamericans are the most likely to be economically secure while Latines are the least likely.[17]

While several government programs have helped reduce poverty, incorrect poverty assessments mask the real extent of poverty in

---

[15] The official definition of poverty masks the true extent of poverty in the United States. Poverty was defined sixty years ago by government statistician Mollie Orshansky, who herself recognized the shortcomings of the definition. The official definition of poverty (PT = 3 x SFB [Poverty Threshold = 3 x Subsistence Food Budget]) fails to consider the radical changes in consumption patterns since the early 1960s. It was originally based mainly on food consumption, which since then has become less expensive in relationship to housing, health care, childcare, and transportation. Changes in consumer patterns have converted the original formula into nonsensical numbers (Blank 2008, 233–39, 49–50).

[16] "Report: Minimum Wage Workers Have to Work 95 Hours a Week to Make Rent in Colorado," ABC Denver, June 9, 2017.

[17] Institute for Women's Policy Research, "Basic Economic Security in the United States: How Much Income Do Working Adults Need in Each State?," October 2018.

America. Misrepresenting the true level of poverty within the United States does serve a purpose. Politicians can argue that public spending on the poor has had little evidentiary effect, and it, therefore, should be discontinued. For example, citing flawed calculations of the poverty level during his 1988 State of the Union address, Ronald Reagan was able to declare, "My friends, some years ago the federal government declared a war on poverty and poverty won." With this flawed citation, he justified the dismantling of the social safety net. And yet, it is that same safety net (Social Security; food stamps; earned income tax credits; the Women, Infants, and Children [WIC] program; and more) that has kept some 40 million people out of poverty, according to the Center on Budget and Policy Priorities.[18] If we were to recalculate the definition of poverty to mean less than the figure required for economic security, we would discover that millions more Americans live in actual poverty than published government figures convey.

The dismantling of the New Deal meant that, over the long haul, working families are unable to earn a living wage. Many are forced to skip meals, forgo paying rent, or postpone necessary medical care. A study conducted by the National Low Income Housing Coalition titled "Out of Reach 2021" found that low-income workers are unable to find an affordable, modest one- or two-bedroom rental in any state of the union. Most real estate professionals calculate that rents or mortgage payments must be less than 30 percent of total family income to consider housing expenses affordable, yet the average renter's hourly wage ($18.78) means that the average renter must work fifty-three hours per week to afford a modest two-bedroom apartment. Households headed by people of color are more likely than white households to have renters who earn extremely low incomes. Not surprisingly, the task of finding a rental is a greater challenge for people of color who also face housing discrimination (Aurand et al. 2021, 2, 7).[19] With the onset of inflation during the spring of 2022, rents are outpacing wages, only exacerbating an already difficult predicament.

Many of the wealthy, and those who represent them politically, oppose safety-net programs like Social Security, welfare, Medicare, the more recent Affordable Care Act (aka Obamacare), or the Build Back Better-based

---

[18] Peter Edelman, "Poverty in America: Why Can't We End It?," *New York Times*, July 29, 2012.

[19] Twenty percent of Black households, 18 percent of Native American or Alaska Native households, 14 percent of Latine households, and 10 percent of Asian households are extremely low-income renters, compared to just 6 percent of white households.

initiatives, claiming that such government programs interfere with the private market. Nevertheless, the dismantling of safety-net programs has had devastating effects on the US family. With each passing year, the poor sink deeper into despair. Society's most vulnerable find it difficult to simply survive. Once the benefits associated with the COVID-19 government relief packages expired, 7.8 million Americans fell into poverty; this included many who lost jobs, homes, and retirement funds—especially people of color—who never recovered (Han et al. 2020, 1). Yet a minority of the population appeared to have benefited from our culture's economic structures during the pandemic and other times of crises. Why are there fortunes to be made during an era of global deaths? Consider that, during the pandemic, American billionaires saw their collective wealth soar by more than 70 percent, or about $5 trillion.[20]

The ten richest men in the world doubled their wealth during the first two years of the COVID-19 pandemic, from a combined $700 billion to $1.5 trillion—or roughly $15,000 per second. Meanwhile, the income of most of humanity dropped during this same time as 160 million more people were forced into poverty. By 2030, some 3.3 billion people will be living on $5.50 per day. If these 10 men were to lose 99.999 percent of their wealth tomorrow, they would still be richer than 99 percent of all the world's inhabitants (Ahmed et al. 2022, 7–8, 19–21). Some experienced historically unparalleled increases in their net worth, like Elon Musk (Tesla) who went from being worth $27 billion at the start of the pandemic to $294.2 billion by January 2022 (up 1,016 percent). Steve Bezos (Amazon) saw his wealth increase during this same period to $202.6 billion from $113 billion (up 67 percent).[21] For these uber-rich, spaceships have replaced yachts as the ultimate status symbol.

How quaint it now seems that, during the early 1960s, CEOs made only twenty times as much as their average worker. George

---

[20] Tami Luhby, "Billionaires' Wealth Has Soared 70% in the Pandemic." CNN, October 28, 2021.

[21] The other nine who financially benefited during the pandemic are: Bernard Arnault (LVHM) at $187.7 billion (up 130 percent); Bill Gates (Microsoft) at $137.4 billion (up 31 percent); Larry Ellison (Oracle) at $125.7 billion (up 99 percent); Larry Page (Google) at $122.8 billion (up 125 percent); Sergey Brin (Google) at $118.3 billion (up 125 percent); Mark Zuckerberg (Facebook) at $117.7 billion (up 101 percent); Steve Ballmer (Microsoft) at $104.4 billion (up 85 percent); and Warren Buffett (Berkshire Hathaway) at $101.5 billion (up 40 percent). Larry Elliott, "World's 10 Richest Men See Their Wealth Double during Covid Pandemic," *The Guardian*, January 16, 2022.

Romney—CEO of American Motor Association and father of the 2012 presidential candidate Mitt Romney—declined a $100,000 annual bonus in 1960 (among other incentives) because he believed he was making too much money. As he told his board of directors at the time, no executive should be paid more than $225,000 a year—almost $2.1 million in today's money. Mr. Romney was not alone in this way of thinking. When John O. Ekblom, CEO of Hupp Corporation, was offered a $110,000 bonus to his $42,000 salary, he refused, stating, "The total sum of $152,000 far exceeds my needs and my appetites."[22]

Damage to human existence goes beyond just an increasing wealth gap. This obscene concentration of wealth in a few hands contributes to the deaths of at least 21,300 people each day, or one person per second (Ahmed et al. 2002, 12–13).[23] Additionally, the 20 richest billionaires are responsible, on average, for emitting eight thousand times more carbon into the environment than the billion poorest people on the planet (7, 13, 22).[24] So, we must again ask: why do we continue to maintain and sustain this unjust economic arrangement?

The Rich Get Richer

Who supposedly benefits from the present economic system? Why does the income gap continue to widen? We can begin to answer these questions when we first consider that the pay schedule of CEOs has increased at the expense of workers' wages. In 1975, corporate leaders made forty-four times as much as the average factory worker. During the early 1980s, CEOs such as Roberto Goizueta of Coca-Cola and Michael Eisner of Disney convinced stockholders to link their compensation to company stock prices. As a result, by 1985, the average CEO's salary rose to seventy times that of the average worker; by 1990 it was one hundred times that worker's annual income.[25] Between 2003 and 2007, the average chief executive salary increased by 45 percent, compared with a measly 2.7

[22] "Romney Cuts Pay to $225,350, Refusing $100,000 of His Bonus," *New York Times*, January 6, 1960.

[23] Inequality of resources is responsible for an estimated 5.6 million people dying each year in poor countries due to lack of health care, and in a world of plenty, 2.1 million die each year from hunger.

[24] It is conservatively estimated that, by 2030, some 231,000 people will die each year due to climate change in poor countries.

[25] David Leonhardt, "The Imperial Chief Executive Is Suddenly in the Cross Hairs," *New York Times*, June 24, 2002.

percent increase for the average worker (Ebert, Torres, and Papadakis 2008, 7). When the Great Recession occurred in 2008, corporate leaders were earning 299 times as much as the average worker. Two years later, when many workers lost their jobs to outsourcing or were forced to take pay cuts, the earnings of CEOs increased to 325 times that of the average worker (Anderson et al. 2011, 3). A decade later, the income gap only grew more, to 670 times the average worker's wage. Amazon's new CEO is being paid 6,474 times the company's median pay. Meanwhile, workers' wages nationwide fail to keep up with the average 4.7 percent inflation (Anderson and Pizzigati 2022, 1–2).

At the start of the 2000 down market, compensation rules were rewritten once it became obvious that production goals would not be met. This pattern of increasing pay during bear markets was modified after the 2008 Great Recession. While CEOs took pay cuts (11 percent in 2008, 15 percent in 2009, and 30 percent in 2010) due in part to stockholder revolts, they still made a major portion of their earnings on the value realized from exercised stock options.[26] Hence, by 2011 top executive pay levels had rebounded nearly all the way back to pre-2008 recession levels (Anderson et al. 2011, 4). Profits are privatized while losses are socialized. That year, the nation's two hundred top-paid CEOs enjoyed a median income of $14.5 million, a 5 percent pay raise over the previous year.[27] In spite of all the news concerning stockholders' revolts and holding CEOs accountable for outsized compensation—which led to their salary cuts— the fact remains that most CEOs had better financial packages in 2012 than they did in 2007, the year before the Great Recession. Additionally, many executives have created exceptionally profitable exit strategies amounting to $100 million (and up). For example, Gene Isenberg of Nabors Industries received $126 million when he exited as CEO and IBM's CEO Sam Palmisano received $170 million, while Google's CEO Eric Schmidt received $100 million.[28]

A trend that was identified as far back as 2001 continues today. Increases of CEO wages became tied to decreased workers' wages as the latter were understood as an expense. Those CEOs who announced layoffs of one thousand or more workers earned higher compensation than those who did not announce layoffs, one study found (Anderson et al. 2001, 6–7).

---

[26] Scott DeCarlo, "What the Boss Makes," *Forbes*, April 28, 2010.

[27] Nathaniel Popper, "CEO Pay, Rising Despite the Din," *New York Times*, June 17, 2012.

[28] Gary Strauss, "The Golden Parachute Is Evolving into the Platinum Kiss," *USA Today*, November 8, 2011.

For example, the CEO of Best Buy, Corie Barry, enjoyed a 30 percent raise ($15.6 million) and a $4.7 million cash bonus after she laid off five thousand employees, most of whom had full-time employment with benefits, effectively increasing her CEO-to-worker pay ratio to 521:1 (Anderson and Pizzigati 2022, 7). David Calhoun of Boeing, which reported a $12 billion loss in 2020, received $21.1 million (up from $422,390 in 2019) after firing thirty thousand workers. Frank Del Rio of Norwegian Cruise Line had his pay doubled to $36.4 million (from $17.8 million in 2019) after reporting a $4 billion loss and laying off 20 percent of the company's workforce, and Chris Nassetta of Hilton received $55.9 million (up from $21.3 million) after a reported $720 million loss and eliminating a quarter of the corporate staff.[29]

Workers suffered in other ways as well. The 1938 Fair Labor Standards Act established a forty-hour workweek, discouraging employers from assigning longer hours by forcing them to pay time-and-a-half on any worker's weekly hours that exceed the standardized forty. By 1975, exemptions were added that excluded "highly paid executives" who could work up to seventy hours a week with no additional pay. The problem is that "highly paid executive" was defined as anyone who supervised two other employees and was being paid as little as $13,000 a year. This loophole, exploited by the service and retail industries, has meant longer work hours for the average American without an increase in wages.[30]

Racism

The 2019 poverty rate for euroamericans was 7.3 percent, compared to Black people at 23.8 percent or Latines at 28.1 percent. The 2019 median household income for euroamericans was $76,057. Contrast this figure with Latines' median income of $56,113 and $45,438 for Blacks (Semega et al. 2020, 4, 15). Accumulated wealth during that same year illustrated these severe disparities. Compare the median and mean wealth of euroamerican families at $188,200 and $983,400 respectively, with that of a typical Black family at $24,100 and $142,500, or a typical Latine family at $36,100 and $165,500 (Bhutta et al. 2020). The pandemic only made matters worse. According to an analysis conducted by the Federal Reserve Bank of St. Louis, for every dollar that a typical euroamerican household

---

[29] David Gelles, "C.E.O. Pay Remains Stratospheric, Even at Companies Battered by Pandemic," *New York Times*, April 24, 2021.

[30] Rose Eisenbrey, "Just What the Worker Needs—Longer Days, No Overtime," *Los Angeles Times*, February 14, 2003.

had in 2021, a Latine household had 21 cents, while a Black household had 12 cents.[31]

Predatory banking contributes to the poverty of Black and Latine people. For example, Wells Fargo Bank former loan officer Beth Jacobson claimed in her 2009 affidavit that her employer saw Black neighborhoods as fertile ground for high-interest subprime mortgages, pushing customers who could qualify for prime loans into subprime agreements. One of her colleagues referred to the subprime mortgage applicants as "mud people" and to the loans as "ghetto loans." Jacobson, the bank's top-producing subprime loan officer, noted, "Wells Fargo's mortgage had an emerging-markets unit that specifically targeted Black churches, because it figured church leaders had a lot of influence and could convince congregants to take out subprime loans."[32] A racial divide existed as to the type of loans people obtained. Eric Halperin, director of the Center for Responsible Lending, pointed out, "We've known that African Americans and Latinos are getting subprime loans while whites of the same credit profile are getting the lower-cost loans."[33]

In 2006 Wells Fargo's subprime mortgages charged an interest rate of at least three percentage points above the federal benchmark, financing costs were higher, and prepayment penalties were imposed, making refinancing to lower interest rates to keep one's house out of foreclosure a financial impossibility.[34] The bank has admitted that, since 2016, it forced customers to pay unnecessary fees and opened millions of fake accounts in their names. At one branch, employees were told that if they did not meet their targets, they would be "transferred to a store where someone had been shot and killed." In 2020 former chief executive John G. Stumpf was fined just $17.5 million for his role in creating a toxic environment that foisted unwanted products and sham accounts on millions of customers.[35]

When the housing bubble burst in 2007, most of those who took on these subprime loans, disproportionately those of color, were left

---

[31] Ana Hernández Kent and Lowell Ricketts, "Has Wealth Inequality in America Changed over Time? Here Are Key Statistics," Federal Reserve Bank of St. Louis, December 3, 2020.

[32] Michael Powell, "Suit Accuses Wells Fargo of Steering Blacks to Subprime Mortgages in Baltimore," *New York Times*, June 7, 2009.

[33] Ibid.

[34] Gretchen Morgenson, "Baltimore Is Suing Bank over Foreclosure Crises," *New York Times*, January 8, 2008.

[35] Stacy Cowley and Emily Flitter, "Former Chief of Wells Fargo to Be Penalized with Rare Fine," *New York Times*, January 24, 2020.

destitute—widening the wealth gap between them and euroamericans. Furthermore, municipalities like Baltimore, Cleveland, and Buffalo faced waves of foreclosures, experienced reduced tax revenues, and saw increased costs for city services. Abandoned houses cost such cities more in services as they attempted to ward off crimes like arson, sex work, and drug use. The chief solicitor for the Baltimore City Law Department, Suzanne Sangree, best explained the damage banks like Wells Fargo have caused neighborhoods of color: "This wave of foreclosures in minority neighborhoods really threatens to undermine the tremendous progress the city has made in developing distressed neighborhoods and moving the city ahead economically."[36]

People of color are relegated to inner-city poverty and segregated from the middle class, making it difficult for them to break through barriers that foster and maintain their poverty. Last to be hired, they are also among the first to lose their jobs during downsizing, as was the case during the pandemic in 2020. For example, Latinas and Black women faced disproportionately higher unemployment than any other populations a year after the start of the pandemic.[37] Although numerous studies demonstrate the reality of racism (and sexism), for our purposes it suffices to acknowledge that racism leads to lower wages, greater financial burdens, and fewer opportunities to transcend the consequences of poverty.

Corporations:
The Unfair Distribution of the Tax Burden

In 1952, corporate taxes represented 32 percent of taxes collected by the federal government; by 2012, the corporate share was only 7.9 percent. After the 2017 passage of the Tax Cuts and Jobs Act, the corporate income tax was cut to 21 percent from 35 percent. This contributed to the corporate share to drop further to 7 percent, with some corporations obtaining a windfall that eliminated their tax liability altogether. For example, in 2017, FedEx owed more than $1.5 billion in taxes. After the passage of Trump's $1.5 trillion tax cuts, FedEx owed nothing. Instead, the multibillion-dollar corporation was due a rebate. FedEx was not alone. One year after Trump's corporate tax cuts took effect, 91 profitable Fortune 500 companies (including Amazon, Chevron, Halliburton, and IBM) had a tax bill of $0 on their US income; another 56 companies had an effective tax rate of 2.2

---

[36] Morgenson, "Baltimore Is Suing Bank over Foreclosure Crises."

[37] Ella Koeze, "The Job Recovery Is Slowest for the Disadvantaged," *New York Times*, March 10, 2021.

percent, and 195 profitable companies in the Fortune 500 had an effective tax rate of slightly over half the 21 percent rate under the new law. Five companies (Bank of America, JP Morgan Chase, Wells Fargo, Amazon, and Verizon) collectively enjoyed $16 billion in tax breaks (Gardner, Roque, and Wamhoff 2019, 4–5).

One of the arguments used to justify the 2017 passage of the Tax Cuts and Jobs Act was that corporations that have moved their operations abroad to avoid taxes would be incentivized to bring those jobs back to the United States. They did not. The expectation was that the new tax savings would position companies to increase investment in new equipment and other job-creating assets. This, too, did not happen. Two years after the tax cuts went into effect, no statistically meaningful relationship was found between the size of the tax cut a company received and the investments it made. What helped FedEx convince the government to provide these tax cuts was the $10 million it spent in 2016 on tax-focused lobbyists. These same lobbyists played a pivotal behind-the-scenes role in shaping the final bill, meeting regularly with Senate and House committee staff responsible for writing its provisions and working with the Treasury in shaping the regulations of the tax-cut implementation.[38]

Three years after the tax cuts were issued, not much has changed. Fifty-five of the largest US corporations still paid no federal corporate income taxes during the 2020 fiscal year despite enjoying substantial pretax profits within the United States. These include companies like Charter Communications, Duke Energy, and Salesforce. Through the manipulation of deductions and legal loopholes, these 55 corporations avoided paying a collective total of $8.5 billion in taxes that would have been due that year if they would have paid the legislated 21 percent tax rate. Instead of paying their share, they received $3.5 billion in tax rebates. This means that their total corporate tax breaks for 2020 ($8.5 billion in tax avoidance and $3.5 billion in rebates) came to $12 billion (Gardner and Wamhoff 2021, 1, 3). According to a US Treasury report, from fiscal year 2017 when the Trump tax cuts took effect to 2018, the federal budget deficit increased by $113 billion (US Department of the Treasury 2019, 2). Meanwhile, corporate tax receipts dropped by approximately $90 billion, accounting for nearly 80 percent of the deficit increase.[39] At the time, the Congressional Budget Office projected that the Trump corporate tax cuts would increase deficits

---

[38] Jim Tankersley, Peter Eavis, and Ben Casselman, "Intense Lobbying by FedEx Slashed Its Tax Bill to $0," *New York Times*, November 17, 2019.

[39] Galen Hendricks, Michael Madowitz, and Seth Hanion, "Trump's Corporate Tax Cut Is Not Trickling Down," Center for American Progress, September 26, 2019.

by about $1.9 trillion over eleven years. By 2019 the debt rose to $23.2 trillion, making the debt-to-GDP ratio the highest since the Second World War. By the end of 2020, the national debt increased to $27.75 trillion, up 39 percent from $19.95 trillion when Trump took office.[40]

Another route many corporations take to eliminate paying the appropriate portion of their taxes is by registering their companies in tax havens like the Cayman Islands while keeping their working headquarters in the United States. The Cayman Islands' population in 2022 was 67,250.[41] According to the British territories' Chamber of Commerce, it is home to 117,000 companies.[42] This means there are 42.5 percent more companies on the island than there are people. One Cayman Islands building, the Ugland House, is the business address for more than 20,000 companies. Many of the largest corporations within the United States maintain subsidiaries in such offshore tax havens. Seventy-three percent of the Fortune 500 (about 366 companies) collectively operate 2,213 tax haven subsidiaries. They hold more than $2.6 trillion in accumulated profits offshore for tax purposes (with four companies—Apple, Pfizer, Microsoft, and General Electric—accounting for a quarter of the total). These maneuvers have led to an annual $100 billion avoidance of federal income, meaning individual taxpayers must make up every dollar these corporations avoid paying (1–2).

Apple and Citigroup provide us with examples on how these tax havens operate. Apple has shielded $246 billion offshore, a greater sum than any other company's offshore cash pile. The company structured two subsidiaries in Ireland that resulted in them being neither taxable residents of the United States (from where they are managed and controlled) nor of Ireland (where they are incorporated). In 2017, before the implementation of Trump's tax cuts, Apple utilized their subsidiaries to avoid paying $76.7 billion in US taxes on their earnings. The company used this tax haven structure to pay a rate of just 0.005 percent on its European profits in 2014 to Ireland. The financial services company Citigroup maintains 137 subsidiaries in offshore tax havens. It reported $47 billion offshore for tax purposes on which it would have owed $13.1 billion in US taxes. Instead, in 2017, Citigroup only paid a 7 percent tax rate on its offshore profits, which went to other foreign governments. They paid little to no tax on most of the money that they parked in tax havens (2).

---

[40] Allan Sloan and Cezary Podkul, "Trump's Most Enduring Legacy Could Be the Historical Rise in the National Debt," *Washington Post*, January 14, 2021.

[41] Worldometer, "Cayman Islands Population," online database.

[42] Vanessa Burke, "Almost 117,000 Companies Registered in Cayman," Cayman Island Chamber of Commerce, January 18, 2022.

Apple and Citigroup are not alone in their quests for the greatest possible tax avoidance scheme. In 2017, some of the major corporate abusers of tax havens were Nike, Pfizer, PepsiCo, and Goldman Sachs. Through its offshore tax haven in Bermuda, Nike sheltered $12.2 billion, avoiding $4.1 billion in US taxes. The corporation only paid a 1.4 percent tax rate to foreign governments. Ironically, although they operate 1,142 retail stores globally, none are in Bermuda. Pfizer, the world's largest drug manufacturer, operates 157 subsidiaries holding $198.9 billion in profits, thus saving the company from remitting $40.7 billion in US taxes. PepsiCo, with its 133 subsidiaries, avoided paying US taxes on $44.9 billion, and Goldman Sachs, with 905 subsidiaries, avoided paying $31.2 billion (2–3).

These foreign subsidiaries are not just leveraged for tax avoidance. Before Dick Cheney resigned his tenure as CEO of Halliburton—a major war profiteer—to become George W. Bush's vice president, he used the company's offshore tax haven subsidiaries to circumvent US laws and conduct business with Iran during the trade embargo.[43] According to a Congressional Research Service report, American multinational companies collectively reported 43 percent of their foreign earnings at five small tax-haven countries: Bermuda, Ireland, Luxembourg, the Netherlands, and Switzerland. These countries accounted for 4 percent of the companies' foreign workforces and 7 percent of their foreign investments (2). In effect, multinational corporations, thanks to numerous loopholes, choose what they want to pay in taxes.

At the time of this writing, attempts are being made to globally close these tax havens through a negotiated international agreement aimed at ending the race to the bottom of international tax rates. The Group of 7 agreed on a global minimum tax rate of 15 percent regardless as to where a corporation headquarters its office. Additionally, some of the largest companies (e.g., Amazon, Facebook, and Google) would pay taxes to countries based on where their goods and services are sold, not the tax haven where their headquarters are located.[44] If the Senate ratifies this agreement, along with closing other loopholes as per Biden's 2021 tax plan, it can add $700 billion of current tax avoidance to the US coffers over ten years.[45] The 2022 razor-edge division of the Senate, however, was dooming the

---

[43] Robert M. Morgenthau, "These Islands Aren't Just a Shelter from Taxes," *New York Times*, May 6, 2012.

[44] Alan Rappeport, "G7 Finance Leaders Reach a Deal to Curb Offshore Tax Havens," *New York Times*, June 6, 2021.

[45] Jim Tankersley and Alan Rappeport, "Biden Tax Plan Aims to Curtail Use of Havens," *New York Times*, April 8, 2021.

process as one senator, Joe Manchin (D-WV), announced his intention to scuttle the global tax agreement, siding with all Republicans in the Senate to protect US corporations' ability to continue using tax havens.[46] The global tax agreement failed to be included in the Inflation Reduction Act of 2022, meaning that major multinational corporations will continue to avoid contributing their fair share to the federal and local tax bases.

The Inflation Reduction Act signed by President Biden on August 16, 2022, contained a watered-down version of a corporate minimum tax. US corporations will no longer depend on multiple deductions, credits, and loopholes to report no income or negative income to tax authorities while reporting profits to shareholders. Starting in 2023, companies will have to calculate their taxes using two methods: the 21 percent income tax as before and the 15 percent corporate minimum tax. Whichever figure is higher is the tax that is due. This will impact around 150 of the world's largest companies, including Apple, Citigroup, Nike, Pfizer, PepsiCo, and Goldman Sachs. However, to get the last Senate holdout, Kyrsten Sinema (D-AZ), to support the bill and ensure fifty votes (plus the vice president as the tie-breaking vote), the bill had to include a provision that allowed companies to carry forward prior year losses to offset future income, credit for research and development expenses, and deductions on capital investments such as machinery, vehicles, and buildings. Still, according to the Joint Committee on Taxation, the new tax will add approximately $222 billion to government coffers over the next ten years.[47]

Billionaires:
The Unfair Distribution of the Tax Burden

The current US tax code continues to harm the poor, specifically those who are of color. Euroamericans represent 67 percent of all taxpayers. They earn approximately 77 percent of the total US income, yet they received 79.5 percent of the $1.9 trillion individual and business tax cut benefits generated by the 2017 Tax Cuts and Jobs Act. African Americans, who represent 10.2 percent of taxpayers, earn 6 percent of the nation's income but received 5 percent of the same benefits. Latines, who represent 11.9 percent of taxpayers, earn 8 percent of the income but receive 7 percent of the benefits. This means that in 2018, the first year the tax-cut bill went

[46] Alan Rappeport and Jim Tankersley, "How Joe Manchin Left a Global Tax Deal in Limbo," *New York Times*, July 19, 2022.

[47] Rose Horowitch and David Lawder, "Explainer: How Could the New U.S. Corporate Minimum Tax Affect Companies?," Reuters, August 11, 2022.

into effect, whites received $218 billion in tax cuts while Blacks and Latines received a combined total of $32 billion. These disproportionate rates held true regardless of economic class (Wiehe et al. 2018, 4–5).

Neoliberal doctrine asserts that entrepreneurs and business owners should control the economy, for they are, after all, the so-called job creators. Because the rich supposedly have specialized or exceptional entrepreneurial skills and experience, they receive greater disposable income through tax cuts. A trickle-down effect is supposed to result. Unfortunately, this has never happened. A study conducted by the London School of Economics examined eighteen industrial countries (including the United States) over a fifty-year period (1965–2015). The study explored economic outcomes by comparing countries that implemented tax cuts with those that did not. They discovered that the per capita gross domestic product and unemployment rates were nearly identical after five years in countries that reduced taxes on the rich and in those that did not. One difference did emerge. The incomes of the wealthy grew at a faster rate in countries where tax rates were lowered. Rather than trickling down to the middle class, tax cuts for the wealthiest just helped them keep more of their riches while exacerbating income inequality (Hope and Limberg 2020, 4–6).

Lyndon B. Johnson was the president who lowered the top marginal tax rate to 70 percent. Ronald Reagan, who ushered in the tumbling of tax rates, lowered it further to 50 percent. Since then, the top rate has hovered between 30 and 40 percent. From 1980 to 1990, the poorest 20 percent of the population saw their tax liability increase by 10 percent while the richest 5 percent of the population enjoyed a 12.5 percent reduction in taxes (Cooper 1998, 345). By 2000, the top four hundred wealthiest taxpayers in the United States represented 1 percent of all income obtained, a figure that had quadrupled in the eight years since 1992. Yet their tax burden dropped from 26.4 percent in 1992 to 22.3 percent by 2000.[48]

According to Internal Revenue Service data obtained and published by ProPublica in 2021, the wealthiest Americans—including plutocrats like Warren Buffett, Elon Musk, and Jeff Bezos—paid little in federal income taxes despite their soaring fortunes. The wealthiest Americans only paid on average 3.4 percent in taxes in recent years. For example, Buffett officially paid 19 percent ($23.7 million) in federal income taxes on his reported total income of $125 million from 2014 through 2018. However, if his actual income of $24.3 billion during that period would have been taken into

---

[48] David Cay Johnston, "Very Rich's Share of Wealth Grew Even Bigger, Data Show," *New York Times,* June 26, 2003.

consideration, his "true tax rate" was only 0.10 percent. Others fared even better than Buffett. Bezos, the world's richest man, paid no taxes in 2007 and 2011 (the latter year receiving a $4,000 tax credit). The second-richest man in the world, Elon Musk, paid no taxes in 2018. Michael Bloomberg, Carl Icahn, and George Soros, among others, had years when they did not pay a penny in taxes. Even the former president, Donald Trump, paid no income tax for ten out of the fifteen years prior to becoming president. One year, he only paid $750.[49]

Taken collectively, the twenty-five richest Americans from 2014 through 2018 paid a true tax rate of 3.4 percent, somewhat less than the 14 percent tax rate for those earning $70,000 or the 37 percent rate for those earning $628,300.[50] For the first time in US history, thanks to Trump's 2017 tax cuts, billionaires paid a lower tax rate in 2018 than the working class.[51] The wealthy can aggressively bend tax laws with lowered (or eliminated) anxiety about being audited. When Congress asked the IRS why it disproportionately audited the poor rather than the wealthy, the agency responded that it simply lacked the funds and staff to properly audit the affluent, and that auditing the poor was relatively easy.[52] Congress has slashed funding to the IRS each year since 2010. The IRS workforce in 2022 was 80,000, the same size as in 1970. Not surprisingly, audits of millionaires have declined by more than 70 percent since 2010. Lack of resources and personnel makes it impossible to crack down on those who push the legal limits of the law to lower their tax bills and have the means to hire armies of accountants to fend off any audit.[53] Only 10 audits were conducted in 2019 on households that reported income over $10 million, compared to 16,607 and 6,578 audits conducted on households that reported less than $25,000 and $25,000 to $50,000, respectively (Internal Revenue Service 2022, 36).

---

[49] Russ Buettner, Susanne Craig, and Mike McIntire, "The President's Taxes: Long-Concealed Records Show Trump's Chronic Losses and Years of Tax Avoidance," *New York Times*, September 27, 2020.

[50] Jesse Eisinger, Jeff Ernsthausen, and Paul Kiel, "The Secret IRS Files Trove of Never-Before-Seen Records Reveal How the Wealthiest Avoid Income Tax," ProPublica, June 8, 2021.

[51] In 2018, the four hundred wealthiest families paid an average effective tax rate of 23 percent, as opposed to the bottom half of American households that paid a rate of 24.2 percent. See Dominic Rushe, "Trump's Tax Cuts Helped Billionaires Pay Less Than the Working Class for First Time," *The Guardian*, October 9, 2019.

[52] Paul Kiel, "IRS: Sorry, But It's Just Easier and Cheaper to Audit the Poor," ProPublica, October 2, 2019.

[53] Alan Rappeport, "Trump Tax Case Shows a Squeeze in IRS Funding," *New York Times*, December 23, 2022.

Financially starving the IRS led to a $7 trillion "tax gap" during the 2010s, as tax revenue is owed by the uber-wealthy but goes uncollected.[54] Because everyone does not pay their fair share of taxes, the middle class is squeezed, contributing to their downward financial spiral.

The main reason the super-rich pay so little is that the United States places an emphasis on taxing income derived from labor rather than wealth. Most of the income of the richest among us is in the form of capital gains, which is taxed at a maximum rate of 15 percent, far below the maximum tax rate applied to salaries and wages. Some progressive legislators, like Senator Elizabeth Warren (D-MA), have championed a 2 percent tax on individual net worth above $50 million, but her proposal has garnered little support, even within her own party. With the passage of the 1986 tax bill, President Reagan equalized the top rate on capital gains (28 percent) with earned income. The real decline of capital gains tax rates began with the Clinton administration in 1997 to assure passage of the Children's Health Insurance Program. The drop of the capital gains tax to levels lower than when Herbert Hoover was president occurred under George W. Bush's administration, in the Job and Growth Tax Relief Reconciliation Act of 2003.

The tax cuts—advocated by then-president Bush—to the wealthiest Americans at the start of the millennium were reportedly based on a trickle-down economic theory that promised a higher rate of economic growth that never materialized. Although real gross domestic product (GDP) growth peaked in 2004 at 3.6 percent with the implementation of tax cuts to the wealthiest, it quickly faded. Even before the Great Recession, the real GDP was growing at an annual rate of less than 2 percent.[55] The same occurred with the Trump tax cuts to the wealthiest. Although Trump promised 3 percent growth with his tax plan, the GDP only grew by 2.3 percent. By the end of his term, the Gross National Product (GNP) showed that the championed tax cuts for the uber-wealthy did nothing to substantially boost the economy. In fact, real business investment declined for three quarters in a row during 2019, the worst stretch since the last recession.[56] Contrast these dismal economic results due to tax cuts with the robust growth that occurred with the 1982 and 1993 US tax increases. In 1984, real GDP rose 7.2 percent and continued to rise at more than 3

---

[54] Ibid.

[55] Bruce Bartlett, "Are the Bush Tax Cuts the Root of Our Fiscal Problems?," *New York Times*, July 26, 2011.

[56] Jared Bernstein, "It's Official: Trump's Tax Cuts Were an Economic Bust," Insider, February 1, 2020.

percent per year for the remainder of the 1980s; in 1994, real growth averaged 4 percent for the remainder of the 1990s.[57]

Recalling that George W. Bush inherited a projected $6 trillion surplus when he took office, we are left wondering how we arrived at a $6 trillion cumulative deficit by the close of his presidency. Tax cuts for the wealthiest Americans had and continue to have a devastating effect. By 2011, more than 90 percent of the tax savings went to taxpayers in the top quintile of the population, and nearly half of all the benefits went to the top 10 percent (Fieldhouse and Pollack 2011, 1–2). Revenue, according to the Congressional Budget Office (CBO), was reduced by at least $2.9 trillion below what it would have been between 2001 and 2011.[58] The CBO also notes that lower-than-expected growth further reduced revenue by $3.5 trillion; additionally, a higher-than-expected $5.6 trillion in spending helped create the country's fiscal dilemma.

The Trump tax cuts—as already noted—also went to the wealthiest individuals. Sixty percent of the tax savings went to those in the top quintile.[59] Revenue, according to the CBO, was reduced by 7.6 percent the following year (2018) or some $275 billion.[60] Corporate tax revenues fell by 31 percent in the first year after the tax cuts were passed. By the end of Trump's term, the federal deficit was at almost $1 trillion.[61] The CBO predicts that the budget deficit will grow to 5.4 percent by 2030, approximately 27.8 percent greater than projections before the Trump tax cuts.[62]

Tax cuts to the wealthy negatively impact the federal deficit. Higher interest payments are required to finance the deficits. Implementation of the Bush tax cuts from 2001 to 2010 added $2.6 trillion to the public debt, or 50 percent of the total national debt accrued during this period (Fieldhouse and Pollack 2011, 3). The Trump tax cuts' impact on the federal deficit was just as damning. His tax cuts contributed $1.8 trillion through 2029 to the federal debt. If we factor in his spending policies, the debt will

---

[57] Bartlett, "Are the Bush Tax Cuts the Root of Our Fiscal Problems?," July 26, 2011.

[58] Ibid.

[59] Scott Horsley, "After 2 Years, Trump Tax Cuts Have Failed to Deliver on GOP's Promises," NPR, December 20, 2019.

[60] William G. Gale, "Did the 2017 Tax Cut—the Tax Cuts and Jobs Act—Pay for Itself?," Brookings Institution, February 12, 2020.

[61] Horsley, "After 2 Years, Trump Tax Cuts Have Failed to Deliver on GOP's Promises."

[62] Christian Weller, "Trillion-Dollar Deficits in Expanding Economy," *Forbes*, January 29, 2020.

mushroom by an additional $3.4 trillion to $3.8 trillion.[63] And here is the irony: as Trump ran up the budget deficits during his first prepandemic years in office to levels not seen except during major wars or financial crises, Biden faced Republican deficit hawks, in addition to two Democratic senators, when he sought tax cuts through his Build Back Better bill for the poor.

In the final analysis, the only thing that the Trump tax cuts (and those of Bush before him) accomplished was to place more money in the hands of the uber-wealthy and multinational corporations. Why, then, defend tax cuts to the wealthiest when it clearly is detrimental to most Americans? Those who benefit from the upward transfer of wealth wield tremendous political power. According to the CBO, fully eliminating the Bush tax cuts for the wealthiest 2 percent of Americans would have immediately increased national revenues by about $690 billion over the following ten years, in addition to $140 billion in debt service that otherwise would have been needed to maintain the tax cuts. That comes to $830 billion in savings (Bogusz et al. 2010, xi–xv). As to Trump's tax cuts, 60 percent of Americans at the lowest end of income distribution gained less than $1,000 in tax savings; the top 1 percent saved $51,000. These numbers are due to the rate changes and the reduction of corporate taxes coupled with the rise in corporate profits that created higher incomes for the wealthiest households. Hence, the biggest winners of Trump's tax cuts were corporations and the households that receive income from corporate profits. Those who benefited were the wealthiest 10 percent of Americans, those who own 84 percent of all stocks. Along with the richest Americans, congressional representatives also profited. Cutting tax rates on companies in which many lawmakers (mainly Republicans) own stock contributed to them enriching themselves, according to a Center for Public Integrity analysis of legislature members' financial disclosure forms.[64]

The Biden administration sought to reverse much of the 2017 tax-cut legislation passed by his predecessor, whose legacy was enriching the wealthy. Generally, Republicans believe economic growth trickles down from the top to the bottom while Democrats believe growth is built from the bottom up. For Republicans, cutting taxes on corporations and wealthy individuals would stimulate businesses to expand, create

[63] Committee for a Responsible Federal Budget, Budgets & Projections, "President Trump's $4 Trillion Debt Increase," June 25, 2019.

[64] Teresa Ghilarducci, "Five Good Reasons It Doesn't Feel Like the Trump Tax Cut Benefited You," *Forbes*, April 9, 2019; Peter Cary, "Republicans Passed Tax Cuts—Then Profited," Center for Public Integrity, January 24, 2020.

more jobs, and generate greater wealth for everyone. This is known as the Laffer Curve, developed by Arthur Laffer to theoretically justify the Reagan tax cuts of the 1980s. Unfortunately, when the principles of the Laffer Curve were implemented by Reagan, Bush, and Trump through tax cuts on the wealthy, no data prove that new jobs were created, businesses expanded, or growth materialized. Instead, the rich got richer and the poor poorer. For most Democrats, the best way to generally stimulate economic growth and spur global competitiveness is to make huge financial investments in infrastructure, technology, and education by raising taxes on corporations and the wealthiest Americans. Educating women, preventing child poverty, and leveling the playing field are prerequisites for national economic success.

In March 2021, Biden signed into law the American Rescue Plan, which delivered a large tax cut to lower-income Americans. This was a temporary, one-year plan in which taxpayers with an income under $75,000—on average—were exempt in 2021 from paying taxes, with most among lower-income Americans receiving refunds instead.[65] The administration's hope of making these cuts permanent, along with increasing corporate taxes and the tax rate on the top 1 percent, seems hopeless in the divided Congress that marks Biden's administration.

Step 3: Meditating

How relevant are the words of the prophet Jeremiah, who said, "Woe to those who build their palace on anything but integrity, their upper rooms by injustice, making their compatriots work for nothing, not paying them for their labor" (22:13)? Historically, individuals who commit themselves to a life of Christian service would renounce all earthly possessions so as to be used by God. But are today's Christians required to renounce their riches to become disciples of Jesus? The early church wrestled with issues of wealth, concluding that any riches possessed by Christians were to be used for the betterment of the community. Yet this concept is not well accepted within a capitalist economic structure. Individuals pursue their own economic self-interests, believing that an "invisible hand" will ensure economic benefits for all of society.

Perhaps Adam Smith's economic theories of supply and demand may be relevant in a society dominated by small businesses and petty merchants, where no one seller can control the market but must compete with others.

---

[65] Stephen Silver, "Biden Tax Cut and Stimulus Checks vs. Trump Tax Cut: Which Was Better?," *National Interest*, April 27, 2021.

In today's economy, however, Smith's theories are outdated. In the United States today, the corporation controls the means of production, sets the pricing for the merchandise or service, and determines the wage for producing the merchandise or service. Prices are often kept artificially high and wages artificially low.[66] Defenders of our present system of capitalism see no inherent conflict between Christian morality and the pursuit of profit by whatever means necessary. It is assumed that each person has an absolute right, if not a moral obligation, to follow economic self-interest as a duty in creating a more just society. Yet the biblical text calls us to "Be subject to one another in the fear of the Lord" (Eph. 5:21). We are called to put the needs of the other before our own. How, then, can these two opposing views be reconciled within a wealthy Christian community?

Some prosperity gospel televangelists have proclaimed a "name it and claim it theology," and some ministers preach that God wants God's children to be rich. Poverty, for these, is the consequence of a lack of faith on the part of the disenfranchised. For example, televangelist Benny Hinn proclaimed, "Poverty is from the devil and God wants all Christians prosperous." During several of his sermons he has led his congregation in repeating the phrase "The wealth of the wicked is mine" (McConnell 1995, 175). Kenneth Copeland begged his virtual audience to make donations to his ministry so that he could maintain his private jet. He did not want to deal with the hassles of travel during a time of COVID-19, which required safety protocols like masking. He believed that the "mark of the beast" was the COVID-19 vaccine.[67] Should it be surprising that such a theology finds fertile soil within a capitalist "Christian" culture? It even explains why the poor are still with us; obviously they lack faith in God. Nonetheless, throughout the Gospel of Luke, we read the opposite of what today's prophets of wealth proclaim. The poor both inherit the reign of God and become the instrument by which the rich can discover their own salvation.

In Luke 16:19–31, Jesus tells the story of a poor man named Lazarus. According to the biblical text, there once was a very wealthy man who was accustomed to feasting on only the very best. At the gate of his mansion lay Lazarus, a poor man covered with sores, dreaming of a future that provided him with scraps that fell from the rich man's table. When both

---

[66] Karl Marx did predict that, with the passage of time, small businesses and petty merchants would gradually be absorbed by larger industries until a concentration of industrial power rests in the hands of a few capitalists.

[67] Jennifer Lee, "Kenneth Copeland Wants Private Jet to Avoid Vaccine Mandate," *Christianity Today*, September 25, 2022.

men died, Lazarus was carried by the angels to the bosom of Abraham while the prosperous man was sent to hell to be tormented for all eternity.[68] The rich man, seeing Lazarus held in Abraham's arms, pleaded for mercy. He begged to have a few drops of water placed on his tongue to cool the agony of the flames. But Abraham refused, for a great gulf separated heaven from hell. The rich man then asked to have Lazarus go back to his family to warn them of the danger of their "mammon." This, too, was denied, for, as Abraham stated, "If they were not willing to hear Moses and the prophets, even if one from the dead should rise, they will not be persuaded."

Nowhere in the text does it tell us that the rich man's wealth was accumulated unjustly or that he was directly oppressing Lazarus; his judgment and condemnation to hell were because he failed to share his resources with those such as Lazarus who lacked the basics for survival. To ignore the plight of the dispossessed is to deny one's humanity. In this case, God's judgment was not based on anything the rich man did, or any belief system he confessed, or any particular church he attended. He was condemned for failing to give to the very least of God's children. He failed to use his resources so that others could also enjoy an abundant life. If we are truly to love our neighbor, and if this commandment is to be the biblical basis that informs our ethics, then it is immoral to ignore our neighbor's hunger as we continue to store away our riches. To do so is to be called a fool by Christ (Lk. 12:16–21).

Although the Lazarus story condemns the rich, we must ask then, who in our time will proclaim the good news of salvation from materialism? While an analysis of this text and others that focus on the plight of the rich has become commonplace, all too often our gaze remains fixed on the wealthy man and not others. Perhaps this is because most of us read the text from the social location of the middle class, and the message of this story in Luke is reduced to a charitable act demanded of the wealthy. But what happens if we read the text from the perspective of Lazarus? We may discover that it wasn't a sin of commission that resulted in the eternal condemnation of the rich man but a sin of omission.

What if Lazarus had been the subject instead of the object of the story? What if, instead of sitting by the gate dreaming about the scraps that might fall from the rich man's table, Lazarus had been proactive? What if Lazarus had demanded food, shelter, and clothes—not out of a sense of

---

[68] It is interesting to note that, while the text provides us with the name of Lazarus, the one from the margins, it does not name the rich man, who, no doubt, was known and honored by the community at large.

pity, but based on his human right to survive? What if Lazarus had sought solidarity with others made poor by the prevailing economic structures, and joined forces with them to demand structural changes within society? What if Lazarus had confronted the rich man with his sin of greed and hoarding? What if the rich man, upon hearing Lazarus's demands, had repented? Then salvation as liberation from sin would have also come to the rich man, and he too could have found comfort in the arms of Abraham.

Even though the rich man forfeited salvation by refusing to fulfill his ethical responsibility to the poor man, the poor are still responsible for acting as moral agents to create a just society. Those who are privileged by the way society is constructed are in need of liberation and salvation because they are also created in the image of God. God desires all, the rich and the poor, to enter into a saving knowledge of God's grace. When the marginalized seek out the liberation of the oppressors, they verify the humanity of both the privileged and themselves (De La Torre 2003).

Jesus of Galilee, coming from the margins, challenged the rich in the hope that they would find their own salvation through solidarity with the poor. To say one is a disciple of Christ is to commit one's life to those without—those for whom the gospel message claims Christ opted. Such a commitment to the poor is not ideological but praxological, a practiced expression of faith. In the Gospel accounts, some wealthy persons did find God's salvation, as in the case of Zacchaeus (Lk. 19:8–10), who, when confronted with his sin of hoarding wealth, pledged to repay back four times over what he received through fraudulent means; he then split the remainder of his wealth between himself and the poor. These actions led Jesus to proclaim that, on that day, salvation had come to the house of Zacchaeus. For others, the path to heaven was impossible to achieve, as in the case of the rich young ruler (Lk. 18:24–25), who, while pious and virtuous in keeping the commandments, still walked away from salvation out of reluctance to share his wealth with the poor.

According to Christian theology, Jesus incarnated himself into the lives and plight of the poor. For the church to discover its own salvation, it must do likewise. If not, those who refuse to walk in solidarity with "the least of these," the marginalized, join the rich young ruler and renounce a basic principle of Christianity regardless of how moral they may appear to be. Simply stated, one cannot be a Christian and remain complicit with social structures that privilege wealth. In our world, the privileging of wealth has been and continues to be insidiously entwined with privileging whiteness and masculinity. The gospel message says that it is the people on the margins who are the salvific agents for the recipients of society's power and privilege. They are the stone rejected that becomes the builder's cornerstone. In other words, no one gets into heaven without a letter of recommendation from the dispossessed, the disinherited, the disenfranchised.

Perhaps the rich man's salvation did not occur because Lazarus failed to demand a place at the banquet table. Those who exist on the margins of society also bear a burden in that they have a sacred trust and ethical responsibility to evangelize the dominant culture about the danger of power and privilege. But how? By coming together, organizing, and demanding that those in power obey God's command not to sell the poor "for a pair of sandals" (Amos 8:6). Not only will the rich find their salvation through their solidarity with the poor, but the poor will also facilitate this process by demanding from the rich their rightful share, working out their own salvation in "fear and trembling." Additionally, the humanity of the dispossessed is regained as they actively seek the humanity of their oppressors. Through repentance can come salvation.

Step 4: Case Studies

1. The Protestant work ethic is interwoven into the essence of being an American. Hard work leads to prosperity while laziness leads to poverty. With a combination of intelligence and ingenuity, anyone can climb out of poverty and strike it rich. In the land of opportunity where the American Dream is possible for anyone, those who are poor have no one to blame but themselves. After all, as the saying goes, "God helps those who help themselves." Financial success has come to be interpreted as favor within God's eyes, while economic disenfranchisement is understood as the consequence of sin (sloth) or simply not being elected or chosen by God. And yet, according to Jerome Powell, chair of the Federal Reserve under the Trump and Biden administrations, "We think of ourselves and we've always been a country where anybody can make it from the bottom to the top. But the data show now that actually the chances of making it from the bottom to the top in the United States are lower than they are in many other comparable countries."[69]

• Is Powell right? Or can anyone make it? Is poverty due to character flaws or structural classism and racism? How then do we deal with poverty?

• What does it say about the United States, the richest country in the world, that on any given night, over half a million Americans lack housing, forced to sleep in public spaces? Another 18 million spend more than half

---

[69] Zachary B. Wolf and Will Houp, "Inequality Is an Undeniable Fact in America," CNN, September 12, 2019.

of their income on housing, causing financial insecurity. The government calculates that $600 for housing is the most someone living at the poverty line can afford and still have something left over for food, health care, and other necessities. Houselessness will only increase as inflation and an unstable economy take their toll. Is houselessness a consequence of unforeseen personal tragedies, or is it the systemic symptom of a savage capitalism that generates and perpetuates a preferential option for the rich through a reverse Robin Hood tax structure?

• A cure for houselessness exists; the nation is simply unwilling. Our tax laws are written to privilege the rich, especially those who invest in real estate by means of interest deductions and depreciation write-offs. If these billions of dollars in subsidies to the rich were to be shifted toward the houseless, every American would be able to be housed. If this is true, why don't we do it? Is it because we have been hardwired to interpret subsidies to *us* as earned, while if they are for *them*, is it a handout making them dependent on the government? Or is the reason greed and indifference?

• Should housing be defined as a human right?

2. The United States does not have a spending problem; what it has is a revenue-collecting problem. Tucked away in the 2017 Tax Cuts and Jobs Act was the creation of "opportunity zones," a law that allowed the wealthy to avoid taxes if they invest in projects or companies in designated geographical locations that supposedly are low-income. Investors could sell their stocks and other investments and plow their proceeds into opportunity zones, thus delaying capital gains taxes for seven years. After ten years the investor can cash out (i.e., sell the opportunity zone real estate) and owe nothing in taxes. Profits from those projects in which they invested could avoid federal taxes altogether. The purported aim was to coax investors to channel funds into poor neighborhoods with the goal of creating opportunities for the poor. Instead, opportunity zones served as a tool for the rich to avoid paying capital gains taxes on safe and lucrative projects as they poured investment profits into luxury apartments, hotels, and storage facilities—employing relatively few workers in the process.

• Republican campaign donor and billionaire Wayne Huizenga Jr. built a luxury condominium development in a superyacht marina in West Palm Beach (a short drive north of Mar-a-Lago) thanks to former Florida governor Rick Scott, who designated this upmarket peace of real estate as an opportunity zone after a direct appeal from Huizenga. In making his choice, the governor rejected poorer tracts that the city of West Palm Beach asked to be named opportunity zones. The law authorizes governors to distribute valuable tax breaks that have been wielded to benefit the politically connected, rewarding political donors. Such misuse of power may be unethical, but it is not illegal. Should it be? Should such opportunity zones be rescinded? What recourses, if any, exist for such a once-in-a-lifetime bonanza to the wealthiest among us? Only those with unrealized and thus untaxed capital gains can invest—in other words, the wealthy. Is it problematic to help the poor by financially benefiting the rich through incentives?

• It is hard to gather information on opportunity zones because reporting requirements were stripped from the bill that created them. Why? Who benefits from this obscurity? The creation of these opportunity zones has led to the creation of almost nine thousand domestic tax havens. Half of all funds went to the best-off 1 percent of zones. Projects like the Ritz-Carlton Hotel and complex in downtown Portland, Oregon, benefited from being located in an opportunity zone, while 84 percent of truly needy zones received no money.[70] Can these opportunity zones be reformed as President Biden vowed to do, or are they so corrupt that they are beyond reform?

• Those connected to Trump—like his son-in-law Jared Kushner, former governor Chris Christie, Richard LeFrank, and Anthony Scaramucci—were among the first to benefit from opportunity zones. These friends and family of Trump profited from laws Trump enacted. Although legal, is it ethical? Do public servants have a right to make money in the private sector? Should the wealthy who hold political office be penalized by laws preventing them from profiting from investments? If such laws existed, would we have politicians who are economically closer to the average people who vote than the plutocrats? Or should fiscal investment of all politicians be mandatorily placed in blind trusts?

3. In 1993, 28 percent of children lived in poverty. Prior to the pandemic, the percentage of children in poverty—across all races and ethnicities—experienced a downward trend, reaching 14.4 percent (10.5 million), the lowest level in forty years.[71] During the pandemic, the trillions of dollars in stimulus payments provided income guarantees for families

---

[70] David Wessel, "Another Tax Loophole for the Rich," *New York Times*, October 12, 2021.

[71] Still, two in ten Latine children (21%) lived in poverty in 2019, down from 35 percent in 2010. Also, 26 percent of Black children remained impoverished, dropping from 39 percent in 2010. Even so, Black and Latine children were three times more likely than Asian (7 percent) and white (8 percent) children to be living in poverty. See Deja Thomas and Richard Fry, "Prior to COVID-19, Child Poverty Rates Reached Record Lows in U.S.," Pew Research Center, November 30, 2020.

with children. The American Rescue Plan of 2021 was signed into law by President Biden to further reduce child poverty to 12.1 percent through the expanded monthly child tax credit payments to families (Parolin, Collyer, and Curran 2022, 1–2). The impact was significantly felt by Black and Latine children who saw their poverty rates drop by 3.8 and 6.1 percentage points, respectively.[72] However, with the expiration of the monthly payments in January 2022, child poverty spiked to 17.5 percent (12.5 million children) as 3.7 million children entered or reentered poverty (Parolin, Collyer, and Curran 2022, 1–2). Seventy-one percent of children living in poverty are Indigenous, Latine, or Black.[73] An attempt was made by Congress to extend payments, but it failed because Senate Republicans, along with Democratic senator Joe Manchin, worried that parents would spend the money on drugs.[74] Out of forty countries, the richest nation in the world ranks thirty-eighth in child poverty.

• Some of the reasons for our dismal standing regarding child poverty include the lack of universal health care, minimal spending on early childhood education, and a lack of direct child allowances. These shortcomings contribute to the high rate of food insecurity that dangerously impacts child development.[75] What other reasons exist? Is the American Dream that children will enjoy a better standard of living than their parents no longer attainable? How do we reverse the increased poverty rate of children?

• The 2017 tax bill doubled the federal child tax credit to $2,000. A quarter of Americans who filed for the credit (parents to 35 percent of eligible children) earned too little to fully qualify for the full credit, receiving but a portion of the full amount, with the poorest receiving the smallest portion. Ten percent received nothing. Those excluded from a full credit represent 53 percent of Blacks, half of Latines, and 70 percent of single mothers. Because the credit was expanding to those earning as much as $400,000, wealthy taxpayers are receiving the full credit, costing the govern-

---

[72] Bryce Covert, "There Is a Solution to Child Poverty," *New York Times*, May 8, 2022.

[73] Organisation for Economic Co-operation and Development, "Poverty Rate," 2021.

[74] Ibid. Poverty rates among Latine children rose to 27.3 percent while among Black children, the increase was to 29.2 percent. In contrast, the rates of white and Asian children in poverty remained relatively stable. See Yiyu Chen and Dana Thomson, "Child Poverty Increased Nationally during Covid, Especially among Latino and Black Children," Child Trends, June 3, 2021.

[75] Organisation for Economic Co-operation and Development, "Poverty Rate."

ment $127 billion a year. How is this tax cut an antipoverty initiative? Or is it not? How are such programs systematically racist, sexist, or classist? Or are they not? Has the 2017 Tax Cuts and Jobs Act been good for the country? Why or why not? If not, what changes should be considered? How can such changes be enacted in the present political climate?

Chapter 10

Politics

Step 1: Observing

As the nation emerged from the Great Depression, the US business community, resentful of powerful labor unions and government regulation of their industries, was left demoralized and in disarray. President Franklin Roosevelt successfully used religious imagery to sell his New Deal, which was picked up by liberal ministers and preached from their pulpits. How, then, could the business community counter what they perceived to be the New Deal's so-called socialist leanings? They understood resistance to New Deal policies could be effective if it could be tied to religiosity.

Their efforts began in 1940, when five thousand titans of industry (the heads of such companies as Standard Oil, General Motors, Sears, General Electric, and Mutual Life) gathered at the Waldorf-Astoria Hotel for the annual meeting of the National Association of Manufacturers (NAM). They experienced their own revival—what would become the foundation of a white Christian nationalist modern manifestation. At the meeting, Reverend James W. Fifield preached against the sins of Roosevelt's New Deal, arguing that salvation could only be found through free enterprise and deregulation. The titans of industry were not the cause of the Great Depression; they were the saviors of the nation from ungodly socialist policies. Fifield suggested that clergy could be the means to regaining the upper hand in the capitalist struggle against Roosevelt's liberal policies. This watershed moment bound Christianity and capitalism as soulmates (Kruse 2015: 6–8).

The Pew brothers, J. Howard and Joseph N., ran Sun Oil and reviled Roosevelt, believing he was leading the nation toward socialism and secularism. Committed to Christian libertarianism, they became Fifield's patrons during the mid-1940s, outsourcing the task of persuading citizens to embrace capitalist ideology to the church. They would later back an obscure tent revivalist and fiercely pro-capitalist preacher named Billy Graham to continue the work of preaching not just against the New Deal but also the Fair Deal, the New Frontier, the Great Society, and civil rights. The solution to racism, Graham preached, could only be remedied with Christ's second coming. The Pews were committed to using their petroleum fortune to remake the Republican Party by driving out moderates. The religious movements they financed believed that, once religious leaders realized they had something to fear from the liberalism of the New Deal, they would eagerly join the capitalists in the battle for the soul of the nation (17–18). Advocates of outsourcing pro-capitalist ideology to the church prepared fertile ground that would give rise to a nationalist Christianity that merged the state with the growing power of a corporate-connected group of wealthy, white male capitalists steadfast in their opposition to social gospel–inspired policies.

With the eventual capture of the White House by Ronald Reagan, wealthy, conservative white Christians set out to reclaim a greater influence in directing the nation. Flush with victory, the Council for National Policy (CNP) was created on May 18, 1981, and tasked with bringing together conservative religious, business, political, and media leaders. Paul Weyrich, who was responsible for establishing the Moral Majority and Heritage Foundation, was a cofounder of the CNP.[1] His goals were clear: "We are talking about Christianizing America. We are talking about simply spreading the gospel in a political context" (Lambert 2008, 224). The CNP successfully merged the antigovernment, low-tax, fringe wing of the Republican Party with the Religious Right. A symbiotic relationship developed in which the business community provided financial funding for Religious Right grassroots organizations who, in turn, supported capitalist ideals. As David Kirkpatrick, the *New York Times* reporter who attended the CNP's August 2004 meeting, noted, the group consists of "a few hundred of the most powerful conservatives in the country [who meet] behind close[d] doors at undisclosed locations . . . to strategize about how to turn the country to the right."[2]

This turn to the right, however, became difficult due to the changing national ethos. With the start of the new millennium, white births declined, resulting in less than 50 percent of all births; same-gender-loving marriages became the law of the land; abortion was a constitutional right; law enforcement started to be held accountable for decades of abuse; and white affirmative action began to be dismantled. Worse, as the first decade

---

[1] David D. Kirkpatrick, "Club of the Most Powerful," *New York Times*, August 28, 2004; David Von Drehle, "Social Conservatives' Ties to GOP Fraying: Weyrich's Disillusion 'Touched a Chord,'" *Washington Post*, February 28, 1999.

[2] Kirkpatrick, "Club of the Most Powerful."

of the new millennium neared its last two years, a Black man occupied the White House. CNP members, and whites in general, felt they were losing their country.

The election of Barack Obama to the presidency in 2008 and his reelection in 2012 were warning shots across the bow of white nationalism. Minoritized communities went to the polls in mass and voted. Obama was elected in 2008 in part by a surge of new voters, many of whom were people of color registered to vote for the first time. This scared those who assumed the political arena was their birthright, those who feared the unraveling of a white affirmative action program that—since the foundation of the republic—secured their unearned power, privilege, and profit. America needed to be great again. For many, Donald Trump's ascension to the presidency made him their great white hope for reclaiming lost territory. Making the White House white again was the undergirding objective, even if it meant many Republicans literally held their noses as they cast their votes and provided unquestioning support for Trump.

If the Republican minority ideology was to have dominance in the political arena of the future, if the goal was to "own the libs," then a strategy was required that would hamper fair elections. From the moment Barack Obama took the oath of office, a national political strategy was developed that led to political structural advantages where Republicans could control the federal government without ever needing to win a majority of votes. These advantages were only strengthened by Republican-controlled state legislatures and a Republican-appointed majority on the Supreme Court. The resurgence of an extreme right-wing political ideology that led to the rise of the Trump presidency and the further oversized influence of corporations in the political process can be traced to a seminar held for wealthy donors at the St. Regis Resort in Aspen, Colorado, by the libertarian industrialist Koch brothers.

Corporations and the wealthy, like Charles and Fred Koch, took over the mantle from the Pew brothers. In 2010, the Kochs, two of the richest men in the world, with a calculated net worth at the time of $50 billion each (per *Forbes* calculations, up from $532 million in 1982), laid out a ten-year strategy to shift the United States to a smaller and less regulated country with fewer taxes. First, they proposed conducting grassroots activist education, best demonstrated in financing the formation of Americans for Prosperity, the political action group responsible for galvanizing Tea Party organizations and their causes. Second, they influenced the political electoral process, contributing more than $60 million during the 2000s ($275 million since 1986) to foundations, think tanks (e.g., the Cato Institute, founded by Charles Koch in 1974), front groups (e.g., Americans for

Prosperity, founded by David Koch in 2004), and state political candidates (through political action committees) to mold public opinion and legislators along libertarian positions (Barlett and Steele 2012, 29–30). For example, one of the organizations they created—Citizens for the Environment—advocated the notion that many of the environmental problems supposedly faced by the United States, like acid rain, were myths.

The strategy that got us as a nation to this point began locally. By controlling state governments, laws can be changed and oppositional voices suppressed and silenced to facilitate control of federal government entities, positions, and offices. In turn, control of the federal government would provide the means to control the courts, which would possibly render decisions that could move the nation further to the far right. The goal was not to elect those who put the nation first or even to uphold a eurochristian agenda, but to strengthen extreme conservative business ideologies that would put the interest of the privileged few first, an interest shamelessly wrapped in the flag and concealed in the Bible.

The Koch brothers were always less interested in the religious issues of conservative movements (e.g., the Religious Right) than in the economics of less government and lower taxes. What truly mattered to them was realization of their economic goals, moving the center of the discourse closer to their corporate ideology. Differences between candidates may be noticeable on social issues, but on the goals and aims of big business, differences are measured by minor degrees. The strategy the Koch brothers laid out bore fruit with the election of Donald Trump.

Control of State Government

A whitelash against the election of a Black man two years earlier led Republicans to spend $30 million to flip 680 state legislative seats and 20 state chambers. Winning state legislatures in 2010 was crucial because that was the year when voting maps were redrawn based on the new census report. This electoral success allowed Republicans to redraw 55 percent of congressional districts to their favor and control national politics for a decade—regardless of a Democrat capturing the White House. What was behind this political tidal wave? While many factors contributed to the shift in power, one underexplored major contribution is the Koch brothers' financial support of local candidates.

Drawing new voting maps positions the party in power to gerrymander, ensuring a hold on power even if the party creating the new maps receives fewer partisan votes. For example, in the 2012 congressional election—the first election employing new maps drawn after the 2010 state victories—

most Americans cast their votes for Democrats rather than Republicans, meaning that the 113th Congress, if majority ruled, should have been a Democratic-controlled House. Yet, due to gerrymandering, it was instead a Republican-controlled House. Sophisticated gerrymandering created safer district seats for the party in power.

Gerrymandering effectively minimizes the demographic shifts toward greater representation of minoritized communities. Imagine a state with five congressional districts comprising only one hundred voters—sixty of whom are euroamericans and forty of whom are Black. Equal congressional representation would mean two of the congressional districts would lean toward representing the interests of African Americans while three would be representative of euroamerican views. But let's say that Republicans, who tend to be white and conservative, control the state legislature and are thus charged with redrawing the political map. Fearing people of color, who tend to be more liberal and vote Democratic, Republicans redraw the map to minimize those more left-leaning voices. They draw district lines to ensure that each of the five districts have twelve euroamericans and eight African Americans; thus all five congressional seats are safely within the Republican column. This process is known as "cracking." But what if Democrats control the state legislature? They then can redraw the maps so that two districts solely comprise Republicans and thus reduce their influence to just two congressional representatives while increasing their minority party to represent three districts. This process is known as "packing."

Gerrymandering, an antidemocratic strategy that allows legislators to choose their voters—thus creating safe seats for themselves—is employed by both parties, negatively impacting communities of color.[3] Since 2010, the greater damage has been wrought by Republicans. Once Republicans controlled a state legislature, they turned to a little-known redistricting expert, Thomas B. Hofeller, to play a central role in redrawing the voting maps in 2011. After his death in 2018, tens of thousands of maps and documents were discovered on his computer. Once publicized, they demonstrated the role that race and ethnic discrimination played in gerrymandering. Hofeller's success can be noted, for example, in North Carolina—an emerging swing state that was safely kept in the Republican column by using racial statistics, making Latine ethnicity and race a constant when drawing district lines on a map.[4] In 2012, Democrats won

---

[3] Nick Corasaniti and Reid J. Epstein, "Map by Map, G.O.P. Erasing Black Districts," *New York Times*, December 18, 2021.

[4] Michael Wines, "G.O.P. Gerrymanderer and His Broad Reach," *New York Times*, September 11, 2019.

50.6 percent of North Carolina's statewide congressional vote but only picked up four of the thirteen House seats. Even though racial gerrymandering is illegal, a five-to-four decision by the 2019 Supreme Court[5] made it difficult for federal courts to hear challenges. Stating that partisan gerrymandering is legal, the court's Republican-appointed majority ignored how often racial and ethnic demographics play roles in partisan gerrymandering. For example, because 90 percent of Georgia's African American voters cast their votes for Democrats in 2020, officials drawing gerrymandered voting maps could argue they were only considering politics and not race.[6]

In states that were becoming swing states in 2010 (Michigan, Wisconsin, and Pennsylvania), GOP supermajorities were created through gerrymandering, leaving voters powerless to change state legislative leadership even though these states were narrowly divided along the lines of partisan registered voters. During the decade after redistricting, none of these states lost any of the two chambers even as voters elected Democrats as governors, senators, or president. As regressive as 2010 was, redrawing of the voting maps after 2020 would be worse. Texas, North Carolina, Ohio, and Georgia are being added to the list of states in a Republican stranglehold. Through gerrymandering, these state legislatures will be able to withstand a blue wave, ensuring political dominance for the rest of the decade.[7]

Because Republicans controlled the redrawing of 187 congressional seats as opposed to the 84 seats Democrats got to redraw in 2020 (the rest are drawn by independent panels), a further decade-long devaluation of the electoral voice of communities of color should be expected. Consider North Carolina, where Trump carried the state by only 1.3 percentage points. This evenly split state does not reflect the voting map drawn by Republicans, who have given themselves an advantage in 10 of the 14 congressional districts.[8] In 2010, of 435 congressional districts, 73 of them were competitive. Based on how the voting maps were drawn in 2020, fewer than 40 are competitive.[9] As effective as gerrymandering is, it is not enough. Political dominance for the minority political party can also be assured by making the voting process burdensome through

---

[5] *Rucho et al. v. Common Cause et al.*

[6] Corasaniti and Epstein, "Map by Map."

[7] Nick Corasaniti, "Maps Give G.O.P. a Stranglehold in Swing States," *New York Times*, November 26, 2021.

[8] Reid J. Epstein and Nick Corasaniti, "Jagged Maps Tilt Key Races toward G.O.P." *New York Times*, November 15, 2021.

[9] Reid J. Epstein and Nick Corasaniti, "New Voting Maps Erase Competitive House Seats," *New York Times*, February 7, 2022.

demanding voter identification, purging voter rolls, restricting early voting, and employing intimidating poll watchers.

Given that poor people of color disproportionately lack drivers' licenses, the demand for voter identification is a major tactic used to suppress voters of color. Requesting some form of identification may seem like a good idea; however, a 2017 study showed that, when thirty-four states implemented some form of ID restriction (prior to 2006, no state required such identification), voter turnout of racial and ethnic minorities in both primary and general elections was suppressed—with Latines being most negatively affected. The main burden associated with strict voter identification is not showing an ID but obtaining one. For example, in 2016 Alabama made it harder for people of color to obtain a state-issued ID by shutting down thirty-one driver's license offices in predominately low-income neighborhoods, neighborhoods that are predominately of color.[10] To demand an identification card to vote and then make it difficult to obtain one best illustrates structural racism. This has led former US attorney general Eric Holder to equate strict voter ID requirements to a poll tax (Hajnal, Lajevardi, and Neilson 2017, 363–64, 372–73).

Another tactic employed to shut people of color out of voting is purging voting rolls. And while a need exists to keep rolls updated, purging the rolls has targeted those living in large metropolitan areas that lean Democratic, especially in states like Florida, Texas, and Ohio. For example, prior to the 2016 election, Ohio targeted Cleveland, Cincinnati, and Columbus, all cities that had twice the rates of Democrats than Republicans. At least 144,000 voters were removed from the rolls of these cities.[11] By 2019 Ohio sought to purge 235,000 voters for failing to vote in previous elections under the "use it or lose it" rule. A careful analysis of the names purged revealed that almost one in five names should not have been taken off the rolls. When voters of color are targeted for purging, an election can be thrown. Consider the 2018 gubernatorial race in Georgia, when Democrat Stacy Abrams lost to Republican Brian Kemp by just 55,000 votes. Contributing to her lost was the purging of 500,000 voters from the rolls a year before the election by Kemp, who was, at the time, secretary of state.[12] Or consider the Wisconsin purge of approximately 232,000 voters prior to

---

[10] Associated Press, "New Rules in These States Are Frustrating Voters," *Fortune*, November 7, 2016.

[11] Andy Sullivan and Grant Smith, "Use It or Lose It: Occasional Ohio Voters May Be Shut Out in November," Reuters, June 2, 2016.

[12] Sam Levine, "Voter Purges: Are Republicans Trying to Rig the 2020 Election?," *The Guardian*, December 31, 2019.

the 2020 election. Trump won the state in 2016 with less than a tenth of that amount (22,748 votes). When checking the zip codes of those targeted for purging, they were areas that leaned Democratic—predominately Black neighborhoods and areas populated by students. Purged voters of color outnumbered by a factor of two the numbers of euroamerican voters, even though they disproportionately represent a smaller segment of the population.[13] From 2016 through 2019, 17 million voters were purged from the nation's voter rolls. Many found out they could not vote when they arrived at the polls on election day. And while there were names that needed to be purged due to deaths or voters leaving the state where they were registered, the overwhelming evidence shows that purging has been weaponized to keep voters, predominately voters of color, from voting.

Keeping many off the rolls to begin with is another strategy to suppress voter power. By 2020, 5.17 million Americans could not register to vote because they were classified as convicted felons, even after paying their debt to society. Disenfranchisement of felons is a relic of nineteenth-century racism and was designed to disenfranchise the freed-but-just-recently-enslaved population of Black people. Thanks to the prison industrial complex today, one in sixteen African Americans are negatively impacted (3.7 times more than non-Blacks) along with 2 percent of the Latine voting population.[14] To correct this injustice, the voters of Florida—one of three states that at the time imposed a lifetime voting ban on former felons—passed a 2018 ballot referendum restoring voting rights to 1.4 million former felons (a quarter of all disenfranchised felons in the country). The Republican-controlled legislature, however, quickly passed a bill delaying full voting rights until the former felons repaid the state any and all court-ordered monetary sanctions without enacting any procedure by which to inform former felons the amount due and how to satisfy said debt, thus keeping 1.1 million former felons from voting.[15]

Even when registered and possessing a valid form of voter identification, voters remain targeted for suppression. Expanding election "day" by opening polls early or facilitating other "early voting" practices has been shown to increase electoral participation. Early voting opportunities reduce the length of lines and wait times on "election day," thereby reducing a

---

[13] Erin McCormick, Spenser Mestel, and Sam Levine, "Revealed: Wisconsin's Black and Student Populations at Highest Risk of Voter Purge," *The Guardian*, April 6, 2020.

[14] Christopher Uggen, Ryan Larson, Sarah Shannon, and Arleth Pulido-Nava, *Locked Out 2020: Estimates of People Denied Voting Rights Due to a Felony Conviction* (Washington, DC: The Sentencing Project, 2020), 4.

[15] Ibid.

significant deterrent, specifically in neighborhoods of color. Disruptions in early voting procedures, then, discourage and even suppress the vote in these neighborhoods and similar settings. One study shows that, during the 2016 election, people of color were seven times more likely than euroamericans to wait longer than one hour to vote (Pettigrew 2021, 1); another study showed that lines in communities of color were about twice as long as those in predominantly white communities (Chen et al. 2019, 4). The votes of African Americans can further be minimized by limiting—if not banning—the ritual affectionately known as "souls to the polls." After church, Black worshippers would pile into church vans and head to the polls to fulfill their civic duty. Three months after Georgia narrowly sent two Democrats to the Senate—a Jewish man and a Black man—thus flipping the Senate, the Republican legislature responded in March 2021 by banning Sunday voting. While making it more difficult for Blacks to vote, the legislature, in the same bill, made it easier for euroamericans to vote by expanding early voting access in smaller, more rural counties.[16]

Mail-in ballots provide another form of early voting. Almost half of all ballots cast during the 2020 presidential election were by absentee ballot.[17] Still, Republicans attacked mail-in ballots under the false and unproven assertion of possible fraud. President Trump, however, explained the real reason for the suppression. When Democrats proposed expanding mail-in balloting during the COVID-19 pandemic, Trump—who was running for reelection—explained during a live call-in to *Fox & Friends* that if the bill was enacted, it would lead to "levels of voting that, if you ever agreed to it, you'd never have a Republican elected in this country again."[18] He was not alone. During *Lou Dobbs Tonight*, Congressman Matt Gaetz (R-FL) noted, "If we accept this universal mail-out balloting to people who didn't even request ballots, I don't think Republicans will ever win another national election again. That's why we have to stand and fight now."[19] One way of fighting back is eliminating the selectivity as to who gets to use mail-in ballots. For example, Nebraska automatically sends mail-in ballots in rural areas populated by fewer than ten thousand people (predominately white and Republican) but forbids this practice in large urban areas (predominately

---

[16] Adam Brewster and Caitlin Huey-Burns, "What Georgia's New Voting Law Really Does—9 Facts," CBS News, April 7, 2021.

[17] Michael Wines, "Republicans Mount Attack on Mail-In Voting Rules," *New York Times*, December 11, 2020.

[18] Aaron Black, "Trump Just Comes Out and Says It: The GOP Is Hurt When It's Easier to Vote," *Washington Post*, March 30, 2020.

[19] Angelica Stabile, "Gaetz Warns Republicans Will Never Win 'Another National Election Again' If Mail-in Balloting Persists," Fox News, November 30, 2020.

Democratic, where people of color congregate and live). Texas allows no-excuse absentee voting for those sixty-five years old and older, a group that skews toward Republicans.[20] Ironically, no evidence exists that mail-in ballots favor Democrats, a fact proven by the 2020 election.[21]

The broader scheme against full democracy further requires that the agency responsible for delivering the ballots must have its capacity diminished or impaired. In addition to reducing the number of ballot drop-off boxes in the lead-up to the 2020 election, President Trump pushed to defund the United States Postal Service in an effort to limit mail-in ballots from being delivered and counted. As he explained at the time: "[The Post Office] need[s] that money in order to make the post office work, so it can take all of these millions and millions of ballots. If we don't make a deal … that means they can't have universal mail-in voting."[22]

Yet even casting and successfully delivering a mail-in ballot does not ensure that it will be counted. In Washington State, auditors discovered that the votes of African Americans were four times more likely than euroamerican votes to be disqualified and rejected during the 2020 election cycle because of so-called problematic signatures. The ballots of Latines, Asians, Native Americans, and Pacific Islanders also experienced elevated rejection rates.[23] During the 2022 Texas primary election, eighteen thousand ballots were rejected, disproportionately those of African Americans. Areas with high concentrations of Black people—like Harris County, encompassing Houston—were 44 percent more likely to have their ballots rejected than counties with predominately euroamerican populations.[24] In short, the ballots most likely to be rejected are those cast by people of color, younger voters, and first-time voters—groups that skew Democratic.

---

[20] Reid J. Epstein and Stephanie Saul, "Shifting to Vote-by-Mail Hasn't Hurt the G.O.P. Despite Trump's Claims," *New York Times*, April 11, 2020.

[21] Anecdotally, Colorado sends a ballot to every registered voter whether they request one or not. Although the state leans Democratic, in 2014, the voters ousted the Democratic senator, Mark Udall, replacing him with Cory Gardner. Additionally, Republicans won three of the four statewide races. For more information, see Jesse Yoder, Cassandra Handan-Nader, et al., "How Did Absentee Voting Affect the 2020 U.S. Election?," *Science Advances* 7, no. 52 (December 22, 2021): 135–49; Nicholas Riccardi, "Study: No Partisan Benefit from Mail Voting in 2020 Election," Associated Press, March 5, 2021.

[22] "Trump Tells on Himself," *New York Times*, August 16, 2020.

[23] Mike Baker, "Race Seen to Coincide with Higher Rejection of 2020 Mail Ballots," *New York Times*, February 3, 2022.

[24] Nick Corasaniti, "Rejected Mail Ballots in Texas Disproportionately Affect Black People," *New York Times*, March 19, 2022.

Poll watchers are also being weaponized. The Harris County (Texas) Republican Party, in preparation for the 2022 midterm elections, trained euroamericans who believe the Big Lie that the 2020 election was stolen[25] to serve as poll watchers in Black, Latine, and Asian American Houston neighborhoods. According to the precinct chair of a northeastern suburban white neighborhood, white poll watchers were being sought with "the confidence and courage" to inundate precincts comprised mainly of voters of color to prevent imaginary fraud. This Jim and Jane Crow tactic was on full display in 2020, where at least forty-four incidents were reported of inappropriate behavior by poll watchers in Harris County. One nonpartisan election official, Cindy Wilson, shared, "Two poll watchers stood close to the black voters (less than three feet) and engaged in what I describe as intimidating behavior."[26]

Control of Federal Government

These tactics on the state level ensured that the minority party would have dominance on the federal level—the requisite power to achieve the ultimate purpose of controlling the courts. But not all forms of voter suppression lie with the state; the federal government also has its tools. Consider the Electoral College, a relic from slaveocracy. In this century alone, two different candidates who lost the popular vote, George W. Bush by 543,895 votes in 2000 and Donald Trump by almost 3 million votes in 2016, were awarded the presidency via the Electoral College system. Not trusting direct democracy, the Constitutional Convention of 1787 devised an apartheid-type political mechanism as a last-minute compromise to satisfy and benefit slave-holding states. In short, individual voters would not vote for the president. Instead, they would vote for party delegates, even if their names do not appear on the ballot, who, in turn, would vote for the candidate that carried the state. In a winner-takes-all structure, the candidate who wins the state's popular vote is given all the state's electoral votes. When Hillary Clinton garnered 43 percent of the votes in Texas in 2016, all thirty-eight electoral votes went to Donald Trump. Maine and Nebraska, notably, do not follow the winner-takes-all pattern.

---

[25] It should be noted that, after sixty lawsuits claiming voter fraud allegations (many of which were issued before Trump-appointed judges) since the 2020 election, and after offering financial incentives for anyone with information concerning fraud, not a single case was found of someone voting twice, of an undocumented immigrant voting, or of someone who is dead voting—hence the Big Lie.

[26] Nick Corasaniti, "Republicans Aim to Expand Power of Poll Watchers," *New York Times*, May 2, 2021.

Today, this mechanism disenfranchises millions of voters who live in about forty "safe" blue or red states, where the outcome as to who would be awarded the electoral votes is never in doubt. This disenfranchises around 100 million Americans. For the next president, the vote of a Democrat in Wyoming or a Republican in the District of Columbia simply does not count. Only about 20 percent of the population, those living in the five to ten battleground states, gets to choose the president and vice president. The loser of the popular vote in a presidential election can still be sworn in, changing the direction of the nation, because we do not operate as a democracy under majority rule. The person who garners the most Electoral College votes wins.

During the 2020 election, Trump lost the popular vote by 8 million votes. Yet, if he would have garnered 5,229 additional votes in Arizona, 5,890 more in Georgia, and 10,342 in Wisconsin, he would have been reelected. This minor shift in the tally would have tied the electoral vote at 269 each, throwing the decision, according to the Constitution, to the House of Representatives. Even though Democrats controlled the House as a whole on election night, their voting process to break an electoral tie is also not based on the votes of individual representatives. Instead, state delegations vote as one unit. Thanks to gerrymandering, Republicans have the advantage in state delegation majorities. Under the current system, then-president Donald Trump did not lose the 2020 election by 8 million votes. He lost by 21,461.

In the eight presidential elections since 1988, Republicans have won the popular vote once: George W. Bush's second term in 2004. If Al Gore, who won the popular vote in 2000 but lost the electoral vote, would instead have been president, there would not have even been a second term for which George W. Bush could have run. While Democratic candidates have received more votes than Republicans, Republicans have nonetheless served as president in three of those elections.

The antidemocratic processes in the Electoral College system further disenfranchise voters of color by effectively weighting the votes cast by euroamericans. For example, during the 2016 presidential election, when Trump lost the popular vote to Clinton by almost 2.9 million votes,[27] one electoral vote representing 508,000 voters from a racially and ethnically diverse city like Los Angeles was equal to one electoral vote from Wyoming representing 143,000 mainly euroamerican conservative voters. The Constitution may have codified the worth of an African American to three-fifths of a euroamerican man, but today (using the above example), a person

---

[27] "Presidential Results," CNN Politics, 2016.

of color is worth less than a third of a euroamerican when it comes to voting. This race-based math ensured Trump's 306 electoral votes to Clinton's 232. The influence of a president who fails to receive the majority of the popular votes cast is not confined to the four years they serve. The candidate who lost the popular vote in the 2016 election, for example, had a profound influence on the shape of the Supreme Court of the United States, an impact that could last for the next three to four decades—if not the rest of this century.

Control of the Courts

The Koch brothers' interest in exercising a controlling influence over the Supreme Court was due to the pivotal role the court plays in determining the degree of regulatory power that corporate America faces from federal and state governments. From 1997 to 2017, the Koch brothers gave more than $6 million to the Federalist Society, a nonprofit institute that recruits conservative and libertarian judges. They also paid for junkets for judges to Utah ski resorts and Florida beachfront properties so that they could attend seminars on the importance of market forces in society. Through their work, the brothers established a grassroots army of volunteers called Americans for Prosperity. Following the election of President Trump, that organization mobilized to take advantage of a Republican-controlled Senate and White House. Controlling both steps in the process of confirming a Supreme Court justice provided a once-in-a-lifetime opportunity to change the court's ideological balance. Americans for Prosperity undertook national campaigns to ensure the appointments of Neil Gorsuch and Brett Kavanaugh. On Kavanaugh alone, the efforts ran into "seven figures."[28]

When Amy Coney Barrett was nominated to the Supreme Court to replace Ruth Bader Ginsburg, Charles Koch was less interested with her stance on *Roe v. Wade* and more concerned with her opposition to the 1984 *Chevron v. Natural Resources Defense Council*. Barrett obtained Koch's support, and that of his vast network, because she signaled that some precedents should be overturned and that she ascribed to the judicial philosophy of the late justice Antonin Scalia. Overturning *Chevron v. Natural Resources Defense Council* would be the culmination of decades of Koch political activism. Since the 1984 decision, the court applied the "Chevron deference" to government agencies' interpretation of the law whenever a related law enacted by Congress appeared dubious. This precedent allowed

---

[28] Christopher Leonard, "A Koch Brother's Big Bet on Judge Barrett," *New York Times*, October 13, 2020.

government agencies—like the Environmental Protection Agency (EPA)—to establish and implement complex regulations on corporations that may not have necessarily been explicit in the laws established by Congress. The EPA specifically has always been a thorn in the side to the Koch brothers' multinational corporation that—among other ventures—engages in the manufacturing, refining, and distribution of petroleum.

Once Justice Barrett and other Trump-appointed justices were on the court, they delivered the *West Virginia v. EPA* decision, weakening the 1984 *Chevron* decision. This court determined that Congress never gave the EPA broad authority to shift the country away from fossil fuels, rendering the EPA powerless to address climate change. Specifically, the EPA became toothless to enact regulatory policies that negatively impacted Koch Industries. Fortunately, Democrats controlled both chambers of Congress at the time and were able to include a provision in the Inflation Reduction Act empowering and authorizing the EPA to enact such regulatory policies.

The current Republican-appointed Supreme Court will continue to dismantle the safeguards against savage capitalism and the guardrails that protect democratic values and institutions. The Big Lie of 2020 set in motion major voter suppression initiatives that the Supreme Court has already agreed to deliberate. In 2021, conservative justices, in the case *Brnovich v. Democratic National Committee*, upheld Arizona laws designed to make voting for those from communities of color more difficult.[29] Emboldened, Arizona passed a new law (HB 2492) requiring proof of US citizenship in order to vote in 2022.

The slew of suppression laws since 2020 are designed to be a "corrective" to President Trump's inability to undermine the election and remain in power after losing both the popular and electoral votes. The main reason that he failed was because safeguards existed that protected the integrity of the election process. Secretaries of state and state legislators were powerless to overturn the will of the people and appoint a slate of electors contrary to the results. This protection, too, is being dismantled. As of this writing, legislators from fourteen states have enacted laws that give Republican state officials control of county election boards, especially in states where the

---

[29] In *Brnovich*, the Supreme Court upheld two laws. The first discounted ballots that had been cast by a voter outside of the voter's precinct. The second banned nonrelative neighbors or friends from delivering mail-in ballots on someone's behalf. The laws themselves challenged the prohibition of state laws that deny equal participation in the voting system for minoritized voters in Section 2(a) of the Voting Rights Act of 1965. The conservative majority argued that Arizona's interest as a state to prevent voter fraud was a more important factor for upholding the laws than the disparities laws caused on people of color.

Trump campaign narrowly lost (Arizona, Georgia, Michigan, Wisconsin, and Pennsylvania). Other states (Texas and Florida) are following this lead. In at least one state, Republican officials are able to overturn the legitimate election results if they cite—without any need to prove—election fraud. Other states are poised to follow this lead.

Since the Big Lie, the single most important domestic policy of the Republican Party has been legalizing the subversion of elections by stripping independent election officials of their duties and responsibilities, replacing them with people loyal to the party. Democratic guardrails are weakened by shifting the authority of supervising elections from administrators to partisan politicians. In some cases, election officials have been threatened with felony prosecution for doing their jobs. Comprehensive voting rights in the form of the Freedom to Vote Act or the John Lewis Voting Rights Advances Act have gone nowhere in Congress as of 2022, thanks to a Senate parliamentary procedure known as the filibuster, which was employed during the 1960s as a means of frustrating civil rights legislation.

Entrusting more election oversight power to partisan politicians may very well be upheld by the Supreme Court, who announced they will hear *Moore v. Harper* during the fall 2022 session (with a decision slated to be issued in early summer 2023), a case concerned with how federal elections are conducted. Based on four justices of the Republican-appointed Supreme Court already voicing tentative support for partisan gerrymandering, it appeared they would rule to give state legislatures powers that would not be subject to state courts,[30] thus eliminating protections against partisan influence.[31] In theory, such a decision could have vested state legislatures with the right to refuse to certify an election, instead naming their own slate of electors contrary to the will of the people. In control of thirty state legislatures in 2022 compared to seventeen Democratic-held legislatures, Republicans have locked Democrats out of power through gerrymandering and other voter suppression tactics, strengthening their dominance for decades to come. Although the Supreme Court did not rule in their favor, they did not settle the issue of partisan dominance in certifying elections. No doubt this issue will reemerge in future cases.

"Election integrity" has become coded language for the suppression of votes—mainly the votes of communities of color because they

---

[30] During the 2020 redistricting cycle, state courts in North Carolina, Ohio, and New York rejected the redrawn maps as partisanly gerrymandered. This case arises from the North Carolina decision.

[31] Adam Liptak and Nick Corasaniti, "Supreme Court Could Reshape Election Rules," *New York Times,* July 1, 2022.

skew Democratic. And while the integrity of elections should always be a concern, passing laws that disenfranchise major constituencies of voters to fix a problem that does not exist is a tactic from the playbook of would-be authoritarian regimes. The question before us is, can a major political party maintain dominance in the twenty-first century based on voter suppression? At what point does established disenfranchisement of the majority of the population—specifically communities of color—become a neo-apartheid system?

Step 2: Reflecting

Since the early 1900s, corporations have been banned from making campaign contributions to federal candidates to prevent their deep pockets from subverting the democratic process. The coercive impact of money on the democratic process became obvious during the Watergate era, leading to political reforms such as public financing of presidential elections. From 1976 until 2008, both Republicans and Democrats took public money for the general election, adhering to spending limits that reduced the influence of campaign contributions. In 2008, then-candidate Barack Obama became the first presidential candidate since the Watergate era to refuse public financing, instead raising as much money as possible without any restrictions or limitations. By the 2012 election, the post-Watergate reforms were dead as both candidates unashamedly raised hundreds of millions more than the public system could provide. Our electoral process has been transformed from trying to limit the role money plays in determining who would be president to one of super political action committee (PACs), unlimited contributions, and secret donors.

This is not to state that public financing was a panacea. Individuals within corporations and their families were still allowed to make individual donations. In many cases, this was and continues to be accomplished through a process known as "bundling," where a multitude of individual checks written by executives and their families within a corporation are bundled together and presented to the candidate. In addition to bundling, the Federal Election Campaign Act in 1974 allowed large corporations to form PACs for the express purpose of pooling funds from a group of individuals who voluntarily join to support a candidate. The express purpose of PACs was to influence the political sphere by helping elect public officials friendly to the PAC's ideology. PAC contributions are made to those aligned with the interest of the corporation, or as a reward to incumbents who have continuously acted in the best interest of the corporation. Although somewhat eclipsed in the 1990s by direct contributions to candidates' campaigns through "soft money," PACs are still an important component in influencing political officials.

Raising campaign donations secures incumbency. The ability to raise great sums of money for a sufficiently large war chest can scare off potential rivals. Not surprisingly, politicians become beholden, more or less, to those responsible for raising the funds needed to mount successful campaigns. Once elected, indebtedness to the corporate leaders who placed them in power makes them advocates of neoliberal policies favorable to the corporations, policies that usually maintain the status quo and safeguard privilege. Being supported by PAC monies does not necessarily mean that the recipients will vote a specific way, although how they vote on public issues can determine how much money they will receive from a PAC during the next election cycle. While laws do exist to prevent corporations from unfairly influencing elected officials, enough loopholes also exist to weaken such regulations.[32]

The laws concerning corporate contributions to political campaigns were radically changed on January 21, 2010, with the Supreme Court five-to-four decision in *Citizens United v. Federal Election Commission*. Corporations—like Koch Industries—were no longer prohibited from directly making contributions to candidates during election cycles. The decision was based on a broad interpretation of the First Amendment principle of free speech. Those Republican-appointed justices who supported the decision overturned earlier court precedent, arguing that campaign contributions constitute political speech, and the government has no right to regulate any

---

[32] During the mid-1980s, I served as chairperson of the Real Estate Political Action Committee for the Miami Board of Realtors. My job was to serve as a pseudo-lobbyist, traveling to both the state and nation's capitals, to relay our organization's positions on specific legislation and target candidates to whom we would give support and provide funding. It was very common to hedge one's bets by giving monies to both candidates. Regardless of who won, we would be on the winning team. When there was a particular candidate we really liked, we were always able to funnel additional monies to them through bundling. Our support bought us access. I always had a direct line to the representatives we supported with a phone call or visit, access that I lost when I was no longer representing the PAC. While in my position, it was common for me to hear candidates state, "Just tell me what you guys want and I'll support it." One candidate in particular who was running for reelection once threatened to vote against a measure we supported because he had not yet received our organization's financial endorsement. We quickly stated that an oversight was made and cut a check to his reelection committee. Within hours, he voted for the bill we supported. While this was not the norm, it is still the way the system legally operates.

form of free speech.[33] In effect, political reliance on large corporate donations posed the probability that the influence of the average voter would be overwhelmed. Those opposing the decision argued that the flood of corporate money would corrupt the democratic process. At the time of the decision, President Obama called it "a major victory for big oil, Wall Street banks, health insurance companies and the other powerful interests that marshal their power every day in Washington to drown out the voices of everyday Americans."[34] Regardless of his protestations, Obama created his own super PAC, Priorities USA Action, raising $78 million following the *Citizens United* decision.[35]

Because 2012 was the first presidential election since the *Citizens United* ruling, we saw how the ruling made it possible to give in secret. Even though public support exists for public disclosure of campaign giving and decades of legal precedent supports the right for the public to know who is funding campaigns, 2012 saw the rise of "dark money." Dark money comes from innocuously named nonprofits engaged in "social welfare," 501(c)(4)-designated organizations that do not disclose their funding sources. During the 2012 election, shell corporations that did not disclose their funding sources funneled at least $17 million to super PACs. Contributions to super PACs via identified shell corporations represented almost 17 percent of all business contributions. During 2012, dark money nonprofits reported spending over $299 million running "issue ads" that only needed to be reported when aired just before primaries or the day of the election. Thanks to both dark-money nonprofits and shell corporations, it is now almost impossible to identify violations of election or tax law, such as the infiltration of foreign funds (Fischer and Bowie 2013, 1). Among the loudest opponents of dark money since the *Citizens United* case have been Democrats who have repeatedly expressed moral indignation; still, during the 2020 election, Democrats outstripped the GOP in raising millions in dark money. Fifteen of the most politically active nonprofits aligned with Democrats spent more than $1.5 billion, as opposed to the

---

[33] *Citizens United v. Federal Election Commission* in effect overturned two earlier Supreme Court precedents: *Austin v. Michigan Chamber of Commerce*, which decided in 1990 to uphold campaign spending decisions that supported or opposed candidates; and *McConnell v. Federal Election Commission*, which in 2002 upheld the Bipartisan Campaign Reform Act (aka McCain-Feingold) that restricted corporations and unions from campaign spending.

[34] James Vicini, "Landmark Supreme Court Ruling Allows Corporate Political Cash," Reuters, January 21, 2010.

[35] Nicholas Confessore, "Results Won't Limit Campaign Money Any More Than Ruling Did," *New York Times*, November 12, 2012.

fifteen most politically active nonprofits aligned with Republicans, which spent $900 million.

An April 2018 dinner party held at the Trump International Hotel in Washington, DC, demonstrates how the *Citizens United* ruling operates in the political arena. President Trump attended the event, as did Lev Parnas and Igor Fruman. Parnas and Fruman, associates of Rudolph Giuliani, pressed Trump to remove Marie Yovanovitch, who was blocking their ability to profit from natural gas, as the ambassador to Ukraine. The owner of a steel-making company gave $1.75 million for Trump's reelection, asking in return to tighten restrictions on steel imports and allow longer work hours for truckers. An Ohio executive was asking that the natural gas engines his company made would be regulated like the less polluting electric engines.[36] Pay-to-play is irreconcilable with draining the swamp.

In most cases, however, the return on corporate political contribution investments can be made via matters that do not appear to be so quid pro quo. A beneficiary of campaign contributions might choose to abstain from voting altogether if the corporation and the political official disagree on how they were originally planning to vote on the proposed legislation. The beholden politician can, behind the scenes, encourage certain witnesses to testify at a committee hearing or block those whose testimony may be perceived as harmful. Corporations can greatly benefit when public officials they support encourage or block someone's appointment to a post that oversees or regulates the benefactor's industry. In effect, the corporation transforms the relationship from regulator and regulated to a more symbiotic one between parties with mutual interests.

Citizens United has done more than legalize the influencing of politicians with unlimited funding; it has also opened the door to the financing of ballot initiatives by the wealthy few. Once considered a progressive exercise in direct democracy, ballot initiatives, in a post–*Citizens United* era, have become a means by which laws could be challenged with private funding. For example, Tom Steyer, founder of the hedge fund Fallon Capital Management, spent $22 million to advocate for California Proposition 39, rescinding a three-year-old tax benefit given to out-of-state companies. Billionaire insurance executive George Joseph funneled $16 million to change—singlehandedly—the state's auto insurance laws. While the wealthy have used their money to advance pet projects in the past, now it has become a more common method of setting governmental policies.[37]

---

[36] "More Money, More Political Problems," *New York Times*, February 2, 2020.

[37] Norimitsu Onishi, "California Ballot Initiatives, Born in Populism, Now Come from Billionaires," *New York Times*, October 17, 2012.

Besides negatively impacting the democratic process, *Citizens United* also negatively impacts capitalism. Maybe the ultimate paradox is that entrepreneurial capitalism, which rewards the one who can build a better mousetrap and get it to market quicker, is being destroyed by monopolistic capitalism whose winner-takes-all philosophy is sustained through a bought government whose electability is dependent on corporate donations. In return for corporate PAC monies—like those doled out by Koch Industries—less government and lower taxes are advocated to the detriment of average citizens who develop a false consciousness that blames government and those on the margins for their difficulties rather than the elite who profit from the laissez-faire vision of libertarians. "Class warfare" is a term used by politicians and political pundits whenever the public (rich or poor) questions the disparity of wealth in this nation. To raise concerns about the ever-growing economic gap in this nation is to risk being accused of fomenting social unrest—or worse, to be labeled a socialist.

Many may wish to avoid the term "class warfare" lest they too be labeled socialists (as if the term were synonymous with evil), yet the truth remains that the massive infusion of corporate political contributions, thanks to *Citizens United*, only strengthened the class warfare waged by politicians protecting the super-rich. This war began in the 1980s, when Reagan, followed by George H. W. Bush, occupied the White House. In quick succession, deregulation and the granting of massive tax cuts to the richest Americans occurred. This new era was most responsible for the greatest transfer of wealth in human history from the poorest Americans to the richest, as explored in the previous chapter. When Bill Clinton was elected in 1992, the national deficit was $300 billion. And while he worked to control this, ending his term with a surplus (the first in decades), he still participated in the transfer of wealth, specifically in his "ending welfare as we know it." More important was his administration's role in deregulating the banking industry, a charge led by his Treasury secretary Larry Summers and Senator Phil Gramm (R-TX) in the form of the 1999 Financial Service Modernization Act. The safeguards put in place to prevent another 1930s Depression were basically gutted. Not surprisingly, nine years later, our nation experienced the 2008 Great Recession. Aggregating that situation was a greater transfer of wealth under tax cuts in the George W. Bush administration of 2001.

Despite inheriting the budget surplus, Bush's $1.3 trillion tax cut to the richest Americans grew the deficit by $400 billion a year. Beginning two wars and fighting them on credit further aggravated the country's debt situation under Bush. When the Obama administration began, during the worst economic crisis since the Great Depression (a crisis rooted in deregulation), he signed an $800 billion spending increase to stimulate the economy—the growth in spending needed to stave off the Great Recession and a drop in revenue due to the Bush tax cuts having exploded the deficit to $1.4 trillion (down to $1.1 trillion by 2012). Under the Trump administration, the deficit grew to $27 trillion during his four years, thanks mainly to tax cuts that transferred more wealth to the wealthiest Americans and a total lack of spending restraints. As of July 2022, halfway through Biden's first term, the deficit is at $30.5 trillion.

As discussed earlier, neoliberalism has succeeded greatly in transferring wealth from the bottom of society to the top, as witnessed by the growing income disparity between the poor and the rich—a process brought about by reducing available social services (such as welfare, support for education, and health care) and increasing tax breaks for the wealthiest citizens. Neoliberalism poses a distinct threat to democracy. When concentrated wealth influences legislation, it is only a matter of time until political inequality follows, something witnessed today as state after state imposes voter suppression legislation. True democracy is replaced with a democratic façade, and the public is led to believe that it is exercising its right to choose leaders. Because corporations funnel large sums of money to candidates from both parties, the corporations win regardless of who wins the election.

For example, many celebrated the 2008 election of our first Black president, creating an illusion that we live in a postracial society. But was there truly a difference between Barack Obama, Hillary Clinton, or John McCain, the main 2008 candidates? Because of unregulated campaign contributions, all three can be considered as ontologically white males. One cannot become the leader of the world's most powerful country (empire?) unless they are committed to what male whiteness symbolizes within the colonial process. Barack's "whiteness" and Hillary's "maleness" raise concerns and questions and, as such, make their ascension in the political process an issue of class. The power of corporate monies contributed to candidates subjugates the collective will of feminists and the Black community regardless of "one of their own" winning the election.

Campaign contributions can easily negate the importance of electing a Black man or a white woman to the presidency. If the national politics and economics of the captains of industry were to be threatened by the needs of marginalized US constituencies—be they Black, women, or poor white—the future president would rally all the forces at their disposal to maintain the prevailing economic power structures that exist, even if those structures are detrimental to communities that share their gender or skin pigmentation.

This raises a major concern. Has the democratic system been reduced to a choice among pro-empire individuals who throughout political campaigns show no significant difference in their commitments to protecting the rights of multinational companies to expand globally? Will future presidents, regardless of race or gender, protect the interests of Mobil, Microsoft, and McDonald's, even at the expense of establishing justice, and even at the cost of committing US troops? Any presidential candidate who questions free-market policies or who seriously addresses the undemocratic distribution of wealth, resources, and privileges in this country would never be a serious contender because they would be unable to attract the needed corporate campaign contributions to mount a potential run. Campaign contributions from multinational firms and Wall Street have the corroding power of transforming hopeful politicians like Obama or Clinton into the Black or female face of a global neoliberalism that continues to privilege the few at the expense of most of the world's population.

The question seldom pondered is, who would benefit by less government regulation? The answer is obvious: large corporations benefit the most by fewer labor, environmental, or safety regulations along with lower taxes—thus explaining why *Citizens United* is such a bonanza to companies. It opens the political donation floodgates needed to peddle libertarian political goals like those advocated by Koch Industries, which saw their holy mission as using their millions to change the political environment toward a pre–New Deal America. Given the continuing influence of corporations through super PACs, we are now moving away from a representative democracy toward an oligarchy, a system in which unequal wealth creates political inequality. The excessive wealth enjoyed by the privileged few provides them the right, through the funneling of campaign contributions, to influence—and in some cases to determine—laws and regulations, often for their own benefit. Wealth funneled to political campaigns, especially through super PACs, serves to obscure and complicate the will of the privileged few with the will of the majority. And who suffers most from *Citizens United?* The vast majority whose ability to influence the political process is greatly diminished.

Step 3: Meditating

The marginalized concept of ethics is far different than that of politicians beholden to PACs. Any law or regulation is ethical if it produces a more human existence as a response to *agape*—meaning unconditional love. Proper public policy promotes a more human existence by providing opportunities for all citizens to participate in the abundance of life promised by Christ (Jn. 10:10), specifically and especially those citizens who are the most vulnerable within society. PACs, whose purpose is to have laws and regulations reflect private rather than public interests, prevent the societal goal of *fiat justitia, ruat coelum*—let justice be done though the heavens should fall. Although the elimination of super PACs will not usher in a new dawn of justice, their continuation prevents the disenfranchised from participating equally in what society has to offer.

According to W. E. B. Du Bois, the best way to prevent the rich from controlling the political process is for democracy to be allowed to modify industry. In seeking an alternative to the present disjointedness between economics and electoral democracies, Du Bois advocated a proper relationship between the two. He wrote, "While wealth spoke and had power, the dirtiest laborers had voice and vote." Or, as restated by Dwight Hopkins, "The power of wealth submits and succumbs to the will of a collective, conscious, common folk" (2000, 136). The ethical question to ponder is: how do super PACs subvert and pervert the proper relationship between economics and electoral democracies? Hopkins may very well be correct in stating,

> The federal government (the presidential, judicial, and legislative branches) often appears to be a competing system of objective checks and balances. But if the national politics and economics were threatened with a reversal, that is, if the pyramidal monopoly capitalist structure in the United States began to move bottom to top, then so-called checks and balances system would rally to prevent such a movement. The present system would immediately stop the realization of genuine democracy in which the majority of the citizens—the people at the bottom in the United States—would own all the economic resources as well as the military industrial complex, and would, therefore, control the federal government. (187)

For Christians, God calls political leaders to do justice by linking justice with how the disenfranchised are rescued from the oppressor's hand, with how the least in society are treated,[38] and with how those who are innocent are protected. Speaking to the prophet Jeremiah, God said,

---

[38] The biblical phrase "alien, orphan, and widow" can be understood as a euphemism for the marginalized.

Go down to the house of the king of Judah, and there speak this word—say, Hear the word of God, O king of Judah who sits on the throne of David, and also your servants and your people who enter through these gates. Thus says God—Do justice and practice righteousness; deliver the one wronged from the hands of the oppressor; do not oppress the alien, the orphan, or the widow; do no violence; and do not shed innocent blood in this place. (22:1–3)

Throughout his ministry, Jesus proclaimed that God's reign was at hand. What did he mean by this phrase? Those doing ethics from the margins believe that Jesus, and all the prophets before him, understood God's reign to mean a striving toward establishing a social order where justice prevails for all. God's reign is not limited to the otherworldly. It exists in the here and now. This reign of God can best be understood by what Jesus did: he fed the hungry, healed the sick, and proclaimed the good news to the poor. But while Jesus anchored his good news with the experience of the disenfranchised of his time, he still emphasized the ethical responsibilities of those who possess power and authority over others, warning of the importance of moral diligence.

During Jesus's earthly ministry, he and his disciples lived from a common purse (Jn. 13:29). The early church continued by creating a church where "all the believers were together, and held all things in common, they sold their goods and possessions and distributed them to all, each according to their need" (Acts 2:44–45). Nonetheless, there were those who tried to create a façade of Christianity while holding on to the material possessions that secured their privilege. The apostle Peter challenged Ananias and his wife, Sapphira, who publicly agreed to participate in community but privately attempted to secure their wealth. Their sin was not that they withheld a portion of the proceeds of the sale of their property. As Peter said, it was their property to keep or dispose of as they saw fit (Acts 5:1–11). Their sin was to claim to be part of the faith community while attempting to maintain an uneven distribution of the power that comes from wealth.

Ananias and Sapphira have become the patron saints of today's eurocentric Christianity, a façade of a faith that seeks to secure their unearned profit, power, and privilege by claiming victimhood. The nationalist Christianity that has emerged since that 1940 annual meeting of the National Association of Manufacturers has led us to today's Q-infused faith based on messianic loyalty to Donald Trump. The fact that most whites who identify as Christians voted for Trump creates a cognitive dissonance between how eurocentric Christianity is defined and how communities of color have understood Christianity. Although insufficient space exists here to reveal how Trump is the antithesis of the Gospel message, suffice it to simply say he has demonstrated racist tendencies ("there are good people on both sides" during Charlottesville's Unite the Right rally); unapologetic xenophobia (Mexican migrants are "a people with lots of problems, bringing drugs, bringing crime, and being rapists"); and avowed misogyny ("grab them by their pussies"). Whatever God Trump and those who voted for him worship is detrimental, if not deadly, to marginalized communities.

Four years of masculine toxicity was rewarded with greater support by eurochristianity. Trump garnered more votes in 2020 from eurochristians who witnessed his antigospel words and actions played out on the national stage. Consider that 84 percent of white evangelicals, 57 percent of white Protestants, and 57 percent of white Catholics cast their votes for Donald Trump in the 2020 election. In the 2016 election, the count was, respectively, 77 percent, 57 percent, and 64 percent.[39] Through their votes, the majority of white Christians supported a white nationalist Christianity. Eurochristianity and Trumpism are, after all, twins of white supremacy. As such, they require rejection by those seeking to do ethics from the margins.

Step 4: Case Studies

1. Politicians hype fear and expand ignorance to secure the votes of euroamericans. Since 2020, the tactic employed is scaring euroamericans with the threat of being replaced by advocates of a so-called racist ideology known as critical race theory (CRT). During the 2021 Virginia gubernatorial race, Glenn Youngkin rode the fear of CRT to the state mansion, promising, "There's no place for critical race theory in our school system, and why, on day one, I'm going to ban it." He vowed to end something that did not and never did exist in Virginia's public schools.[40] Not to be outdone, Governor Ron DeSantis of Florida proposed following nine other states in codifying a ban on CRT through his Stop WOKE Act, which took effect on July 1, 2022. The legislation he proposed allows parents to sue school districts that teach critical race theory, recouping from the public schools any legal fees incurred. Additionally, diversity training by corporations would be banned because it "creates a hostile work environment" for whites.

---

[39] Justin Nortey, "Most White Americans Who Regularly Attend Worship Services Voted for Trump in 2020," Pew Research Center, August 30, 2021.

[40] Graham Colton, "Glenn Youngkin Vows to Take Bold Stand against Critical Race Theory as Governor," Fox News, October 31, 2021.

• Critical race theory has become a red herring, doubling as a dog whistle whose purpose is to create fear and anxiety that euroamericans are going to be oppressed. What is critical race theory? How was it developed? What was its goal? If the Civil Rights Act of 1968 outlawed discrimination, why, then, do people of color still face death-dealing racism and ethnic discrimination? Is racism a consequence of individual bias or is it structural? Who benefits by outlawing discussion on how racism and ethnic discrimination function in society?

• Gerrymandering politicians, cognizant of how power works, have obsessed over critical race theory. Why? Throughout Republican states, laws have been enacted prohibiting diversity training by state contractors, banning literature that tackles racism by authors of color, and disallowing the teaching of critical race theory in public schools. Some states, like Texas, banned teachers from even discussing racism, white supremacy, or current events in the classroom. How successful will these initiatives be? When the voices of communities of color are silenced as critical race theory is demonized, does a eurocentric education for students of color becomes a form of corrective therapy?

2. The withering away of democracy begins with an inaccurate census count. Every ten years—as per the US Constitution—a census is to be taken of all living in the nation, regardless of documentation or status, to determine the allocation of resources and the reallocation of political representation. Whoever controls the state legislature determines the demarcation of political power. Who is counted and who is not determines who will be privileged and who will be marginalized for the next decade. Following his ascension to the presidency, Trump actively sought to undermine the accuracy of the 2020 census.

He specifically sought to accomplish the following: (1) Add a divisive question on citizenship to reduce participation from immigrant communities. According to a stash of documents obtained by Congress, the purpose of the citizen question—as per partisan appointees in the Commerce Department—was aimed to exclude noncitizens from the count to favor Republicans in congressional apportionment.[41] (2) Exclude undocumented residents from the population to shift Democratic House seats to Republican states doing reapportionment. (3) Stop the counting a month early and before the work was finished despite delays caused by the pandemic. In addition to Trump's interference, the pandemic made house-to-house counting unattainable as door-knockers willing to go into areas with high

---

[41] Miriam Jordan, "Documents Suggest Trump Plan to Steer Census for Party Gain," *New York Times*, July 21, 2022.

COVID-19 infection rates were hard to find. Considering that minoritized communities were disproportionately struck with the virus, they were more likely to be undercounted or not counted at all.

• All of these acts were unprecedented. They sought to insulate the minority political party from demographic shifts. What groups were most impacted by these schemes? For the better? For the worse? According to the Census Bureau, the 2020 Census seriously undercounted Latine, Black, and Native American residents and overcounted Asians and euroamericans.[42] Can Trump's interference be blamed? Is this a recurring structural dilemma? What does it mean for those groups to not only be absent from the nation's consciousness but from the nation's physical count?

• People are counted depending on where they sleep and eat. Those in prison, who cannot vote and have no attachment to where the prison is located, are counted as part of a local population to which they do not belong. The prison industrial complex disproportionately houses Black and Brown people from urban centers; nevertheless, they are counted to the detriment of the neighborhoods to which they have ties because prisons are often sited in rural areas. Counting in this way benefits the predominately euroamerican rural areas, especially as voting maps are redrawn. This is known as "prison gerrymandering." Is this fair? Should the prison inmates be counted? If so, how? Should the "usual residence" rule for counting be changed? Is so, how? If not, why not?

• Bill O'Hara, a demographer and author of two books on the accuracy of censuses, stated, "Having watched census for fifty years, there is no doubt in my mind that this is the most politicized census in my lifetime."[43] Is he right? What does manipulation of census numbers mean for democracy? What safeguards can be put in place to better protect the 2030 Census? What does it mean that Thomas Hofeller, responsible for using race and ethnicity to draw voting maps that benefit Republicans, played a role in pushing for the Census Bureau to include a question concerning citizenship?[44]

---

[42] US Census Bureau, "Census Bureau Releases Estimates of Undercount and Overcount in the 2020 Census," news release number CB22-CN.02, March 10, 2022. The Census missed 4.99 of every 100 Latines, 5.64 of every 100 Native Americans, and 3.3 of every 100 African Americans while adding 1.64 for every 100 Euroamericans and 2.62 for every 100 Asians.

[43] Michael Wines, "Growing Fear of a 2020 Census Tailored for One Party's Gains," *New York Times*, August 7, 2020.

[44] Michael Wines, "Disclosures Hint at Politics Behind Census Question," *New York Times*, December 1, 2019.

3. According to an extensive analysis conducted by the *New York Times* concerning stock trades by members of Congress from 2019 through 2021, they discovered that ninety-seven congresspersons—Republicans and Democrats—reported more than thirty-seven stock trades by themselves or their immediate family that directly intersected with the work of the committees on which they serve, raising the potential for conflicts of interest.[45] Many members of Congress or office holders in former administrations become lobbyists when they leave office, or they obtain lucrative jobs in the very industries they once regulated. For example, when Senator Phil Gramm (R-TX)—former chair of the Senate Banking Committee—left office, he became vice president of UBS, a Swiss banking giant and a benefactor of the Financial Services Modernization Act, the banking deregulation legislation Gramm championed.

• Is any of this ethical? Can this be construed as bribery? Should former public officials be allowed to become lobbyists or obtain employment in the industries they once regulated? If not, is this restricting their rights to employment? Lobbyists can be paid an annual $200,000 salary at the low end, and on the high end, over $1 million. Should limits be placed on what a lobbyist can earn? Why or why not? Why are firms willing to pay lobbyists such high fees? Are these reasons ethical, even if they are detrimental to those who cannot afford lobbyists?

• A month before the stock market nosedived due to the COVID-19 pandemic, losing 30 percent of its value, congressional members who were privy to confidential reports divested themselves of stocks. Then-senator Kelly Loeffler (R-GA) dumped $4.38 million, selling twenty-seven stocks which lost on average 32 percent of value a month later. Others who also profited included Senators Richard Burr (R-NC), Dianne Feinstein (D-CA), David Perdue (R-GA), and Jim Inhofe (R-OK).[46] No evidence exists that the sale of these stocks violated any laws; still, were they unethical? Should political officials profit off confidential government reports? Or does a free market imply that anyone should be free to participate in it, including political officials?

• Audrey Ellis and Adam Feuerstein worked together at PricewaterhouseCoopers (PwC), a mega accounting firm. In mid-2018, one of Feuerstein's clients was trying to persuade the government that the association of real estate companies they represented should qualify for the

---

[45] Kate Kelly, Adam Playford, and Alicia Parlapiano, "In Congress, Thousands of Potential Conflicts in Stock Trading," *New York Times*, September 14, 2022.

[46] Jeremy Herb, "Senators' Stock Sales under Fire after Coronavirus Tanked Markets," CNN, March 20, 2020.

new Trump federal tax break. Feuerstein contacted his former colleague, Ellis, who was now at the Treasury Department, working on drafting the rules for this particular deduction. A week after making contact, Feuerstein's client received the deduction, worth billions of dollars. A year later, Ellis returned to PwC, where she was immediately promoted to partner. This example is not an outlier, but rather, the norm.[47] Is this revolving door between business and government problematic? If so, how can the door be shut? Moving from the private sector to the government entails a pay cut, but the return to the private sector is lucratively rewarded. How does one prevent government officials from financially helping their former employers, or, upon leaving their post, financially benefiting from those they supposedly regulated? How is this not, at best, a conflict of interest— or at worst, bribery?

• As this book goes to press, revelations of corruption at the Supreme Court is coming to light. For example, Justice Clarence Thomas has accepted millions of dollars in gifts over the decades from his "friend" Texas billionaire and conservative megadonor Harlan Crow. Likewise, Justice Neil Gorsuch sold a property to Brian Duffy that he had difficulties selling over the past two years. The sale occurred right before Gorsuch's confirmation. Duffy, CEO of a prominent law firm, has had at least twenty-two cases heard before the Court since the sale. Unlike other public servants, none of these acts are illegal. Additionally, Supreme Court justices are not held to the same "ethic" as other lower court justices. Why? Should they be? Are such gifts and sales ethical even if legal? Or is the Court corrupt?[48]

---

[47] Jesse Drucker and Danny Hakim, "A Revolving Door Keeps Tax Policy on Clients' Side," *New York Times*, September 21, 2021.

[48] Moira Donegan, "The US Supreme Court's Alleged Ethics Issues Are Worse Than You Probably Realize," *The Guardian*, April 28, 2023.

Chapter 11

Life and Death

Step 1: Observing

Hopefully, there is more general agreement on the universality of the basic human right to good health than there is on the political actions to take when addressing issues that ensure a more just society. Nearly everyone would argue that human beings have a right to have their health and well-being unthreatened by exterior forces. Although we may disagree as to how to accomplish this goal, humans can expect not to have government or business impose upon them hazardous conditions that produce illness or death. Yet, for many within the United States, the quality of health care—considered among the most advanced in the world—ranges from poor to nonexistent. In 2020 the United States spent approximately 17 percent of its gross domestic product on health care. This is the highest percentage compared to other countries, mainly because most nations set the rates for health care as if it were a public utility. Health spending per US inhabitant came to $11,945 in 2020, which is more expensive than any other industrialized nation. The average amount spent on health per person in comparable countries ($5,736) was about half that of the United States.[1] Such a large discrepancy is mainly due to operating under a capitalist belief that the private market is the best way to provide health care and coverage. Besides a lack of adequate health care, specifically for the poor who are disproportionately people of color, those with darker skin also face a greater risk of being incarcerated or executed by the state. This chapter explores how issues of life (adequate health care) and death (capital punishment) impact marginalized communities.

---

[1] Emma Wager, Jared Ortaliza, and Cynthia Cox, "How Does Health Spending in the US Compare to Other Countries?" Health System Tracker, January 21, 2022.

Life: The Quality of Health Care

Native American, Alaskan Native, African American, Latine, and Pacific Islander populations in the United States disproportionately experienced higher mortality rates from COVID-19 than did euroamericans (Lundberg et al. 2022, 2–4). Furthermore, Latine and Black people have died from COVID-19 at three times the rate of whites.[2] By November 2020, they represented 50 percent of the country's COVID-19 hospitalizations.[3] Over three-quarters of children in the United States who died from COVID-19 were of color—45 percent Latine, 29 percent Black, and 4 percent Indigenous (Bixler et al. 2020, 1324). Obviously, we were not all in this together.

The pandemic, according to a federal report, reduced US life expectancy for the first time since World War II. While life expectancy dropped overall by a year and a half, Latines experienced a greater drop by three years while Black people saw a decrease by 2.9 years. Native Americans faced the most misery as their life expectancy dropped by 6.5 years. Euroamericans, by comparison, experienced a decrease of 1.2 years (Arias et al. 2021, 2). When a vaccine became available, euroamericans were being administered the antidote at 2.3 times the rate as Black people and 2.6 times the rate of Latines. When a site for administrating the vaccine was established in New York to serve the Washington Heights Latine community that was being devastated by the virus, it vaccinated more euroamericans who traveled from other areas to Washington Heights for the vaccine.[4] Furthermore, euroamericans disproportionately benefited more from the CARES Act federal housing aid during the pandemic than people of color.[5]

Lessons from COVID-19 vaccinations in preventing future racial disparities when administrating vaccine doses were not learned. When "mpox"[6] spread through the United States in 2022, New Yorkers represented

---

[2] Nicquel Terry Ellis and Deidre McPhillips, "White People Are Getting Vaccinated at Higher Rates Than Black and Latino Americans," CNN, January 26, 2021.

[3] Abdullah Shihipar, "Racism Is a Health Emergency," *New York Times*, March 9, 2021.

[4] Nicquel Terry Ellis, "A Vaccination Site Meant to Serve a Hard-Hit Latino Neighborhood in New York Instead Served More Whites from Other Areas," *CNN*, January 30, 2021.

[5] Taylor Miller Thomas, "Coronavirus Relief Favors White Households, Leaving Many People of Color at Risk of Being Evicted," *Politico*, August 7, 2020.

[6] Changing the name of an existing disease is an exceptional occasion and is the responsibility of World Health Organization, in consultation with WHO Member States. On November 28, 2022, WHO announced, "Following a series of consultations with global experts, WHO will begin using a new preferred term 'mpox' as

45 percent of those with a heightened risk of infection. While New York did receive 46 percent of the national vaccine doses, Black people—who represent 31 percent of the at-risk population—received but 12 percent of doses administered. These types of imbalances also occurred in other parts of the nation. In North Carolina, where 70 percent of mpox cases impacted Black men and 19 percent impacted euroamericans, 24 percent of the vaccines went to African Americans while 67 percent went to euroamerican people during the summer of 2022.[7]

This should not be surprising. When it comes to health care, people of color are at greater risk of dying from illnesses. Across the board, people of color in the United States receive less care and worse care than euroamericans. A serial cross-sectional survey of US adults conducted from 1999 to 2018 demonstrated a nearly two-decade lack of progress to eliminate racial and ethnic differences in health status and healthcare access. The study of more than half a million adult participants showed that, in 2018, low-income African Americans had the highest estimated prevalence of poor or fair health care (24.9 percent); low-income Latines had the highest estimated percentage of not having health insurance (27.3 percent); and middle- and high-income euroamericans had the lowest percentage in both categories (Mahajan et al. 2021, 637–39). Why? What role does a person's race or ethnicity play in the quality of US health care received?

When insurance coverage and access to medical treatments are comparable, quality of care received varies due to one's race or ethnicity. According to a 2015 study appearing in *American Journal of Public Health*, one of the contributing factors for racial healthcare disparities is the implicit bias of most healthcare providers, who appear to have positive attitudes toward euroamericans while harboring negative attitudes toward people of color (Hall et al. 2015, 60–61). Unsurprisingly, patients of color rate the interpersonal quality of care received from physicians more negatively than euroamerican patients. Patients of color also experience poorer communication with medical providers, particularly in race-discordant

---

a synonym for monkeypox. Both names will be used simultaneously for one year while 'monkeypox' is phased out." Significantly for this book, they further noted, "When the outbreak of monkeypox expanded earlier this year, racist and stigmatizing language online, in other settings, and in some communities was observed and reported to WHO. In several meetings, public and private, a number of individuals and countries raised concerns and asked WHO to propose a way forward to change the name." World Health Organization, "WHO Recommends New Name for Monkeypox Disease," news release, November 28, 2022.

[7] Sharon Otterman, Joseph Goldstein, and Liam Stack, "In Replay from Covid, Disparities over Access," *New York Times*, August 19, 2022.

patient-clinician relationships. A systematic compilation of several studies concerning implicit bias among physicians conducted between 2007 and 2016 revealed that many physicians, regardless of specialties, demonstrated "an implicit preference for white people" (Dehon et al. 2017, 895).

And it's not just human practitioners. According to a study published in the *New England Journal of Medicine*, the numerous medical formulas, digital calculators, and decision-making tools employed to determine treatment disproportionately divert medical resources away from Black patients, steering them from procedures and denying treatment options available to white patients. For example, the osteoporosis risk calculator is calibrated to give Black women a score that makes qualifying for the prescription of osteoporosis medication less likely than among white women who are similar in all other respects except color or race (Vyas, Eisenstein, and Jones 2020: 878–90). Researchers at the University of Chicago note the existence of a pervasive algorithmic bias that impacts countless daily decisions concerning how patients of color are treated by hospitals, insurers, and other businesses. The biases of society have been unconsciously (or consciously) coded into the very programs and protocols on which health professionals rely when deciding health care for their patients. Furthermore, the mere suspicion held by patients of color concerning prejudices of healthcare providers—or the AI programs upon which they rely—is enough to result in exacerbated psychological and physiological stress—specifically threat cognitions, threat emotions, and increased cardiovascular reactivity (Obermeyer et al. 2021, 2). According to a 2012 study, over time, such stressors can lead to coronary and carotid atherosclerosis and hypertension. The study concluded that the mere anticipation of prejudice from one's care provider leads to health hazards for the patient (Sawyer et al. 2012, 1020).

A 2015 *American Journal of Public Health* study also demonstrates how people of color have difficulties in accessing health care, including preventive services, acute pain treatment, and chronic disease management. The negative attitudes expressed by physicians toward patients of color were dominant in their communication styles. Doctors' demonstration of positive emotions was limited, requests for patient input concerning treatment decisions were infrequent, and patient-centered care seemed unavailable. Not surprisingly, patients of color experienced longer waiting time with shorter treatment time (Hall et al. 2015, 61). In making treatment decisions, physicians demonstrating a pro-white bias were more likely to recommend thrombolysis (a blood clot prevention treatment) to euroamericans than to Black patients. Even pediatricians were more likely to recommend the ideal management of pain for white patients when responding to their complaints than when patients were Black (72).

In a 2017 study published by the *American Journal of Health-System Pharmacy*, pharmacies in predominantly nonwhite neighborhoods were significantly less likely to stock medication to treat patients with severe pain than those pharmacies located in predominantly white neighborhoods. According to a survey conducted in Shelby County, Tennessee, pharmacies located in areas with a high percentage of racially minoritized residents had lower pharmacy density than areas with a high percentage of euroamerican residents. Pharmacies located in communities with low average income levels, low employment rates, and high scores for personal crime risk were less likely to offer home medication delivery services (Chisholm-Burns et al. 2017, 667).

The result of a systematic empirical study indicates that, when a medical professional gazes upon a "dark" body, they tend to superhumanize the person. Clinicians assume darker bodies possess supernatural "magical" mental and physical abilities that allow them to supposedly manage pain better than whites. Hence, medical professions tend to undertreat African Americans when they express pain (Waytz, Hoffman, and Trawalter 2014, 1–2). When health professionals were presented with a facial photo of an African American prior to considering the medical situation that patient was supposedly experiencing, they responded by prescribing less treatment for pain when compared to viewing a photo of a lighter-skinned face. The study concludes that the disparities in pain treatment are largely due to automatic (below-conscious-level regulation) as opposed to deliberate awareness (subject to conscious regulation), and are independent of general prejudices (Mathur et al. 2014, 476–77). Studies such as these suggest that the diagnosis and treatment of African Americans may indeed be biased. Physicians' stereotypes were also evident among pediatricians in prescribing treatment recommendations for pain management, urinary tract infections, attention deficit hyperactivity disorder, and asthma among children of color.

The first comprehensive study of racial disparities in health care was conducted by the Institute of Medicine, an independent research agency that advises Congress on healthcare issues. Reviewing more than one hundred studies conducted from 1992 to 2002, the report concluded that the disparities in health care due to race and ethnicity contribute to higher death rates among people of color from cancer, heart disease, diabetes, and HIV infection.[8] The empirical evidence overwhelmingly indicated that, all factors being equal, those from racial and ethnic communities receive a lower quality of health care than their white counterparts. Not

---

[8] Sheryl Gay Stolberg, "Minorities Receive Inferior Care, Even If Insured, Study Finds," *New York Times*, March 21, 2002.

much has changed since the start of the millennium when this study was concluded. In some cases, the situation worsened. Race, ethnicity, and place of residency continue to be major indicators of the quality of health care received. For example, we have known for decades that, with the right medication, diet, and lifestyle changes, diabetic patients can learn how to manage their disease, making amputations unnecessary. Yet close to 140,000 diabetes-related amputations are conducted each year, with Black patients being four times more likely to have an amputation than euroamericans (Mizelle 2021, 1256). Overall, those with diabetes who live in neighborhoods ranking in the nation's bottom quartile by income—comprising primarily residents of color—were nearly 38.5 percent more likely to undergo major amputations compared with people living in the highest-income communities, which mainly comprise euroamericans (Skrepnek, Mills, and Armstrong 2015, 2).

Women from the eight states[9] making up the Delta region have a lower rate of utilizing mammograms than those in the rest of the country. Among these women, those who are African American have higher mortality rates due to breast cancer than their euroamerican counterparts, as well as higher rates than Black women in the rest of the country. For women within the Delta region, the median accessibility to mammograms is higher in Illinois compared to other states in the region, with Louisiana having the lowest access (Zahnd et al. 2019, 551, 555). Although breast cancer incidence rates are slightly higher among euroamericans (130.8 per 100,000) than African Americans (126.7 per 100,000), Black women have the highest breast cancer death rate (28.4 deaths per 100,000) and are more likely to die from it at every age with a mortality rate that is 40 percent higher than that of euroamerican women (American Cancer Society 2019, 4, 7).

A direct correlation exists between the death of Black people from cancer and the neighborhoods in which they live. For example, African Americans have a greater likelihood (49 percent) of being diagnosed with an advanced stage of lung cancer than their white counterparts if they live in a segregated county. This disparity disappears for those Black people when they live in less segregated areas. Black patients with early-stage lung cancer living in highly segregated areas were also 47 percent less likely to receive necessary surgery (Annesi et al. 202). These data raise questions concerning the link between living a healthy life, the race or ethnicity of those who get to live that healthy life, and where they must reside to live that healthy life.

---

[9] Alabama, Arkansas, Illinois, Kentucky, Louisiana, Mississippi, Missouri, and Tennessee.

Even children of color experience a lower quality of health care than white children in a health system that already ranks 39th (lowest among industrialized nations) out of 180 nations (Clark et al. 2020, 641–42). A study surveying more than 172,000 children found that the odds of African American children dying within thirty days after surgery were 3.43 times more likely than white children. Black children also have 18 percent greater odds of developing postoperative complications and 7 percent higher odds of developing serious adverse events (Nafiu et al. 2020, 1–2). Unsurprisingly, from 2016 through 2019, euroamerican children (34.4 percent) admitted to children's hospitals across the country were more likely than Latine (25.5 percent) or Black children (28.4 percent) to be given CT scans for the risk of head trauma (Marin et al. 2021, 5). When it came to prescribed narcotic medications, their usage decreased for children of color when compared to euroamerican children. A study discovered that an annual average of 2.3 percent of children received opioid prescriptions; however, white children received a higher rate (3.0 percent) of prescribed opioids when compared to Black children at 1.7 percent, Latine children at 1.4 percent, or Asian children at 0.9 percent (Groenewald et al. 2018).

If a patient of color complains about unfair treatment, they risk having their medical records noted with them being uncooperative or exhibiting problematic behaviors through coded words like "non-adherent," "agitated," or "non-compliant." Such terms, while not commonly used, appear more commonly in the medical records of Black patients. Surveying over forty thousand electronic medical records, Black patients were 2.54 times more likely than white patients to have at least one negative descriptor in their official medical records (Sun 2022, 203). Even when patients of color are "compliant," another study of thirty thousand electronic medical records found "stigmatizing language" was used to describe nonwhite patients. While 2.6 percent of medical notes of euroamerican patients contained such terms, they were present in 3.15 percent of Black patient records (Himmelstein, Bates, and Zhou 2022, 1–13).

Discrimination within the medical profession cannot be easily dismissed as the consequence of individual discriminatory bias. A discriminatory ethos exists that has been internalized and institutionalized throughout all levels of the medical profession—an ethos that creates and maintains a negative health effect on patients of color. For example, a 2016 study revealed that 40 percent of first-year medical students believed Black people have thicker skin than non-Black people, while 14 percent of second-year students surveyed believed Black people have less sensitive nerve endings—thus concluding they biologically feel less pain than euroamerican people (Hoffman et al. 2016, 4298). Such assumptions mean that the present-day healthcare system in the United States is structurally designed to bring better health to middle- and upper-class euroamericans than it does to people of color. One could go so far as to say that it tends to bring ill-health or even death to poor people of color. Even the largest doctors' group, the American Medical Association, which is overwhelmingly white, has publicly acknowledged its racist history and current imbedded biases and, in response, implemented a strategic plan in 2021 to tackle health inequities.[10]

This reality has historical roots. Since the early twentieth century, sterilization of those deemed "mentally inferior" or otherwise "unfit to propagate" became common procedures in keeping with the dominant medical philosophy of eugenics. In 1907, Indiana passed the world's first eugenics-based sterilization law, which was soon followed by similar laws being enacted in thirty-one other states. Under these laws, approximately sixty thousand women of color were sterilized. The "success" of protecting whites in the United States from being overrun by defective races and ethnic groups led Nazi Germany to implement similar laws.[11] During the 1950s, a third of the women of Puerto Rico were sterilized after their second child—many involuntarily. In California, from 1909 to 1964, the state sterilized twenty thousand people—mostly African Americans, immigrants, and those of Mexican descent (the latter at higher disproportionate rates).[12] During the 1970s, more than a quarter of Native American women of childbearing age were sterilized under the Family Planning Services and Population Research Act of 1970.[13] In 1975, working-class Mexican immigrant women were, according to a filed class-action lawsuit, sterilized at Los Angeles County General Hospital without their consent.[14] More recently, migrant women in the 2020s have faced unnecessary hysterectomies without their consent at the Irwin County Detention Center in Ocilla, Georgia, before being deported back to their countries of origin.[15] In

---

[10] See the American Medical Association's *Organizational Strategic Plan to Embed Racial Justice and Advance Health Equity*, May 2021.

[11] Catherine E. Shoichet, "In a Horrifying History of Forced Sterilization, Some Fear the US Is Beginning a New Chapter," CNN, September 16, 2020.

[12] Natalia Molina, "Forced Sterilization of Mexican-Americans: When US Lawmakers Took a Page from the Nazi Playbook," The History Channel, October 23, 2017.

[13] Brianna Theobald, "A 1970 Law Led to the Mass Sterilization of Native American Women. That History Still Matters," *Time*, November 27, 2019.

[14] Molina, "Forced Sterilization of Mexican-Americans."

[15] Priscilla Alvarez, "Whistleblower Alleges High Rate of Hysterectomies and Medical Neglect at ICE Facility," CNN, September 16, 2020.

addition to being sterilized, women of color were also used as birth control test subjects without being told that they were part of a trial or the risks involved. This occurred when the first birth control pill—Enovid—was tested on Puerto Ricans from the poorest neighborhoods of San Juan. A strong formulation of the drug (higher doses of hormones than today's pills) led to illnesses, depression, and several deaths.[16]

Besides medically preventing the birth of people of color, those who were alive—like the women of Puerto Rico—were routinely used as guinea pigs for medical experimentation. In the mid-1800s, James Marion Sims, considered the father of gynecology, perfected his knowledge and techniques by experimenting on enslaved women, operating on them without anesthesia, under the assumption that they didn't feel pain to the same degree as euroamerican women. Probably the most infamous modern example of US human experimentation is the forty-year-long (1932–1972) Tuskegee research study, which the US Public Health Service (PHS) conducted on 412 poor Black sharecroppers in the late stages of syphilis. They were told by government researchers that they were being treated, when in fact they were not. The data that researchers hoped to obtain from the experiment were gathered from autopsies. Consequently, these poor Black men were deliberately left to degenerate under the ravages of tertiary syphilis, the symptoms of which include tumors, heart disease, paralysis, blindness, insanity, and death.

US medical experiments such as these were not limited to domestic subjects. Between July 1946 and December 1948, US doctors—with the full backing of US health officials and Surgeon General Thomas Parran—deliberately infected thirteen hundred unsuspecting Guatemalans (out of the fifty-five hundred in the study) with venereal diseases to explore methods and approaches to control sexually transmitted diseases. Federico Ramos was one of the thousands who, as a low-ranking soldier in the Guatemalan army, was ordered to report to a clinic run and operated by US doctors. There, over the course of two visits, he was injected with what he now suspects were syphilis and gonorrhea. After leaving the armed forces, he returned to his rural village, where he suffered from the effects of the disease for decades, unable to pay for medical treatment. Worse, he infected his wife and children. These medical human experiments were uncovered in 2010. Ramos and others sued the US government, and, while President Obama's official apology contained flowery words, the US Department

---

[16] Erin Blakemore, "The First Birth Control Pill Used Puerto Rican Women as Guinea Pigs: Eugenics and Unethical Clinical Trials Are Part of the Pill's Legacy," The History Channel, May 9, 2018.

of Justice requested that the compensation case be dismissed. In June 2012, the case was rejected by the US District Court. Instead of settling with those whose personhood was violated, the US government pledged $1 million to study new rules protecting medical research volunteers and $775,000 to help fight STDs in Guatemala.[17]

Race and ethnic identity were major components in the Tuskegee and Guatemalan experiments; ironically, the experiments were conducted at the same time that the United States was prosecuting Nazi officials at the Nuremberg trials immediately following the Second World War for carrying out medical experiments on human beings (primarily Jewish people). The conclusion of the Nazi doctor trials led to the establishment of what eventually became the Nuremberg Code of medical ethics. Medical practitioners cannot participate in human experimentations without first obtaining voluntary consent from participants. Additionally, unnecessary harm to the subject should be avoided. Such accounts of US medical experiments on humans are especially troubling in the shadow of the Nuremberg trials.

Nonetheless, during the mid-twentieth century, conducting medical experiments on prison inmates and disabled people remained common. Reports exist of mental patients in Connecticut being infected with hepatitis, prisoners in Maryland having the pandemic flu virus squirted up their noses, and the chronically ill at a New York hospital being injected with cancer cells. At least forty such cases of human medical experiments were carried out by the US government within the country's borders from the 1940s through the 1960s. It was legitimate in the minds of health professionals to experiment on those who lacked full rights within society, specifically prisoners, the mentally disabled, and poor people of color.[18]

In June 1990, about fifteen hundred six-month-old, predominantly Black and Latine babies in Los Angeles were given an experimental measles vaccine developed by Kaiser Permanente. The parents of these children were never informed that the vaccine was experimental, even though they were used before in two-thirds-world countries with devastating results.[19] Another troubling example of human testing in that decade occurred at the Kennedy Krieger Institute, which is affiliated with Johns Hopkins University. The prominent Baltimore medical institute knowingly exposed more

[17] Matthew Walter, "First, Do Harm," *Nature*, February 9, 2012; Brian Vastag, "US Pledges $1.8 Million in Response to Unethical Guatemalan Medical Studies," *Washington Post*, January 10, 2012.

[18] Mike Stobbe, "Past Medical Testing on Humans Revealed," *Washington Post*, February 27, 2011.

[19] Marlene Cimons, "US Measles Experiment Failed to Disclose Risk," *Los Angeles Times*, June 17, 1996.

than one hundred Black children as young as one year old to lead poisoning for periodic testing of their blood to study the cumulative hazards of lead poisoning. The children were endangered in homes with high levels of lead dust even while the Kennedy Krieger Institute assured parents that the houses were "lead safe." The six-year program of human testing led to permanent neurological injuries among some of the children.[20]

Human medical experiments continue to occur, using the world's poor as subjects. According to a report by the Office of Inspector General of the Department of Health and Human Services, 80 percent of approved marketing applications for drugs and biologics contained data from clinical trials conducted outside the United States. Two-thirds-world nations with lower medical standards, less regulatory oversight, and inadequate patient protection lack the means to effectively enforce the minimum rules already on the books for medical trials. In such places, foreign drug companies have been accused of often testing their experimental drugs on the poor and illiterate without obtaining their consent or properly explaining the risks involved in their participation (Yang, Chen, and Bennett 2018, 226). Is it any wonder that the world's poor and non-whites have a healthy suspicion of euroamerican medical professionals and distrust the US government? Is it any wonder that communities of color experienced COVID-19 vaccine hesitancy?

Disparities in the Legal System

Like the health system, the US legal system negatively impacts marginalized communities of color. A disproportionate number of people of color face prison and capital punishment. At the close of the twentieth century, the United States had incarcerated more than two million of its citizens, 70 percent of the incarcerated being of color. The first twenty years of the new millennium revealed that not much has changed. According to statisticians with the Federal Bureau of Prisons, 38.4 percent of the prison population was Black even though they represent 12.6 percent of the US population, while 30.3 percent were Latine (regardless of race) although they represent 18.7 percent of the country's population.[21] Black and Latino males had respective imprisonment rates that are 5.7 and 2.5 times higher than that of euroamerican men, while Black and Latina females' imprisonment rate was respectively 1.7 and 1.2 times that of euroamerican women

---

[20] Timothy Williams, "Racial Bias Seen in Study of Lead Dust and Children," *New York Times*, September 16, 2011.

[21] Federal Bureau of Prisons, "Statistics," July 30, 2022.

(Carson 2021, 24). That people of color unduly fill our prisons should not be surprising when we consider that people of color are more likely to experience unjustifiable stops, insulting language, excessive force, or corrupt activities by police.

Perceiving people of color as suspicious was best illustrated in New York City during the so-called liberal Bloomberg administration. He did reduce the homicide rate in the city to its lowest levels since reliable data were kept in the early 1960s. Credit for this accomplishment is given to programs like the controversial "Stop, Question, Frisk." As the name of the initiative implies, "suspicious" individuals were stopped by the police, questioned, and then frisked. However, of the 685,724 street stops conducted in 2011, 41.6 percent of them were of young Black and Latino males (ages fourteen through twenty-four) who, combined, represent only 4.7 percent of the city's population.[22]

And while "Stop, Question, Frisk" was a race-based inconvenience, seeing Blacks and Latines as dangerous can prove deadly. Of the 4,653 fatal shootings by the police over a five-year period (2015–2020), BIPOC had significantly higher death rates than euroamericans. Native American (3.06), Black (2.62), and Latine (1.29) populations had even higher rates when we consider those who were unarmed—respectively at 3.95, 3.49, and 1.55 (Lett et al. 2021, 394).

Lacking proper documentation complicates the Latine experience in the penal system. Reporting on 4,130 interviews with 12,895 individuals held in Border Patrol custody from fall 2008 to spring 2011, No More Deaths paints a disturbing portrait of the depth of human rights abuses that occur.[23] According to the study, Border Patrol agents denied food to 2,981 people and gave insufficient food to 11,384 people who were held in custody. Only 20 percent of those in custody for more than two days received a meal. Water was denied to 863 people, and 1,402 individuals received insufficient water. Children were more likely to be denied water or not provided enough. These are individuals who were recently picked up traversing a desert; hence many were suffering from moderate to severe dehydration when apprehended (No More Deaths 2011, 4–9). When three children died in detention during 2019 of influenza, probably due to the

---

[22] Al Baker, "New York Police Release Data Showing Rise in Number of Stops on Streets," *New York Times*, May 13, 2013.

[23] Although I did not participate in this report, my own work on the borders, interviewing deported migrants in Mexico who were also held by the Border Patrol, corroborates the rampant abuses that exist. I spoke to many migrants, saw the recent scars and bruises on their bodies, and heard their testimonies of physical and psychological abuses.

routine practice—per detainee complaints—of maintaining overcrowded and cold temperature conditions, the CDC recommended distributing the flu vaccine at the point of entry into the system. Such precautions would save lives—specifically the lives of Brown children exposed to infectious respiratory illnesses due to congested and extremely cold facilities. The Customs and Border Protection agency refused to put a vaccination program into effect.[24]

Physical abuse was reported by 10 percent of interviewed migrant inmates, including teenagers and children. Of the 433 incidents in which emergency medical treatment or medications were needed, Border Patrol provided access to care in only 59 cases. The study recorded 2,926 incidents of failure to return personal belongings. Border Patrol deported 869 family members separately. This means that families were deported through different ports of entry, a costly practice designed to separate families by distance. Furthermore, 1,051 women, 190 teenagers, and 94 children were repatriated in the middle of the night, with no money, to dangerous border towns, when Mexican humanitarian service agencies are closed. Increasing reports of psychological abuse were also reported, including threatening detainees with death, depriving them of sleep, keeping vehicles and cells at extremely hot or cold temperatures, playing traumatizing songs about people dying in the desert, and forced holding of strenuous or painful positions for no apparent reason other than to humiliate (No More Deaths 2011, 4–9).

Because most people cannot tell the difference between a documented and undocumented Latine, all face discrimination in the hands of law enforcers. They do not belong until proven otherwise. A 2020 study focusing on the border state of Texas, which has a substantial Latine population, found that they—39 percent of the time—were more likely to be stopped and searched than any other racial or ethnic group. Ironically, those searches found less contraband among Latines (32 percent) than with euroamericans (36 percent) when they were searched (del Carmen et al. 2022, 2). We are challenged to ask: What does a person who is undocumented look like to raise suspicion? What is it that makes Blacks and Latines look more suspicious to trained law enforcement than euroamericans?

Being seen as more dangerous by those who have the power of life and death over you is highly problematic. Take, for example, the comments of Judge Edith H. Jones of Houston, who sat on the US Court of Appeals for the Fifth Circuit and served as its chief justice. During a speech at the University Law School in February 2013, she said that

---

[24] Miriam Jordan, "Doctors with Vaccines Ready, but Immigration Officials Turn Them Away," *New York Times*, December 12, 2019.

Blacks and Latinos were "predisposed to crime." According to an affidavit concerning the event, Judge Jones went on to state, "Sadly, some groups seem to commit more heinous crimes than others.... [There is] no arguing that Blacks and Hispanics far outnumber Anglos on death row.... Sadly people from these racial groups do get involved in more violent crimes." The victim of institutionalized racism and ethnic discrimination is blamed rather than the system that accounts for the disparity. Judge Jones went on to suggest that a death sentence would be a service to them, for it allows them to "make peace with God." Arguments against capital punishment based on "mental retardation" [sic] or systemic racism were dismissed by the judge as "red herrings."[25]

Black and Latine people posing as inherent threats to white peace and security is a theme that launched a successful presidential campaign. During his announcement speech for the White House, then-candidate Donald Trump claimed, "When Mexico sends its people, they're not sending their best. They're sending people that have lots of problems.... They're bringing drugs. They're bringing crime. They're rapists. And some, I assume, are good people."[26] Trump tapped into a way of seeing and defining bodies of color that resonated with a segment of the population. According to a Reuters/Ipsos poll at the time, almost half of Trump supporters were more likely to describe African Americans as "criminals," "unintelligent," "lazy," and "violent," than supporters for other Republican candidates during the primaries.[27]

When defendants who are of color go to trial, most stand before an all-white or nearly all-white jury. When Black defendants are tried for murder, prosecutors routinely dismiss Black jurors. Jurors of color are often dismissed from serving due to what is known as the "death qualification," that is, unlike most euroamericans, they are deemed to have a stronger opposition to capital punishment. Others are dismissed due to the high levels of unexamined (or examined) racial biases of judges and prosecutors. In a study conducted in South Carolina, 51 percent of Black jurors were dismissed for cause in capital cases as opposed to just 33 percent of potential euroamerican jurors (Ndulue 2020, 39). Nonracially diverse juries adversely affect the outcome of trials and sentencing. All-white juries are more likely to convict defendants of color than juries that are racially

---

[25] Ethan Bronner, "Complaint Accuses US Judge in Texas of Racial Bias," *New York Times*, June 4, 2013.

[26] Michelle Ye Hee Lee, "Donald Trump's False Comments Connecting Mexican Immigrants and Crime," *Washington Post*, July 8, 2015.

[27] Emily Flitter and Chris Kahn, "Exclusive: Trump Supporters More Likely to View Blacks Negatively—Reuters/Ipsos Poll," Reuters, June 28, 2016.

and ethnically diverse, and juries with an overrepresentation of euroamerican men are more inclined to sentence defendants to death. In one study, participants were given the same facts concerning a conviction, except they were provided with a photograph of the accused with either a light skin tone or dark skin tone. The results were that the darker-skinned person was rated more culpable as participants interpreted ambiguous facts as being more consistent with guilt (46).

A 2020 study demonstrated that, between 1973 and 2019, those convicted of killing euroamerican people were seventeen times more likely to be sentenced to death than those convicted of killing Black people (Phillips and Marceau 2020, 587, 607). In deciding who will be charged with a capital offense in death penalty states, it is important to note that, as of 2019, 95 percent of elected prosecutors were euroamericans (Ndulue 2020, 37). Euroamerican prosecutors are not the only problem. Most capital defense attorneys are also euroamerican, usually appointed to defend clients of color. Studies show that they, too, share the implicit biases of the general population (43). Hence, we should not be surprised that at least one out of every five executed African Americans were convicted by an all-euroamerican jury (Amnesty International 2003, 3). Not much has changed since the start of the millennium. More recently, Amnesty International wrote, "From initial charging decisions to plea bargaining to jury sentencing, African-Americans are treated more harshly when they are defendants, and their lives are accorded less value when they are victims. All-white or virtually all-white juries are still commonplace in many localities" (Amnesty International 2017, 1).

Because bodies of color are not trusted in the euroamerican imagination, euroamerican bodies have greater worth. The United States places a greater worth on the life of a euroamerican person than it does on the life of a person of color. According to the Marshall Project, of four hundred thousand homicides committed by civilians between 1980 and 2014, euroamerican people who kill Black men in the United States often face no legal consequence. No criminal sanction occurred in one in six of such killings. While an average 2 percent of murders—regardless of the victims' or perpetrators' race—are classified as justified, when it comes to euroamerican people killing Black men, almost 17 percent of such murders are deemed justified, while 3.1 percent are considered justified when euroamerican people kill Latines. But when Black people kill euroamerican people, only 0.8 percent of the deaths are deemed justifiable.[28]

---

[28] Daniel Lathrop and Anna Flagg, "In Deeming a Killing 'Justifiable,' Race Is a Factor," *New York Times*, August 23, 2017.

An irrational fear interprets dark bodies as "threatening" in the euroamerican mind and influences policy decisions that transform willful killing into a justifiable act. Laws of self-defense—e.g., "Stand Your Ground" legislation—become legal justification to employ deadly force whenever the would-be killer feels threatened by a person of color. Predominately euroamerican juries are probably more inclined to give euroamerican defendants who kill Black men the benefit of the doubt because they, too, can relate to the fear of darker, dangerous bodies. Defense attorney Laura Hogue played to this inclination when she described Ahmaud Arbery, the Black jogger who was chased down and killed in Satilla Shores, Georgia, by three euroamerican men after he took a sip of water at a house under construction in 2020, "in his khaki shorts with no socks to cover his long, dirty toenails."[29] When tropes of dirtiness can stoke fears of monstrosity and danger, Black lives—as well as Brown, Indigenous, Asian, or any combination thereof—simply do not matter.

When racism and ethnic discrimination play such leading roles in who is executed and who is not, we should also expect the innocent to be put to death. We should not be surprised that defendants of color are over-represented among those wrongly convicted of capital murder, spending, on average, four years longer on death row than euroamerican defendants before being exonerated. Furthermore, Black defendants who are exonerated were 22 percent more likely to be so due to police misconduct. One can only wonder how many innocents have been executed based on the inherent racism and ethnic bigotry of the judicial process.

The arbitrary and discriminatory manner by which the death penalty is imposed has meant that, even if it could be argued that the state has the right to execute our worst criminals, the state has lost its moral authority and ability to do so due to how our judicial system enforces executions based on race and ethnicity. And yet, regardless of the overwhelming statistics that indicate the inherent biases present throughout all aspects of the US judicial system, in the wake of the George Floyd murder (when euroamerican police officer Derek Chauvin suffocated Floyd by pressing a knee on his neck), US attorney general William Barr—the top law enforcement agent in the land—responded, "I don't think that the law enforcement system is systemically racist." Chad Wolf, acting secretary of the Department of Homeland Security, went on to confirm that "systematic racism" was not an issue for law enforcement.[30]

---

[29] Theresa Waldrop, "Defense Lawyer Prompts Outrage for Bringing Up Ahmaud Arbery's Toenails in Closing Arguments," CNN, November 24, 2021.

[30] Katie Benner, "Barr Says He Sees No Systemic Racism in Policing and Won't Limit Immunity," *New York Times*, June 8, 2020.

Both the health system and the legal system function on the underlying assumption that life can be reduced to a commodity, the value of which can be determined based on its proximity to whiteness. Not all human life has equal value in the United States. The life of a euroamerican person has, historically, been more valued than that of a dark-skinned person; the life of a wealthy person more valued than that of a poor person; and the life of a heterosexual man more valued than the life of a cisgender woman or queer person.

This nation's judicial system is rooted in the violent birth of the country, influencing how the very definition of justice is determined. Since its foundation, the United States has forged and continues to champion an economy designed to benefit the invading European immigrants through the violent appropriation of Indigenous people's land, the labor of Africans and people of African descent, and the stolen natural resources of the Global South. Thus, those who have suffered under the unjust US judicial system cannot rely on or look to the dominant eurocentric culture for guidance on defining justice. The persistence of discriminatory social structures like the healthcare or legal systems remains an indictment of the dominant eurocentric culture.

Step 2: Reflecting

During the early months of the COVID-19 pandemic, when the painful economic toll on the nation was becoming apparent, lieutenant governor of Texas Dan Patrick proposed that "senior citizens" should return to work at the height of COVID infections and deaths, "[taking] a chance on [their] survival in exchange for keeping the America that all America loves for [their] children and grandchildren."[31] Patrick's sentiments clearly demonstrate the commodification of life and the marginalization of commodified lives. For Patrick, the elderly should be offered up on the altar of capitalism as sacrifices to ensure the economic privilege of the few. In our current system, claims of "pro-life" become valid when they do not impact stock dividends. Human life within the United States is dispensable when it comes to saving the wealth of the few, when it is the wealth of the few that should be dispensable to save the lives of the many.

Why is it that, for millions within the United States, the quality of health care has consistently ranged from poor to nonexistent, a phenomenon disproportionately experienced by the poor and people of color, although in the past few years, many middle-class euroamericans have been rapidly joining their ranks? The US healthcare system has been structured within

---

[31] "Tucker Carlson Tonight," Fox News, March 23, 2020.

a neoliberal economic philosophy. In other words, health care was and continues to be a profit-making venture. This explains why the US health-care system cost four times more than the single-payer system of Canada. The average American spends $933 in hospital administration, $844 on insurance company overhead, and $465 for physicians' insurance-related costs. Compare this to what Canadians spend—$196, $146, and $87, respectively.[32] The question ignored during the debates that led to the Health Care and Education Reconciliation Act of 2010 (aka Obamacare) was: are afford-able health care and profit-making capitalism mutually exclusive?

The problem is not obtaining coverage; the problem is the high health-care costs in this country. For 85 percent of low-income enrollees, federal subsidies make health insurance premiums slightly affordable. But, for those who are middle-class (an annual income of $47,720 for an individual and $97,200 for a family of four), premiums are expensive and high deduct-ibles make coverage unaffordable. In 2015, 46 percent of uninsured adults attempted to gain coverage through Obamacare, but that coverage was too expensive.[33] Attempting to offer universal health care within a capitalist paradigm means that those who are not poor enough will find the cost of health insurance cost prohibitive. If we decide that health care should be provided through so-called free-market forces, then it is moral for an insur-ance company to determine treatment based on cost outweighing profit. If we decide that health care should create a profit, then it is ethical when pharmaceutical companies charge whatever the market can bear for life-saving medicine, or—through political action committees (PACs)—donate to politicians who legislate against the same medicine that is sold at cheaper prices in other countries to be sold in the United States for similar prices if it is even sold at all. If health care should be ruled solely by market forces, then we should be satisfied with a system where healing is available only for those to whom it's affordable. Complaining about the affordability of health care betrays our capitalist economic structures.

Rather than philosophically questioning the principles upon which we, as a society, determine who gets to live and who gets to die due to who receives and who does not receive health care, Obamacare instead attempted to reform a system that, for some, might be beyond reform. In fact, this legislation sought reform of a system whose very purpose is to make money, remaining inherently unattainable to large segments of the

---

[32] Igor Derysh, "American Health Care System Costs Four Times More Than Canada's Single-Payer System," Salon, February 15, 2020.

[33] Tami Luhby, "Is Obamacare Really Affordable? Not for the Middle Class," CNN: Business, November 4, 2016.

population. Jesus tells us that no person can serve two masters; nevertheless, that is exactly what Obamacare has tried to do: heal all who are ill and still turn a profit.

Just as there are areas within society where principles of entrepreneurship may better serve the broader population, there are areas where a more communal approach might be needed. Could it be that a communal approach to health care (socialized medicine) provides the greatest number of people more affordable health care than Obamacare would be able to do? If we recognize a basic human right to good health, then we must also have a frank conversation to determine which economic structures frame institutions and practices of health care.

One of the consequences of the US economic structure is the subjugation of its own citizens, particularly the marginalized, to social systems such as our healthcare and legal labyrinths that do not foster abundant life. The social structures of a society are established around or to support certain social and moral values. But the question must be asked: Whose or what social and moral values are the foundation of these structures? Is the morality of any given society whatever the dominant culture of that society decides is correct social behavior?

To a great extent, any judicial system that is established by the dominant culture exists to legitimize the social and moral values of that culture, which, in the case of the United States, is privileged by whiteness and economic class. These values are then imposed upon the marginalized, who may well perceive them to be unjust and oppressive. We should, therefore, not be surprised when ethical issues concerning health care or the legal system represent the perspectives of the dominant eurocentric culture. Seldom explored are the perspectives of the disenfranchised, usually those ill-treated by the present systems. When bioethicists focus on the ethical issues raised by scientific and technological advances that may prolong or secure a richer quality of life, attention is seldom given to how or why those on the margins fail to benefit.

Generally, the marginalized are excluded from the benefits of medical advances, or the fair application of justice within the legal system, mainly because of how they are socially perceived or seen. "Seeing" can transform human beings into things, into objects. Once social structures adopt this form of seeing, it becomes normalized and legitimized within society. Seeing (or defining) dark-skinned bodies as dangerous occurs unconsciously. This is demonstrated by simply consulting a dictionary for a definition of the word "black." When the dominant culture gazes upon a dark-skinned male body, that body is automatically defined as something evil, wicked, harmful, and dangerous. If the act of seeing is used to mask the power and privilege of those who benefit from how reality is constructed, then gazing upon dark bodies as dangerous is the first crucial step in maintaining a system that continuously seeks to punish or confine those dangerous dark bodies.

Actions taken upon people of color based solely on appearance are illustrated by a study published in 2022 that demonstrated how cultural stereotypes play an integral role when individuals engaged in mock shooter simulations. White participants were quicker to "shoot" both armed and unarmed Black targets compared to white targets (Splan and Forbes 2022, 442). How our culture teaches us to see dark bodies shapes the behavior of people responding quickly and automatically when confronted by those from the margins who are dark-skinned.

In most cases, racist behaviors are seldom conscious. No doubt, there are those within the medical profession or those involved in law enforcement who are not always or even often outwardly racist who, nonetheless, subscribe to white supremacy. The face of racism and ethnic discrimination has changed from a more direct bigotry of frequently spewed derogatory slurs toward an ambivalence characterized by many who are probably well-intentioned, liberal, highly educated euroamerican folk whose unexamined attitudes nonetheless disenfranchise communities of color. Studies show how socialization practices and normal cognitive biases contribute to aversive racist and discriminative perspectives that exist under the surface of consciousness, even when this aversive racism and ethnic discrimination conflict with positive, consciously held, and life-affirming beliefs concerning justice and equality.

Aversive racism and ethnic discrimination are more likely expressed in the forms of prejudice and discrimination during ambiguous situations, when attitudes or behavior that negatively impact people of color can be attributed to causes other than discrimination or could be justified on nonracial grounds. Aversive racism and ethnic discrimination can also be manifested in terms of pro-ingroup bias that favors one's own group compared to the more recognizable anti-outgroup bias that negatively affects people of color in more obvious ways (Hodson, Dovidio and Gaertner 2009, 2). A politically correct racism that is seldom personally recognized is no less damning to communities of color and society as a whole.

Step 3: Meditating

Basic Christian doctrine maintains that the *imago Dei* (image of God) is present in every person (every living creature) created by God, thus establishing the infinite worth of each human being if not every sentient being. To ignore this *imago Dei* violates the inherited rights of all humans. Because the spark of the Absolute exists within every human, all possess inherent dignity. Even so, social structures are constructed to deny the worth of those who are relegated to the margins or, worse, cause the oppressed to question if they even possess the *imago Dei*. As Desmond Tutu observed, "The ultimate evil is not the suffering . . . which is meted out to those who are God's children. The ultimate evil of oppression . . . is when it succeeds in making a child of God begin to doubt that he or she is a child of God" (1991, 131). How is the *imago Dei* denied? Assigning more worth to one human life than to another because of race, class, orientation, or gender ignores the *imago Dei* of the least among us and rejects the God of life.

Taking capital punishment as an example, we can note that biblical texts, specifically in Leviticus, prescribe capital punishment for such crimes as murder and rape. But Leviticus also prescribes that a disobedient, stubborn child who curses his or her parent is subject to the death penalty (20:9). So is the adulterer (20:10), the one who lays with a man as if a woman (20:13), the person who curses (24:16), and the Sabbath breaker (Ex. 31:14–15). Still, biblical texts also provide examples of murderers and rapists who were not condemned for their transgressions. Moses, who killed an Egyptian (Ex. 2:11), is chosen to lead his people to liberation. King David, a man chosen by God, uses his power as king to force himself on Bathsheba and then, to cover his transgression, has her husband murdered (2 Sam. 11). In this particular case, not only is David acquitted (2 Sam. 12:13), but the ancestry of Jesus can be traced back to this adulterous union (Mt. 1:6). Such apparent contradictions between God's law and how those chosen by God fell short of the law, yet were greatly used by God, can be understood by affirming the basic principle of the sacredness of human life due to its reflection of the *imago Dei*.

Based on the *imago Dei*, Jesus turned many rules upside down. For example, Jesus said, "You have heard that it was said, an eye for an eye and a tooth for a tooth, but I say unto you, do not resist evil" (Mt. 5:38–39). It could be argued that Jesus was "unjust," as that term is defined by our present culture, for he refused to punish the wrongdoer. Rather than accommodating the current definition of justice by meting out deserved punishment, he was quick to provide undeserved mercy. In John 8, he is confronted with an adulterous woman caught in the very act itself (where, then, was the man?), a capital offense. Asked to judge her, he instead balanced justice and mercy with the famous line, "Whoever is without sin should cast the first stone." Throughout the New Testament, Jesus provides a model that should prompt us not to look toward the law for justice principles, but rather ground moral guidance and principles upon relationships, always cognizant that all human beings contain the image of God. Thus, to take a life is to extinguish the spark of the Divine that all possess.

Step 4: Case Studies

1. During the 1950s, the United States ranked third among all nations in its ability to prevent infant mortality.[34] By the 1990s, the United States had the highest infant mortality rate of all the Western European countries (10.2 deaths per 1,000). Although great strides have been made since then to reduce infant mortality, bringing incidents to their lowest levels, the United States has not kept pace with other industrialized countries. While the 2019 global average was 3.8 deaths per 1,000, the United States was at 5.8 deaths for that same 1,000 (Andrulis et al. 2019, 21, 40). Among US communities of color, the infant mortality rate was higher than those of many nations.

Among the largest disparities found in health care, according to the US Department of Health and Human Services, are the racial and ethnic differences found in infant mortality. In 2020, the mortality rate for Black infants (10.6 per 1,000) was 2.4 times the rate for euroamerican infants (4.5 per 1,000).[35] Black babies are more than twice as likely to die before reaching their first birthday as euroamerican babies.[36] Even when Black mothers are as rich as white mothers, their baby is twice as likely to die.[37] American Indians (7.9 per 1,000), Pacific Islanders (8.2 per 1,000), and Latine (5.0 per 1,000) populations also had relatively high infant mortality rates.[38] Your chances of survival if born Black in America, the richest country ever known to humanity, are worse than if you were to be born in economically struggling countries like Libya, Romania, or Botswana. Part of the problem is the absence of prenatal care among some communities of color. Not only are the lives of infants of color endangered, so too are the lives of their mothers. Black women face a higher risk of dying than

---

[34] The infant mortality rate indicates the number of deaths occurring among children under the age of one per one thousand live births in a given year.

[35] Centers for Disease Control and Prevention, "Infant Mortality," 2020.

[36] Anna Flagg, "Black American Deaths, and a Paper from 1910," *New York Times*, September 7, 2021.

[37] Claire Cain Miller, Sarah Kliff, and Larry Buchanan, "Childbirth Is Deadlier for Black Families Even When They're Rich, Study Finds," *New York Times*, February 19, 2023.

[38] Centers for Disease Control and Prevention, "Infant Mortality."

white women due to pregnancy complications. Maternal mortality rates for Black women are 41.7 per 100,000 live births, compared with 13.4 per 100,000 for euroamerican women.[39]

• Do these statistics indicate that the value of euroamerican infants' lives is greater than that of infants of color? If not, how do we explain the continuous gap between the mortality rate of euroamerican infants and infants of color? If women of color are unable to afford prenatal care or vaccination shots once the child is born due to lack of insurance or low-paying wages, should they be provided by the state?

• Are euroamerican babies simply more valuable than Black babies? Consider that the cost of adopting a euroamerican child is approximately $35,000, plus legal expenses, while the cost of adopting a fully Black child is $18,000, with a biracial child's adoption expenses racking up $24,000 to $26,000.[40] If the value of life is not correlated by skin pigmentation, then how do we explain the cost difference?

• The United States has the highest infant mortality rate among industrial countries and the costliest maternity care. For substantially less, other industrialized countries provide similar access to high-tech care. Why does the richest nation have the most inferior healthcare system among industrial nations? Who benefits from a privatized healthcare system? Is the marketplace the best means of providing adequate health care? Should health care remain privatized? Should the United States have universal healthcare insurance? If so, who would pay for it?

2. During the war on terror, a hospital—Loqman—set itself up in Herat, Afghanistan, as the country's first kidney transplantation center. In five years, they performed more than one thousand transplants. There, the poor who find themselves in dire financial straits can go and sell a kidney. Organ selling dates to the 1980s in India and in 2021 accounted for 10 percent of all global transplants. Afghanistan joins China, Pakistan, and the Philippines, all countries more prolifically engaged in the organ trade.

Mir Gul Ataye, a twenty-eight-year-old construction worker from the slums of Herat, was earning $5 a day and responsible for thirteen family members. He sold his kidney for $3,800 in November 2020. "It is difficult, but I had no choice," he said. "Nobody wants to give up a part of his body to someone else. It was very shameful for me." Now, he is unable to lift

---

[39] Roni Caryn Rabin, "Racial Inequities Persist in Health Care Despite Expanded Insurance," *New York Times*, August 17, 2021.

[40] NPR staff, "Six Words: Black Babies Cost Less to Adopt," NPR News, June 27, 2013.

more than ten pounds, constantly in pain, and unable to control his urine. Unemployed, he has racked up $4,000 in accumulated debt. One night, the pain was so severe that he banged his head against the wall and fractured his skull.[41]

- Is selling one's organs a way for the poor to gain financial security? In a commoditized global economy, why not let supply and demand among willing adults operate unfettered? Does the phrase "My body, my choice" apply? Should any governmental authority restrict what a consenting adult can do with their own body, especially in deciding a medical procedure? If we own our bodies, why can't we sell off parts of them?

- A seventeen-year-old high school student in China named Wang sold his kidney for $3,500 so that he could buy an iPad and an iPhone.[42] Should economic safeguards exist? Is this an indication that something is wrong with our global economy?

- Each day, about thirteen people die waiting for a kidney donor. Because Medicare covers approximately 6 percent of the dialysis cost, a single transplant can save about $300,000 over the first five years after the transplant. These savings lead to about five hundred US patients a year obtaining kidneys.[43] Kidneys sell on the black market for about $200,000, even though the donor of the organ receives a couple of thousand dollars. Should the selling of organs be globally legalized? Would its decriminalization lead to providing a greater return to the organ seller and reduce prices for the buyer?

3. George Allen Jr., an African American, was convicted in 1983 for the murder of a young court reporter, along with rape, sodomy, and first-degree burglary, in St. Louis, Missouri. He was sentenced to ninety-five years. On January 18, 2013, he was exonerated after serving more than thirty years in prison. Allen was convicted based in part on a false confession, police "tunnel vision," and blood-type evidence that was said to include Allen's, but, in reality, eliminated him as a possible contributor. According to the Innocence Project, by 2021, in the United States, 375 people have been exonerated thanks to DNA testing, including 21 who served time on death row after

---

41 Adam Nossiter, Najim Rahim, and Kiana Hayeri, "'Everything Has a Value': Afghanistan's Kidney Trade Preys on the Poor," *New York Times*, February 7, 2021.

42 "Five Face Charges in China over Sale of Youth's Kidney," *New York Times*, April 8, 2012.

43 Eilene Zimmerman, "Is it Ever OK to Sell (or Buy) a Kidney?," *Stanford Business*, March 13, 2017.

averaging fourteen years of imprisonment before their release.[44] By 2021, the death penalty had been abolished in twenty-three states and the District of Columbia.

• What obligations does the state have toward the wrongfully convicted? Should the state provide financial restitution, counseling, job placement, and so on to these individuals? If so, who should pay for it? Should the state's legal liabilities for wrongful convictions be limited? Is the fact that most are poor and of color relevant or significant? Why or why not?

• Even if capital punishment was equitably applied, it is financially unsustainable. A California study revealed that, from 1978 to 2012, the state spent $4 billion to carry out thirteen capital punishment sentences. Two individuals in 1978, John V. Briggs and Donald J. Heller, are most responsible for the success of Proposition 7, which reinstated the death penalty. Today, Mr. Heller, along with Briggs's son Ron, are the two biggest advocates to reverse what they have come to recognize as the biggest mistake of their lives, mainly due to the fiscal cost.[45] If not for moral reasons, should capital punishment be abolished due to budgetary prudence?

• What about those who are rightfully convicted of a felony and serve their time? Upon being released, in most states, they are barred from receiving welfare or food stamps, public housing, voting, and obtaining certain jobs in plumbing, education, barbering, or health care (just to name a few). Should such restrictions exist, even after people have paid their debt to society? Are these former prisoners simply getting what they deserve for the crimes they committed? What consequences, if any, exist for society if these former felons are not reintegrated into society?

---

[44] Innocence Project, "Exonerate the Innocent," 2021.

[45] Adam Nagourney, "Seeking End to Execution Law They Championed," *New York Times*, April 7, 2012.

PART IV

CASE STUDIES OF BUSINESS RELATIONSHIPS

Chapter 12

Introduction to Business Relationships

Each society must determine for itself how the goods and services the community needs and/or wants are to be produced, who will be responsible for producing these goods or providing these services, where production will occur, and how the goods and services will be distributed within the community. Within the present global marketplace, the responsibility for answering these questions generally belongs to multinational corporations. In theory, an employee has a right to accept or reject employment at a given company. If a corporation treats its employees poorly or refuses to pay a living wage, the employee is free to find a job elsewhere. But what if the two parties negotiating are not equal in power, which is true of the average worker and the typical company? Or what if, through monopolistic dealings and political connections, one company can determine how a particular good or service is to be produced, who will produce it, where it will be produced, and how it is to be distributed? What effects will this have on employees and consumers?

Corporations, which are legal entities with limited liabilities, consist of three groups of people. First come the stockholders who provide capital; their liabilities are limited to the money invested. In theory, the raison d'être of the corporation is to create profit for these shareholders. Second, there are the directors and officers charged with administering the corporation's assets and running the day-to-day activities. And, finally, there are the employees who provide the labor necessary to produce the goods or provide the services.

Corporations are recognized by society as "artificial persons"; they are able to enter into agreements and to be sued when those agreements are broken. Then-governor Romney, while campaigning for president in Iowa, best captured this sentiment in his now famous retort to a heckler, "Corporations are people, my friend."[1] In effect, the corporation is a "soulless" person. Can it, then, be expected to follow moral dictates and practices? Even if it were to operate according to some moral standards, we are again forced to ask, whose or which standards? If a multinational corporation has offices in the United States, the Middle East, and Asia, should it follow Christian, Muslim, or Buddhist ethics? Should it adhere instead to a system of secular humanist ethics? How should it operate if it has a branch office in a society that believes women have a moral obligation to stay at home and raise children? Should the corporation not hire women or pay them less? Should corporate ethics be defined by what is customary or legal in the country in which it operates? Should "when in Rome, do as the Romans" be the basic rule to follow?

For example, laws regulating the disposal of corporate byproducts, which are stringent in the United States to protect the environment, are lax in many two-thirds-world countries. Likewise, the safety regulations in the United States that protect employees from physical hazards at the workplace are nonexistent in some other countries. Yet, on the other hand, a practice like bribing government officials to facilitate the navigation of bureaucratic red tape, while illegal in the United States, is considered an acceptable and necessary business procedure elsewhere. Because certain safety and environmental regulations that are mandatory within the United States cut into corporate profits, relocating to two-thirds-world nations with less stringent laws may be desirable for a corporation. Do these practices in different countries require a system of business ethics in which what is moral depends on where one conducts business?

Noble Prize–winning economist Milton Friedman argues for restricting moral obligations overall, limiting corporate responsibilities to obeying the laws in whatever nation a corporation finds itself pursuing profit:

> There is one and only one social responsibility of business—to use its resources and engage in activities designed to increase its profits so long as it stays within the rules of the game, which is to say, engage in open and free competition, without deception

---

[1] James Oliphant, "Romney in Iowa: 'Corporations Are People' Too," *Los Angeles Times*, August 11, 2011.

or fraud.... Few trends could so thoroughly undermine the very foundations of our free society as the acceptance by corporate officials of a social responsibility other than to make as much money for their stockholders as possible. (1962, 133)

Friedman ignores any connection between corporate profitability and the quality of life of the general public or of the corporation's employees. Corporations are legally created entities responsible for abiding by the law to ensure individual legal rights, but their participation within society also subjects them to certain moral rights beyond simply making "as much money for their stockholders as possible." Corporate responsibility that goes no further than making as much money as possible can produce a vacuum in ethics and clearly lead to abuse. Nonetheless, danger lurks if such moral rights are established from the perspective of the dominant culture that has a vested interest in corporate profit, in securing "as much money as possible." Moral rights must be a product that includes the disenfranchised community from which many employees are drawn. And, if we speak of Christian moral rights, then it is the responsibility of the marginalized faith community to spearhead the formulation of what these moral rights should be.

The definition of moral rights should never be too tightly limited, and it must include positive actions as well as proscriptions. Conservatives generally maintain that the government should not demand that businesses become responsible for the welfare of their employees and that businesses simply not interfere with the employees' pursuit of their rights. For example, if it is determined that individuals who work for a corporation have a moral right to a wage that supports the basics of human existence (food, clothes, and shelter), then the concept of positive rights would insist that corporations have a duty to pay a living wage. The employer cannot simply claim the worker's right to freely choose to work elsewhere, for while workers may indeed have the right to reject a job, they cannot reject every job if they hope to survive. Because workers cannot bargain as equals with multinational corporations to arrive at mutually beneficial arrangements, they are limited to the types of wages that corporations are willing to pay. When the heads of corporations increase their wealth at the expense of the labor pool because they have the power to control wages, the corporation, even though it is an artificial person, is acting immorally. By extension, those who are privileged by the actions of the corporation are also acting immorally—whether they are the officers, directors, stockholders, or consumers.

In Part II of this book, we considered case studies that explored the impact of neoliberalism upon the global stage. Part III provided case studies that narrowed our exploration to the field of US national policies. In this fourth and last part, we consider case studies that explore the ethics of business within a global marketplace by focusing on three areas: the moral accountability of corporations, the overall treatment of women, and affirmative action.

Chapter 13

Corporate Accountability

Step 1: Observing

In his classic text, *The Wealth of Nations*, the Scottish economic philosopher Adam Smith wrote, "It is not from the benevolence of the butcher, the brewer, or the baker, that we expect our dinner, but from their regard to their own self-interest" (1976 [1776], 13). US modern economic principles are based on Smith's concept of laissez-faire economics. He argued that pursuit of economic self-interest within the context of a competitive society benefits all persons. Thus, he implies that no restraints should be placed on the accumulation of wealth. For him, land ownership by individuals is a fundamental if not sacred building block of civilization, and to suggest the resumption of land as common property is paramount to advocating a regression toward some premodern, uncivilized existence.

Smith's model creates problems. For example, the privileged will be in an economic position to acquire immense portions of land. Through their holdings, they can stunt competition. They can also impose laws upon those who need land for basic subsistence. In exchange for the use of the land, tenants must recognize the supreme authority of the land*lord*, whether the landowner is an individual, a multinational corporation, or a civil government.

When society is constructed on the fundamental principle of laissez-faire wealth accumulation, the state must protect the property rights of the wealthy by privileging laws against trespassing and theft over and against basic human rights for the nonwealthy's life's necessities. Franz Hinkelammert, the theologian and economist, reminds us that unconditional recognition of the right to private property deprioritizes all other rights, leading to global disenfranchisement and dispossession. Protecting private property is maintained at the expense of rights "to satisfy basic needs in food, shelter, medical attention, education, and social security" (1986, 120). Jumping a fence to take a fallen apple rotting on the ground, the hungry are convictable of trespassing and theft offenses even if the motivation of the trespasser was to feed their hungry child. Greed defends the right of hoarding rotting fruit as a virtue.

Gordon Gekko, the fictional character played by Michael Douglas in the 1987 movie *Wall Street*, best summarizes Adam Smith's sentiments in his now famous speech:

> The point is, ladies and gentleman, that greed, for lack of a better word, is good. Greed is right, greed works. Greed clarifies, cuts through, and captures the essence of the evolutionary spirit. Greed, in all of its forms—greed for life, for money, for love, knowledge—has marked the upward surge of mankind.

Real-life personality Fabrice P. Tourre, better known as "Fabulous Fab," captures the fictional Gekko's mantra. The former Goldman Sachs trader became infamous for an email he wrote to his girlfriend as the US economy approached the brink of economic collapse in 2008 due to the rapidly expanding mortgage crises. In the message, he bragged about unloading toxic real estate bonds to "widows and orphans."[1]

Trading Money for Influence

One of the fundamental purposes of neoliberal governments—which usually operate in individualistic and capitalist societies—is to preserve an open market economy. In many locales and at different times in US history, the Christian faith has been artificially linked to a laissez-faire philosophy. This connection has then been used to create ethical and moral truths concerning freedom and rights, often allowing the dominant culture to prosper freely, even or expressly at the expense of others. The application of freedom and rights to human dignity has often been missing from the equation. Rights to unfettered capital have become a battle cry in any serious conversation about correcting the wealth disparities within the United States. César Chávez explained how rights' slogans can be used to mask oppression:

> When the racists and bigots, the industrialists and the corporation farmers were not shedding our blood, they were blocking our way with all kinds of stratagems. We have heard them all—"Property Rights," "States Rights," "Right to Work." All of these slogans, as

---

[1] Susan Craig and Ben Protess, "Symbol of Crises from Goldman Getting Day in Court," *New York Times*, July 15, 2013.

you will have noticed, and as you will still notice, have been uttered in ringing tones of idealism and individual freedom. But that is the special genius of those who would deny the rights of others and hoard the fruits of democracy for themselves: They evade the problems and complex challenges of equal justice by reducing them to primitive oversimplifications that plead for nothing else but the perpetuation of their own special, exploitative interests. (Dalton 2003, 67–68)

The danger in hiding behind rights' slogans is that, when wealth is concentrated in the hands of a few, democracy is threatened if the privileged few use their wealth to control the direction and policies of the society. And this often happens. Economic power leads directly to political power.

At the start of the twenty-first century, the American business community was rocked by corporate scandals. The business shenanigans that occurred in corporations like Enron, Arthur Andersen, Global Crossing, and Adelphia Communications (to name just a few) revealed how a privileged elite was able to amass great fortunes by subscribing to a laissez-faire capitalism that justified greed. Unfortunately, these fortunes were usually made on the backs of shareholders, the middle class, and the poor. We begin with the example of Enron CEO Ken L. Lay, who had close ties with the Bush family. The Texas energy giant hired prominent members of the first Bush administration (such as James Baker and Robert Mosbacher) and was also among the largest donors to the second Bush presidential campaign.

Then–newly elected President George W. Bush appointed two of Ken Lay's nominations to the Federal Energy Regulatory Commission (FERC), and one, Pat Wood, was named chair of the commission. FERC maintains oversight of the nation's electricity and gas markets, markets in which Enron made most of its money. The commission failed to act during the winter of 2000–2001 when Enron manipulated the price of gas and electricity during California's energy crisis. Enron's price-gouging maneuvers ensured that the company made the bulk of its profits ($7 billion in net trading profits during the energy crisis) at the expense of Californians who endured rolling blackouts and higher energy prices.[2] The demise of Enron after the company was caught up in massive financial fraud cost thousands of jobs, more than $60 billion in market value, and more than $2 billion in

---

[2] David Barboza, "Despite Demand, Enron Papers Show Big Profit on Price Bets," *New York Times*, December 12, 2002; Adam Zagorin, "The Trail out of Texas," *Time*, February 18, 2002, 41.

pension plans. Investors hoping to recoup some of their losses through the legal system were dealt a setback when the US Supreme Court refused to review the investors' lawsuit.[3]

Then again, we should not be surprised by the decision of the Supreme Court. After all, those who appoint and confirm Supreme Court justices (as well as all other federal justices) are the same politicians beholden to corporate political contributions to mount their election or reelection campaigns. The Roberts Court, which started in 2005, has been the most pro-neoliberal, pro-corporate court since World War II. Not since the early twentieth century, during the "Lochner era,"[4] has the Supreme Court struck down such a wide range of federal regulations on businesses, ensuring a truly laissez-faire-generated economy. According to the Constitutional Accountability Center—a nonprofit, progressive think tank in Washington, DC—since Justices John Roberts and Samuel Alito joined the court, the Chamber of Commerce has prevailed in 70 percent of its cases. In the earlier Rehnquist Court's stable membership period (1994–2005), the chamber prevailed only 56 percent of the time; in the stable membership period of the Burger Court (1981–1986), the chamber only won 43 percent of its cases.[5]

A study conducted on cases since the start of the Taft Court in 1921 demonstrates that the current Roberts Court is the most pro-business of all time. In 2020 alone, when the court heard a case featuring business on one side and a non-business entity on the other, it found in favor of the business 83 percent of the time. Based on court rulings, the six justices with the most pro-business voting records *ever*—all nominated by Republican presidents—were sitting on the bench in 2022.[6] Even the least business-

---

[3] "Supreme Court Won't Hear Complaint by Enron Investors," *New York Times*, January 23, 2008.

[4] The Lochner era is named after the 1905 egregious *Lochner v. New York* decision in which the Supreme Court struck down a law that prevented employees from working more than ten hours a day and sixty hours a week. Interpreting the Fourteenth Amendment verbiage of "freedom of contract" to mean people were free to enter contracts without governmental involvement, the decision ushered in a set of pro-business decisions by courts that upheld laissez-faire capitalism—an era that lasted until the 1930s during the Great Depression and the implementation of the New Deal.

[5] Brian R. Frazelle, "Big Business Powers Ahead with Another Successful Term at the Roberts Court—2019–2020 Term," Constitutional Accountability Center, October 1, 2020.

[6] Amy Coney Barrett, Brett Kavanaugh, Neil Gorsuch, Samuel Alito, John Roberts, and Clarence Thomas.

friendly justice, Sonia Sotomayor, found in favor of business 48 percent of the time. Late justice Ginsburg wasn't that far behind with business-friendly rulings 42.7 percent of the time. In contrast, Earl Warren of the Warren Court (1953–1969) sided with business only 25.3 percent of the time (Epstein and Gulati 2022, 7, 11, 17). A barrage of pro-business rulings allows companies to operate without fear of litigation by those harmed by their actions, products, or wrongdoing, be they employees, customers, or the public at large. Peddling of political favors, specifically who gets nominated and confirmed to the federal courts, for campaign support continues to plague and threaten US democracy.

Yet governmental power to protect laissez-faire capitalism is not the most egregious corporate peccadillo. Corporate scandals that enrich the privileged are not limited to accounting shenanigans or trading money for influence. More grievous is the commodification of human beings for the sake of profit, a process that, at times, results in the loss of human life—usually the life of the disenfranchised and dispossessed. Some baby food manufacturers' practices illustrate this point.

The Commodification of Human Life

Those on the margins—as multiple examples throughout this book have verified—face greater hazards from the dominant eurocentric culture. However, when it comes to turning a profit, all consumers—regardless of race or ethnicity—are at the mercy of corporations, reduced to a commodity to be exploited. Corporations are more concerned with making a profit than with discriminating against any one particular group. If a corporation decides that its first responsibility is to create profit for its stockholders, then it must redefine what is just and ethical to allow the maximum profit to be made. If people are hurt in the pursuit of profit, their national origins or whether they be euroamerican or of color matters little. This does not mean that racism and ethnic discrimination do not continue to play roles in deciding who benefits from corporate decisions; it just reiterates that classism is colorblind if it means greater power and privilege for the dominant culture's elite. In this country, those elites are disproportionately euroamerican.

Take, for example, the four leading baby food manufacturers, the trusted names of Gerber, Beech Nut, Happy Baby, and Earth's Best Organic. A congressional investigation into internal company documents discovered that they knowingly sold baby food that contained high amounts of toxic heavy metals. According to a Heathy Babies 2019 internal report, 95 percent of the baby food randomly pulled off supermarket shelves that were tested contained toxic metals. An additional three companies (Spout Organic Foods, Plum Organics, and Walmart's Parent's Choice) refused to fully cooperate with congressional investigators, raising concerns that their products might contain even higher amounts of toxic heavy metals.

Babies—euroamerican babies as well as Black, Latine, Asian, and Indigenous babies—were fed baby food by their loving parents that contained dangerous levels of arsenic, lead, cadmium, and mercury. All these metals are linked to cancer, chronic disease, and neurotoxic effects. Innocent babies were slowly poisoned for the sake of profits because on the spreadsheets, they are seen as a means to obtain profits. Regardless of race or ethnicity, during a crucial time of their brain development, babies fed what were certainly toxic-laced products were likely exposed to life-impacting toxic metals, where the full extent of the physical damage may not be fully known for decades. Sadly, though the Trump-era Food and Drug Administration (FDA) learned of the presence and risk of toxic metals in baby food in a secret industry presentation on August 1, 2019, no action was taken (US House 2021, 2–6).

While we can argue that the pursuit of profit does not necessarily see race or ethnicity, management definitely does. As previously discussed, Wells Fargo is well known for its predatory behavior toward communities of color. Such maleficence created a public image of the bank that needed repair. To that end, according to six former employees from Wells Fargo's large wealth management unit, managers were encouraged to interview more women and African Americans for employment. The candidates, however, were being interviewed for jobs that were already filled. The purpose of the interviews was not to actually hire anyone and diversify the financial entity's workforce, but rather to appear on paper as having made a genuine attempt to diversify. Furthermore, when the company failed to diversify, they blamed the very applicants who were women and of color. Charles W. Scharf, the CEO, sent a 2020 memo to the company's employees informing them that, while the bank was committed to hiring a wider array of workers, they simply struggled to find any "qualified Black candidates."[7]

Focusing blame on corporate management, however, is futile in the current neoliberal structure. Regardless of the racial, ethnic, gender, disability, or sexual-orientation diversity of management, true corporate power lies in corporate boardrooms and executive offices. Decisions that financially benefit shareholders and those sitting around the confer-

---

[7] Emily Flitter, "At Wells Fargo, a Quest to Increase Diversity Leads to Fake Job Interviews," *New York Times*, May 19, 2022.

ence table are made by strikingly homogeneous groups of people. At the start of the twenty-first century, euroamerican men held 96.4 percent of the Fortune 500 CEO positions—just over 480 of 500. Twenty years on, they still hold 85.8 percent of the Fortune 500 CEO positions—just under 430 positions. Since those euroamerican men mostly lost their spots to euroamerican women, and, since euroamerican women comprise 6.8 percent of those new CEOs, euroamericans still represented 92.6 percent of Fortune 500 CEOs. Only 1 percent of these CEOs were African American, 2.4 percent Asian, and 3.4 percent Latine.[8] Boardroom membership is not much different. Of the 3,000 largest publicly traded companies, only about 12.5 percent of their members were from underrepresented ethnic and racial groups in 2020, even though they represent more than 40 percent of the country's population.[9] The question remains: If the CEOs and corporate boards were as racially and ethnically diverse as the nation, would classism continue to trump sexism, racism, and ethnic discrimination? Would it really matter if the CEO is of color or a woman if the mantra continues that greed is good?

Demonstrating its settler-colonial convictions, whiteness in the US corporate boardroom embodies the goodness of greed by incentivizing theft on a massive scale and insulating the executive thieves from retributive consequences. Law enforcement focuses on street crimes, with deadly consequences for communities of color, and is supported in its efforts to ignore the crimes of the boardroom. The dichotomy between "blue-collar" and "white-collar" crime allows politicians to spout "tough on crime" rhetoric that ignores significant criminal statistics. According to the FBI, street-level crimes (burglary, larceny, and theft) are estimated to cost victims $16 billion annually. Appropriately named white-collar crimes (fraud, embezzlement) are estimated to cost $300 billion to $800 billion a year. Corporations, when "caught" in the larceny, cannot be jailed. If a CEO is convicted, he (because it is usually a "he" and identifies as such) will likely face a light sentence because many judges consider his fall from grace sufficient punishment.

Wells Fargo provides another example. From 2009 to 2016, they schemed to open 3.5 million checking, savings, and credit card accounts without customer consent. They then hit customers with overdraft fees and other unauthorized charges. When caught, corporate management

---

[8] Richie Zweigenhaft, "Fortune 500 CEOs, 2000–2020: Still White," The Society Pages, October 28, 2020.

[9] Peter Eavis, "Boardrooms Barely Move the Needle on Diversity," *New York Times*, September 16, 2020.

responded by firing honest employees who brought the maleficence to light rather than by stopping the fraud. When the white-collar crime became public, John Stumpf, then-CEO, resigned in "disgrace." But on his way out the door, his board of directors awarded him a $134 million exit payment. By the time the Office of the Comptroller of the Currency—the banking industry's primary regulator—banned Stumpf from ever working in banking again, the sixty-six-year-old had already retired (Taub 2020, xix–xxi).

At times, CEOs get away with murder. Consider Boeing's problems with its 737 Max jets. In October 2018, one of its jets plunged into the ocean off the coast of Indonesia, killing 189 passengers and crew. Less than five months later, another 737 Max crashed in Ethiopia, killing another 157 individuals. The company quickly blamed its software. But the software was not the main problem. The real culprit was corporate greed.

During the production of the 737 Max jet, executives and engineers ignored serious warning signs during development and refused to adopt additional precautions, making their decisions based on increasing profits rather than ensuring safety. The cause of the eventual crashes was evident during an early development stage of the aircraft's construction, but Boeing plowed onward. Relying on just one sensor (an engineering failure), the new software had the power to push the plane's nose downward. If the pilot does not act within ten seconds, the outcome could—and ultimately did— prove catastrophic. Rather than adding an alert for activating the automated flight-control system that corrects altitude in abnormal flight conditions (the MACS), Boeing persuaded the Federal Aviation Administration (FAA) to remove mentions of MACS from training manuals. Furthermore, Boeing refused to invest in costly training of pilots on simulators to deal with this potential risk.

An investigative inquiry by the Transportation Department found that the FAA had "too close of a relationship with Boeing officials," leading to the corporation essentially regulating itself—a key factor leading to the crashes. When Boeing became aware that the cockpit warning light, which could have alerted pilots on the Indonesian and Ethiopian flights of the imminent danger of the equipment, was not properly functioning, the airlines were not informed. While none of these singular-but-connected issues were solely responsible for the crash, the cumulative effect of constantly placing profit over safety certainly was responsible. After the Indonesia crash, Boeing knew of the danger but kept their planes in the air, making the Ethiopian crash, at the least, manslaughter.[10] We live in a nation

---

[10] Thomas Kaplan, "FAA Faulted for Delegating to Air Industry," *New York*

where a Black man can be shot for a broken taillight and a euroamerican CEO can steal millions or be responsible for the death of hundreds and never see the inside of a jail.

Corporate Welfare

"Welfare queen" entered the US lexicon during the 1980 presidential campaign, when then-candidate Ronald Reagan described an alleged case from Chicago's South Side of a Cadillac-driving woman who fraudulently received excessive welfare assistance. Reagan's welfare queen, who was never found by the media to prove his point, had 12 Social Security cards, received benefits from four nonexistent dead husbands, and collected food stamps—all to the tune of $150,000 a year (equivalent to more than $500,000 in 2022). Another race-based, fictitious accusation made by Reagan was of a "strapping young buck" using food stamps to buy T-bone steaks at his local grocery store. For southern whites, "young buck" usually denoted a large Black man. These were pejorative terms meant to conjure up images of the proverbial lazy Blacks taking institutional advantage of hard-working whites, thus justifying to the conservative base that the so-called welfare state had gone amok.

While Americans focus on social welfare programs, few discuss where most tax dollars go: corporate welfare in the form of subsidies and tax breaks, to a tune of about $80 billion a year. States and cities that compete against each other to lure business, in the hope of securing the new jobs that corporations promise to create, dole out large financial breaks. For example, in 2018 Maryland offered Amazon an $8.5 billion incentive bid to build its second headquarters in the state. The bid included cash grants for the company to relocate, subsidized land, and forgiving company taxes—from property to sales taxes. They even offered to return the maximum state income tax (5.75 percent) levied on workers' salaries to the company.[11] New York fell short, only offering Amazon $1.525 billion in incentives, which included $1.2 billion over ten years as part of the state's Excelsior tax credit. Over and above these figures, the state pledged to assist with infrastructure upgrades, job-training programs, and securing access to a helipad.[12]

Times, March 27, 2019; David Gelles, "Boeing's Saga of Capitalism Gone Awry," *New York Times,* November 29, 2020.

[11] Nathan M. Jensen, "Do Taxpayers Know They Are Handing Out Billions to Corporations?," *New York Times,* April 24, 2018.

[12] Ben Casselman, "A $2 Billion Question: Did New York and Virginia Overpay for Amazon?," *New York Times,* November 13, 2018.

Unfortunately, throughout the United States, the jobs promised in exchange for tax breaks fall short of benefiting the communities. Since Amazon opened a fulfillment center in Campbellsville, Kentucky, two decades ago, median income has barely kept pace with inflation. More people now (one in five) live in poverty than when Amazon first came to town. Part of the reason that the town financially struggles is that 5 percent of workers' paychecks, normally destined for county and state taxes, go to Amazon. Since the warehouse is located just outside the town limits, the city school system is deprived of collecting tax revenues from Amazon.[13]

Boeing—whose headquarters are in the state of Washington—affords another example. In 2017 Boeing threatened the state legislature to provide a $227 million share of the state tax cut or see twenty thousand jobs eliminated. The state gave in to their demands. And yet, since the announcement of the tax cut to the end of that year, Boeing still eliminated some thirteen thousand Washington jobs. Governor Jay Inslee expressed that he was not happy with Boeing, describing the experience as crime victimization: "If you've ever been mugged, you understand what it feels like."[14]

Instead of providing $80 billion in tax breaks to corporations, the public at large might be better served if these funds were invested in education, rebuilding infrastructures, or providing incentives for local small-business entrepreneurs to create greater long-term community economic growth and stability. Is it wise to provide such incentives to major corporations that simply pit one government agency against another to obtain the greatest incentives of benefit to their bottom line and shareholders? The impact of well-paid lobbyists for these large corporations, who obtain the ears of politicians who ultimately decide what these incentive packages could or will look like through generous political contributions, further complicates the situation.

Corporations also receive welfare when they can cheaply finance major business projects through government bonds that are exempt from federal taxes. While these types of low-interest tax-exempt bonds were once utilized by cities and states for public works such as building bridges, roads, and schools, for-profit corporations now take advantage of these instruments. Corporate gains come at the expense of taxpayers, who, in effect, subsidize the interest paid to bondholders. Through tax subsidies, a Corvette museum was built in Kentucky, a winery was planted in North

---

[13] David Steitfeld, "Town Feels Tech Giant's Influence, but Tastes Little of Its Profits," *New York Times,* December 28, 2019.

[14] Paul Constant, "It's Time to End Corporate Welfare. Boeing is Exhibit A for Why," *Business Insider,* January 23, 2020.

Carolina, a golf resort was created in Puerto Rico, and offices for Barclays and Goldman Sachs were constructed in Brooklyn and Manhattan, respectively.[15] These types of corporate subsidy programs become a form of socialism in reverse, where profits are privatized while risk is spread among the general public. "Too big to fail" has become the new norm as government bailouts of mismanaged corporations become the responsibility of taxpayers.

Step 2: Reflecting

English philosopher John Locke (1632–1704), the father of classical political liberalism, is responsible for advancing certain "self-evident natural rights," one of which is the exclusive use of property. He viewed property as an institution of nature, not a social construct based on human laws (1952 [1689], 17). Property became the third of the inalienable rights, along with "life and liberty." Locke argued for the right of each person, based on self-preservation and personal interest, to keep whatever property they possessed, despite the means utilized in its acquisition or an individual's ability to use all the property's resources. Locke first limited the accumulation of property to what would not spoil, rust, rot, or decay (23). However, with the introduction of a cash economy, previous limits were no longer applicable. Eventually, currency became the common denominator for property, as well as for labor. While property can spoil, rust, rot, or decay, money as a commodity does not. Wealth, accumulated in the form of gold or silver (money), became unlimited (29), and so did the accumulation of wealth.

The state, constructed to preserve the individual's right to life, liberty, and property, is duty-bound to ensure these inalienable rights (5–6). And the state is needed by the property holders to guarantee their interests in this particular mechanism. The sacredness of property was reaffirmed in the young US republic, reserving the right to participate in the political discourse to only those euroamerican males owning property. Rather than the traditional right to property being derived from the power to rule, the Federalist Papers inverted this concept to reflect a right to rule in order to protect said property. Property became owned by "legal" individuals possessing a title that conferred rights protected by the state's judicial system. Still, property equality remained a seditious idea to be quashed because it created the possibility that the wealthy might lose their privilege.

---

[15] Mary Williams Walsh and Louise Story, "A Stealthy Subsidy Aiding Big Businesses Is Growing," *New York Times*, March 5, 2013.

The goals of the young republic were fully identified by and with the interest of the property holders (Madison 2001 [1787], 48).

According to Locke, who had a vested interest in the colonial venture,

> God and his reason commanded him to subdue the earth, i.e., improve it for the benefit of life, and therein lay out something upon it that was his own, his labour. He that in obedience to this command of God, subdued, tilled and sowed any part of it, thereby annexed to it something that was his property, which another had no title to, nor could without injury take from him. (1952 [1689], 31)

Missing from most analysis of the Western concept of private property is how the property was acquired in the first place. Most of our modern Western understanding of private property is based on Locke, who was an international trader of the enslaved[16] through working as a business manager for a colonial land-holding corporation that held interests in North America. He eventually moved beyond being a mere colonial bureaucrat to owning a minority share in the Carolina Province along with a seat in the colonial legislature of the Carolina territory. As Osage scholar Tink Tinker reminds us, Locke's ethical philosophy justified the international theft of Indigenous land via a façade of legal and moral propriety. God, according to Locke, wanted the English to take the "vacant" lands of North America. Even though Indigenous people lived on the land, their failure to develop the land forfeited any legal rights to it. The original inhabitants did not own the land they lived upon because, in the "state of nature," it was owned by all. The superior English succeeded because the Indigenous people failed to labor upon the land (agriculture), thus developing and transforming it into private property. Labor conducted upon the land makes it private, and those who simply used the land for eons (Native Americans) held no claim. The taking of Indigenous land was philosophically justified (Tinker 2011, 56).

The strong economic positions of the elite led to control of all aspects of political life. When free markets secure the liberty of the wealthy class, with the help of the government, it is generally secured at the expense of a marginalized class (or multiple marginalized classes) that becomes increasingly alienated. The interests of the common people (specifically those who are poor and of color) become subordinated to the interests

---

[16] Locke was part owner in a slave-run plantation, Bahamian Adventurers, and a slave acquisition and selling firm, Royal Africa Company.

of this ruling class. Questioning the ruling class becomes paramount to revolution or treason. Even though there is a guise of universal participation in government, the wealthy class is instrumental in deciding by its political contributions who becomes governmental officers. This holds true whether the property owners are individuals or corporations. In return, governmental officers protect the power and privilege of the wealthy class and the businesses that maintain and sustain their wealth, ignoring the plight workers face.

The exploitation of labor dehumanizes workers by reducing their existence to expendable commodities. Workers become nonpersons who are prevented from living the abundant life promised to them by Christ in the Gospel of John (10:10). What the economic order values is how cheaply their labor can be extracted, regardless of whether their wages afford the necessities of clothing, food, and shelter. Hence, what are perceived as moral vices (stealing and lying) may appear more as virtues than vices to the marginalized when dealing with those of power and privilege. As mentioned in previous chapters, since the twelfth century, theologians have recognized the rights of the poor, specifically "theft arising from necessity." This right to steal for survival's sake was proclaimed within the context of the famines and plagues common in those eras.

Ethicist Cheryl Sanders explains this understanding of ethics in her analysis of testimonies by the enslaved. Slave masters would hire ministers to preach to the enslaved about the virtues of speaking honestly and of not stealing from the owners of their bodies (1995, 14–15). A former enslaved person, commenting on a sermon preached against stealing, said,

> I did not regard it as stealing then, I do not regard it as such now. I hold that a slave has a moral right to eat and drink and wear all that he needs, and that it would be a sin on his part to suffer and starve in a country where there is plenty to eat and wear within his reach. I consider that I had a just right to what I took, because it was the labor of my hands. (Raboteau 1978, 296)

The ethics of the slaveholder, which defined the stealing of food by the enslaved as a vice, was a socially constructed ethics designed to protect their privilege within the social order. The real question to ask is if the enslaved have a moral right to steal from their masters. Do the oppressed, whose labor is stolen from them, have an ethical right—or one could say, duty—to take what is produced through their labor to feed themselves and their families? Updating this question leads us to ask if employees today who are not paid a living wage also have a right to "steal" from their employers for the purpose of meeting their basic needs for food, clothes, and shelter.

For the formerly enslaved, stealing items necessary for survival (food and clothing) was justified on the grounds that they had been victimized by a worse sin, namely, the theft of a human being. An ethics developed among the disenfranchised of "stealing from thieves and deceiving the deceiver." But stealing and lying had their own constraints. It was understood that such actions were only to be done against those who were privileged. Stealing from a fellow enslaved person led to the accusation of being "just as mean as white folks" (Sanders 1995, 14–15). Scripture scholar Brian Blount observes that, while there was agreement among the enslaved not to steal from each other, it was, however, "not only appropriate but also moral to 'take' from an owner . . . because owners often fed their slaves as little as possible in order to increase their margins of profit, [and thus the slave had no] other means of assuaging the hunger of their children and kin" (2001, 40–41).

Although one cannot compare the institution of slavery with the situation of marginalized employees, the same motivation of maximizing profit at the expense of others remains. When the economy experiences a downturn, as was the case with the 2008 Great Recession or the 2020 COVID-19 pandemic, some companies continued to grow and prosper on the backs of their employees. Businesses like Walmart, Kroger, Lowe's, and Amazon had increased, often record-breaking, revenues during the pandemic, yet they did not provide hazard pay to their employees for risking their lives while working to generate those profits.[17] While many of these retail workers were being heralded as heroes, their employers treated them as disposable commodities, as they barely receive a living wage. Walmart was probably among the most egregious companies. One of the largest winners of the pandemic, announcing a 9.3 percent increase in store sales and a whopping 97 percent rise in e-commerce in 2020, Walmart rolled out a new plan that they named the Great Workplace. Amid the pandemic, as their revenues were growing, the program restructured staffing through the consolidation of departments and roles. This included layoffs, significant cuts in workers' hours, increased workloads, and pay cuts.[18] Not receiving a living wage contributes to individuals living a less than human existence. In effect, denying workers a living wage is stealing. Corporations steal from

---

[17] Michael Corkery and Sapna Maheshwari, "Virus Cases Rise, but Hazard Pay for Retail Workers Doesn't," *New York Times*, November 19, 2020.

[18] Michael Sainato, "Walmart Cuts Worker's Hours but Increase Workloads as Sales Rise amid Pandemic," *The Guardian*, September 24, 2020.

employees when they extract a full week of labor and refuse to compensate them with what is needed to pay for the basic necessities of the week.

Mistreating and undervaluing their workforce are not the only wrongdoings that Walmart commits. The corporate behemoth is the world's largest retailer, with more than 4,735 stores throughout the United States (plus 600 Sam's Club stores) in 2022 and employing more than 1.6 million workers (Walmart likes to call them "associates"). Their total worldwide sales of $567.76 billion (in the fiscal year ending January 31, 2022) was greater than the economies of most of the world's nations. Worldwide, a total of 2.3 million employees work in 10,585 stores operating under forty-six different banners in twenty-four countries.[19] While for the purposes of this chapter we will focus on Walmart, it is important to acknowledge that the practices employed at Walmart exist, in varying degrees, throughout other corporations that predominantly employ the marginalized.

On December 20, 2002, a federal jury in Portland, Oregon, found Walmart guilty of forcing its employees to work unpaid overtime. Employees in twenty-seven other states have filed similar class-action suits against the giant retailer. These employees were pressured to clock out after working forty hours then continue working, violating the Federal Labor Standards Act that requires employees receive time-and-a-half pay for all hours worked over forty within a week. According to testimony given during the Oregon trial, timecards were falsified by erasing hours that would reach or exceed a total of forty for a week, thus helping the company avoid paying time and a half. Any employee failure to comply negatively affected their promotions, raises, and employment security.[20]

Why would an employee willingly work off the clock? Liberty Morales, a woman with limited job skills and only a high school diploma, stated that she routinely worked off the clock without complaining. She knew through the experience of fellow "associates" who did complain that, if she did not comply, she would be fired, given fewer hours, demoted, or reassigned to the night shift. Compliance, on the other hand, led to desirable schedules and promotions. In her words, "I put up with it because I needed to work."[21]

In 2010 Walmart agreed to a settlement that provided about $4 million to some twenty-eight thousand former Oregon employees. Despite agreeing to the settlement, Walmart maintained its innocence. Of the $4

---

[19] Walmart, "Location Facts," 2022.

[20] Steven Greenhouse, "U.S. Jury Cites Unpaid Work at Wal-Mart," *New York Times*, December 20, 2002.

[21] Steven Greenhouse, "Suits Say Wal-Mart Forces Workers to Toil off the Clock," *New York Times*, June 25, 2002.

million agreed upon, claimants could expect to receive payouts ranging from $50 to $241.[22] Paying for its misdeeds did not deter the company from future wage theft. In 2017, Walmart agreed to pay workers in California $60.8 million to settle a lawsuit that accused the company of compelling employees to work off the clock. In 2020, $8.7 million was paid to settle a decade-old lawsuit of Walmart's refusal to pay overtime to those working more than forty hours a week.[23]

In addition to the practice of forcing employees to work off the clock, the retailer also faced a sex-discrimination lawsuit that accused it of denying equal pay and promotions to seven hundred thousand of its female employees from 1996 to 2001. The suit claimed that female employees made $1,150 less per year than men in similar jobs, while female managers made $16,400 less. According to one of the women who testified, her department manager in South Carolina explained that Walmart pays men more than women because the Bible says God made Adam before Eve.[24] In June 2011, the US Supreme Court threw out the employment discrimination class-action suit (*Dukes v. Wal-Mart*) on behalf of 1.5 million female employees. In a five-to-four decision along ideological lines, the court ruled that the suit failed to satisfy the requirement that "there are questions of law or fact common to the class" of female employees.

The Court did not decide if Walmart discriminated against women; it only stated that the suit could not move forward as a class action because the case was improperly certified. Specifically, writing for the majority opinion, Justice Scalia said that the women who brought forth the case failed to point to any specific companywide policies that had a common effect on all the women covered by the class action, even though Justice Ginsburg noted that the overwhelming evidence and testimonies demonstrated that "gender bias suffused Wal-Mart's corporate culture." Not only did the court decision immediately impact the claim of Walmart female employees negatively, but it also made it more difficult for employees or consumers to join together and challenge institutionalized biases that do not arise from a clear company policy. Joseph M. Seller, the attorney for the plaintiff, explained that the court decision "reversed about forty years of jurisprudence that has in the past allowed for companywide cases to be brought challenging common practices that have a disparate effect, that

---

[22] Ibid.

[23] Philip Mattera, "Wal-Mart: Corporate Rap Sheet—Wal-Mart Stores," Corporate Research Project, December 7, 2020.

[24] Steven Greenhouse, "Wal-Mart Faces Lawsuit over Sex Discrimination," *New York Times*, February 16, 2003.

have adversely affected women and other workers."[25] Not surprisingly, people of color are also discriminated against by the company. In 2009 Walmart paid $17.5 million to settle a class-action lawsuit that accused the retailer of discriminating against African Americans during the recruitment and hiring of truck drivers for their private fleet.[26]

Not only are women and people of color discriminated against; so too are the disabled. In 2017, more than one thousand employees accused Walmart of violating the American with Disabilities Act and the Family and Medical Leave Act. The "associates" claimed they were punished for absences due to medical situations. As a rule, Walmart "routinely refuses to accept doctors' notes, penalizes workers who need to take care of a sick family member and otherwise punishes employees for lawful absences." Katie Orzehowski, a North Huntingdon, Pennsylvania, cashier, returned to work after suffering a miscarriage despite her doctor's documented advice and hospitalization records even while still heavily bleeding for fear of being fired.[27] In 2019, the company settled its disability allegations by paying $5.2 million.[28]

When employees at Walmart attempted to unionize to have more leverage with management, union supporters were fired, intimidated, and threatened with the loss of bonuses. A union supporter at a Jacksonville, Texas, store was fired for, supposedly, stealing a banana. The only successful effort at organizing Walmart employees occurred in the meat department in a Texas store. Within two weeks of unionizing, the department was disbanded by the company. When a Walmart outlet unionized in Jonquière, Quebec, becoming the first store to be unionized on the North American continent, the headquarters in Bentonville, Arkansas, closed that store's doors a few months later. A former Walmart store manager who now works as a union organizer summed up the company's attitude: "They go after you any way they can to discredit you, to fire you. It's almost like a neurosurgeon going after a brain tumor: We got to get that thing out before it infects the rest of the store, the rest of the body."

According to Walmart's then–senior vice president Jay Allen, the reason Walmart remains nonunion is because the company has done a great job in keeping its employees happy and paying them competitive

---

[25] Adam Liptak, "Justices Rule for Wal-Mart in Class-Action Bias Case," *New York Times*, June 20, 2011; Joan Biskupic, "Supreme Court Limits Wal-Mart Sex Discrimination Case," *USA Today*, June 21, 2011.

[26] Kathy Shwiff, "Wal-Mart Settles Discrimination Lawsuit," *Wall Street Journal*, February 20, 2009.

[27] Rachel Abrams, "Walmart Is Accused of Punishing Workers for Sick Days," *New York Times*, June 1, 2017.

[28] Mattera, "Wal-Mart: Corporate Rap Sheet."

wages.[29] Human Rights Watch disagrees, asserting that Walmart's aggressive tactics to keep out labor unions has often violated federal laws while infringing on workers' rights. The retail giant, when faced with (what it considers) the threat of unionization, often broke the law by eavesdropping on workers, turning surveillance cameras on them, infiltrating anti-Walmart organizational meetings, or firing those who favored unions.[30] A favorite technique of the retailer, which administrative law judges ruled as illegal, is transferring out or firing pro-union workers and replacing them with antiunion employees to skew the vote whether to unionize, as was successfully done at the Walmart tire and lube shop in Loveland, Colorado.[31]

Walmart's refusal to unionize negatively impacts those who work for Walmart and threatens to undermine the wages being paid to workers by competitors like Costco, who can demand contract concessions from unions so they can compete with Walmart. They cite their inability to compete with Walmart's wages and benefits, which are 20 percent below theirs. In effect, Walmart, the nation's largest corporate employer, is lowering the living standards for everyone by aggressively and artificially keeping wages depressed for the sake of profit. Because Walmart can cut the cost of operations by paying employees less, the retail giant has been able to push over two dozen national chains into bankruptcy. The list of now defunct chains includes Grand Union, Bruno's of Alabama, Homeland Stores of Oklahoma, Winn Dixie, and F.A.O. Schwarz, to name but a few. The Walmartizing of America means that, to compete, other stores must race against Walmart to the lowest labor compensation or face their own demise.

According to a study conducted by the UC Berkeley Labor Center, empirical evidence exists that Walmart employees earn lower average wages and receive less generous benefits than comparable employees working for other large retailers (evidenced by a 17.4 percent earning gap with other general merchandising employees and a 25 percent gap with large

---

[29] Laura Gunderson, "In-House Audit Says Wal-Mart Violated Labor Laws," *New York Times*, January 13, 2004; Anthony Bianco, "No Union Please, We're Wal-Mart," *Business Week*, February 12, 2006.

[30] Steven Greenhouse and Stephanie Rosenbloom, "Wal-Mart Settles 63 Lawsuits over Wages," *New York Times*, December 24, 2008; Ann Zimmerman and Gary McWilliams, "Inside Wal-Mart's 'Treat Research' Operations," *Wall Street Journal*, April 4, 2007.

[31] Steven Greenhouse, "At a Small Shop in Colorado, Wal-Mart Beats a Union Once More," *New York Times*, February 26, 2005.

general merchandise companies). Research indicates that better-paying jobs are replaced with lower-paying jobs whenever a new Walmart store opens in a community. Walmart openings drive down wages of competing industry segments within the new store's proximity. When Walmart enters a new marketplace, the total county's mean income declines along with the average wage. Similar effects also appear on the state level. The presence of fifty new Walmart stores in any given state means a 10 percent reduction of average wages (Dube, Lester, and Eidlin 2007, 1, 3, 6).

The task of disenfranchising Walmart workers (or workers in general) is not carried out by the company's highly paid executives but by those who themselves are disenfranchised. The connection between the privileged elite and the poor and marginalized workers is maintained through a corporate system that enriches the former at the expense of the latter. The privilege of top executives is shielded through the creation of a professional-managerial class that serves as a buffer zone between top management and those employees living in poverty due to low wages. The function of a professional-managerial class was ignored by Marxist economic theorists who centered their analysis on only two classes: the bourgeoisie and the proletariat.

Barbara and John Ehrenreich (a journalist and psychology professor, respectively) argued that the middle class, composed of technical workers, managerial workers, "culture" producers, and so on, must be understood as constituting a distinct class in an advanced capitalist society. They call this group the professional-managerial class (1972, 8–11). Middle-class managers, who are responsible for ensuring that employees work at the lowest possible wage with few or no benefits, consist of salaried employees who do not own the means of production but function within the social division of labor as the reproducers of capitalist culture and class relations. Not surprisingly, the relationship between this professional-managerial class and the employees is usually antagonistic.

This professional-managerial class is, in effect, a contradictory class. Like the poor, they are excluded from owning the means of production, but their interests are still opposed to the workers because of their managerial positions within the corporate organization. Although supposedly materially comfortable, they remain associated with the processes of exploitation (Wright 1985, 285–86). The excessive profits made by the heads of multinational corporations make it possible to "bribe" this contradictory class, through higher salaries, into maintaining the status quo, strengthening the marginalization of the disenfranchised. The rise of the professional-managerial class has contributed to two sets of business ethics, both constructed to benefit the economic elite.

The marginalized who work at the bottom rungs in companies like Walmart are expected to be upright, honest, and loyal. They must pass drug tests to prove they are responsible and take personality tests to ensure their submissiveness. It is good for corporations to promote ethical behavior among its personnel, for the business cannot survive if its employees are not maintaining the company's best interests. It also becomes profitable for companies to maintain a public persona of being ethical, and while no doubt some firms are, this is all simply an issue of public relations for others. The professional-managerial class is responsible for maintaining the ethical façade for the benefit of top executives who are ultimately responsible for the "bottom line," even at the expense of those upright, honest, and loyal employees.

The professional-managerial class can take comfort in knowing that, while things may be economically bad, at least they are not the marginalized. Nevertheless, the professional-managerial class is also susceptible to unemployment, underemployment, and low wages. A downwardly mobile professional-managerial class presents an additional problem as the distinction between them and the marginalized becomes blurred. Not surprisingly, the no-longer-upwardly mobile are angry. Rather than blaming the elite who sit above them, they blame those under them, specifically the marginalized. "Illegal" immigration or affirmative-action policies easily become scapegoats for the economic conditions that have led to the professional-managerial class's financial reversals.

Walmart's corporate ethos of disenfranchising and marginalizing workers is not limited to North America; the giant retailer is having a negative global impact. In 2019 Walmart settled a seven-year global corruption probe when it paid out $282 million. The company had allegedly violated the US Foreign Corrupt Practices Act when it paid bribes in Mexico, Brazil, China, and India to open stores abroad.

In Mexico, Walmart, the country's largest private employer, wanted to build a store barely a mile from the ancient pyramid of Teotihuacán. A 2003 zoning map that prohibited commercial development close to the ancient site stood in their way. A $52,000 bribe was paid to change the zoning map in Walmart's favor before it was published in the newspaper. Months later, Walmart broke ground on its new store, which opened in 2004. Additional bribes amounting to about $221,000 were paid to ensure that the store was built. Total bribes paid in Mexico amounted to more than $24 million.[32] The driving force behind years of bribery, Eduardo Castro-

---

[32] David Barstow, "Vast Mexico Bribery Case Hushed Up by Wal-Mart after Top-Level Struggle," *New York Times*, April 22, 2012; David Barstow and Alejandra

Wright, was promoted to vice chairman of Walmart in 2008. Eventually, it became apparent that Walmart was not some reluctant victim of a corrupt Mexican culture, where bribes are an inherent cost of doing business. Walmart aggressively and routinely used bribes as the means to subvert governance and to procure what the law otherwise prohibited.

For example, through a $341,000 bribe, a Sam's Club was able to be built in a densely populated Mexico City neighborhood without a construction license, environmental permit, an urban impact assessment, or a traffic permit. A $765,000 bribe facilitated the building of a refrigerated distribution center at an environmentally fragile flood basin in Mexico City where electricity is so limited that smaller developers were not permitted to build at the site.[33] Even if caught and found guilty of bribing officials, it was still worth breaking the law because, according to the company, it does not think the repercussions will have a "material adverse effect" on its business. In a note to investors, Janney Capital Markets analyst David Strasser wrote, "This is clearly a bad action, if found guilty, but we believe these issues and penalties will not dramatically impair their balance sheet and its ongoing business model," especially in the United States.[34]

At a Uniden plant in Shenzhen, China, young women, who are mainly recruited from China's poor interior provinces, make the wireless phones supplied to Walmart. These women claim that they are required to work eleven hours a day plus three hours of mandatory overtime for a monthly salary of about $58, half of which must be returned to the company as payment for the drab company dormitories in which they must live. These women accuse the company of hiring many minors and being forced to pay about half of a month's salary as a job-finder fee to be hired.[35]

In India, regulators began an informal inquiry into allegations that Walmart violated rules restricting foreign investments in 2012. Specifically, they investigated $100 million invested by Walmart in the countrywide Indian supermarket chain Bharti Retail. The interest-free, so-called debt security converted into a 49 percent ownership stake thirty months after issue, in violation of India's law. This has allowed Walmart to enter a retail sale market that is estimated at $500 billion annually and is presently dominated by small, family-owned stores. In November 2012, the US Justice

---

Xanic von Bertrab, "The Bribery Aisle: How Wal-Mart Used Payoffs to Get Its Way in Mexico," *New York Times*, December 18, 2012.

[33] Ibid.

[34] Associated Press, "Wal-Mart Says Loss Likely from Bribery Probe," *Denver Post*, March 27, 2013.

[35] Howard W. French, "Workers Demand Union at Wal-Mart Supplier in China," *New York Times*, December 16, 2004.

Department expanded an internal bribery investigation that was originally focused on Mexico to include India, China, and Brazil under political pressure of irregularities.[36]

It would be erroneous to caricature the top executives of Walmart as demonic or wicked people. In fact, many are considered virtuous, upright, leading citizens and churchgoers. "Is Walmart a Christian company? No," said a former Walmart vice chairman during a prayer breakfast. "But the basis of our decisions was the values of Scripture." The stores cater to churchgoing customers, sanitizing questionable products (like keeping *Cosmopolitan* magazine covers out of view) while being the largest retailer of Christian-themed merchandise.[37] Nevertheless, in his exposé of Walmart culture, Bob Ortega revealed the disconnect between the Christian virtues expounded by the company's top officials and their actual corporate practices. He concluded,

> David Glass [then Walmart's president] was considered by his friends to be a fine, upstanding, morally correct, and honest man. Don Soderquist [then Walmart's vice chairman] was a devout Christian once named lay churchman of the year by a national Baptist organization. And yet these two ran a company that profited from the exploitation of children—and, in all likelihood, from the exploitation of Chinese prisoners, too. Time and again it was put before them, by *Dateline* [NBC revealed that some Wal-Mart products made in Bangladesh used illegal child labor], by Harry Wu [former Chinese political prisoner for nineteen years who alleged some Wal-Mart products were made with slave labor], by the *Wall Street Journal*, by others. And yet their response was to do the very least they could, to hold up, time and again, their feeble code, as if its mere existence—forget monitoring, forget enforcement—was enough; as if by uttering once more "our suppliers know we have strict codes" would solve any problem. And nothing would change. (1998, 258–59)

It is of little comfort to the marginalized that these top officials have certain personal virtues while ignoring the Hebrew Bible's condemnation of "those who cheat workers of their wages" (Mal. 3:5), or the New

---

[36] Vikas Bajaj, "India Puts Wal-Mart Deal with Retailer Under Scrutiny," *New York Times*, October 19, 2012; Vikas Bajaj, "India Unit of Wal-Mart Suspends Employees," *New York Times*, November 24, 2012.

[37] Jeff M. Sellers, "Deliver Us from Wal-Mart?," *Christianity Today*, April 22, 2005.

Testament rebuke of those who "cheated the worker who mowed [the employer's] fields" (Jas 5:4). Just as faith without works is dead (Jas. 2:20), so, too, are right virtues without right praxis meaningless.

Step 3: Meditating

In teaching about the day of final judgment, Jesus tells a parable of two stewards in charge of the master's household—one conscientious, the other self-absorbed. The conscientious steward fulfilled his ethical obligations to both the master and his fellow servants. The self-absorbed steward beat those under his authority. Rather than providing his fellow servants with their fair share of profits from the work performed, the self-absorbed steward ate and drank what was stolen from the laborers. The steward's master came home unexpectedly and, seeing how both stewards had behaved, rewarded the conscientious one while condemning the oppressive one (Mt. 24:45–51). Through the parable, Jesus prescribes the ethical responsibilities of those with power over workers. Increasingly, laws and government regulations tend to legitimize the power and privilege of multinational corporations—who have become the stewards of today's world. Because these new oppressive stewards "lord it" over the disenfranchised majority and contribute to their poverty, their salvation becomes ever more elusive.

Rather than looking at the CEOs responsible for setting the wages of the employees, as well as their own compensation, our culture teaches us to blame the workers for their lot. Sometimes we justify this callousness through an ideology based on Charles Darwin's findings that argue for a natural selection that supposedly ensures the "survival of the fittest." Some economic philosophers, misreading Darwin's assertions, have proposed that, just as animals compete to survive, so do (and should) humans. Social Darwinists maintain that free markets guarantee that only those who are aggressive enough will survive because they are the fittest—in effect, they are the best human beings. Hence, those who fail deserve to fail because they are neither the fittest nor the best. There is no reason then for the government to provide them with assistance (such as welfare, unemployment compensation, and so on) because preserving these economic "losers" or "moochers" would perpetuate inferior qualities into the next generation.

Christian ethics from the margins runs counter to the exploitation of labor. When corporations create conditions that contribute to the poverty of workers—whether being disguised as a defense of democracy, open economic markets, or Christian virtues, these corporations are complicit in establishing and maintaining institutionalized violence. Violence is never limited to the use of physical force but incorporates power used to achieve wealth and privilege at the expense of others. Violence is anything that prevents an individual from fulfilling what Christ said was the purpose of his mission: to give life and give it abundantly (Jn. 10:10).

Such violence (usually manifested as racism, classism, heterosexism, and sexism) becomes institutionalized when it is built into the very structure of the corporation. The violence experienced by the working poor through inadequate food, clothes, health care, and shelter brings profit to those within the corporation, specifically its officers, directors, and to a lesser extent, stockholders. Such exploitation of workers dehumanizes them, turning them into just another resource, another commodity. Contrary to such common practices, biblical texts call for workers to be treated humanely and justly:

> You shall not oppress a poor and needy hired servant, neither among your compatriots nor an alien who is in your land or within your gates. You shall pay them for their work on the same day. The sun shall not set upon them, for they are poor and upon these wages their heart is lifted up. Let them not cry out against you to God, and it be sin against you. (Deut. 24:14–15)

As we survey the plight of the global poor, the global privileges enjoyed in the so-called first world are linked to economic disenfranchisement elsewhere. The prophet Amos warns us not to "sell the just for silver, or the poor for a pair of sandals" (2:6). Those who get to live in the West, along with the few within the Global South who are in cahoots, enjoy middle- and upper-class lifestyles because the just are sold for silver and the poor for a pair of sandals—or more typically, a pair of Nike sneakers.

Consider the rural farmers harvesting rice on the island of Java in Indonesia. Those wielding the sickle are usually barefoot. Men who are over sixty spend the entire day scrunched over, harvesting rice for about 55,503 rupiahs, equivalent to $3.81 a day, which is about a third of the official minimum wage of $10.90. Of course, there is an underground economy that relies on trading goods and services, thus complicating the livability of the people; nevertheless, the day's wage of an Indonesian rice farmer is equivalent to the pocket change most Americans carry.[38]

---

[38] Information concerning rice farmers in Indonesia is based on the author's fieldwork in Java.

If these rural workers have children wishing to go to college, their families would be unable to pay tuition and fees for a year of attending a low-end school that would still cost less than a pair of Nike sneakers. Add books, housing, and meals, and it becomes impossible. These rural workers' children are relegated to find similar types of employment on farms or in the city. What would happen if this fieldhand was to secure a job at one of the Nike's factories in Indonesia? They could expect a salary of about $102 a month. What can $102 buy you in Indonesia? Barely enough to pay rent for a tiny, bare room, buy two meager meals a day, and pay bus fare to get to work. The worker would not be able to buy the Nike sneakers that they are producing.[39] Westerners get to buy $100+ sneakers because the poor of the earth make them at abusive wages.

The riches of so-called first-world nations are directly connected to poverty in the Global South. The CEOs and the stockholders in such companies, who are directly rewarded by keeping expenses (meaning the salaries of those who make the product, not those of the CEO's leadership team) as low as possible, are those who truly benefit. And here is the internal contradiction of capitalism: as corporations search throughout the globe for the lowest possible wage to pay, the day will come (if it hasn't already) when workers will not be able to purchase what they produce, causing an abundant surplus of unaffordable goods whose weight could crush capitalism. Could it be that the 2008 Great Recession began the death pangs of this global economic system we created—death pangs that may whimper out in just a few more generations? The great irony of all this is that the US Congress has moved to protect the so-called job creators from taxation, when, in reality, their bonuses are calculated on how many jobs they can eliminate, outsource, or maintain at the lowest possible wage. In effect, they receive large bonuses when they sell the poor for a pair of sandals.

Step 4: Case Studies

1. One possible reason that the United States has a dysfunctional immigration system might be that imprisoning the undocumented is a billion-dollar industry. Since 2011, nearly half the beds in the nation's civil detention systems were in privately owned facilities. The two major corporations that benefit from this arrangement are CoreCivic ($1.97 billion in Q3, 2019) and the GEO Group ($2.45 billion). The average nightly cost

---

[39] Kieran Guilbert, "Adidas, Nike Urged to Ensure Fair Wages for Asian Workers Making World Cup Kits," Reuters, June 11, 2018.

to detain an undocumented immigrant, according to the US Immigration and Customs Enforcement's 2018 budget, is $133.99 per day. However, the number is closer to $200 a day (up from $166 in 2012). To house a mother and children together at a family facility is about $319 a day.[40] Additionally, these companies rake in profits from subsidiaries that provide health care and transportation. Because these facilities are paid by the day, no motivation exists to quickly repatriate the undocumented.

In 2000 Correction Corporation of America—renamed CoreCivic in 2016—was on the verge of bankruptcy. At the time, the Federal Bureau of Prisons signed contracts worth $750 million to house thirty-three hundred immigrants. By 2019 the agency paid private companies $3 billion to house approximately fifty thousand immigrants, the majority of whom had no criminal record.[41] The corporate desire to maintain, if not increase, the bottom line has led to fierce competition on Capitol Hill (and among statehouses throughout the nation) to increase incarcerations. CoreCivic and GEO have spent millions on campaign donations and lobbyists to maintain and introduce laws that ensure a steady stream of undocumented persons flowing though detention centers.

• Should we really feign surprise that the undocumented face inhumane conditions during their US incarceration? In 2019 a USA Network investigation found that, during 2019, there were four hundred allegations of sexual assault or abuse and inadequate medical care, eight hundred instances of physical force employed against inmates, twenty-nine fatalities (including seven suicides), and nearly two hundred thousand filed grievances.[42] Over the years, Amnesty International has documented how these inmates are routinely denied food, water, and medical attention, while being exposed to verbal, physical, and psychological abuse. Many human rights organizations, legal scholars, and the United Nations have meticulously documented how the United States consistently violates international human rights. Do inmates deserve such treatment because, after all, they broke the law and entered the United States illegally? What should be our response to such human rights violations?

• Should prisons, a responsibility of the government, be privatized? Are there certain tasks that only the government should do? Should other

---

[40] Jaden Urbi, "This Is How Much It Costs to Detain an Immigrant in the US," CNBC, June 20, 2018.

[41] Monsy Alvarado et al., "'These People Are Profitable': Under Trump Private Prisons Are Cashing In on ICE Detainees," *USA Today*, December 19, 2019.

[42] Ibid.

governmental tasks be privatized? Military? Environmental protection? Mail service? If not, should some companies profiting at the government's expense be nationalized?

• Fixing a broken immigration system could bankrupt these for-profit prisons. If detention numbers were to decrease, their stock values would drop. The main concern is not to provide humanitarian living conditions but to increase corporate profits. This can only occur when basic services are cut to reduce actual costs. Substandard living conditions can be maintained because there are no substantive legislative or regulatory standards governing detention conditions. Those more likely to complain, or even bring legal proceedings against these firms are deported out of the country. Are these corporations at fault for seeking the highest profits for their stockholders? Should noncitizens be protected by US laws? Is it problematic that these facilities that house the undocumented lack proper oversight?

2. In Victor Hugo's classic, *Les Miserables*, Jean Valjean smashed the window of Maubert Isabeau, the baker on Church Square in Faverolles, to steal a loaf of bread to feed his widowed sister's seven hungry children. Even though he and his sister worked several jobs, what they earned was not sufficient to place food on the table. The story of Jean Valjean is the story of many today who live on the margins of society.

• Is it moral to steal property (bread) to meet a basic human need and avert the greater evil of malnutrition? Is stealing food any greater a sin than stealing Jean Valjean's labor by refusing to pay him a living wage?

• What about the rights of Maubert Isabeau, the baker? Does stealing property, even if it is food, destroy community because it destroys trust? Are property laws designed to protect the property of those who can afford property while ignoring the intangible property of the poor in the form of their labor? Do property rights supersede the rights of humans to consume the daily requirement of calories needed to sustain life?

3. Papa John's former CEO John Schnatter declared shortly after the reelection of President Obama that the cost of implementing the Affordable Care Act (aka Obamacare) for his company would force him to increase the price of his pizza pies by 10 to 14 cents (even though an independent analysis conducted by *Forbes* placed the cost at 3.4 to 4.6 cents per pie). Papa John's cost of providing health care at $5 million to $8 million annually, from total revenue of $1.218 billion at that time, represented a 0.4 percent to 0.7 percent increase in the company's total expenses. Schnatter threatened to scale back employees' schedules to fewer than thirty hours

a week to qualify for the health insurance exception and avoid paying for the health care.[43] He backed away on his threats in an opinion piece he wrote for the *Huffington Post* after a public outcry led to a drop of Papa John's stock values. Meanwhile, Schnatter lives in a forty-thousand-square-foot castle/mega-mansion with a twenty-two-car garage, a golf course, a drawbridge, an office for valet parking, a car wash, and even a motorized turntable to move limousines.[44] He claimed that his annual salary during the last year he worked for Papa John as CEO was $3.5 million. He resigned from the company amid a teleconference call scandal in 2018 when he used the n-word but still retained 25 percent of the business's worth, which—at that time—was $531 million. Forbes estimated his worth then at $801 million.[45] The starting hourly wage of one of his pizza delivery drivers is $7.50. It can be argued that the "value" of what he owns (e.g., his castle/mega-mansion) does not exist within the commodity itself, for such value is secondary. Rather, the conspicuous consumption of such a commodity mainly seeks recognition by others of the consumer's higher social standing. Hence, conspicuous consumption fails to satisfy any particular need of the consumer; instead, the display of commodities, in and of itself, enhances the reputation of the consumer (Veblen 1953, 21–80).

• Is conspicuous consumption moral? Does a person have a right to spend their money on any commodity they choose to own, even when the sole purpose of owning that commodity is to flaunt a higher social standing? Should people be allowed to accumulate luxury items while their neighbors go hungry? If so, is this a governmental responsibility? If not, are there any ways to create a more balanced society?

• What responsibility do CEOs have to their corporation, their stock-holders, the community at large, and the poor? Should Schnatter employ every legal means possible to increase his company's profits? Is this so even or especially if it means reducing employees' weekly hours to fewer than thirty to avoid providing health care?

---

[43] Steven Greenhouse and Reed Abelson, "The Cost of Change: Small Employers Weigh Impact of Providing Health Insurance," *New York Times*, December 1, 2012.

[44] "John Schnatter House: Kentucky Mansion," Urban Splatter (blog), February 2022.

[45] "How Rich Is 'Papa John'? Answers to All Your John Schnatter Questions," *Courier Journal*, July 18, 2018; Noah Kirsch, "Papa John Loses Dough: Pizza Chain Founder Loses $70 Million in Hours, Blames NFL," *Forbes*, November 1, 2017.

Chapter 14

Sexism

We are a nation that celebrates and rewards misogyny. The forty-fifth president provides an excellent example of how one can surmount the pinnacle of power in the United States even while debasing women and bragging about his ability to sexually harass them. "When you're a star," he was caught boasting on tape, "they'll let you do it.... You can do anything ... grab them by the p*ssy."[1] A month later, he was elected president—his comments did not seem to impact his electability. Multiple examples exist of how he judged women by their looks—for example, commenting that political opponent Carly Fiorina was too ugly to be president. "Look at that face," he said. "Would anyone vote for that?"[2] As to his Democratic opponent Hillary Clinton, he tweeted, "If Hillary Clinton can't satisfy her husband, what makes her think she can satisfy America?"[3] When women challenged him, like Megyn Kelly, he dismissed them as "bimbos." In response to critical questions asked by Kelly concerning his sexist comments during a presidential debate, he mused these inquiries were the result of "blood coming out of her eyes, blood coming out of her wherever."[4] And in a creepy comment about his own daughter, Ivanka, he said it was okay to call her a "piece of ass."[5]

The issue here is not Donald Trump's brutish comments concerning women. His sexism is a symptom of a misogynist culture that institutionalizes

---

[1] Susan Dominus, "Donald Trump: King of the Old Boys' Club, and Perhaps Its Destroyer," *New York Times*, October 7, 2016.

[2] Jessica Estepa, "Donald Trump on Carly Fiorina: 'Look at that Face!,'" *USA Today*, September 10, 2015.

[3] Associated Press, "Some of Donald Trump's Most Insulting Comments about Women," October 8, 2016.

[4] Philip Rucker, "Trump Says Fox's Megyn Kelly Had 'Blood Coming out of Her Wherever,'" *Washington Post*, August 8, 2015.

[5] Andrew Kaczynski, Chris Massie, and Nate McDermott, "Donald Trump to Howard Stern: It's Okay to Call My Daughter a 'Piece of Ass,'" CNN Politics, October 9, 2016.

the oppression of women. The fact that he was able to capture the presidency in 2016 and had more people voting for him in 2020 than four years earlier despite multiple sexist (as well as racist) comments, indicates that he personifies the misogynist (and racist) views of a major portion of the US population. When we consider that his election would not have been possible if not for the support of euroamerican women, we are left wondering to what degree they are complicit with their own repression. Does racism trump sexism? From their purview, is finding one's secure space "below" euroamerican men preferable as long as one remains "on top" of people of color? This chapter explores this intersection of sexism, racism, and ethnic discrimination as well as how it undergirds white US Christianity.

Step 1: Observing

As troublesome as sexist comments are, when they are voiced by politicians, they are especially damning because of the power such people hold to enact legislation based on their beliefs—in most cases, their religious beliefs. Discussion of this war on women can easily be explored through the political, economic, social, and traditional acts taken by broader society in multiple areas of daily life. Due to limited space, this chapter focuses on (1) US workplace opportunities (e.g., equal pay); (2) violence toward women (e.g., rape) within the United States; (3) control over American women's bodies (e.g., reproduction rights); and finally (4) global manifestation of socially engrained misogyny.

Workplace Opportunities

Sexism has historically been the norm of the US workplace. "Sexism" is the term assigned to social structures and systems where the "actions, practices, and use of laws, rules and customs limit certain activities of one sex, but do not limit those same activities of other people of the other sex" (Shute 1981, 27). Sexism becomes obvious when we compare the wages of women to those of men. According to a report by the US Bureau of Labor Statistics, the 2018 working-poor rate, which represents the ratio of the working poor to all individuals who were in the labor force for at least twenty-seven weeks, was 5.3 percent for women (3.9 million) and 3.7 percent for men (3.1 million). Thus, 64 percent of those who live below the poverty line are working poor women, while 36 percent are working poor men. Even though women represented almost half (47 percent) of the US labor force, they were paid less than men in every labor category and at every education level. Of course, Black women and Latinas were most likely to be among the working poor. In 2019, women who worked full-time had a median weekly income of $821, which represented 82 percent of men's median weekly earnings of $1,007. Euroamerican women, at $840, fared better than Black women ($704) and Latinas ($642).[6]

After sixty years since the passing of the Equal Pay Act on June 10, 1963, euroamerican women still earned an average wage ratio of 79 cents for every dollar earned by a euroamerican man.[7] At our present rate of progress, pay parity will eventually be achieved in the year 2069[8]—more than a century after the law was originally passed. Not surprisingly, women of color were paid less, with African American women making 58 cents for every dollar paid to a euroamerican man, Native women making 50 cents, and Latinas making 49 cents. Asian American women fared the best, at 75 cents for every euroamerican man's full dollar.[9] While Latinas represent 18.1 percent of all women in the United States, they constitute 27.1 percent of women living in poverty. Likewise, Black women represent 22.3 percent of women in poverty but are only 12.8 percent of all women in the United States. The highest rates of poverty are experienced by Indigenous women, with approximately one in four living in poverty—the highest rate among women or men of any racial or ethnic group in the United States. Nine percent of euroamerican women, by contrast, live in poverty.[10]

Although the situation has improved for euroamerican women since the law was signed in 1963—at which time women earned 60 cents for every dollar made by a man—the narrowing of the gap over the past sixty years had more to do with wage losses among men than wage gains among women. Nevertheless, euroamerican women needed to work until March 24, 2021, to make the same income that a man earned within the year 2020. For Black women and Latinas, the date was farther on the horizon. A Black woman had to work until August 3, while a Latina had to work until October 21.[11] Another way to calculate this disparity is that if the wage gap

---

[6] Bureau of Labor Statistics, *Women in the Labor Force: A Databook*, April 2021.

[7] National Partnership for Women & Families, "Quantifying America's Gender Wage Gap by Race/Ethnicity," May 2022.

[8] Katie Allen, "Gender Pay Gap Won't Close until 2069, Says Deloitte," *The Guardian*, September 23, 2016.

[9] National Partnership for Women & Families, "Quantifying America's Gender Wage Gap."

[10] Center for American Progress, "The Basic Facts about Women in Poverty," fact sheet, August 3, 2020.

[11] Francesca Donner and Emma Goldberg, "In 25 Years, the Pay Gap Has Shrunk by Just 8 Cents," *New York Times*, March 24, 2021.

was eliminated, full-time working euroamerican women would have earned enough for approximately twenty-five months of food, fourteen months of rent, and nineteen months of childcare. In this equitable scenario, Black women's labor would have afforded them thirty-eight months of food, two years of rent, and twenty-nine months of childcare; Latinas would have earned enough for pay for forty-six months of food, two years of rent, and thirty-six months of childcare; and Indigenous women's wages or salaries would pay for forty-one months of food, two years of rent, and thirty-two months of childcare.[12]

Most of the national progress made in income parity occurred among single women, making a woman with children, or motherhood status, the greatest predictor of wage inequality. Substantial decades of research indicate that what is mostly perceived as a gender wage gap is more often a motherhood wage gap. While women, regardless of race or ethnicity, made 82 cents when compared to euroamerican men, mothers made 75 cents, with euroamerican mothers being paid 71 cents; Black mothers, 52 cents; Native mothers, 50 cents; and Latina mothers, 46 cents. Asian mothers fared the best at 90 cents (Tucker 2021, 2). This becomes especially problematic when we consider that, in 2017, 41 percent of mothers were either the primary or sole source of income for their family. This percentage includes single mothers and mothers with higher incomes than their husbands. Historically, women of color were always more likely than euroamerican women to work outside of the home. They are also more likely than euroamerican women to be raising children outside of a marriage, even though the majority of unmarried mothers in the United States are euroamericans.[13]

If we were to solely consider white-collar employment, women do not fare any better. In the highest hierarchical levels of management, the sixth level, women represent just 15 percent of this workforce segment and are paid 77.3 percent of their male colleagues' salary (with just 19 percent representation on the fifth level while being paid 77.6 percent, and 23 percent representation on the fourth level at a comparable 81.7 percent of male colleagues' pay). With only half of 1 percent of all US workers reaching the three highest levels of management, the underrepresentation and underpayment of women are highly problematic (Yildirmaz, Ryan, and Nezaj 2019, 6). The highest-paid female CEO in 2021 was Dr. Lisa Su of

---

[12] National Partnership for Women & Families, "Quantifying America's Gender Wage Gap."

[13] Sarah Glynn, "Breadwinning Mothers Continue to Be the U.S. Norm," Center for American Progress, May 10, 2019.

Advanced Micro Devices, with an annual compensation package worth $40 million. Compare this to the highest-paid male CEO, Alexander Karp of Palantir, who made $1.1 billion.[14]

Studies also indicate that as an occupation becomes more dominated by women (e.g., social workers and primary school teachers), wages for those jobs begin to decline when compared with similar job skills associated with occupations dominated by men.[15] Women can also expect to be among the last hired. According to John Challenger, CEO of a Chicago-based global outplacement firm, men snagged three of every four of the 2.4 million new jobs created between 2009 and 2012—leading him to nickname the recovery from the 2008 Great Recession as the "he-covery" or "mancovery." The threat of a continuing mancovery is that the minimum gains women made in the workplace prior to 2008 could be reversed, as occurred in the 1940s when men returning from war pushed women out of jobs.[16]

Discrimination against women, especially in the workplace, has been based on the popular adage that women could not be fulfilled wives and successful mothers while pursuing a career. In 1962, psychiatrists maintained that "normal" women renounced aspirations outside the home to meet their feminine need for dependence. Two-thirds of Americans, according to a University of Michigan survey around that time, agreed with this view. The survey revealed that the most important family decisions "should be made by the man of the house."[17] Since then, a revolution of attitudes concerning women in the home and workplace has occurred.

In 1977, two-thirds of Americans believed it was "better for everyone involved if the man is the achiever outside the home and the woman takes care of the home and family." By 1994, two-thirds of Americans rejected this notion. Yet this 1994 trend of thinking began to reverse. From 1994 to 2004, the model of male breadwinner / female homemaker rose in popularity among North Americans from 34 percent to 40 percent.[18] By 2019, the trend again began to change. When given a choice, 66 percent of adults preferred work outside the home—men at 75 percent and women

---

[14] Peter Eavis, "Meager Rewards for Workers, Exceptionally Rich Pays for CEOs," *New York Times*, June 11, 2021.

[15] Stephanie Coontz, "The Myth of Male Decline," *New York Times*, September 30, 2012.

[16] Aldo Svaldi, "Men Winning More Jobs Than Women in Economic Recovery," *The Denver Post*, August 10, 2012.

[17] Stephanie Coontz, "Why Gender Equality Stalled," *New York Times*, February 17, 2013.

[18] Ibid.

at 56 percent.[19] The historical patriarchal assumption that the woman's domain is found within the domestic sphere while men were charged to be the primary breadwinners continues to be challenged in today's era. The economic realities that women face in the workplace (e.g., lack of paid paternity leave and minimal maternity leave) become forms of institutional violence. Unfortunately, women also face physical violence.

Violence toward Women

In 2014, nearly three women a day were murdered by their husbands or boyfriends in the United States. By 2019, the number was closer to four a day.[20] According to the Centers for Disease Control and Prevention (CDC), more than one in five women in the United States have experienced physical violence and one in eleven were raped by an intimate partner at some point in their life. Additionally, 9.2 percent have been stalked by an intimate partner (Breiding et al. 2015, 1). By 2017, Black women were twice as likely as euroamerican women to be murdered in general, with 91 percent of them knowing who their murderer was (Violence Policy Center 2019, 6). A 2016 study showed that homicide was the third most frequent cause of death among pregnant women, with 190 cases over a six-year period (2005–2010), behind natural causes (n = 1150) and injury (n = 430, transport-related and other injuries combined). Pregnancy-associated homicide was more than three times as likely to occur among Black women compared to euroamericans (Wallace et al. 2016, 364e2). No doubt: a woman's life is far safer with a man she does not know than with a man she does know.

According to the US Department of Justice, during 2019, 1,258 rapes occurred every day—that's almost a rape a minute (Morgan and Truman 2020, 3). The CDC estimates that, during their lifetime, nearly one in five women have experienced completed or attempted rape. One in four experienced sexual violence at the hands of an intimate partner, and one in three have reported unwanted sexual contact (e.g., groping) at least once in their lifetime (Smith et al. 2018, 2, 7). While all women are at risk of abuse, those with the highest rate of rape or sexual abuse are women who are seventeen years old or younger (43.2 percent) with the second largest risk group (38.1 percent) being those in the eighteen- to twenty-four-year-old range (4). According to another CDC report, from 2017, approximately

---

[19] Megan Brenan, "Record-High 56% of U.S. Women Prefer Working to Homemaking," Gallup, October 24, 2019.

[20] Carol A. Lambert, "The Number of Women Murdered by a Partner Is Rising," *Psychology Today*, September 3, 2019.

10 percent of high school students were sexually assaulted that year, with females (15 percent) enduring higher rates than males (4.3 percent).[21] Yet according to estimates by the Justice Department, only 31 percent of rapes and attempted rapes are reported to law enforcement, leading to just 5.7 percent with arrests due to accusations, and only about 0.7 percent ending with a felony conviction for the perpetrator.[22]

Violence becomes the means by which control is maintained over the conduct, thoughts, beliefs, and actions of the Other, specifically women. The possibility of violence—say, simply being threatened with a glance—is often sufficient to secure docile obedience of the abused. Such internalization of power teaches the marginalized to police themselves. As a form of survival or self-preservation, the one on the actual and potential receiving end of the violence (often women, but also girls and boys) learns to behave in the appropriate matter—a manner that reinforces their status of imposed inferiority. Self-disciplining leads to justifying one's oppression (i.e., "I deserved to be punished"), thus undermining one's sense of self-worth and dignity, which is crucial for the development of well-adjusted personhood.

One common form of violence that men usually categorize as benign is sexual harassment. Sexual harassment occurs whenever sexual favors are demanded to ensure professional or economic gain or when refusal to provide sexual favors threatens one's professional or economic security. Sexual harassment is not limited to physical violence; it also encompasses economic deprivation, intentional degradation, public humiliation, spiritual manipulation, and verbal intimidation (e.g., "grabbing them by their p*ssy"). The abuse of women—whether manifested physically, sexually, spiritually, or psychologically, and whether committed by a family member, acquaintance, or total stranger—is, first and foremost, about power. Sexual harassment or violence (even in the case of rape) often has little to do with sex, even though sex becomes how power is enhanced.

We should recognize that sexual abuse encompasses more than harassment carried out by economically powerful men against women in their employ. Sexual abuse is also a threat to wives and young children, sex workers and the incarcerated, college students, the elderly, and young teenagers—crossing all economic, gender, orientation, and racial lines. And while all men are not sexual predators, almost all women have experienced sexual harassment at least once. Although a thorough and comprehensive

---

[21] Nan D. Stein and Bruce Taylor, "Stop Pretending Sexual Assault Can't Happen in Your School," *Education Week*, October 4, 2018.

[22] Andrew Van Dam, "Less Than 1% of Rapes Lead to Felony Convictions," *Washington Post*, October 6, 2018.

analysis of violence toward women in the workplace could prove productive, for the purposes of this chapter, I focus on just one institution: the US
Armed Forces.

The acceptance of women within the Armed Forces has been resisted
by many means, including, perhaps most disturbingly, sexual assault.
According to Executive Director Elizabeth Van Winkle of the US Department of Defense Office of Force and Resiliency, the prevalence of sexual
assault in the Armed Forces rose in 2018, with about 20,500 service
members—13,000 women and 7,500 men—reporting a sexual assault. This
is up from a total of about 14,900 in 2016. Overall, 6.2 percent of service-
women of all ranks in 2018 reported being sexually assaulted, as did 0.7
percent of servicemen.[23] By 2019, assaults at the nation's military service
academies rose by 50 percent from 2016 figures, driven almost entirely by
assaults on women.[24] The situation was just as dire at military bases. For
example, male and female personnel at Fort Hood, Texas, have described
the base ethos as a culture of sexual harassment and bullying ignored by
the leadership. Eighteen out of fifty-three women surveyed said that, in
2020, they were sexually harassed. Not until a soldier from the base—
Aaron Robinson—kidnapped, murdered, dismembered, and burned the
remains of fellow soldier Vanessa Guillen was an independent review panel
formed.[25] The final report confirmed what has always been the norm on
the base: a "permissive environment for sexual assault and sexual harassment" exists.[26]

The climate of fear reigning in the military branches led then–defense
secretary Leon Panetta to acknowledge that the number of sexual assaults
is probably far higher in the military than what official statistics show. The
Defense Department believes one in three women in the military have
been sexually assaulted, compared to one in six civilian women during

---

[23] Jim Garamone, "Report Points to Need for New Programs to Counter
Sexual Assault," US Department of Defense, May 2, 2019. While the focus of this
chapter remains on women, it should be recognized that women are not the only
victims of sexual violence. Because men represent the largest proportion of armed
service personnel (85 percent), one would expect that most service members who
experienced unwanted sexual contact would be men. But as these numbers show,
that was not the case.

[24] David Phillips, "Pentagon Survey Finds Increase in Sexual Assaults Reported
by Women," *New York Times*, May 3, 2010.

[25] Helene Cooper, "Army Inquiry into Soldier's Killing Expands to Base's Chain
of Command," *New York Times*, September 2, 2020.

[26] Helene Cooper and Jennifer Steinhauer, "Video Pushes Austin to Grapple
with Sex Harassment in the Military," *New York Times*, February 20, 2021.

that same period. About 20 percent of female soldiers who served in Iraq and Afghanistan experienced a sexual assault, yet only 3,374 reported their abuse in 2012, likely due to the fact that fewer than one in ten sexual assault reports result in any court-martial conviction (US Department of Defense 2012, 3, 12, 71). Not much had changed by 2019, when an internal military report showed a gap between the number of sexual abuses officially reported and the number of incidents reported as a result of an anonymous survey.[27] Coming forward with an accusation can be a career-ending decision for a solider, especially a servicewoman; worse yet, the victim could face administrative retribution and reprisals, especially given that reports are handled within the military chain of command. A woman choosing to report an assault or abuse within the military is very often forced to continue to serve under the command of her assailant. Unsurprisingly, many refuse to report their abuse—and if they do report being raped, it is usually covered up—at times by the officer assigned to the case.

Sexual assault is not restricted to the military. The US Equal Employment Opportunity Commission received 7,609 complaints of sexual harassment in 2018 and 7,514 in 2019. And while the numbers dropped to 6,587 in 2020, this probably had more to do with the empty offices and facilities while working remotely during COVID-19 than anything else.[28] Because most attacks are not reported, the numbers are no doubt higher and the true magnitude of the situation more prevalent than is known or assumed. Women who leave their relegated domestic space of the household have faced, and continue to experience, all form of abuse solely because they are seen as invading the male public domain.

Control over Women's Bodies

Throughout history, women have always had access to abortions. During the seventeenth and eighteenth centuries, abortion was legal under common law until "quickening," which occurs when the pregnant woman can feel the fetus move—usually between the thirteenth and sixteenth weeks. Abortion before the second or third week of the second trimester was neither considered murder nor immoral.

Historian Jessica Furgerson notes that abortion services and contraceptives were regularly and openly advertised in US newspapers. Physicians

---

[27] Helene Cooper, "More Assaults Unreported on Campuses of Academies," *New York Times*, February 1, 2021.

[28] Iris Hentze and Rebecca Tyus, "Sexual Harassment in the Workplace," National Conference of State Legislatures, August 12, 2021.

in the 1850s, seeking to codify their professional expertise, persuaded state legislatures to criminalize abortion and birth control. The Comstock[29] Act of 1873 classified advertising or information about abortion and contraceptives as legal obscenity. By the twentieth century, state legislatures had passed laws restricting, if not outlawing, abortion and contraceptives. One motivation for such legislation was what was then called "race suicide," the concern that euroamerican women were not having as many babies as women of color (Furgerson 2022, 1–28, 72). Although *Roe v. Wade* made abortion legal again in 1973, a concerted effort was made to move the country toward a political stance where the reproductive organs of women would, once again, be regulated by the government. Presidential candidate Donald Trump's promise was to only nominate so-called pro-life justices to the Supreme Court. He kept that promise with the appointments of Amy Coney Barrett, Brett Kavanaugh, and Neil Gorsuch, reconfiguring the court to have a majority of justices hostile to *Roe*.

For decades, overturning *Roe* was the single-minded obsession of the Religious Right. Their tenacity paid off. On June 24, 2022, the constitutional right to an abortion was nullified, thanks in part to President Trump's bargain with the so-called pro-life movement and political maneuvering in the Senate by Mitch McConnell, who denied President Obama a Supreme Court appointment. *Dobbs v. Jackson Woman's Health Organization* provided states with the "freedom" to determine for themselves the legality or illegality of the procedure. In more than half of the nation's states, abortion will continue to remain legal and protected by state government. However, in the South and Midwest (about twenty-two states), women, especially those who are predominately poor and thus of color, are most negatively impacted due to "trigger" laws that automatically reinstated pre-*Roe* laws, some over 173 years old, upon the overturn of *Roe*. Criminalizing abortion places some doctors at risk of prison if they misdiagnose the risk to the mother as justification for terminating a pregnancy. Women may be forced to carry unwanted pregnancies to full term even if doing so endangers their

---

[29] Anthony Comstock (1844–1915), for whom the 1873 act is named, led a powerful movement, as a crusader of Christian values, against anything he considered obscene being distributed through the postal service. He began his attacks on pornography but quickly moved to literature (including some classics) and information about abortion and contraceptives. Against women's suffrage and highly vindictive, he would boast of the number of persons he would drive to suicide—mostly women, like spiritualist Ida Craddock, who wrote sex manuals from a feminist perspective. His actions were responsible for preventing generations of women accessing information on sexual health and reproduction issues. His more creditable work included crackdowns on medical quackery and the financing of fraudulent schemes.

lives or is the result of rape or incest. Forty-one percent of women of child-bearing age will witness the closure of their closest abortion clinic, making the nearest center about 279 miles away, as opposed to 35 miles pre-*Roe*.[30] Women with means can always afford to cross state lines for the procedure.

Justice Samuel Alito wrote in the majority opinion for *Dobbs*, arguing that "*Roe* was egregiously wrong from the start." He argued that "the Constitution makes no reference to abortion, and no such right is implicitly protected by any constitutional provision." Such logic, wielded for the first time in US history, justified eliminating the constitutional right to autonomy of one's own body for about half of the population. The success of overturning *Roe*, which had been legal precedent for almost fifty years, appears to be the first step toward greater societal restrictions. The ink had not yet dried on the *Dobbs* decision when, within minutes, Missouri banned all abortions and clinics in Alabama and North Dakota were shut down.[31] Such restrictions are apparently not enough. The next battle lines have begun to be drawn. So-called pro-life advocates are calling for the fetus, upon conception, to receive full protection under the Fourteenth Amendment of the US Constitution, which, if successful, will make all forms of abortion—for whatever reason (including rape or incest)—illegal in all fifty states.

Moving beyond sole focus on the abortion implications of the *Dobbs* decision, Supreme Court Justice Clarence Thomas said that the legal reasoning originally used to establish the *Roe* decision is the same logic employed to establish access to contraception rights (*Griswold v. Connecticut* [1965]), the right to engage in same-gender intercourse (*Lawrence v. Texas* [2003]), and marriage equality rights (*Obergefell v. Hodges* [2015]). He advised that "at the earliest opportunities," these cases that rely on the Fourteenth Amendment protection should be reconsidered.[32] It is interesting to note that Justice Thomas, who is a Black man married to a euroamerican woman, didn't also include the right to interracial marriage (*Loving v. Virginia* [1967]), which was also based on the Fourteenth Amendment.

Thomas is not alone. Texas attorney general Ken Paxton said that, after *Roe*'s reversal, he is "willing and able" to defend any law criminalizing sodomy. Utah State Senate president Stuart Adams wants his state to

---

[30] The Upshot, "What a 'Post-Roe' Nation Might Look Like," *New York Times*, May 20, 2021.

[31] Kate Zernike, "Ending One Fight and Starting Another in a Polarized America," *New York Times*, June 25, 2022.

[32] Charlie Savage, "A Conservative Supermajority May Be Just Getting Started," *New York Times*, June 25, 2022.

join others in pressing the Supreme Court to reverse same-gender-loving couples from legal marriage. Combined with more than three hundred bills restricting LGBTQI+ civil rights introduced in twenty-three different states, these statements are key components of a frightful trend in 2022.[33]

If the true goal is to reduce the number of abortions, what better way to prevent unintended pregnancies than sex education and the availability of birth control? Since 2010, the US abortion rate has been declining, reaching its lowest point in 2019, with only 18 percent of all pregnancies ending in an induced abortion. Among teenagers (fifteen to nineteen years old), the birth rate decreased by 51 percent over that past decade; overall abortion rates decreased by 50 percent (Kortsmit et al. 2021, 7). A study conducted by the Guttmacher Institute found that four states that enacted legal restrictions to abortions between 2011 and 2017 saw an increase in the number of procedures performed, while those states that increased the number of clinics saw a decline in abortions (Jones, Witwer, and Jerman 2019, 1, 7). The Guttmacher Institute also found that, over the course of thirty years (1990–2019), in countries (excluding China and India) where legal restrictions on abortions exist, the rates of completed abortions were actually higher than in those countries with fewer restrictions (Bearak et al., e1152–53). If these trends hold, we can expect the opposite of what the so-called pro-life movement claims it wants. The *Dobbs* Supreme Court decision will lead to an increase in abortions, not a decrease.

Another study on adolescent health found that teenagers who were sexually active but did not use contraception had an 85 percent chance of becoming pregnant within a year of being sexually active. Commenting on the accelerated decline in US adolescent fertility since 2007, the study concluded that "improvements in contraceptive use appear to be the primary proximal determinants of declines in adolescent pregnancy and birth rates" (Lindberg, Santelli, and Desai 2016, 582). Not surprisingly, disparities are persistent between euroamerican (11.4 per 1,000 in 2019) and Black (25.8 per thousand), Native American (29 per 1,000), and Latine (25.3 per 1,000) populations. While teen pregnancies, per the CDC, had declined to their lowest recorded level in 2019, a trend that appears to be continuing, the rate continues to remain substantially higher than in other industrialized nations.[34] Yet those most opposed to abortion are, paradoxically, also opposed to the availability of contraceptives and sex education.

---

[33] Trip Gabriel, "Roe's Reversal Stokes Attacks on Gay Rights," *New York Times*, July 23, 2022.

[34] Centers for Disease Control and Prevention, "About Teen Pregnancy," November 15, 2021.

The opposition to contraceptives by religious organizations can be noted by the 2012 actions of thirteen Roman Catholic dioceses, evangelicals, Mennonites, several related religious groups, and some private corporations, including Hobby Lobby. Together, they filed more than forty-five lawsuits across a dozen federal courts, claiming that the inclusion of contraceptives in basic healthcare coverage was a violation of their religious freedom, even though the contraception-coverage mandate exempts houses of worship.[35]

Should religious-affiliated organizations (e.g., hospitals, schools, or charities) that believe contraceptive usage is a sin be forced to provide such options via their insurance coverage to their female employees? Most patients (71.3 percent), according to a recent study, noted that they did not care whether a medical facility was religiously affiliated because most (71.4 percent) believed that their health choices should take priority over an institution's religious affiliation when it came to the services offered (Guiahi et al. 2019, e4). This raises some interesting questions. Are religious hospitals imposing their faith's dictates upon women's bodies, or are they simply being faithful to their convictions? Can a pharmacy refuse to fill contraceptive medication because a pharmacist's personal convictions consider its usage to be sinful?

David Green, founder of Hobby Lobby, pays his employees almost twice the minimum wage, forsakes profits on the Sabbath, and provides a comprehensive health insurance that has no objection to covering contraception, except for the "morning-after pill," which he considers an abortion-inducing procedure. Green, who considers himself a conscientious Christian capitalist, believes that the morning-after pill is irreconcilable with the Christian principles upon which he operates his company. He was sued, and the case made it to the Supreme Court, which ruled in his favor.

According to the court, in *Burwell v. Hobby Lobby*, owners do not lose their religious liberties when they go into business.[36] But do companies have souls? The Supreme Court ruled in *Citizens United v. Federal Election Commission* that corporations are protected by the First Amendment's freedom-of-speech clause. Does the *Hobby Lobby* case mean that the First Amendment's freedom-of-religion clause can be extended to protect corporations' conscience? After all, the First Amendment allows churches and religious organizations to preach and speak against contraceptives, declaring their usage to be a sin. Still, in an earlier 1990 decision, Justice Scalia wrote

---

[35] "The Politics of Religion," *New York Times*, May 27, 2012.

[36] Carey Lodge, "Hobby Lobby and the Morning-After Pill: A Victory for Religious Liberty?," *Christianity Today*, July 1, 2014.

that, to make "the professed doctrines of religious beliefs superior to the law of the land [would allow] every citizen to become a law unto himself. Government [w]ould exist only in name under such circumstances."[37]

When the Obama administration declined to renew the contract with the United States Conference of Catholic Bishops (USCCB) to aid victims of human sex trafficking, the administration was charged as being anti-Catholic. The contract, however, was not renewed because the bishops required its subcontractors to use no federal monies to pay for their employees' or subcontractors' contraceptives or abortion referrals and services.[38] Furthermore, according to Federal District Court Judge Richard Stearns, the bishops' requirements violate the First Amendment because they impose religion-based restrictions on use of taxpayer dollars.[39]

Controlling a woman's reproductive choices by criminalizing abortions, denying contraception, or forcing sterilization is problematic. Sterilization, as discussed in chapter 11, becomes a form of genocide, an unbloodied means of preventing the growth of a racial or ethnic group seen as a threat to the dominant culture. Since 1979 China enforced a one-child policy in an attempt to deal with a growing population that was believed to place a strain on national and global resources as well as the environment. Village officials were charged with charting the menstrual cycle of every childbearing woman and providing pelvic exams within their rural region. Women who were impregnated without government permission were levied exorbitant fines or risked a forced abortion. Feng Jianmei, who was carrying a second child in violation of the national policy, was forced by local officials to abort a seven-month-old fetus. Until she ceded to official demands, peasants in her village of Yuping were led in a march that denounced her family members as "traitors." Her husband was even beaten. She could have kept the second child if she would have paid the $6,300 fine, which averaged anywhere from three to ten times a household income depending on the province.[40] China's one-child policy proved disastrous, creating demographic crises due to declining birth rates. Across China, authorities are now encouraging women to have more children, except in the Xinjiang region, where ethnic Muslim minorities live. There, China is forcing women to have fewer children, hoping that, over generations, a lower birth rate will

---

[37] *Employment Division, Department of Human Resources of Oregon v. Smith.*

[38] It should be noted that the Hyde Amendment bars the use of federal money for abortions except in the case of rape or incest, or when the life of the woman is endangered.

[39] "Sex Trafficking and the First Amendment," *New York Times*, April 3, 2012.

[40] Edward Wong, "Forced to Abort, Chinese Woman under Pressure," *New York Times*, June 27, 2012.

create a demographic shift. There, doctors at government clinics, with the use of metal forceps, insert an intrauterine device to prevent pregnancies, even on women in their fifties.[41]

Global Sexism

Subjugating women is not limited to the United States or China. The oppression of women, which is based on male supremacy, is a global phenomenon and problem. According to a UN study conducted in seventy-five countries, where approximately 80 percent of the world's human population reside, almost half of respondents believe men are superior to women, and about a third of men *and women* believe it is acceptable for a man to beat his wife. Ninety-one percent of men and 85 percent of women hold at least one negative bias toward women in relation to politics, economic, education, violence, or reproduction rights. When it comes to equal pay for equal work, it is estimated that the global gap will be eliminated—at our current pace—by the year 2277 (Conceição et al. 2019, 1, 8–9). Millions of women and girls worldwide suffer from some form of daily violence. Violence can manifest itself as rape, sexual abuse, a tool of repression in war-ravaged regions, early arranged marriages, dowry-related murder, honor killing, sex trafficking, female infanticide, female genital circumcision, or acid attacks. The violence can be physical, but it also can be verbal, economic, spiritual, and psychological. Women from all cultures, all religious faiths, all economic strata, and all racial and ethnic groups are at risk of experiencing violence at the hands of men.

Women on every continent—including Antarctica[42]—have experienced and continue to experience some form of sexual harassment. Women around the world face life-threatening situations simply because they were born as women. Violence toward females occurs early in life in the form of female infanticide, prenatal sex selection, and the systematic neglect of girls, an acute problem in South and East Asia, North Africa, and the Middle East. For some 3 million girls a year who survive infancy, the horror of genital mutilation awaits them. It is estimated that, in 2021, at least 200 million girls and women in thirty-one countries across three continents were subject to female genital mutilation, with more than half of them living in Egypt, Ethiopia, and Indonesia (UNICEF 2022, 5, 8). As

---

[41] Amy Qin, "China Is Forcing Birth Control on Muslim Women in Xinjiang," *New York Times*, May 11, 2021.

[42] National Public Radio, "Sexual Harassment and Assault Plague U.S. Research Bases in Antarctica, Report Says," *All Things Considered*, September 1, 2022.

these girls mature, they still face grave dangers if they rebuff the advances of a potential suitor or become the perceived cause of a husband's, lover's, or boyfriend's jealousy. Globally, some fifteen hundred acid attacks against women by men (throwing sulfuric or nitric acids into a woman's face to disfigure her) are reported yearly. Afghanistan, Bangladesh, India, Pakistan, and, more recently, Columbia, report acid attacks as a cheap and quick way of destroying a woman's life.[43]

According to the World Health Organization, some 736 to 852 million women (age 15 and older)—almost three in ten—have been subjected to sexual violence at least once in their life. Most of the violence experienced by women was perpetrated by current or former husbands or intimate partners. In 2018, about one in seven women experienced physical or sexual violence from an intimate partner or husband during the past twelve months (World Health Organization 2021, 20–21, 33). In 2020, according to the United Nations, eighty-one thousand women globally were killed by men; forty-seven thousand of them (58 percent) by a member of their family. This means that a woman or girl is murdered by someone they know every eleven minutes (Gibbons 2021, 3, 18). Fear of stigma prevents many women from reporting the violence they face; hence, the current data are, expectedly, underrepresentative. Rather than concentrating on the men who perpetrate this violence, there has been a historical trend to blame the victim. Women, in the minds of some, are to blame for their victimization because of the way they dress, showing off too much skin by wearing revealing clothes or creating an irresistible allure by wearing too much cloth; because they drink; because they work outside the home; or because they lead men on via flirtation (flirtation as perceived and defined by men).

While women face risk every day, they experience greater unrestrained targeting during times of military conflict. Women have always faced abuse at the hands of the military as rape has been and is used as an instrument of war designed to terrorize communities, destroy the bonds of families, create fissures in communities, and, in some cases, change the ethnic composition of an area. The US liberators (known as the Greatest Generation) who landed in Normandy on D-Day to oust the Nazis instituted their own "regime of terror" on local women. According to historian Mary Louise Roberts's archival research, soldiers were "sold" on the invasion by its portrayal as an erotic adventure involving oversexed French women. The so-called adventure was an excuse to unleash a "tsunami of male lust" (Roberts 2013, 9). According to Roberts,

---

[43] Anastasia Moloney, "Colombia Acid Attack Survivor Calls for Greater Action to Help Other Victims," Global Citizen, November 15, 2018.

Rape posed an even greater threat to the myth of the American mission as sexual romance. In the summer of 1944, Norman women launched a wave of rape accusations against American soldiers, threatening to destroy the erotic fantasy at the heart of the operation. The specter of rape transformed the GI from rescue-warrior to violent intruder. Forced to confront the sexual excess incited by its own propaganda, the army responded not by admitting the full range of the problem, but by scapegoating African American soldiers as the primary perpetrators of the rapes. (10)

According to the United Nations, between 100,000 and 250,000 women were raped in Rwanda during the three months of the 1994 genocide; more than 60,000 women were raped during the 1991–2002 civil war in Sierra Leone; more than 40,000 between 1989 and 2003 in Liberia; 60,000 in 1992–1995 in the former Yugoslavia; and at least 200,000 in the Democratic Republic of the Congo since 1998 (UN Department of Public Information 2013, 1). In Ethiopia, rape as a weapon of war has been deployed targeting Tigrayan women from 2020 to 2022. More than 500 have formally reported sexual violence, accusing soldiers of forcing them to have sex with their parents, their children, and other close relatives.[44] A study released in 2022 found that, when Russia invaded Ukraine, conflict-related gender-based violence such as rape, sexual violence, or sexual harassment were employed by the invading forces, constituting war crimes and crimes against humanity (Benedek, Bílková, and Sassòli 2022, 1–2).

In addition to rape as a war strategy, women are also forced into sex slavery. Toru Hashimoto, leader of a populist political party in Japan, has even argued that sex slavery during war is a necessary evil. Referring to the usage of "comfort women" during World War II, he upheld the popular belief among many Japanese people, including then–prime minister Shinzo Abe, that no evidence exists of women being forced to serve in brothels, thus ignoring the voices and testimonies of women from many countries who claimed to have been sexual slaves. Historians estimate that 200,000 women were rounded up to serve as "comfort women" by the Japanese imperial forces.[45]

---

[44] Declan Walsh, "In Ethiopian Rebel Region, Rape Has Become 'a Weapon of War,'" *New York Times*, April 2, 2021.

[45] Hiroko Tabuchi, "Japanese Politicians Reframes Comments on Sex Slavery," *New York Times*, May 27, 2013.

Rape is not confined to war. The custom of early marriage (male adults marrying girls) is a common practice worldwide, generally considered a human rights violation if the girl is under eighteen years of age. Globally, 21 percent of young women—according to UNICEF—were married before their eighteenth birthday. It is expected that 110 million additional girls will be married before their eighteenth birthday over the next decade.[46] Rape of children in these cases is masked under the term "marriage," marriages that are often against the wishes of the bride. And while we think this is a problem plaguing so-called underdeveloped cultures in Africa, Asia, and the Middle East, it is worthwhile to note that, as of 2022, domestic child marriage is legal in forty-three US states.[47]

More problematic is when overseas child marriages end in the death of the wife, what is known as dowry deaths, when married women are either killed or driven to suicide over disputes concerning their dowry, usually a desire by the groom's family for a larger sum. The UN estimates that more than seven thousand dowry-linked deaths occur every year, usually because of a kitchen "accident," where the wife ends up being burned to death.[48] For some, an attempt is made to avoid paying a dowry by aborting female fetuses so as not to have daughters in the first place.

Honor killings are another life-threatening danger faced by women. An honor killing occurs whenever a woman is accused of diminishing a man's family honor, reinforcing an ancient binary honor/shame understanding of one's place within society. Because of patriarchy, a woman is understood as property, and one can do with one's property as one sees fit. A woman as property who (or rather that) belongs to one man, if used or perceived as used by another, brings shame to the "owner" of her body—even if that trespass was nonconsensual, as in the case of rape. The woman, regardless of complicity in welcoming male attention, brings shame to the family and must be held responsible and punished. Through women's deaths, honor is restored. It is estimated that some five thousand women are killed each year in the name of honor.[49]

When Qandeel Baloch, a Pakistani social media celebrity, posted ideas that challenged the tradition of a woman marrying the man chosen for her by her family, her brother drugged and strangled her to preserve

---

[46] UNICEF, "Child Marriage around the World," March 11, 2020.

[47] Alba Ibraj, "Massachusetts Becomes 7th State to End Child Marriage," *Forbes*, August 5, 2022.

[48] Diane Cole, "UN Report: 50,000 Women a Year Are Killed by Intimate Partners, Family Members," National Public Radio, November 30, 2018.

[49] Stéphanie Thomson, "5,000 Women a Year Are Still Being Killed in the Name of 'Honour,'" World Economic Forum, July 22, 2016.

their family honor.[50] In another Pakistani town, a twenty-six-year-old woman named Madiha was murdered by her mother and brothers for marrying against their wishes.[51] Syrian eighteen-year-old Aida Hammoudi Saeedo was executed by a firing squad composed of relatives for refusing to marry her cousin.[52] Forty-year-old Ahlam, a divorcee who was engaged in a love affair, had her skull crushed with a concrete block by her father in Jordan.[53] And in Khuzestan, the Iranian husband of seventeen-year-old Mona Heydari was recorded walking through the town's street with a grin on his face, a blade in one hand, and the severed head of Mona in the other hand—considered an honor killing because she fled their marriage.[54]

In regions where such murder is normalized, for a woman to be alone with a man who is not her relative is shameful. For a woman to choose her own spouse is shameful. For a woman to seek an education (the first step toward any hope of liberation) is shameful. When she was fifteen years old, Malala Yousafzai was a Pakistani pupil who was shot point-blank in the head and neck by the Taliban in October 2012, so as to silence her. Her crime? Not only did she dare to defy the Taliban's ban against girls going to school, but she was also vocal about the rights of girls to an education. According to UNICEF, there are 129 million girls out of school worldwide[55]—almost twice as many as a decade ago when the number was 66 million.[56] In June 2013, some six months after the attack on Malala, eleven students were killed and twenty wounded in a bomb that exploded on a university school bus for women in the city of Quetta, in western Pakistan. As the victims were taken to the hospital, gunmen showed up and continued the assault.[57]

---

[50] Malaka Gharib, "'Honor Killings' Are a Global Problem—And Often Invisible," National Public Radio, July 19, 2016.

[51] Imtiaz Ahmad, "A Daughter Killed by Her Family—a Story of Love and 'Honor,'" *Deutsche Welle*, November 11, 2018.

[52] Edy Cohen, "18-Year-Old Girl Executed for Refusing to Marry Cousin," *Israel Today*, July 15, 2021.

[53] Nabih Bulos, "After Woman's Brutal Killing by Her Father, Jordan Asks at What Price 'Honor'?" *Los Angeles Times*, July 28, 2020.

[54] Yaron Steinbuch, "Appalling Video Shows Iranian Man Carrying Wife's Head after 'Honor Killing,'" *New York Post*, February 8, 2022.

[55] UNICEF, "Girls' Education: Gender Equality in Education Benefits Every Child," 2022.

[56] Kyle Almond, "Malala's Global Voice Stronger than Ever," CNNWorld, June 17, 2013.

[57] "Pakistan Blast Kills Female Students," BBC News, June 15, 2013.

Many may read of such horror inflicted upon women in other countries with some latent belief that those people "over there" are somewhat uncivilized, if not barbaric—all the while ignoring our own form of uncivilized and barbaric behavior. The danger in making comparisons between the United States and other cultures is the tendency of inferring that "our" sexism is not as bad as "theirs" and that "our" women are treated better than "theirs." Although the concern of making the racial or ethnic Other more misogynist exists, the fact remains that other cultures and societies engage in their own wars on women. Although sexism may appear differently with and within varying degrees of oppression, we must avoid the temptation of ranking sexist acts in a way that redeems eurocentric expressions as not being "so bad" in comparison to those of Others. To the oppressed and repressed victims of the war on women, all forms of marginalization are damning.

Probably the most collective barbaric act of all is the failure of Congress, as of this writing, to pass the International Violence Against Women Act,[58] which would name and shame those countries that tolerate acts of violence toward women. As we explore the war on women overseas, it is important to remember that we here in the United States have not been and often continue to not necessarily be on the side of women during the global enactment of misogyny.[59]

As horrific as these global and domestic situations are, muting worldwide outcries is a disappointing endeavor. Attempts by international institutions to band together in solidarity with women facing life-threatening situations are usually opposed in the name of religion. In March 2013 the work of the UN Commission on the Status of Women was hampered by delegates from Iran, Russia, and the Vatican due to their religious sensibilities. They sought to eliminate any admonition to nation states that refrained from their obligations to condemn all forms of violence against women by invoking custom, tradition, and religious considerations from the final communiqué.[60] Delegates from Poland, Egypt, several Muslim states, and conservative Christian groups based in the United States objected to

---

[58] The International Violence Against Women Act (I-VAWA) is proposed legislation intended to address violence against women through the foreign policy of the United States, specifically by providing best practices that prevent violence, protect victims, and prosecute offenders.

[59] Nicholas D. Kristof, "Is Delhi So Different from Steubenville?," *New York Times*, January 13, 2013.

[60] Iran, Russia, and the Vatican failed in their attempt to exclude the language, which appears as paragraph 14 of the 2013 document *The Elimination and Prevention of All Forms of Violence against Women and Girls*.

other parts of the document, including but not limited to references to abortion rights and references to the term "rape" when describing forcible sexual behavior by a woman's husband or partner.[61] It appears that, as long as women are kept from participating in education, society, and the political arena, men who dominate in these spheres of human life will continue to define what is abuse and liberation for women.

Step 2: Reflecting

Since ancient times, goes conventional thinking, the woman's domain was the home while the man's domain was the public sphere. The root of this assumption is found in the ancient honor/shame code that we've briefly discussed. A family's place and reputation within any given society were based on either acquiring honor or inducing shame. Honor is a male-centered activity, for through the man's participation in the public sphere, honor was or could be increased or decreased by how he interacted with other men. Men were obligated to maintain or improve the public honor of their family while simultaneously avoiding anything that could bring shame on their family name. From this purview, while honor is achieved in the public sphere, shame occurs or at least initiates within the private sphere— the domain of the woman.

In a preventive measure to protect one's honor, the man often confines the woman to the household, where she can remain secure and protected from enemies wishing to bring shame on the good name of the one who owns her body. If she ventures into the public domain, she can be covered up, often from head to toe, to avoid shaming her husband if other men lustfully glance in her direction. This honor/shame code helps explain the binding of feet in some Asian countries, the societal pressure to wear a burqa in some Islamic countries, the forced medical procedure of female genital mutilation in some African countries, or simply the required custom of chaperoning unattended women worldwide. While this honor/shame code is detected in the custom and traditions of non-eurocentric people, the residue of this ancient value system can be seen throughout the development of Christianity. Eve's association with the fall makes her the counterpoint to Mary, the mother of Jesus and perpetual virgin. Eve represents the ultimate temptress who led men and, by extension, all of humanity astray. Mary, on the other hand, signifies the ideal model for all Christian women to emulate. Christian women have historically been given a choice between the purity that comes with motherhood or the wantonness

---

[61] "Unholy Alliance," *New York Times*, March 11, 2013.

that comes with independence from "benevolent" male authority; in short, their choice is between the virgin and the whore, between the pivotal values of the ancient world: honor or shame.

Keeping women tied to their domestic habitation forestalls the possibility of shame. "As the snail carries its house with it," Martin Luther reminds us, "so the wife should stay at home and look after the affairs of the household, as one who has been deprived of the ability of administering those affairs that are outside and that concern the state."[62] Seeking virtue either through chastity or by becoming a prolific mother redeems a woman from Eve's influence and from the shame she herself could bring on the honor of her man's name. If she is a mother, her worth and respect increase proportionately to the number of males she births. Yet regardless of how much honor the woman brings to her husband's name, she remains inferior, someone who is less than a male.

Women are not the only ones who can be designated as feminine; seeing Others as feminine (whether they be female or not) justifies their subjugation, helping us to better understand the underpinnings of colonialism and imperialism. Sexism also serves as a paradigm for the subjugation of all people groups or demographics that fall short of the euroamerican male ideal. Because inferiority has historically been defined as feminine, all who are oppressed—be they females, males, trans, or nonbinary—are feminized. While this is not an attempt to minimize oppressive and violent structures toward women in communities of color, it is an attempt to stress that all forms of oppression are identical in their intention and attempt to domesticate the feminine (read: inferior) Other, to place the Other in a subordinate position (De La Torre 2010, 222).

The danger that sexist comments made by politicians and pundits pose to society goes beyond some ignorant misogynist remark; they provide us with a blueprint for maintaining and sustaining the racist, elitist, classist, and imperialist structures of society through the sexist paradigms these structures advocate. Theologian Mary Daly quipped, "If God is male, then the male is God" (1973, 19). This truth is likely what undergirds the historical war on women. Because God is male—in other words, because God, like males, has a penis—then the male is as a god, lording over all who lack a penis, physically (i.e., women) or symbolically (i.e., men of color). Women, as well as non-euroamericans (females and males) and the poor (regardless of skin pigmentation), are subordinated to those who possess a penis.

Throughout Judeo-Christian history, God has been thought of as a male, consistently referred to as "he." But if the function of a penis is to

---

[62] "Lectures on Genesis," *Luther's Works*, 1.202–3.

urinate and copulate, why would God need a penis? Or does the penis have societal meaning? Because women were castrated and penectomized by the Almighty, is it not natural for them to submit to men who, unlike women, are created in the very image of God? Is Sigmund Freud's contribution of "penis envy," therefore, accurate? With this in mind, we can understand why Abraham and Israel placed great spiritual value on their penises, swearing oaths upon their genitals (Gen. 24:2–3; 47:29–31), or why King David wins Michal as his wife through the gift of a hundred foreskins from Philistine penises (2 Sam. 3:14). The very sign of the covenant between God and man begins with the penis, specifically cutting off its foreskin through the ritual of circumcision (Gen. 17:10–14). How, then, do women enter a covenant with God if there is no penis to circumcise (De La Torre 2007, 16–17)?[63]

When *the man*, who, like God, has a penis, looks into Lacan's mirror, he constructs his male identity through a distancing process of negation, defining himself through the archetype of "I am what I am not." For example, because women are emotional, when the man looks into a mirror, he does not see a woman, therefore he is not emotional. Because women are inferior and weak, when he looks into a mirror, he does not see a woman, therefore he is not inferior nor weak. In the formation of the subject's ego, an illusory self-representation is constructed through the negation of a penis that is projected upon Others, those who would be identified as non-men.

Ascribing femininity to the Other, regardless of gender, forces feminine identity construction to originate through the domesticating man. In fact, the feminine Object, in and of itself, is seen as nothing when apart from a masculine Subject that provides unifying purpose (Grosz 1990, 115–45).

The resulting gaze of the euroamerican, elite male inscribes effeminacy upon Others who are not man enough to "make" history, "provide" for their family, or "resist" their subjugation. Ironically, no one really has a penis. The man lives always threatened by possible loss, while the non-man is forcibly deprived. The potent symbolic power invested in the penis both

---

[63] Paul Tillich and Paul Ricoeur assert that one can only speak of or describe God using symbols, connecting the meaning of one thing recognized by a given community that is comprehensible (i.e., father) with another thing that is beyond our ability to fully understand (i.e., God). See Ricoeur 1976 and Tillich 1959. As important as symbols are to better grasp the incomprehensible essence of the Divine, they are incapable of exhausting the reality of God. To take symbolic language literally (i.e., God is exclusively male or female) leads to the absurd (i.e., God has a penis or vagina) and borders on idolatry (the creation of hierarchies in relationships by who is closer to the Divine ideal).

signals and veils heterosexual male domination, as well as white supremacy and socioeconomic power. Constructing those oppressed as feminine allows men with penises to assert their privilege by constructing oppressed Others as inhabitants of the castrated realm of the exotic and primitive. Lacking a penis, the Other does not exist, except as designated by the desire of the one with a penis. While non-men are forced to flee from their individuality, the euroamerican man must constantly attempt to live up to a false construction (De La Torre 2012, 125).

Step 3: Meditating

The biblical text has historically been interpreted within Christianity in such a way that it has contributed to the creation and propagation of abuses toward women within many churches today. Probably the best biblical way to maintain control over women is through the construction of the "traditional biblical marriage"—as defined by most religious conservatives—even though such a concept is foreign to the biblical text. In fact, it would be hard to find a modern-day Christian who would abide by a biblical marriage in practice, for the biblical understanding of marriage meant that (1) women were considered property to be owned by men, (2) women were human incubators, (3) women were the weaker sex, and (4) women were the cause of evil.

Male ownership of women meant that women, as the property of men, existed for procreation and fulfilling male desires. Early in the biblical text, we are told that the woman's desire would be for her husband, while he would rule over her (Gen. 3:16).[64] Upon marriage, a woman's property and her body became the possession of her new husband. Women became available for male possession soon after they reached puberty (usually at eleven to thirteen years old), that is, when she became physically able to produce children. Throughout the Hebrew text, it is taken for granted that women (as well as children) are the possessions of men. The focus of the text does not seriously consider or concentrate on women's status but constructs their identity through their sexual relationship to the man: virgin daughter, betrothal bride, married woman, mother, barren wife, or widow. A woman's dignity and worth as one created in the image of God are subordinated to the needs and desires of men.

---

[64] Historically, men have argued that this hierarchy is the divine order of things. Others maintain that the man and woman being naked yet feeling no shame (Gen. 2:25) is the correct pre-fall divine order of things, and the verse stating that the man will rule over the woman (Gen. 3:16) refers to the consequence of sin, not the will of God.

As chattel, women became the extension of men; thus, any trespass against the man's human possession becomes a direct violation of that man. Not surprisingly, women are often equated with a house or livestock (Deut. 20:5–7), which is demonstrated in the Tenth Commandment, "Thou shalt not covet thy neighbor's house, wife, slave, ox or donkey" (Exod. 20:17). Because women are not excluded from being the subject of this commandment, the woman, like a house, slave, ox, or donkey, is reduced to an object—just another possession, another piece of property that belongs to the man, and thus should not be coveted by another man. Therefore, regulations concerning sexual activities appear in the biblical text under the category of property law. If a daughter was raped, the perpetrator had to either pay her father (who owns her virginity until granted to her husband) three times the original marriage price for the loss in value of his property or marry the young girl (Exod. 22:15–16, 23–29).

A man could have as many sexual partners as he could afford. The great patriarchs of the faith—Abraham, Jacob, and Judah—had multiple wives and concubines and delighted themselves with the occasional sex worker (Gen. 38:15). King Solomon alone was reported to have had more than seven hundred wives of royal birth and three hundred concubines (1 Kgs. 11:3). The book of Leviticus, in giving instructions to men wishing to own a harem, provides only one prohibition: not to "own" sisters (18:18). The Hebrew Bible is clear that men could have multiple sex partners. A woman, on the other hand, was limited to just one sex partner who ruled over her, unless of course, she was a sex worker. Sins like adultery never applied to men, who could own multiple pieces of property; they were only applied to women, which explains why the participating man did not need to be brought to Jesus when a woman was caught *in the very act* of adultery.

Second, the biblical understanding for marriage's purpose has historically been reproduction; women were understood to be human incubators. A barren Sarai offers her slave girl Hagar to Abram for rape so that Sarai can give him an heir (Gen. 16:2). Rachel, Jacob's wife, demands of her husband, "Give me children, or I shall die" (Gen. 30:1). If the woman was unable to bring forth a child, the marriage could be dissolved by the man. Besides reproduction, marriage within a patriarchal order also served political and economic means. To ensure that any offspring were legitimate heirs, the woman was restricted to just one sex partner—her husband. Biblical marriages were endogamous, that is, they occurred within the same extended family or clan, unlike the modern Western concept of exogamous marriage, where unions occur between outsiders.

The early shapers of Christian thought believed that the only purpose for a woman's existence was her ability to procreate. Only through childbearing could a woman be saved, a disturbing understanding of salvation as reiterated by Paul: "It was not Adam who was led astray but the woman who was led astray and fell into sin. Nevertheless, she will be saved by childbearing" (1 Tim. 2:14–15). Paul, the promoter of salvation solely through grace, not works, implied that, unlike men, women are saved through childbearing, a concept rooted in patriarchy. Birthing children took precedence over the life of the mother. Or, as Martin Luther instructed women, "Bring that child forth, and do it with all your might! If you die in the process, so pass on over, good for you! For you actually die in a noble work and in obedience to God."[65]

If the only natural reason for participating in sex is procreation, then all sexual activities that do not lead to children are, by definition, unnatural. Hence, for a man to engage in intercourse with a barren woman, a menopausal woman, or a menstruating woman becomes an abomination because of her inability to conceive (Lev. 15:24). Any sexual act that does not directly lead to human conception automatically becomes defined as "unnatural," be it oral sex, anal sex, same-gender-loving sex, the use of contraceptives during sex, or sex for the pure sake of pleasure—hence the admonition from the first-century Christian thinker Clement of Alexandria: "To indulge in intercourse without intending children is to outrage nature" (De La Torre 2007, 22–24).[66]

Third, an underlying assumption found throughout the biblical text is that men are physically and morally superior to women, the weaker sex. According to 1 Peter, "Husbands must treat their wives with consideration, bestowing honor on her as one who, though she may be the weaker vessel, is truly a co-heir to the grace of life" (3:7). Although equal in grace, still the purpose for the woman as the "weaker vessel" is to be ruled by the man. In his first letter to the Corinthians, Paul insisted that women must cover their heads because the woman is the "glory of man." Specifically, he wrote, "For man . . . is the image and glory of God. But the woman is the glory of man. For man did not come from woman, but woman from man. And man was not created for woman, but woman for man" (1 Cor. 11:7–9).

Because man is closer to the spirit, he is a rational subject ordained to rule. And because woman is closer to the flesh, she is an emotional object ordained to be ruled. Thus, subjecting woman to man becomes the natural manifestation of subjecting passion to reason. Paul makes this view obvious when he wrote, "But as the church is subject to Christ, so also are wives to be subject to their husbands in everything" (Eph. 5:24). Just

---

[65] "On Married Life," *Weimarer Ausgabe*, 10.2.
[66] *Christ the Educator*, 2.10.95.

as the body must submit to the spirit, which is superior, and the church must submit to Christ, so too must the wife submit to her husband. Ephesians (along with Col. 3:18–19) sets up the marriage relationship in which husbands are commanded to love their wives while wives are commanded not to love but submit to their husbands. This makes a woman, according to Thomas Aquinas, a "defective and misbegotten male," probably due to "some external influence, such as that of a south wind, which is moist" (De La Torre 2007, 24–27).[67]

Fourth and finally, because women are responsible for the evil in the world, they must be controlled for their own good. One of the major Christian themes is that women, represented by Eve, are the cause of sin and consequently the reason *man*kind was led astray from God's perfect will. She was first to be deceived and was responsible for deceiving the man. Like their mother, Eve, all women today are the incarnation of temptation. Their shapely curves incite passion among holy men. Thus, they are the cause of man's disgrace and downfall. Connecting Eve with all women, the third-century Christian thinker Tertullian proclaimed, "You [woman] are the one who opened the door to the devil.... You are the one who persuaded [Adam] whom the devil was not strong enough to attack. All too easily you destroyed the image of God, man. Because of your desert, that is, death, even the Son of God had to die"[68] (De La Torre 2007, 27–29).

Step 4: Case Studies

1. Melissa Nelson, a ten-year-long dental assistant for Dr. James Knight, was fired from her job because Dr. Knight found her attractive. Both he and his wife were concerned that the woman might become a threat to their marriage, so Dr. Knight fired her to save his marriage. Ms. Nelson sued and lost. The all-male Iowa Supreme Court ruled that employers could fire employees who they found to be an "irresistible attraction," even if the employee did nothing warranting termination. Justice Edward M. Mansfield wrote that such firings are lawful under state law because they were not motivated by gender, rather by feelings and emotions. Dr. Knight's attorney interpreted the decision as a victory for family values. Ms. Nelson's attorney, on the other hand, said the courts failed to recognize the discrimination women consistently experience in the workplace. He went on to state, "These judges sent a message to Iowa

---

[67] *Summa Theologica* 1.92.1.

[68] *The Apparel of Women*, 1.1.2.

women that they don't think men can be held responsible for their sexual desires and that Iowa women are the ones who have to monitor and control their bosses' sexual desires."[69]

• Should Dr. Knight be praised for his fidelity to his wife in going to extreme lengths to save his marriage from temptation? Is it better for men to admit their "irresistible attraction" for certain beautiful female employees rather than to subject them to unwanted attention or sexual harassment? What responsibility, if any, does Ms. Nelson hold in her dismissal? Was the ruling fair and just? Why or why not?

• Can a married female employer fire a man she finds attractive? What about an employer who finds an employee of the same gender attractive, even if the employee is not queer? Does the ruling objectify bodies based on desirability? Can the argument of sexual desire be used as an excuse to dismiss unwanted employees?

2. A ten-year-old Ohio girl became pregnant after being raped. Days after the *Dobbs v. Jackson Woman's Health Organization* decision, she sought an abortion, but lived in one of almost a dozen states[70] that, at the time, banned all abortions, including in the cases of rape and incest. She is not alone. In 2017 (the last year such information was gathered as of this book's publication), approximately 4,460 girls under age fifteen (the age of consent) became pregnant, with 44 percent obtaining an abortion. The ten-year-old Ohio girl had to cross state lines to get an abortion, triggering a national political fight with so-called pro-life groups dismissing the story as "fake," even when the girl's perpetrator was arrested and charged.

• Setting aside, for the moment, the psychological and physical abuse a child experiences by being raped, is forcing the child to carry the pregnancy to term another form of abuse? Why or why not?

• Ten-year-olds' bodies may not be able to carry a pregnancy to full term, putting the life of the child-mother at risk. Does the life or potential life of the unborn trump the life of the mother? Should the matter of life and death remain only in the hands of God? Or are so-called pro-life groups imposing their religious views upon people, some of whom may not believe in God? Still, if abortion is indeed murder, as many claim it is, should they then do everything in their power to uphold this universal claim? Should those who perform abortions be tried for murder?

---

[69] "Iowa: Court Upholds Firing of Woman Whose Boss Found Her Attractive," *New York Times*, December 22, 2012.

[70] Alabama, Arkansas, Florida, Kentucky, Louisiana, Missouri, Oklahoma, Ohio, South Dakota, Tennessee, and Texas.

• Is the *Dobbs* ruling misogynistic? Does the Supreme Court respect the rights of women? Why or why not? What of Justice Amy Coney Barrett's support for the majority opinion? Does it matter that many women also support the *Dobbs* decision?

3. An eighteen-year-old woman was raped in 2016 by five men in a building lobby during Spain's famous Pamplona festival known as the Running of the Bulls. The crime was recorded on a security camera. The men were not convicted because, during the rape, the victim laid there with her eyes shut, not moving. The defense argued that her refusal to resist meant consent. Her predicament inspired the Parliament to pass a new law in 2022. Under the new measure, any sex that occurs without clear consent will be considered rape. Spain joins Canada, Denmark, and Sweden, which have similar laws. Consent ceases to be defined by a male's imagination. Only yes means yes.[71]

• Is such a law a good idea? Should it be adopted in the United States? Men have been taught that women say no when they really mean yes. Is this some old myth justifying forced sex? Is every time that a woman said no but ended up engaging in sex an incidence of rape? Why or why not? If yes only means yes, would this make what is culturally acceptable and what is not easier to decipher?

• Euroamerican women have falsely accused men of color of sexual improprieties or rape in the past and in the present. A malicious whisper, a false accusation, or a gaslit desire have been sufficient to have boys and men of color lynched, burned alive, electrocuted, or thrown into a river with an industrial fan tied with barbed wire around their neck like Emmett Till; entire Black towns like Rosewood, Florida, and sections of cities like the Greenwood District of Tulsa, Oklahoma—"Black Wall Street"—have been destroyed. Even today, euroamerican women call the police, claiming to be threatened by Black men. In 2020 Amy Cooper called the police, falsely accusing a Black bird watcher in Manhattan's Central Park by telling 911 operators that "there's an African-American man threatening my life."[72] Due to centuries-old negative stereotypes about men of color contributing to a culture of fear toward those considered "beastly," should euroamerican women be automatically believed when accusing men of color? What is the danger of not believing euroamerican women's claim of sexual assault by men of color? How much of white liberal feminism is a racist ideology supporting white supremacy?

---

[71] Emma Bubola and José Bautista, "Spain Passes Law Requiring Clear Consent for Sex, Joining Others," *New York Times*, August 26, 2022.

[72] Jonathan Stempel, "Woman Who Falsely Accused Black Bird Watcher in Central Park Sues Ex-Employer," Reuters, May 26, 2021.

Chapter 15

Affirmative Action

Step 1: Observing

Institutions, whether they be governmental, educational, social, political, or ecclesial, are not, nor have they ever been, race neutral. The issue, then, is not how to become more diverse but how to challenge the institutional power currently residing in euroamerican hands. The COVID-19 pandemic clearly demonstrated how the political structures designed since the foundation of the republic to privilege whiteness have worked as euroamerican affirmative action, reinforcing the marginalization of US communities of color. When Congress created the Paycheck Protection Program in March 2020 (an $800 billion relief effort for small businesses), data from several sources (including the Small Business Administration tasked with managing the program) revealed that minority-owned businesses were disproportionately underrepresented and underserved.[1] How the CARES Act was administered ensured that it mainly functioned as a form of affirmative action for small businesses run by euroamericans. This phenomenon reinforced oppressive structures and contributed to the devastation faced by Black and Brown Americans who, as already mentioned, also experienced higher rates of COVID-19 infections, higher proportions of fatalities, and, when the vaccine became available, fewer opportunities for obtaining the lifesaving doses.

As the legitimized historical norm, euroamerican affirmative action substituted meritocracies with social structures that prioritize whiteness. Euroamericans, regardless of abilities, skills, or the availability of qualified applicants of color, jump in front of the line when it comes to obtaining undeserved opportunities. During the Great Depression and World War II, as the nation implemented significant federal policies to lift a middle class through social programs like a minimum wage, Social Security, a GI Bill, and strong unions, African Americans—specifically those from the

---

[1] Stacy Cowley, "How Businesses Led by Minorities Received Less Relief," *New York Times*, April 6, 2021.

South—were excluded. Social welfare programs of the time, according to historian Ira Katznelson, included occupational exclusions demanded by southern Democrats coupled with an absence of antidiscrimination language to prevent the economic advancement of Black Americans. For example, by excluding maids and farmworkers from the 1935 Social Security program, 66 percent of Black Americans nationally, 80 percent of Black people in the South, and an unknown number of Latine people were excluded. Both the New Deal and the Fair Deal created an exclusive middle class by providing whites the ability to attend college, secure good jobs, buy houses, and begin businesses (2005, 43–55, 113–14, 192).

Yet when communities of color push back on an establishment that privileges whiteness in job opportunities or college admission, they are gaslit into believing it is they who are asking for special treatment, to be judged by the color of their skin rather than the content of their character. In a 1997 statement, then-senator Jeff Sessions said it best: "I think it makes people unhappy if they lost a contract or a right to go to a school or a privilege to attend a university simply because of their race."[2] And while it is true that people of color have always been "unhappy" when they were denied access "simply because of their race," no doubt this is not what Sessions meant.

A narrative has been created that says a level playing field already exists. According to this familiar and fictitious story, undeserving minorities, taking their place due to politically correct government officials and liberal social engineering, stand in the way of euroamerican success. America must be made great again by returning to an era of unquestioned white affirmative action.

White affirmative action has been able to operate as the indisputable norm because most minds from communities of color were, for centuries, so colonized that they defined white affirmative action as legitimate. For white affirmative action to operate at full efficiency, communities of color must be taught to see reality and define themselves through the eyes of the dominant euroamerican culture. Carter G. Woodson, son of enslaved Africans and among the first to study Black history, best describes this colonized mindset:

> The opponents of freedom and social justice decided to work
> out a program which would enslave the Negroes' mind inasmuch
> as the freedom of body had to be conceded.... If you control

---

[2] Andrew Kreighbaum, "The Trump Nominees and Affirmative Action," *Inside Higher Ed*, January 11, 2017.

a man's [*sic*] thinking you do not have to worry about his action. When you determine what a man shall think, you do not have to concern yourself about what he will do. If you make a man feel that he is inferior, you do not have to compel him to accept an inferior status, for he will seek it for himself. If you make a man think that he is justly an outcast, you do not have to order him to the back door, he will go without being told; and if there is no back door, his very nature will demand one. (2006 [1933], 84)

To see through the eyes of one's oppressors took centuries to normalize and legitimize. During the period prior to the Civil War, it was illegal to teach African Americans to read. Even after ratification of the Fourteenth Amendment to the US Constitution (equal rights for all citizens), traditions, customs, and local ordinances conspired to prevent Black Americans from receiving an adequate education. Consequently, whites became the interpreters of reality. Those who could read were in a position of power over those who could not because those privileged with an education maintained and manipulated the flow of information. During this time, there was widespread fear, particularly in the South, of educated persons of color, so schools were segregated, job opportunities deprived, and resources to correct these injustices denied.

If knowledge is indeed power, then marginalization can be maintained by limiting, censoring, or fabricating "alternative facts," not just for African Americans, but for any who fall short of the white ideal, a strategy maintained in turn by the dominant culture. As seen by the dominant euroamerican majority, the post–civil rights era has corrected most of the grievances of people of color. They believe that the election of the first Black president in 2008 serves as proof that we now live in some postracial America. The election of Donald Trump in 2016 should have put to rest any such notions. BIPOC communities, after four years of President Trump, continue to face institutionalized violence, specifically manifested in education.

Despite the 1960s' attempt to limit white affirmative action, when some legal gains for communities of color occurred, people of color continued nonetheless to be disenfranchised by political and social institutions. Statistics from the US Census Bureau reveal African Americans and Latines earn substantially lower wages than euroamericans.[3] Black and Latine people are

---

[3] Comparing the 2019 income of non-Hispanic white households with households of color shows that the ratio of Blacks' to non-Hispanic whites' income was 0.60—an increase of .01 since 2010, and the ratio of Hispanics' to non-Hispanic

more likely to be discriminated against when looking for a home in which to live and pay higher interest rates for houses. They are more likely to be racially profiled and arrested for drug charges. Furthermore, they suffer from higher unemployment levels. The impact of racism and ethnic discrimination is not limited to those who are passed up for a job or not admitted into college. Racism and ethnic discrimination expose institutionalized violence in economic and social structures that foster death-dealing policies upon the disenfranchised due to the pigmentation of their skin or their national origins. Discrimination is a multisystem-wide phenomenon that affects employment, education, and advancement within society. It often decides who gets employment, schooling, and health care; who gets to live in "safe" neighborhoods; and who is stigmatized as lazy or sinful (as in Max Weber's *Rise of Capitalism*) because they are unable to "pull themselves up by their bootstraps," never realizing, as so many people of color have said, that they haven't any boots.

The pervasiveness of racism and ethnic discrimination means that people of color often lack the same skills as euroamerican males because they have been locked out of education and employment opportunities. Because of centuries of accumulated racism and ethnic discrimination, people of color are conspicuously absent from the more desirable and prestigious jobs within society. Not surprisingly, almost all the heads of Fortune 500 companies are euroamerican males—not because of superior business acumen, but because of white affirmative action.

How can society mend this structural flaw? One of the means used was to limit white affirmative action. Noting the inadequacy of the 1964 Civil Rights Act to remedy institutionalized racism, President Lyndon B. Johnson signed Executive Order 11246, requiring government contractors to implement policies ensuring that people of color were hired. Johnson argued on June 4, 1965, during the commencement address at Howard University titled "To Fulfill These Rights," that

> You do not take a person who, for years, has been hobbled by chains and liberate him [*sic*], bring him up to the starting line of a race, and then say, "You are free to compete with all the others," and still justly believe that you have been completely fair.

Some, however, believe President Johnson's action was itself discriminatory. For example, Supreme Court Justice Roberts argued in a 2007

---

whites' income was 0.75—an increase of .06 since 2010 (DeNavas-Walt, Proctor, and Smith 2011, 9; Semega et al. 2020, 5).

decision, "The way to stop discrimination on the basis of race is to stop discriminating on the basis of race."[4] By focusing on the impact of white affirmative action within the education system, specifically higher education, this chapter engages the continued effects of race-conscious action on employment, housing, and social services for communities of color in the United States.[5]

During Reconstruction, people of color began to attend school, but due to a racially segregated society, communities would have a white school and a "Negro" school. Because education was segregated, Negro schools lacked resources, thus providing inferior educational opportunities. In the early 1950s, based on a US Supreme Court ruling that justified the "separate but equal" rule, a process began to end segregation, which until then had been the norm. In Topeka, Kansas, a Black third-grader, Linda Brown, had to walk one mile to get to her Black elementary school, even though a white elementary school was only seven blocks away. When her father attempted to register his daughter at the white elementary school, the principal refused to admit her. The US District Court for Kansas heard the case on June 25 and 26, 1951. The school argued that, because segregation in Topeka and elsewhere pervaded many other aspects of life within the United States, segregated schools simply prepared "colored" children for life in America. Losing the case in the District Court, it was appealed to the Supreme Court, which did not rule until 1953.

Today, that ruling is known as *Brown v. Board of Education*. Although the court neither abolished segregation in public areas nor placed a time limit as to when schools needed to desegregate, it did declare segregation to be unconstitutional. Despite the court's decision, most public schools simply ignored the ruling and continued racial segregation. It would take four years and the dispatching of federal troops to Central High School in Little Rock, Arkansas, to provide a few Black students access to a white school. Through the 1960s and 1970s, a battle raged throughout our nation's public school systems, with euroamericans fighting the will of the Supreme Court tooth and nail.

---

[4] *Parents Involved in Community Schools v. Seattle School District No. 1.*

[5] Most Americans (73 percent) say colleges should not consider race or ethnicity in admission decisions, a significant increase when we consider that in 2013 a slightly lesser majority (57 percent) opposed its consideration. Nikki Graf, "Most Americans Say Colleges Should Not Consider Race or Ethnicity in Admissions," Pew Research Center, February 25, 2019; Public Religion Research Institute, *Survey: Americans Divided between Principle and Practice on Affirmative Action, Divided on DOMA* (Washington, DC: Public Religion Research Institute, 2013).

What role did Christian churches play? Many, particularly in the South, which preached that God's saving grace is for all people regardless of race or ethnicity, responded to the moral crisis of segregation by establishing their own "Christian" schools. Christians could now send their white children to a private school where they would not have to sit next to Black or Brown children. Many Christian schools established during these times were founded for the sole purpose of circumventing the Supreme Court's mandate to desegregate. Although such schools were a response to a political situation, their motivation was supposedly religiously based, as they claimed they were seeking a Christ-centered education in an increasingly secular school system.

Almost three-quarters of a century after *Brown v. Board of Education*, most private elementary and secondary "Christian" schools (66 percent Catholic and 71 percent other religions) remain predominately white (Hussar et al. 2020, 31). The role played by these Christian schools—then and now—to maintain the separate-but-equal mindset raises suspicions among people of color about the moral commitment of the dominant culture to create a truly desegregated learning environment. Ironically, the students attending school within a predominately white educational system also suffer because they acquire an education devoid of diversity, limiting their ability to adequately function or succeed in the new global marketplace. Neoliberalism means that our present generation will have to deal with, purchase from, sell to, negotiate with, work for, and supervise people from different races, cultures, and ethnicities.

Although those who are mainly denied a competitive education are students of color, it would be an error not to consider the link between this nation's disparity in wealth and skin pigmentation. According to the 2019 Census Bureau, while 14 percent of US children lived in poverty prior to the COVID-19 outbreak, a disproportionate number were of color; 35 percent of Black and 41 percent of Latine children live in poverty. Children of color are three times as likely to live in poverty as euroamerican children.[6] Both President George W. Bush's No Child Left Behind initiative, which set unrealistic goals that ultimately proved self-defeating, and President Obama's attempted fix of No Child Left Behind, which judged teachers through their students' test scores, failed because they did not consider the driving force for schools' underperformance: the economic class to which the students belong.

---

[6] Deja Thomas and Richard Fry, "Prior to COVID-19, Child Poverty Rates Had Reached Record Lows in U.S.," Pew Research Center, November 30, 2020.

According to data from the National Assessment of Education Progress, more than 40 percent of the variation in average reading scores and 46 percent of the variation in average math scores is directly correlated with the variation in child poverty.[7] A 2015 study demonstrates that the lowest SAT scores are from students living in households with incomes of less than $20,000 while the highest scores came from children living in households with incomes of or over $200,000.[8] Could it be that ignoring class issues while setting high education performance standards undermines public education by either leading many to fail or leading states to lower standards, thus justifying the need for privatization and creating support for a voucher system?

In her 2011 presidential address to the Association for Public Policy Analysis and Management, Helen L. Ladd (2012) argued that initiatives to improve the US education system, like No Child Left Behind, are misguided because they ignore the body of evidence that documents that, on average, students from disadvantaged households perform at a lower academic level than those from more advantaged families. Ignoring class-based data means that educational policy initiatives, thus far, contributed little and more than likely will not contribute much toward the future in dealing with the educational gap existing between those attending schools in poor areas and those attending schools in more affluent communities.

The pandemic spotlighted how such economic disparities contributed to educational barriers for communities of color. For the poor, lacking home internet connectivity and having households managed by low-income working parents made remote learning nearly impossible. Some 16.9 million children lack home internet access, while 7.3 million lack a home computer. March 2020 marked the moment that most public schools shut their doors. It also marked the last time some 3 million of the most marginalized students (approximately the school-age population of the entire state of Florida) experienced any form of formal education—virtually or in person. A disproportionate number of these students are low-income Black, Latine, and Native American students.[9]

---

[7] Helen F. Ladd and Edward B. Fiske, "Class Matters. Why Won't We Admit It?," *New York Times*, December 11, 2011.

[8] Scott Jaschik, "SAT Scores Drop: Declines Take Averages down to Lowest Point in Years," *Inside Higher Ed*, September 3, 2015.

[9] Hailly T. N. Korman, Bonnie O'Keefe, and Matt Repka, "Missing in the Margins: Estimating the Scale of the COVID-19 Attendance Crises," Bellwether Education Partners, October 21, 2020.

Step 2: Reflecting

Is it possible to be colorblind in a society where color still matters? For the past half millennium, racial and ethnic forms of oppression have been normalized and legitimized in the eyes of the overwhelming majority of euroamericans through legal (eugenics was constitutionally upheld by the Supreme Court) and religious (curse of Cain) justifications. The 1960s US civil rights movement (and other antiracist, anticolonial, and democratizing movements throughout the world) ushered a new way for nonwhites to be seen and perceived that radically challenged and changed the legitimized gaze. Nevertheless, a racial hegemony was preserved by advancing a new racial project that repackaged white supremacy and secured structural inequalities and injustices under the ideology of "colorblindness."

Despite the omnipresence of racism in US life, the dominant culture insisted on the construct of colorblindness and the rhetoric of reverse discrimination. According to a March 2021 Pew Research poll, only 14 percent of euroamerican people believe Black people face "a lot" of discrimination, while an additional 26 percent say Black people experience "some" discrimination. Almost half of euroamerican people (48 percent) believe white people face discrimination. Nearly half of white people believe they suffer greater discrimination than Black people.[10] White perception of reality is frustrating when we consider that, according to a 2020 Rutgers University study, Black US teenagers face discrimination on average 5.21 times a day. This barrage of daily discrimination usually leads to depression (English et al. 2020, 5, 7). Racism and ethnic discrimination are not unfortunate aberrations based on individual biases or prejudices. They are a structural norm that has manifested as centuries of a white affirmative action that reinforced white dominance.

When colorblindness is claimed, the euroamerican ideal, consisting of the segregated life whites carved out for themselves, is masked. The racial demographics of most neighborhoods, schools, and social gatherings indicates that color is seen. But by claiming colorblindness, euroamerican people need not be bigots; in fact, they could be very politically correct, even marching with Black Lives Matter or protesting at detention centers holding Brown children in cages. One need not say the n-word or burn crosses to be a racist because the social structures are racist for them, protecting white privilege even while providing the opportunity to lament the lack of diversity. To claim the ideal of colorblindness allows some

---

[10] Andrew Daniller, "Majorities of Americans See at Least Some Discrimination against Black, Hispanic and Asian People in the U.S.," Pew Research Center, March 18, 2021.

Christians, specifically conservative and evangelical Christians, to approach racism on an individual basis rather than on a communal level. Under the Lordship of Christ, they believe different races can come together as true brothers and sisters. Because Christ is Lord, euroamerican Christians can downplay, if not outright ignore, the importance of initiating sociopolitical acts that challenge the present social structures that are detrimental to communities of color and remain embedded within US social, political, and economic structures. For them, reconciliation is achieved through personal relationships across racial and ethnic lines. Stressing acts as individuals over and against changing social structures allows those who are privileged by those same structures to feel righteous because of public apologies voiced for past racist acts. Meanwhile, they can continue to benefit from the status quo due to their eurocentric privilege.

Sociologist Howard Winant argues that the construction of color-blindness has moved the conversation from addressing institutionalized racism (as evident in the education system) to creating a political correctness that attempts to expunge individual bigotry. The New Right racial project, according to Winant, differs from the more racist Far Right by not vocally espousing white supremacy. Unlike the Far Right, the New Right embraces mainstream political activities. The New Right can accept a few nonwhites to participate politically and socially within the prevailing power structures if they are willing to expound colorblindness. A face of color is placed on a pedestal to prove that minorities who work hard enough can be as successful as white people. Participants in this movement differ from outright racists by their willingness to manipulate whites' fear of people of color through "coded language" (Winant 2004, 56–57). (This language appears as Ronald Reagan's complaints about "welfare queens" or "young bucks buying T-bone steaks with food stamps"; as George H. W. Bush's presidential campaign ads in 1988 about Willie Horton as a dangerous Black rapist to smear his opponent Michael Dukakis; as Governor Mitt Romney's post-2012 election remarks concerning "gifts" promised by Barack Obama to Black and Hispanic communities; as then-candidate Donald Trump's efforts to "protect" America from Brown caravans heading toward our borders.) Winant goes on to describe the neoconservative racial project as a discourse wishing to preserve white advantages through the denial of racial differences, which, for the New Right, is best accomplished by advocating colorblindness (57).

But neoliberal economic policies are dismantling the white middle class as white affirmative action becomes insufficient in saving its beneficiaries from a downward economic spiral. Resentment toward the consequences of neoliberalism is channeled away from the 1 percent who benefit by casting blame on the unfair advantages "given" to nonwhites. The bene-ficiaries of historical white affirmative action participate in gaslighting communities of color. The remedy to their economic losses becomes an insistence to treat everyone the same, regardless of how social structures continue to privilege euroamerican people. Establishing a colorblind society becomes the expressed goal.

The problem with expounding colorblindness is that, regardless of euroamericans' best intentions, the disparities between euroamerican people and people of color reveal that social structures are not colorblind. When President Trump was asked by a journalist about the dispropor-tionate rate of African Americans being killed by the police, he provided the perfect colorblind response: "What a terrible question to ask. So are white people. More white people, by the way."[11] His daughter Ivanka, while introducing her father during the 2016 Republican National Convention, said it best by simply proclaiming, "He is colorblind."[12]

Those who "do not see color" remember the civil rights movement fondly as successfully eliminating most of our racist past. But despite claims to colorblindness, racism and ethnic discrimination persist because the radicalness of the civil rights movement was toned down to obtain some significant and important concessions from the dominant white culture. Unfortunately, these compromises simply replaced racial domina-tion with a racial hegemony that poses questions concerning the struggle for justice on a universal rather than on a corporate plane by integrating the opposition to nullify the more radical demands of the movement. Even Martin Luther King Jr.'s dream that his children be judged by the "content of their character" and not "the color of their skin" is co-opted to insist that considering race or ethnicity for college admission violates the spirit of King's "dream" and that true followers of King should, instead, advocate colorblindness. The reconciliation attempting to be forged is a colorblind reconciliation that enacts toothless anti-racist policies while failing to fundamentally change or transform the social structures that maintain and sustain racism. The more radical demands of the civil rights movement (e.g., equitable distribution of wealth, resources, and opportu-nities) were sacrificed in favor of limited economic, political, and cultural access to limited power and privilege for a minority of middle-class people of color.

---

[11] Jeremy W. Peters, "Asked about Black Americans Killed by Police, Trump Says, 'So Are White People,'" *New York Times*, July 14, 2020.

[12] Will Drabold, "Read Ivanka Trump's Speech at the Republican Convention," *Time*, July 21, 2016.

Ironically, whenever those who suffer disenfranchisement raise their voices in protest due to the oppression caused by the segregated society in which they live, they are dismissed and labeled "racist" by those claiming colorblindness. People who have spent most of their lives advocating legislation and policies detrimental to communities of color being among the first to accuse people of color of being racists is a curious phenomenon. Former Speaker of the House Newt Gingrich, echoing radio personality Rush Limbaugh, called for then–Supreme Court nominee Judge Sonia Sotomayor's nomination to be withdrawn because she was, in Gingrich's words, "A Latina woman racist." She was attacked for lacking sufficient intelligence (although she graduated summa cum laude) or for being too abrasive (translated as a nondocile Latina who speaks her mind).[13]

Euroamericans who pine to "Make America Great Again" lament the loss of white affirmative actions that assured that whites, regardless of qualifications, were prioritized to fill empty slots in the workplace, the marketplace, and academic institutions. In a perverse zero-sum rule, every position earned by a person of color was interpreted as a slot "given" to a less deserving applicant—a birthright taken away from a member of the dominant culture. The level of intellectual acumen possessed by students of color matters little because they are never considered as good as or as likely to succeed as a white student. Racism reinforces the societal belief that people of color are inferior because they lack white skin. To such minds, people of color, specifically Black and Latine people, present a threat to the dominant culture.

To consider race and ethnicity for college admission is interpreted by the beneficiaries of white affirmative action as a form of "reverse discrimination." Yet the acceptance to a college of Latine applicant "X" does not mean that euroamerican student "Y" with a higher SAT score was not accepted because Latine "X" displaced them. In reality, if Latine "X" was denied admittance, it would more likely be that another euroamerican student with a lower SAT score than euroamerican student "Y" might be accepted because they belong to one of several subgroups that receive preferential consideration, such as legacy children, athletes, or low-scoring children of potential future donors. Or perhaps the spot going to Latine "X" may instead go to another student of color who scored higher than euroamerican student "Y," or the position might be given to a foreign student. The 2019 college admissions scandal exposed by the FBI's Operation Varsity Blues demonstrates the complexity of factors in collegiate

---

[13] Sheryl Gay Stolberg, "Two Sides Start Plotting Confirmation Strategies," *New York Times*, May 28, 2009.

admissions. In the exposed scheme, thirty-three euroamerican parents of economic means paid more than $25 million in bribes, along with several of them falsifying small to significant components of their children's applications, to get their underachieving children into top universities between 2011 and 2018.[14]

Considering race and ethnicity in college admission decisions is not another form of racism—"reverse racism"—but rather recognizes a historical white privilege that reserved all slots in higher education (and jobs) for euroamericans. Even today, euroamerican people continue to have the advantage, holding a disproportionate number of more desirable jobs and attending more prestigious educational institutions than people of color. No one contends that euroamerican students are excluded from getting a college education simply because they have white skin. The same cannot be said about students of color. Considering race and ethnicity in college admissions is an attempt to provide equal opportunity for all, regardless of race, to achieve the advantage currently reserved for euroamerican people. Its purpose is not to exclude euroamerican students but to serve the missions of colleges and universities in creating diverse learning environments for the betterment of the overall student body and for the good of the general public and future workforce.

Furthermore, the concept of "reverse discrimination" masks the domestic economic disparity caused by neoliberalism, blaming students of color and, in the minds of many among the euroamerican working class, giving Black and Latine applicants an unfair advantage. Those who "do not play by the rules" of eurocentricity and white privilege are conjured up to serve as scapegoats. While reverse discrimination is an illusion for which no empirical data exist, it rhetorically provides "the answer" for why euroamericans are disadvantaged by neoliberalism. Rather than looking toward the top 1 percent as a possible cause for the negative consequences of neoliberalism, most euroamerican people have been taught to blame downward, to scapegoat those perceived as taking their seats in classrooms, their jobs in markets, and even "their" women in bedrooms. Although the United States cannot return to its slaveocracy past, nor is it willing to challenge neoliberalism, it can advocate colorblindness to address and assuage the downwardly mobile euroamerican middle class.

Of course, most would not make the error of publicly voicing racist comments or appearing to violate the rules of political correctness (at least

---

[14] Jennifer Medina, Katie Benner, and Kate Taylor, "Actresses, Business Leaders and Other Wealthy Parents Charged in U.S. College Entry Fraud," *New York Times*, March 12, 2019.

not in the presence of people of color). Nevertheless, wishing to preserve white advantages through the denial of racial differences has led to the advocacy of colorblindness. White resentment toward the 2008 and 2022 economic crises has led many to blame the so-called unfair advantages given to nonwhites, which can only be mediated when everyone is supposedly treated the same, ignoring how social structures continue to privilege euroamerican communities. Rejecting the assumption that people of color are inferior, those on the margins of society recognize that they are locked out of educational and employment opportunities because euroamerican people, the guardians of society's power structures, either consciously or unconsciously bias their decisions in favor of other euroamerican people. Considering race and ethnicity in college admissions was designed as a corrective measure. Nonetheless, numerous studies show that, even when people of color are more qualified, euroamerican males in power still garner higher salaries and positions.

If the goal was to racially and ethnically diversify college campuses, then efforts have failed. College attendance of students of color and those who are economically disadvantaged has fallen off since the early 1970s. Even under current policies, students of color continue to be underrepresented. The underrepresentation of low-income students is even greater. By 2015, African Americans, who represented 15 percent of the college-age population, represented only 7 percent of selective public college students. Latine people, who comprised 21 percent of the college-age population, accounted for only 12 percent of selective public college students (Carnevale et al. 2018, 19). Because attending selective institutions provides advantages, specifically greater likelihood of graduating, greater access to graduate schooling, and higher wages, homogeneous campuses—whether consciously or unconsciously designed as such—serve to further institutionalize racism and classism within society.

Ironically, considering race and ethnicity in college admission decisions is beneficial for neoliberalism, and the "establishment" generally recognizes this fact. Both *Grutter v. Bollinger* and *Gratz v. Bollinger* considered the University of Michigan's admissions policies with regard to race, on behalf of euroamerican women who were denied admission to law school (*Grutter*) and undergraduate (*Gratz*) educations. Both cases argued that promoting racial and ethnic diversity was not a compelling enough reason to justify the university's admission policies in 1997. They also argued that admission policies at the University of Michigan were too broad to promote diversity and were, hence, failing to meet the compelling-interest exemption that the court applies to the Constitution's equal-protection clause.

A record-setting sixty-six friend-of-the-court (amicus) briefs were filed in support of the University of Michigan's admission policies. Those filing amicus briefs in the *Grutter v. Bollinger* and *Gratz v. Bollinger* cases were not liberal or activist organizations, but rather the defenders of the neoliberal establishment, such as the military, including twenty-one retired generals and admirals and three former superintendents of military academies, and some titans of corporate America such as General Motors, Viacom, Microsoft, IBM, Bank One, American Express, Boeing, Shell, General Electric, Coca-Cola, and fifty-four other Fortune 500 companies. They maintained that race should be one of many factors used to achieve a more diverse student body because selective universities train the future leaders of society, and society—presently marred by racial and ethnic tension—will benefit from a diverse and integrated leadership corps.[15]

The Michigan cases were decided in 2003, with the court invalidating the practice of awarding points to minority students in *Gratz v. Bollinger*. In *Grutter v. Bollinger*, the court sided with the university, acknowledging that law school admission policies were needed to aggressively compete on the global stage, where euroamerican students must understand and work with diverse constituencies. Justice O'Connor—the swing voter—expressed the hope that, within twenty-five years of the decision (2028), there would no longer be a need for considering race and ethnicity in college acceptance decisions. A few years short of O'Connor's hopeful future, we know that, despite extensive outreach to students of color and financial investments into the hundreds of millions of dollars, efforts to diversify have been an abysmal failure. Black student enrolment in 2021 at Michigan's flagship school—Ann Arbor—was 4 percent.[16] Failure to consider race and ethnicity during admission will never achieve diversity in the student body.

Unfortunately, at least three obstacles prevent Justice O'Connor's vision from ever being realized. The first obstacle is a reluctance to eliminate class preferences in college admissions, specifically the legacy-type programs that primarily function as the affirmative action for privileged middle- and upper-class euroamerican applicants. Even as Yale brags about the diversity of its class of 2025, where 51 percent of the class identified as students of color, 14 percent of the students were admitted through

---

[15] Justice Powell's written opinion in the court's landmark 1978 case *Regents of the University of California v. Bakke* allowed colleges to consider race in determining admission for the sake of diversity, as long as it did not use quotas.

[16] Stephanie Saul, "Top Colleges Where Affirmative Action Was Banned Says It's Needed," *New York Times*, August 27, 2022.

legacy preferences, students who are predominately euroamerican, wealthy, and well connected.[17] Following the First World War, legacies replaced the quota system that existed at the more prestigious institutions of higher education to limit the influx of immigrant students, particularly Jews and, to a lesser extent, Catholics. Legacies proved a more defendable concept than exclusionary quotas.

This discriminatory system only exists in the United States, preserving an aristocratic right virtually unheard of at universities throughout the world (Schmidt 2010, 34, 39–43). Legacy admissions continue to be used today as an integral white affirmative action method, keeping out most selective college applicants who are students of color. According to a study based on Harvard's data, conducted by Duke University economist Peter Arcidiacono, a white legacy student has a fivefold increase in likelihood of being admitted. The Harvard class of 2024 consisted of 15.5 percent legacy students. Vincent Price, president of Duke University, with an incoming class comprising 22 percent legacy students, further defended the white affirmative action program.[18] If Yale and Harvard were to drop their white affirmative action legacy programs, they would be more diverse than what they are boasting, as unqualified, underperforming students would no longer take the place of more academically rigorous and better-performing students. A relic of white supremacy, legacy programs give admission preference to the sons and daughters of alumni, who, due to historical racism and ethnic discrimination, are disproportionally euroamerican. Of the top one hundred US universities (per *US News & World Report*), almost three-quarters consider legacy in admission decisions. All one hundred top liberal arts schools do so.[19] Though colleges and universities usually downplay the importance of legacy admissions, research suggests that being a legacy is equivalent to a 160-point increase (out of 1,600 points) on the SAT (Espenshade et al. 2004, 1431). Not surprisingly, the admission rate for legacy applicants to Harvard from 2014 through 2019 was 33 percent higher when compared to nonlegacies.[20]

When we consider who was admitted to Harvard during those five years, 43 percent of the euroamerican students were either legacies,

---

[17] Stephanie Saul, "Top Colleges Cling to Favoring Alumni's Children," *New York Times*, July 14, 2022.

[18] Ibid.

[19] Richard D. Kahlenberg, "Letter to Congress: College Legacy Preferences Must Go," The Century Foundation, February 27, 2018.

[20] Delano R. Franklin and Samuel W. Zwickel, "Legacy Admit Rate Five Times That of Non-Legacies, Court Docs Show," *Harvard Crimson*, June 20, 2018.

athletes, children of donors, or children of faculty. The Harvard class of 2019 consisted of 43.2 percent who were legacies and 20 percent who were athletes (regardless of color or ethnicity) from households with reported earned income of at least $500,000 a year. If these white affirmative action admission preferences were eliminated, then only 26 percent of legacies, white athletes, dean's list students, and faculty children would have been admitted from 2014 through 2019 (Arcidiacono, Kinsler, and Ransom, 2019, 1, 24, 29). Even if one's child is not a legacy, the applicant would be treated as if they are a legacy if the ability and capacity to make major financial contributions to the institution exists. The ability of the family to donate to the institution is crucial in admissions decisions. Jared Kushner benefited from a $2.5 million pledge to Harvard from his father, the real estate developer Charles Kushner, when he was admitted even though his GPA and SAT scores were below Ivy League standards (Golden 2006, 45–46).

Legacy admission consideration as a form of white affirmative action is accepted as normative and legitimate, where unqualified wealthier white students are accepted over and against better qualified, but poorer, students of color. Neoliberalism continues to influence all aspects of human life, where today white privilege is, more than ever, trumped by class privilege. One of the major class struggles occurring today is being fought in the admissions buildings of highly selective colleges and universities. Children of the wealthy can afford the SAT tutors and top prep schools that groom their children for marquee colleges. But as previously discussed, as the income gap continues to widen, the once-protected privilege of whiteness becomes less secure for the lower and middle classes and creates a backlash of legislation, referenda, and court decisions that attempt to limit students of color from attending colleges and universities. This privilege is sought and wielded to free up more seats for the beneficiaries of white affirmative action.

During the oral arguments on the University of Michigan cases mentioned above, Justice Breyer asked the attorney representing the students suing the university about the difference between legacy preference and affirmative action. According to the lawyer, the equal protection clause of the US Constitution prohibits race discrimination, not discrimination based on alumni affiliation. Yet because students of color were historically discriminated against when applying to predominately white universities, far fewer of today's students of color have parents who attended Ivy League institutions than white students. Students of color are locked out of legacy opportunities, continuing the racism that privileges euroamerican applicants who claim legacy. In fact, five of the nine

Supreme Court justices (or their children) who determined the *Grutter v. Bollinger* and *Gratz v. Bollinger* cases were themselves legacies of highly selective schools with strong legacy admission programs.[21] It is a given that students with better grades, who made the mistake of not being born white and wealthy, have difficulty entering such selective colleges. Because race and class privilege trump merit, affirmative action serves as a counterbalance to legacy preference.

A second obstacle preventing Justice O'Connor's colorblind vision from being realized by 2028 is the unequal and inequitable distribution of funds for public K–12 education. Justice O'Connor was aware of this obstacle during a rare interview with the *Chicago Tribune* in which she said, "I hope it looks as though we don't need artificial help to fill our classrooms with highly qualified students at the graduate level.... And if we do our job of educating young people, we can reach that goal."[22] Yet despite Justice O'Connor's optimistic hope for the future, the reality is a national refusal to provide a standardized basic public education for all its children.

In the early 1990s, education researcher and author Jonathan Kozol described schools in predominately poor and nonwhite districts as functioning with outdated and secondhand books, gaping holes in their roofs, overcrowded classrooms, inadequate climate control, nonoperational restrooms, running sewage, and in one case, a classroom conducted in an abandoned pool (1991, 23–37). The financial situation faced by these marginalized schools has worsened with the passage of time, exacerbated by how US public school financing continues to be calculated.

According to a study conducted in 2018, school districts that predominately comprise students of color receive, on average, $2,500 per student less than school districts serving fewer numbers of students of color (Morgan and Amerikaner 2018, 10). Studies have consistently shown that districts predominately serving students of color tend to receive less state and federal funding than districts predominately serving euroamerican students (10). Schools outside of the prosperous euroamerican suburbs must contend with fewer funds.

---

[21] Justices Breyer and Kennedy have ties to Stanford University that span three generations; Justice O'Connor's two children benefited from legacy at Stanford University. Stanford admits one-fourth of all legacies compared to just one-eighth of the overall applicant pool. Justice Stevens attended the University of Chicago and Northwestern Law School as did his father, and Justice Ginsburg's daughter benefited from legacy at Harvard Law School. See Daniel Golden, "For Supreme Court, Affirmative Action Isn't Just Academic," *Wall Street Journal*, May 14, 2003.

[22] Jan Crawford Greenburg, "O'Connor Voices Hope for Day Affirmative Action Not Needed," *Chicago Tribune*, June 25, 2003.

Even if the federal and state governments were committed to eliminating the financial discrepancies between schools serving euroamerican and minoritized communities, they would still be unable to do so. On average, state and federal governments have provided less than 54.5 percent of the schools' revenues over the past decades—7.7 percent from the federal government and 46.7 percent from the state. These figures show the government's decreased fiscal contribution from 2008. The remaining funding (45.6 percent) comes from local sources, specifically property taxes.[23] The financial structures created to fund K–12 education are tied to the neighborhoods that children assigned to attend the school live in, which, in turn, have been and continue to be segregated. Historically, reduced tax bases in communities of color were mainly created by the flight of the euroamerican middle class and the exodus of businesses (and I would add churches) to more prosperous neighborhoods when people of color began to move into predominately euroamerican residential areas (Wilson 1987, 56). Because the neediest schools are located in predominately poor neighborhoods where most of the residents are of color, K–12 educational funding will never be equitable unless we radically change how schools are funded. If nothing changes, then the present system of unequal educational opportunities in K–12 will mean most students of color will be unable to compete with white students for college admission, not because they are intellectually inferior, but because institutionalized racism and classism in education have ill-equipped them to do so.

An analytical study that explored how school and neighborhood contexts are jointly related to high school and graduation showed that the level of neighborhood resources positively predicts earned bachelor's degrees, while neighborhood socioeconomic status predicts high school graduation. According to a memo from the assistant secretary of the US Department of Education Office for Civil Rights, children attending K–12 schools with student populations that are predominately Latine and/ or Black are less likely to have adequate facilities, high-quality instruction materials, advanced academic courses, or experienced teachers.[24] Black- and Latine-majority poor schools have lower test scores and serve students who are more likely to drop out of school, contributing to persistent test score gaps with white students.

In other words, residential neighborhood characteristics remain the main indicator for educational attainment. However, simply shipping

---

[23] "U.S. Public Education Spending," EducationData.org, October 28, 2020.

[24] Catherine E. Lhamon, "Dear Colleague Letter: Resource Comparability," US Department of Education, October 1, 2014.

economically deprived students to predominately euroamerican and affluent schools is not the answer either. The study showed that their odds of educational attainment were still reduced in such circumstances (Owens 2010, 287, 289, 307). Reduced educational attainment may be due to the capabilities—or lack thereof—of teachers and administrators, 90 percent of whom are themselves euroamericans in schools with predominately euroamerican student bodies (US Department of Education 2020, 1). Reduced attainment for students of color when taught by euroamerican teachers is possibly due to lack of training and knowing how to educate in integrated settings, or, worse, due to lingering conscious or unconscious racism. Even though 51 percent of US students are of color, just 20 percent of teachers nationwide are of color (Dixon, Griffin, and Teoh 2019, 4). Taking the findings of these studies into consideration leads to the conclusion that educational success for students of color in poor neighborhoods requires both the economic revitalization of these neighborhoods and a more equitable distribution of educational resources among the schools.

A third obstacle to Justice O'Connor's colorblind vision is the recent trend of moving toward a more segregated educational system. On the sixty-fifth anniversary of *Brown v. Board of Education*, despite euroamerican people comprising most of the population and the minority of students across the nation's public schools, they remain the most segregated group. They attend schools in which 69 percent of fellow classmates are also euroamerican students. Black and Latine students attend intensely more segregated schools, making them more isolated from their euroamerican counterparts. They attend schools where 67 percent and 66 percent, respectively, are Black and Brown.

Furthermore, no federal program exists fostering voluntary integration (Orfield et al. 2019, 4–5). Starting with *Board of Education of Oklahoma City v. Dowell* in 1991, the Supreme Court authorized a return to segregated neighborhood schools, maintaining that desegregation was a temporary measure, not a school system's lasting responsibility. Dozens of court-ordered segregationist rulings, an increase of students of color within the overall population, continuing white flight from urban centers, and redlining real estate practices contribute to the resegregation of the nation's schools.

The reemergence of school segregation is as much a class issue as it is a race issue, linking segregation by race with segregation by poverty. Some thirteen thousand school districts throughout the country continue to be drawn based on the skin pigmentation of residents, thus securing that the propertied wealth of euroamerican citizens is allocated to predominately euroamerican K–12 schools. Given that 28 percent of Black students and 19 percent of Latine students live in concentrated poverty (as opposed to 4 percent of euroamerican students), on average, Latine and Black students attend schools with far higher poverty rates than euroamerican students. What this means is that the average predominately nonwhite school district creates a $2,500 wealth deficit per student, or a collective $23 billion less than predominately euroamerican school districts—even though these school districts serve the same number of students. Of course, a more equitable solution can be found if the wealth of the community is pooled and distributed evenly.[25] Implementing such a commonsense solution would dismantle white affirmative action, and ignoring such solutions means that the overlap between poverty and race would only expand over the years, as half the Black and Latine schools with 90 to 100 percent representation continue to have 90 to 100 percent of their students living in low-income households (Orfield et al. 2019, 23).

Unfortunately, multiple studies based on in-depth interviews with euroamericans, coupled with white flight, indicate that the majority of euroamericans do not want to freely integrate with Latine or Black communities (Renzulli and Evans 2005, 398). Justice O'Connor's colleague, Anthony Kennedy, best articulated the new approach to education in a seminal opinion. Writing about a Georgia school district, he said, "Racial balance is not to be achieved for its own sake.... Where resegregation is a product not of state action but of private choices, it does not have constitutional implications." From Missouri to Oklahoma, similar court decisions have reversed *Brown v. Board of Education*, so that once-integrated schools are again becoming segregated.[26] By 2012, just nine years after the University of Michigan decision, the Supreme Court again heard arguments concerning college admissions processes that consider race and ethnicity. Abigail Fisher, a white female student, sued the University of Texas at Austin when the institution where her father and sister attended rejected her application. Using zero-sum logic, she claimed her white race was held against her, even though the university clearly stated that Ms. Fisher would not have been admitted even if race played no role in the process. But even if race did play a role, the university insists on the flexibility to be able to assemble a varied student body as part of its academic mission.[27]

---

[25] Rebecca Sibilia, "School Districts are the Problem," *New York Times*, May 17, 2020.

[26] Allen G. Breed, "Separate but Equal?," *New York Times*, September 29, 2002.

[27] The University of Texas at Austin admits around 80 percent of its students by automatically accepting the top 10 percent of students from every high school in the state. The remaining 20 percent are chosen through individual assessments, considering many factors like legacy, diversity, grades, life experiences, and activities in which they are engaged.

The majority of educators and administrators maintain that students from diverse backgrounds learn from each other, making them better prepared to overcome biases and assume leadership positions within society.[28]

White affirmative action known as legacy is not the issue the justices considered. Rather, in a seven-to-one ruling on June 24, 2013, the Supreme Court continued its skeptical assessment of considering the race or ethnicity of minoritized students for admission purposes. Although the narrow ruling was a reprieve that allowed for the continuation of the policy, the justices ordered the appeals court to reconsider the case under standards that appear to doom considering the race of minority students in the future. Writing for the majority, Justice Kennedy wrote that schools must demonstrate that "available, workable race-neutral alternatives do not suffice" before considering race in admission decisions. Universities must "verify that it is necessary . . . to use race to achieve the educational benefits of diversity."[29] The "strict scrutiny" to be employed by universities considering race allows opponents an easier path to bring new cases before the court, thus providing an opportunity to continue its drift away from the ideal goals that began with *Brown v. Board of Education*.

By 2020, nine states had no race-conscious affirmative action.[30] California was the first to outlaw considering the race of minoritized students for admission in 1996 with the passage of Proposition 209. The first comprehensive study conducted in 2020 considering the impact of Proposition 209 found that, by every measure employed, Latine and Black students were harmed, as evident by their decreased numbers throughout the University of California system (Bleemer 2020, 1–5). In 2020, the state's voters—to the surprise of many—rejected Proposition 16, which would have overturned Proposition 209. Another 2020 study, focusing on all the states that have moved to ban consideration of race and ethnicity of minoritized students, reports a notable long-term drop in the enrollment of underrepresented students in the state's public flagship universities, a trend expected to continue for the foreseeable future. The study concludes "that alternative policies and administrative decisions were unable to fully replace race-based affirmative action" (Long and Bateman 2020, 188–89). Not surprisingly, Latine and Black students, according to a *New York*

---

[28] Adam Liptak, "Race and College Admissions, Facing a New Test by Justices," *New York Times*, October 9, 2012.

[29] Adam Liptak, "Justices Step Up Scrutiny of Race in College Entry," *New York Times*, June 25, 2013.

[30] California (1996); Washington (1998); Florida (1999); Michigan (2006); Nebraska (2008); Arizona (2010); New Hampshire (2012); Oklahoma (2012); and Idaho (2020).

Times study, are more underrepresented at the nation's top universities and colleges than they were at the start of the 1980s.[31]

The Supreme Court agreed to hear two crucial cases during the 2022–2023 term. One challenged the consideration of race during the admission process at public universities (University of North Carolina); the other challenged its usage at private institutions (Harvard). Using the same judicial logic employed when deciding *Dobbs v. Jackson Women's Health Organization*, the decision discussed in an earlier chapter, they outlawed considering race and ethnicity as one factor in determining admission—undoing forty years of precedent by gutting affirmative action. Justice O'Connor's hope of no longer considering race and ethnicity in college acceptance decisions arrived five years earlier. Unfortunately, failure to diversify, from grade school to graduate school, continues the sorry history played out by our education system as it serves as the primary engineer for inequalities within the United States, reinforcing white affirmative action.

Step 3. Meditating

At times, the dominant culture believes that inclusion is an adequate ethical response to structural oppression. Diversity and multiculturalism do not equal justice; they equal political correctness. Even if society were to abide by some politically correct decorum and eliminate the appearance of bigotry and prejudice, it still could neither reverse the damage of centuries of racism wrought upon those relegated to the margins nor eliminate the consequences of (mis)education, which have led to poverty and the misery, bitterness, and hatred that poverty produces. Ethics, when done from the margins, attempts to move beyond political correctness—that Disney-like façade, where different cultures, races, and ethnicities are presented as "a small world after all."

Dismantling white affirmative action while considering the experiences faced by communities of color must be understood as a product of love rather than political correctness. Basing ethics upon the concept of love is not new. Eurocentric ethicists like Joseph Fletcher have attempted to base their deliberations on such a concept. However, many have fallen short because they have applied love primarily to interpersonal relations while ignoring issues of social injustices like segregation within education. Martin Luther King Jr., more so than any other love ethicist, made love the essen-

---

[31] Jeremy Ashkenas, Haeyoun Park, and Adam Pearce, "Affirmative Action Yields Little Progress on Campus for Blacks and Hispanics," *New York Times*, August 25, 2017.

tial theme for both the private and public sector (Williams 1993, 18–23). Nevertheless, for Reinhold Niebuhr and many other ethicists of the dominant culture, unconditional love (*agape*) as an essential theme for the public sector is seen as too problematic to serve as a standard for moral behavior, or as Niebuhr said, an "impossible possibility" (1943, 76).

However, by failing to make *agape* the primary motive for social actions such as the consideration of race in admission decisions, the good intention to love remains separated from the action of love. The transformative power of love remains restricted to the inner soul, rather than the outer social environment. While admirable theoretical models are constructed to explain varied nuances in conceptualizing love, those on the margins complain that, at times, it is difficult to see the connection between the complex models and their practical application within the "everyday" of the disenfranchised. For so many who deal with a daily struggle for dignity, ethical deliberations founded on love as an abstraction provide little help for those marginalized by the educational system.

For example, in his text *Christ and the Moral Life*, James Gustafson stated, "Love as a disposition needs love as an intention, as a purpose, and also love as a norm" (1968, 256). This provides no help for the marginalized. Although Gustafson goes on to define intention as a "basic direction of activity," still one is hard-pressed to find examples in his book of praxis for justice based on love in facing the greatest injustices of his time. When we consider that his book was published in 1968, during the Black community's struggles for civil rights, we are left asking why he didn't connect his ethical perspectives with the moral crises unfolding before him and the Christian community. Did his silence confirm the power of those within the center to determine what is and what is not to become a topic for moral discourse?[32] As James Cone reminds us, white ethicists (of whom Gustafson is just one example) reflect the racism prevalent in society. The "invisibility" of racism is maintained by suggesting the problem of racism is only one social expression of a larger ethical concern (1975, 201).

If it is true that God is love (1 Jn. 4:8), then the only absolute that can be claimed is love. Consequently, love ought to be the prime motive behind every decision taken, including college admissions decisions. But is the biblical concept of love sufficient? Because of the prevalent racism in the US education system, those from the margins remain leery of basing any ethics upon a fixed law or regulation formulated by society, specifically

---

[32] In all fairness, Gustafson does include Martin Luther King's essay "Letter from Birmingham Jail" in a coedited collection of essays published that same year (Gustafson and Laney 1968, 256–74).

the dominant culture. In the end, relying on how the dominant culture defines "love" (either paternalistically or as "tough" love) can mask the self-interest of those with power. The basic flaw of relying solely on love as defined by the dominant culture is one of trust. Can the dominant culture be trusted to act in love? Do they even know how to love? If the history of how people of color have been treated in the United States is to serve as a guide in answering these questions, then the answer is obviously "no."

In addition, love coming from the centers of power and privilege usually focuses on how "they" can love those who are marginalized. But unconditional love is never limited to one direction (in other words, love from the privileged toward the marginalized), lest it reduce the disenfranchised to objects by which those in power can express their paternalistic charity. Love must be mutual. To love the marginalized is to serve them and receive in return God's love through them. Thus, the privileged and powerful find their salvation by discovering God in the lives of "the least of these," their neighbors. In this way, God's love can be experienced, a love manifested in the establishment of just relationships that can lead toward just social structures like college admission policies.

Step 4: Case Studies

1. More than three dozen wealthy white parents, including celebrity Lori Loughlin of the 1990s sitcom *Full House*, were charged with bribing university officials to secure the admission of their children to prestigious universities. Fake credentials were manufactured to have their children accepted as recruited athletes. Loughlin, for example, paid half a million dollars to university athletic officials in exchange for having her children passed off as recruits in a sport they did not play. Another actress, Felicity Huffman, a Golden Globe Award winner, paid $15,000 to an SAT proctor to inflate her daughter's scores. In some cases, parents falsified their student's ethnicities when it was seen to be beneficial. Meanwhile, these same schools, according to disclosed emails, were offering wealthy parents special treatment—including flagging applications—while soliciting donations in connection with their children's applications.[33]

• Lori Loughlin served a two-month sentence for attempting to pass

---

[33] Kate Taylor, "Loughlin Completes Sentence in College Admissions Fraud," *New York Times*, December 29, 2020; Kate Taylor, "U.S.C. Courted Loughlin for Donations," January 16, 2020; Kate Taylor, "Actress Gets 14-Day Sentence in College Admissions Fraud Scandal," September 14, 2019; Dana Goldstein and Jack Healy, "Costly? Always. But Their Help Is Rarely Illegal," *New York Times*, March 14, 2019.

her daughter off as a rower. Felicity Huffman served eleven days. Were these sentences symbolic? Were they treated more leniently than poor and nonwhite defendants accused of educational fraud like Kelly Williams-Bolar, a single, African American mother who was sentenced to five years in prison for using her father's home address to get her children into a suburban school system?

• Loughlin's daughter, who is a social media influencer, didn't understand what all the fuss was about, and posted that she didn't care about school and attended college for "game days, partying." What was all the fuss about? What should happen to the daughter? Is she also a victim? If she didn't know, should she be expelled? Why or why not?

• College admissions is a zero-sum-game procedure. The seats purchased by these wealthy parents who used their economic privilege to secure a spot for their unqualified children meant and still means that other more qualified children were denied entrance. But even if gaming the system ends, even if legacies are abolished, this will not ensure an increase in diversity. Those most likely to benefit are other euroamerican students. Discuss best practices to make higher education reflect the diversity of the nation.

2. The myth is that college is a meritocracy. The reality is that, in a neoliberal economic system, the higher educational admissions system is commodified, distorted by money and privilege. One does not need to engage in illegal activities, like those outlined in the previous case to game the system. For $1.5 million, parents can hire Ivy Coach, a college admissions consulting company that, from eighth grade, steers the student/client as to which classes to take and in which extracurricular activities to engage so as to stand out on their eventual college application—not to mention intense preparation for the SAT or ACT. To truly earn special consideration beyond merit at an Ivy-caliber institution requires an entry-level donation of $10 million. If a parent needs to boost their child's SAT score, seeing the right psychologist can procure a learning disability waiver (like ADHD), which can provide the student additional time to complete their exam and translate to an extra 350+ points.[34]

• During the 2015–2016 school year, each public school counselor was responsible, on average, for 470 students. A need exists for college admissions consulting companies due to the shortcomings of the public school system. What does it mean that the strongest predictor of a student's score is their parents' affluence? Does an ethical and more equitable way exist to

---

[34] Goldstein and Healy, "Costly?"; Eliza Shapiro and Dana Goldstein, "Scandal Highlights Shift away from Entry Exams," *New York Times*, March 15, 2019.

provide this service?

• Accusations of how the SAT is racially and culturally biased have been made over the decades. As a response, more than one thousand colleges and universities have moved toward test-optional admissions. Are such actions enough? How can we reimagine the higher education process to produce more diversity and equality?

3. The existing wealth gap between euroamericans and people of color means that students whose parents lack assets (like homeownership) are unable provide as much financial support for a college education, forcing students of color to incur greater debt. Black graduates, for example, finish their education with on average $25,000 more student debt than euroamericans.[35] Obstacles exist for students of color both seeking financial help and in repaying student loans that often have astronomical interest rates. A recent study shows how lending institutions use educational data in underwriting private student loans to disadvantage racial and ethnic minorities. Banks like Wells Fargo and consumer lending companies like Upstart have been accused of raising the price of credit for students attending traditional nonwhite institutions to the tune of an additional $3,500 per $30,000 five-year loan (*Educational Redlining* 2020, 4–5, 12–13, 16–18).

• Americans owe more than $1.7 trillion in student loans, of which over 45 million people are financially struggling specifically due to student loan debt. Student loans are preventing the next generation from ever achieving financial stability. Worse affected are students of color. Black borrowers are three times more likely to default on their student loans. Racism in the banking industry places heavier burdens on BIPOC students. Can establishing Congressional oversight provide relief? Is the problem the loans themselves or an education system that requires acquiring astronomical debt? Are other industrial countries that provide free higher education a model to be emulated by the United States?

• When financial aid falls short, student loans become the alternative for many people. A lawsuit was filed in federal court accusing sixteen leading private universities and colleges[36] of conspiring to reduce the aid awarded to admitted students. If the allegations are true, how can the financial burdens that have been placed on past students who were victims

---

[35] Ana Hernández Kent and Lowell Ricketts, "Has Wealth Inequality in America Changed over Time? Here Are Key Statistics," Federal Reserve Bank of St. Louis, December 3, 2020.

[36] Brown, California Institute of Technology, University of Chicago, Columbia, Cornell, Dartmouth, Duke, Emory, Georgetown, MIT, Northwestern, Notre Dame, University of Pennsylvania, Rice, Vanderbilt, and Yale.

of price fixing be rectified? Is this practice an indication of the "corpora-tization" of higher education? What other problems exists as more of the practices of higher education emulate business?

• Student loans, which were a means of obtaining an education that can lead to middle-class status, have become a profit-generating venture for banks. Should banking institutions be eliminated from the equation and allow the government to underwrite the loans? Should student debt be forgiven? While loan forgiveness might rectify past abuses, what must be done to prevent future abuses?

Conclusion

Acting—Implementing Praxis

Writing the third edition of *Doing Christian Ethics from the Margins* has given me a unique perspective to better understand some of the major institutionalized policies responsible for the disenfranchisement of minoritized communities. Twenty years of hindsight, informed by revisiting the same topics and issues, has revealed a trajectory of how oppression operates, demonstrating how little has changed since the start of the new millennium. In fact, placing all three editions side by side reveals that the arc of the moral universe has, thus far, not bent toward justice but toward more sophisticated methods of injustices. This realization has informed and reformed my worldview. The hope for the future I held twenty years ago has—in all honesty—been choked out of me, crying out, "I can't breathe." How then does one implement praxis, the fourth step of the hermeneutical circle I present, from a state of hopelessness?

When analyzing social structure, the chapters only explored the first three steps of the hermeneutical circle (observing, reflecting, and meditating). Missing was the fourth step: *acting—implementing praxis*. The original idea was for the reader, through the real-life case studies presented, to consider how they would develop and implement liberative praxis. Yet I see now, in this third edition, that this is not enough. As a corrective, I end this edition with a new conclusion, one that explores a philosophical underpinning to understanding praxis. I have come to realize that a praxis being liberative might not be enough to overturn the tables of oppressions. What *type* of praxis should we seek to implement when the God of liberation fails to liberate? What does one do when one's God seems silent and absent? In this conclusion, situated in a state of hopelessness, I share a type of ethical action, a methodology that I have developed in several of my other books[1] and what I have come to call an ethics *para joder*.

---

[1] Specifically: *Latina/o Social Ethics: Moving beyond Eurocentric Moral Thinking* (Waco, TX: Baylor University Press, 2010); *Embracing Hopelessness* (Minneapolis: Fortress Press, 2017); and *Decolonizing Christianity: Becoming Badass Believers* (Grand Rapids: Wm B. Eerdmans, 2021).

For a moment of US history, hope that a more liberative social order could be established did exist. Embracing their own rhetoric of "liberty and justice for all," great strides were made during the civil rights era when the country's court system was considered an ally of the minoritized. Believing that one's vote counted, a more racially and ethnically diverse populace went to the polls in 2008 and defied what was expected from a nation founded on the principles of white supremacy. They elected a Black man for the White House. But the campaign slogans of "Hope" and "Yes we can" eventually gave way to the reality of a white supremacy infused with Christian nationalism. The Supreme Court, which helped usher in a less discriminative nation, was co-opted as the federal court system's ethos was restructured. Not only was a Supreme Court seat literally stolen from President Barack Obama as the Republican-controlled Senate refused to even consider his nominee to the bench, but President Trump got to appoint with decisively unqualified appointees vacancies to appellate benches that had also been kept unfilled. Many of those judges shared his white nationalist worldview. Obama's call for hope gave way to the reality that, for those on the margins, the situation for the disenfranchised is bleak and hopeless. Since the start of the new millennium, under Republican and Democratic presidents, the situation has only grown worse for those on the margins. Standing before a global neoliberalism and a domestic white supremacy, calls for hope fall short.

A religiosity is required that spiritually justifies repressive and oppressive social structures that repudiate the central themes of good news, a religiosity that advocates a middle-class hope that satisfies any itch to partake in subversive action capable of bringing about social change. The minoritized are sold on the belief in a hope that all things will eventually work for good for those called by God's name and according to God's purposes (Rom. 8:28). Our gaze is directed to the by-and-by of the heavens to obscure seeing the here and now of earthly oppressive structures responsible for stealing the humanity of the disenfranchised. A theology of hope may sound liberating for eurochristians, but for those on their margins, pronouncements of hope reinforce oppression and strengthen the colonizing of minds.

I argue that communities of color within the United States and the colonized of the world live their lives where the promises of eurochristian hope are not apparent. So long as eurochristians claim hope, they can wash their hands of complicity with structures that their forebears designed to protect the unearned power, profit, and privilege of this present generation. From their segregated communities, they can snugly rely on the illusion that God will take care of the least of these, so that they, as good Christians, need not, lest the unfortunate become "dependent" on the state.

Eurochristians may very well be an Easter Sunday people, but those on their margins remain a Holy Saturday people. The colonized of the world, along with communities of color in the United States, occupy the liminal in-between space, where Friday's crucifixion marked by blood-shedding brutality and the not-yet resurrection of Sunday's Easter are constant companions. In this ambiguous space, any good news is easily drowned out by the daily realities faced by the marginalized. Participating in an ethics rooted in the ambiguous space of the marginalized means acting in radical solidarity with the crucified of the world. When we sit with the crucified in the dust of a never-ending Holy Saturday, we quickly discover how hope falls short and how it is used as an opioid to numb Friday's pains, effectively drugging us and ensuring the impotence of any radical liberative praxis.

White supremacy and neoliberalism will not be vanquished in our lifetime or that of our children or even grandchildren. These structures have reigned supreme for centuries and no doubt will endure for centuries to come. The idea that our praxis will bring them crumbling down like the walls of Jericho is a bit naïve. If this is true, why then bother with liberative praxis? We do not struggle for justice because we expect to get an extra ruby in our heavenly crown of glory, nor because we believe our actions will succeed as we win the battle against oppression.

People of color fight for justice, though it is a losing battle, because (1) as a survival tactic, they have little choice, and (2) the struggle is not only a response to the faith we claim, but more importantly, it defines our humanity. Maybe our praxis might move the needle toward a reprieve, allowing social justice to thrive for a season. However, writing on the same unjust policies and oppressive structures for the past twenty-five-plus years has demonstrated that, regardless of how one measures progress, little if any has occurred. In fact, the poor have gotten poorer and communities of color face greater discrimination and repression as this third edition goes to press than when I began writing that first edition.

Hopelessness is the realization that all is lost. As long as the marginalized believe they have something to lose, most will police themselves, avoiding engagement in liberative praxis. *Arbeit macht frei*—work makes you free—hung over the entrance to Auschwitz. This particular lie, that work would set you free, fostered enough hope to restrain rebellion among the condemned who passed through these gates and toward the showers. Hope is among the strongest feelings that reinforce and strengthen complicity with oppressive structures. But when the marginalized conclude they really have nothing to lose, they become a threat to those seeking to prop up oppression as universal norms. Hopelessness is a desperation propelling the marginalized with nothing to lose toward radical praxis.

Embracing hopelessness leads to the realization that, all too often, implementing praxis that seeks justice changes little as oppressive social structures—determined to protect the unearned profits, privilege, and power of the dominant culture—ensure that any protest or rebellion has minimal effect. As I have written elsewhere, we have evolved into a society that must go to the police department to get a permit from the police department to protest the police department about its police brutality. If the purpose of praxis is to bring about liberative change, then we must move beyond rules and regulations legislated and implemented by the dominant eurocentric nationalist culture.

Protestation has become domesticated, rebellion tamed, resistance defanged, oppression normalized, and the movement monetized. We can carry homemade signs and shout pithy slogans demanding liberation as long as the social equilibrium of society is neither disrupted nor seriously threatened. Better yet, we can simply "like" a social media post while patting ourselves on the back for our self-perceived wokeness. Between sips from the comfort of our favorite coffee shop, we post our moral outrage, making us feel better for doing something even though it changes nothing. But if we dare to challenge the status quo—think of the Black Lives Matter movement—the full force of the police state would be mobilized to silence its voice while the prevailing nationalist Christianity would seek to discredit and demonize the movement.

As with antebellum slaveholders, who hired preachers to teach the enslaved to work harder, to obey, and not to steal, spiritual justification for social structures and policies that support the unearned power, privilege, and profit of the dominant culture are needed. Those who stole Black bodies codified rules and laws against stealing. An ethics *para joder* argues that the enslaved have a moral obligation to steal from the master's chicken coop to feed their families, to work as little as possible to conserve their energy, to disobey, and when possible, to free themselves. Laws reinforcing white supremacy, justified by eurochristian nationalism, are required to be disobeyed and broken if the goal remains salvation and liberation. To that end, a eurocentric Christian nationalism, then and now, seeks to limit any liberative spiritual movement, gaslighting it as antichristian.

Furthermore, those on the margins are excluded from and blamed for their disenfranchisement. This, of course, is not a new phenomenon. The United States prides itself as a democracy where anyone can grasp the so-called American Dream—a dream made "great" through stolen land, stolen labor, and stolen resources from all who fell short of whiteness. The residue of these historical acts remains visible to this day in the form of structural racism and institutionalized ethnic discrimination. Communities of color contribute to the colonization of their minds by accepting their exclusion as normative and legitimate. Salvation, understood as liberation from social and structural sins, requires disobeying laws and legislation enacted by a government of euroamericans, by euroamericans, for euroamericans.

Unfortunately, those residing on the underside of a eurocentric Christian nationalism suffer from a Stockholm syndrome, attempting to be as white and as Christian as eurochristians. If minds can be colonized, then bodies can be controlled. The search is always on for a face of color with a white voice willing to be placed on a pedestal to defend eurochristian nationalism and proselytize the disenfranchised. Their support of the white establishment, contributing to the colonization of the minds of those sharing their skin pigmentation, ethnicity, or language, is rewarded with fame and fortune. The salvation they preach can only be found in a white god who gave us a white Jesus to establish a white church with a white liturgy so all can be saved through assimilation to whiteness. A way of being and believing is established where occupied minds conjure the illusion of liberated bodies. A faith that justifies privileging euroamericans as God's will and legitimizes power in their hands as God's design shackles the mind.

Each new generation born to a eurocentric worldview is taught, since childhood, to see and interpret reality through the eyes of those who benefit from how society is structured. They even learn to see and define themselves by how euroamericans define them—through a gaze that has and continues to justify their rape, theft, and enslavement. The eurochristian nationalism morally and spiritually normalizes keeping hungry, thirsty, and naked those falling short of whiteness. Success is achieved when those on the margins regurgitate a worldview, consciously or unconsciously, that expounds eurocentric theological, philosophical, or theoretical paradigms. The decolonization process starts with the full and total rejection of eurochristian nationalist religion. Decolonization of our minds means learning to think our own thoughts from the margins, rooted in our own cultures, apart from eurocentrism. To serve and love eurochristianity or their white god and Jesus, created to spiritually maintain margins, means despising the religious and philosophical wisdom embedded in minoritized communities.

Honestly, can anything be done to address, let alone solve, the issues and concerns raised in this book? Quick and easy solutions may seem to soothe one's conscience, but they are no substitute for bringing about a more just social structure, one not based on creating marginalized spaces. What, then, is the praxis to be implemented? How is this liberative praxis formed?

For several years I have called for an ethics *para joder*. *Joder* is a Spanish verb never to be used in polite company, literally translated as a certain four-letter word beginning with the letter *f* and ending with *k*. To *joder* is a vulgar way of saying, "to screw with." The word connotes an individual who is always purposely causing trouble, who is a pain in the rear end, disrupting the established norm by refusing to stay in their assigned place—a trickster. Before the vastness of structural racism and institutionalized violence, before global neoliberalism and domestic racism, resistance is futile. Liberation for those on the margins is indeed hopeless. Few alternatives exist capable of establishing justice. The only option left for those who occupy the space of Holy Saturday, where few if any options exist, is an ethics *para joder*, an ethics that screws with the prevailing power structures.

Overt rebellion that threatens white affirmative action often leads to death—symbolically, physically, or both. How, then, to be wise as serpents but gentle as doves? If the purpose of law and order is to maintain oppressive structures, then subversion provides opportunities for new strategies to arise. While eurochristians deem maintaining law and order as ethical, those on their margins understand it as oppressive. An ethics *para joder* recalls a table-turning Jesus and refuses to obey and follow the rules created by those who benefit from the rules—rules that currently provide space for orderly dissent that pacifies the need to vent for the marginalized but is designed to change nothing. When the disenfranchised start to *joder*, instability of what has been normalized occurs, allowing opportunities to arise. When marginalized communities begin to *joder*, prevailing power structures are endangered. To *joder* is a subversive praxis, refusing to play by the rules established by those maintaining a social order that protects their privilege, power, and profit. If liberation means bringing forth a just society, then it implies that the current one that is unjust must be overthrown. No choice exists but to move beyond laws and rules established to maintain the current system.

An ethics *para joder* is not some new intellectual concept conjured in my ivory tower, but has been a trickster-based praxis employed by those on the margins for centuries. It appears in the roles of coyote and the spider within the Indigenous community, Br'er Rabbit within the African American community, Cantinflas within the Mexican community, or Elegúa within my own Cuban community. They are all tricksters who, through lies, humor, and tomfoolery, unmasked the hypocrisies of the dominating oppressors. I argue that to do ethics from the margins should consider how to ethically lie to discover truth and morally steal to feed the hungry.

Bibliography

Acevedo-Garcia, Dolores, et al. 2008. *Unequal Health Outcomes in the United States: Racial and Ethnic Disparities in Health Care Treatment and Access, the Role of Social and Environmental Determinants of Health, and the Responsibility of the State.* New York: United Nations.

Ahmed, Nabil, Anna Marriott, Nafkote Dabi, Megan Lowthers, Max Lawson, Leah Mugehera. 2022. *Inequality Kills: The Unparalleled Action Needed to Combat Unprecedented Inequality in the Wake of COVID-19.* Oxford: Oxfam International.

American Cancer Society. 2019. *Breast Cancer Facts & Figures 2019–2020.* Atlanta: American Cancer Society.

Amnesty International. 2003. *Death Penalty and Race.* London: Amnesty International.

———. 2017. *United States of America: Death by Discrimination—The Continuing Role of Race in Capital Cases.* London: Amnesty International.

Anderson, Sarah, Chuck Collins, Scott Klinger, and Sam Pizzigati. 2001. *Executive Excess 2001: Layoffs—Tax Rebates—The Gender Gap.* Washington, DC: Institute for Policy Studies and United for a Fair Economy.

———. 2011. *Executive Excess 2011: The Massive CEO Rewards for Tax Dodging.* Washington, DC: Institute for Policy Studies.

Anderson, Sarah, and Sam Pizzigati. 2022. *Executive Excess 2022: The CEOs at America's Largest Low-Wage Employers Are Grabbing Huge Raises While Workers and Consumers Are Struggling with Rising Costs.* Washington, DC: Institute for Policy Studies.

Andrulis, Dennis P., et al. 2019. *America's Health Ranking Annual Report, 2019.* Minnetonka, MN: United Health Foundation.

Annesi, Charles A., et al. 2022. "The Impact of Residential Racial Segregation on Non-Small Cell Lung Cancer Treatment and Outcomes." *Annals of Thoracic Surgery* 113, no. 4 (April 1): 1291–98.

Aquino, María Pilar. 1999. "Theological Method in U.S. Latino/a Theology: Toward an Intercultural Theology for the Third Millennium." In *From the Heart of Our People: Latino/a Explorations in Catholic Systematic Theology,* ed. Orlando O. Espín and Miguel H. Díaz. Maryknoll, NY: Orbis Books.

Arcidiacono, Peter, Josh Kinsler, and Tyler Ransom. 2019. "Legacy and Athlete Preferences at Harvard." National Bureau of Economic Research Working Paper No. 26316 (September): 1–71.

Arias, Elizabeth, Betzaida Tejada-Vera, Farida Ahmad, and Kenneth D. Kochanek, 2021. "Provisional Life Expectancy Estimates for 2020." *Vital Statistics Rapid Release Report No. 015.* Washington, DC: US Department of Health and Human Services.

Augustine. 1960 [426]. *The City of God against the Pagans, Vol. 6.* Edited by T. E. Page et al. Translated by William Chase Greene. Cambridge, MA: Harvard University Press.

Aurand, Andrew, Dan Emmanuel, Ikra Rafi, Dan Threet, and Diane Yentel. 2021. *Out of Reach 2012: America's Forgotten Housing Crises.* Washington, DC: National Low Income Housing Coalition.

Baker-Fletcher, Karen. 1998. *Sisters of Dust, Sisters of Spirit: Womanist Wordings on God and Creation.* Minneapolis: Fortress Press.

———. 2004. "Spirituality." In *Handbook of U.S. Theologies of Liberation*, ed. Miguel A. De La Torre. St. Louis: Chalice Press.

Barlett, Donald L., and James B. Steele. 2012. *The Betrayal of the American Dream.* New York: Public Affairs.

Barth, Karl. 1928. *The Word of God and the Word of Man.* Trans. by Douglas Horton. Philadelphia: Pilgrim Press.

Bearak, Jonathan, et al. 2020. "Unintended Pregnancy and Abortion by Income, Region, and the Legal Status of Abortion: Estimates from a Comprehensive Model for 1990–2019." *Lancet Global Health* 8, no. 9 (September 1): e1152–61.

Bekkar, Bruce, Susan Pacheco, Rupa Basu, and Nathaniel DeNicola. 2020. "Association of Air Pollution and Heat Exposure with Preterm Birth, Low Birth Weight, and Stillbirth in the US." *Journal of the American Medical Association* 3, no. 6 (June 18): 1–13.

Benedek, Wolfgang, Veronika Bílková, and Marco Sassòli. 2022. *Report on Violations of International Humanitarian and Human Rights Law, War Crimes, and Crimes against Humanity Committed in Ukraine since 24 February 2022.* Vienna: Organization for Security and Co-operation in Europe: Office for Democratic Institutions and Human Rights.

Bhabha, Homi K. 1994. *The Location of Culture.* New York: Routledge.

Bhutta, Neil, Andrew C. Chang, Lisa J. Dettling, and Joanne W. Hsu. 2020. "Disparities in Wealth by Race and Ethnicity in the 2019 Survey of Consumer Finances." *FEDS Notes.* Washington, DC: Board of Governors of the Federal Reserve System. https://doi.org/10.17016/2380-7172.2797.

Bixler, Danae, et al. 2020. "SARS-CoV-2-Associated Deaths among Persons Aged <21 Years—United States, February 12–July 31, 2020." US Department of Health and Human Services: Centers for Disease Control and Prevention, *Morbidity and Mortality Weekly Report* 69, no. 37 (September 18): 1324–29.

Blank, Rebecca M. 2008. "Presidential Address: How to Improve Poverty Measurement in the United States." *Journal of Policy Analysis and Management* 27, no. 2: 233–54.

Bleemer, Zachary. 2020. "Affirmative Action, Mismatch, and Economic Mobility after California's Proposition 209." Berkeley Center for Studies in Higher Education (August): 1–30.

Blount, Brian K. 2001. *Then the Whisper Put on Flesh: New Testament Ethics in an African American Context.* Nashville: Abingdon Press.

Boff, Clodovis. 1987. *Theology and Praxis: Epistemological Foundations.* Translated by Robert R. Barr. Maryknoll, NY: Orbis Books.

Boff, Clodovis, and George V. Pixley. 1989. *The Bible, the Church, and the Poor.* Translated by Paul Burns. Maryknoll, NY: Orbis Books.

Boff, Leonardo. 1997. *Cry of the Earth, Cry of the Poor.* Translated by Phillip Berryman. Maryknoll, NY: Orbis Books.

Boff, Leonardo, and Clodovis Boff. 1988 [1984]. *Salvation and Liberation: In Search of a Balance between Faith and Politics.* Translated by Robert R. Barr. Maryknoll, NY: Orbis Books,

Bogusz, Christine, et al., eds. 2010. *The Budget and Economic Outlook: Fiscal Years 2010–2020.* Washington, DC: Congressional Budget Office.

Bonino, José Míguez. 1983. *Toward a Christian Political Ethics.* Philadelphia: Fortress Press.

Bourdieu, Pierre. 1977 [1972]. *Outline of a Theory of Practice.* Translated by Richard Nice. Cambridge: Cambridge University Press.

Breiding, Matthew J., Kathleen C. Basile, Sharon G. Smith, Michele C. Black, and Reshma Mahendra. 2015. *Intimate Partner Violence Surveillance: Uniform Definitions and Recommended Data Elements.* Atlanta: Centers for Disease Control and Prevention.

Brubaker, Rogers. 1985. "Rethinking Classical Theory: The Sociological Vision of Pierre Bourdieu." *Theory and Society* 14: 745–75.

Brunner, Emil. 1947. *The Divine Imperative.* Translated by Olive Wyon. Philadelphia: Westminster Press.

Bullard, Robert D. 1993. "Anatomy of Environmental Racism." In *Toxic Struggles: The Theory and Practice of Environmental Justice*, ed. Richard Hofrichter. Philadelphia: New Society.

Butler, Smedley D. 1935. *War Is a Racket: The Antiwar Classic by America's Most Decorated Soldier.* Los Angeles: Feral House.

Calvin, John. 1873 [1536]. *The Institutes of the Christian Religion, Vols. I and II.* Translated by Henry Beveridge. Edinburgh: T&T Clark.

Candal, Cara. 2018. *The Case for Education Transformation: Part 1, The Disappointing Reality of American Education.* Washington, DC: Center for Education Reform.

Cannon, Katie. 1988. *Black Womanist Ethics.* Atlanta: Scholars Press.

———. 1995. *Katie's Canon: Womanism and the Soul of the Black Community.* New York: Continuum.

———. 2001. *The Womanist Theology Primer: Remembering What We Never Knew: The Epistemology of Womanist Theology.* Louisville, KY: Women's Ministries Program Area, National Ministries Division, Presbyterian Church.

Carnevale, Anthony P., Martin Van Der Werf, Michael C. Quinn, Jeff Stohl, and Dmitri Repnikov. 2018. *Our Separate & Unequal Public Colleges: How Public Colleges Reinforce White Racial Privilege and Marginalize Black and Latino Students.* Washington, DC: Georgetown University Center on Education and the Workforce.

Carson, E. Ann. 2021. *Prisoners in 2020—Statistical Tables*. Washington, DC: Bureau of Justice Statistics, US Department of Justice.

Carver, Melanie, and Hannah Jaffee. 2020. *2020 Asthma Disparities in America: A Roadmap to Reducing Burden on Racial and Ethnic Minorities*. Arlington, VA: Asthma and Allergy Foundation of America.

Catherine of Siena. 1980 [1388]. *The Dialogue*. Translated by Suzanne Noffke. New York: Paulist Press.

CELAM. 1968. *La iglesia en la actual transformacion de america latina a la luz del concilio— II: Conclusiones, tercera edición*. Bogotá: Secretariado General del CELAM.

Chan, Jenny, Mark Selden, and Pun Ngai. 2020. *Dying for an iPhone: Apple, Foxconn, and the Lives of China's Workers*. Chicago: Haymarket Books.

Chen, M. Keith, Kareem Haggag, Devin G. Pope, and Ryne Rohla. 2019. "Racial Disparities in Voting Waiting Times: Evidence from Smartphone Data." National Bureau of Economic Research Working Paper Series. Cambridge, MA: National Bureau of Economic Research.

Chisholm-Burns, Marie A., et al. 2017. "Evaluation of Racial and Socioeconomic Disparities in Medication Pricing and Pharmacy Access and Services." *American Journal of Health-System Pharmacy* 74, no. 10 (May 15): 653–68.

Clark, Helen, et al. 2020. "A Future for the World's Children? A WHO-UNICEF-Lancet Commission." *The Lancet Commissions* 395 (February 22): 605–58.

Cobb, John B., Jr. 1998. "Liberation Theology and the Global Economy." In *Liberating the Future: God, Mammon and Theology*, ed. Joerg Rieger. Minneapolis: Fortress Press.

Conceição, Pedro, et al. 2019. *Human Development Report 2019: Tackling Social Norms—A Game Changer for Gender Inequalities*. New York: United Nations Development Programme.

Conceição, Pedro. 2020. *Human Development Report 2020: The Next Frontier—Human Development and the Anthropocene*. New York: United Nations Development Programme.

Cone, James H. 1969. *Black Theology and Black Power*. New York: Seabury Press.

———. 1975. *God of the Oppressed*. New York: Seabury Press.

———. 1999a [1979]. *A Black Theology of Liberation, 20th Anniversary Edition*. Maryknoll, NY: Orbis Books.

———. 1999b. *Speaking the Truth: Ecumenism, Liberation, and Black Theology*. Maryknoll, NY: Orbis Books.

Cooper, Mary H. 1998. "Income Inequality." *Congressional Quarterly Researcher* 8, no. 15 (April 17): 339–59.

Crawford, Neta C. 2021. "The U.S. Budgetary Costs of the Post-9/11 Wars." In *20 Years of War: A Costs of War Research Serie*s (September 1), 1–24. Boston: Watson Institute and Boston University.

Dalaba, Maxwell Ayindenaba, Paul Welaga, Abraham Oduro, Laata Latif Danchaka, and Chieko Matsubara. 2018. "Cost of Malaria Treatment and Health Seeking Behaviour of Children under Five in the Upper West Region of Ghana." *PLOS ONE* 13, no. 4: 1–14.

Dalton, Frederick John. 2003. *The Moral Vision of César Chávez*. Maryknoll, NY: Orbis Books.

Daly, Mary. 1973. *Beyond God the Father: Toward a Philosophy of Women's Liberation*. Boston: Beacon.

Dehon, Erin, Nicole Weiss, Jonathan Jones, Whitney Faulconer, Elizabeth Hinton, and Sarah Sterling. 2017. "A Systematic Review of the Impact of Physician Implicit Racial Bias on Clinical Decision Making," *Academic Emergency Medicine* 24, no. 8 (August): 895–904.

de la Cruz, Juan. 1987 [1618]. "Ascent of Mount Carmel." In *John of the Cross: Selected Writings*, ed. Kieran Kavanaugh. New York: Paulist Press.

De La Torre, Miguel A. 2003. "The Challenge of Lazarus." *Celebration: An Ecumenical Worship Resource* 31, no. 3 (March): 99–100.

———. 2007. *A Lily among the Thorns: Imagining a New Christian Sexuality*. San Francisco: Jossey-Bass.

———. 2008. *The Hope of Liberation in World Religions*. Waco, TX: Baylor University Press.

———. 2009. *Trails of Hope and Terror: Testimonies on Immigration*. Maryknoll, NY: Orbis Books.

———. 2010. *Latina/o Social Ethics: Moving beyond Eurocentric Moral Thinking*. Waco, TX: Baylor University Press, 2010.

———. 2012. "Mad Men, Competitive Women, and Invisible Hispanics." *Journal of Feminist Studies in Religion* 28, no. 1 (Spring): 113–25.

———. 2017. *Embracing Hopelessness*. Minneapolis: Fortress Press.

———. 2021. *Decolonizing Christianity: Becoming Badass Believers*. Grand Rapids: Wm. B. Eerdmans.

———. 2021. "Water—A Living Spirit." *Gonna Trouble the Water: Ecojustice, Water, and Environmental Racism*, ed. Miguel A. De La Torre. Cleveland: Pilgrim Press.

del Carmen, Alex, Barry Bowling, Caille Gibson, Kimberly Chism, and Tom Petrowski. 2022. "Additional Analysis of State of Texas 2021 Racial Profiling Data." Hispanic Data Analysis Report. College Station, TX: Institute for Predictive Analytics in Criminal Justice.

Deloria, Vine. 1969. *Custer Died for Your Sins: An Indian Manifesto*. New York: Macmillan.

DeNavas-Walt, Carmen, Bernadette D. Proctor, and Jessica C. Smith. 2011. *Income, Poverty, and Health Insurance Coverage in the United States: 2010*. Washington, DC: US Census Bureau.

Dixon, Davis, Ashley Griffin, and Mark Teoh. 2019. *If You Listen, We Will Stay: Why Teachers of Color Leave and How to Disrupt Teacher Turnover*. Washington D.C.: The Education Trust & Teach Plus.

Dube, Arindrajit, T. William Lester, and Barry Eidlin. 2007. *A Downward Push: The Impact of Wal-Mart Stores on Retail Wages and Benefits*. Berkeley, CA: UC Berkeley Labor Center.

Durkheim, Emile. 1933 [1893]. *Division of Labor in Society*. Translated by George Simpson. New York: Macmillan.

Ebert, Franz Christian, Raymond Torres, and Konstantinos Papadakis. 2008. *Executive Compensation: Trends and Policy Issues*. Geneva: International Institute for Labor Studies.

Educational Redlining. 2020. Washington, DC: Student Borrower Protection Center.

Ehrenreich, Barbara, and John Ehrenreich. 1972. "The Professional-Managerial Class." In *Between Labor and Capital*, ed. Pat Walker. Boston: South End Press.

Eisenhower, Dwight D. 1953, April 16. "Chance for Peace." Speech given before the American Society of Newspaper Editors.

English, Devin, Sharon F. Lambert, Brendesha M. Tynes, Lisa Bowleg, Maria Cecilia Sea, and Lionel C. Howard. 2020. "Daily Multidimensional Racial Discrimination Among Black U.S. American Adolescents." *Journal of Applied Developmental Psychology* 66: 1–12.

Epstein, Lee, and Mitu Gulati. 2022, August 3. "A Century of Business in the Supreme Court, 1920–2020." Virginia Public Law and Legal Theory Research Paper No. 2022-55, Virginia Law and Economics Research Paper No. 2022-16. http://dx.doi.org/10.2139/ssrn.4178504.

Espenshade, Thomas J., Chang Y. Chung, and Joan L. Walling. 2004. "Admissions Preferences for Minority Students, Athletes, and Legacies at Elite Universities." *Social Science Quarterly* 85, no. 5 (December): 1422–46.

Fanon, Frantz. 1963. *The Wretched of the Earth*. Translated by Constance Farrington. New York: Grove Press.

Feinstein, Dianne. 2014. *Report of the Senate Select Committee on Intelligence*. Washington, DC: US Senate.

Feith, Douglas. 2008. *War and Decision: Inside the Pentagon at the Dawn of the War on Terrorism*. New York: HarperCollins.

Fieldhouse, Andrew, and Ethan Pollack. 2011. *Tenth Anniversary of the Bush-Era Tax Cuts*. Washington, DC: Economic Policy Institute.

Fischer, Brendan, and Blair Bowie. 2013, January. *Election Confidential: How Shady Operators Used Sham Non-profits and Fake Corporations to Funnel Mystery Money into the 2012 Election*. Boston: Center for Media and Democracy and U.S. Public Interest Research Group.

Fleischman, Lesley, and Marcus Franklin. 2017. *Fumes across the Fence-Line: The Health Impacts of Air Pollution from Oil & Gas Facilities on African American Communities*. Baltimore: National Association for the Advancement of Colored People.

Food and Agriculture Organization of the United Nations (FAO), International Fund for Agricultural Development (IFAD), UNICEF, Word Food Program (WFP), and World Health Organization (WHO). 2021. *The State of Food Security and Nutrition in the World 2021*: *Transforming Food Systems for Food Security, Improved Nutrition and Affordable Healthy Diets for All*. Rome, FAO.

Foucault, Michel. 1965. *Madness and Civilization: A History of Insanity in the Age of Reason*. Translated by Richard Howard. New York: Pantheon Books.

———. 1984. "Truth and Power." In *The Foucault Reader*, ed. Paul Rabinow. New York: Pantheon Books.

————. 1988 [1982]. *Technologies of the Self: A Seminar with Michel Foucault.* Edited by Luther H. Martin, Huck Gitman, and Patrick H. Hutton. Amherst: University of Massachusetts Press.

Fox, Jonathan, and Libby Haight. 2010. "Mexican Agricultural Policy: Multiple Goals and Conflicting Interests." In *Subsidizing Inequality: Mexican Corn Policy Since NAFTA*, ed. Jonathan Fox and Libby Haight. Santa Cruz: Woodrow Wilson International Center for Scholars, University of California.

Freije-Rodriguez, Samuel, and Michael Woolcock. 2020. *Reversals of Fortune: Poverty and Shared Prosperity 2020.* Washington, DC: International Bank for Reconstruction and Development.

Friedlingstein, Pierre. 2020. "Global Carbon Budget 2020." *Earth System Science Data* 12: 3269–3340.

Friedman, Milton. 1962. *Capitalism and Freedom.* Chicago: University of Chicago Press.

Furgerson, Jessica. 2022. *The Battle for Birth Control: Exploring the Lasting Consequences of the Movement's Early Rhetoric.* Lanham, MD: Lexington Press.

Gardner, Matthew, Lorena Roque, and Steve Wamhoff. 2019. *Corporate Tax Avoidance: In the First Year of the Trump Tax Law.* Washington, DC: Institute on Taxation and Economic Policy.

Gardner, Matthew, and Steve Wamhoff. 2021, April. "55 Corporations Paid $0 in Federal Taxes on 2020 Profits," Report from Institute on Taxation and Economic Policy: 1–8.

Garita, Alexandra. 2016. "Reclaiming Gender and Economic Justice in the Era of Corporate Takeover." In *The Palgrave Handbook of Gender and Development*, ed. Wendy Harcourt. New York: Palgrave Macmillan.

George, Susan. 1987. *Food Strategies for Tomorrow.* San Francisco: Hunger Project.

————. 1999. "A Short History of Neoliberalism." Paper presented at the Conference on Economic Sovereignty in a Globalizing World. Bangkok, Thailand, March 24–26.

George, Susan, and Fabrizio Sabelli. 1994. *Faith and Credit: The World Bank's Secular Empire.* Boulder, CO: Westview Press.

Gibbons, Jonathan, ed. 2021. "Killing of Woman and Girls by their Intimate Partners or Other Family Members: Global Estimates 2020." *Data Matters 3.* New York: United Nations Office on Drugs and Crimes.

Gilligan, Carol. 1982. *In a Different Voice: Psychological Theory and Woman's Development.* Cambridge, MA: Harvard University Press.

Gnanadason, Aruna. 1996. "Toward a Feminist Eco-Theology for India." In *Women Healing Earth: Third-World Women on Ecology, Feminism, and Religion*, ed. Rosemary Radford Ruether. Maryknoll, NY: Orbis Books.

Golden, Daniel. 2006. *The Price of Admission: How America's Ruling Class Buys Its Way into Elite Colleges—And Who Gets Left outside the Gates.* New York: Random House.

González, Justo. 1990. *Mañana: Christian Theology from a Hispanic Perspective.* Nashville: Abingdon Press.

Griffiths, Brian. 2003. "The Challenge of Global Capitalism: A Christian Perspective." In *Making Globalization Good: Moral Challenges of Global Capitalism*, ed. John H. Dunning. Oxford: Oxford University Press.

Grineski, Sara E., and Timothy W. Collins. 2018. "Geographic and Social Disparities in Exposure to Air Neurotoxicants at U.S. Public Schools." *Environmental Research* 161 (February): 580–87.

Groenewald, Cornelius B., Jennifer A. Rabbitts, Elizabeth Hansen, and Tonya M. Palermo. 2018. "Racial Differences in Opioid Prescribing for Children in the United States." *Journal of Pain* 159, no. 10 (October): 2050–57.

Grosz, Elizabeth. 1990. *Jacques Lacan: A Feminist Interpretation.* London: Routledge.

Guiahi, Maryam, Patricia E. Helbin, Stephanie B. Teal, Debra Stulberg, and Jeanelle Sheeder, 2019. "Patient Views on Religious Institutional Health Care." *JAMA* 2, no. 12 (2019): e1–e11.

Gustafson, James M. 1968. *Christ and the Moral Life.* New York: Harper & Row.

———. 1974. *Theology and Christian Ethics.* Philadelphia: Pilgrim Press.

———. 1975. *Can Ethics Be Christian?* Chicago: University of Chicago Press.

Gustafson, James M., and James Laney, eds. 1968. *On Being Responsible: Issues in Personal Ethics.* New York: Harper & Row.

Gutiérrez, Gustavo. 1984 [1979]. *The Power of the Poor in History.* Translated by Robert R. Barr. Maryknoll, NY: Orbis Books.

———. 1988 [1973]. *A Theology of Liberation, 15th Anniversary Edition.* Translated and edited by Sister Caridad Inda and John Eagleson. Maryknoll, NY: Orbis Books.

Haines, John, and Laurel Staley, eds. 2004. *Risk Management Evaluation for Concentrated Animal Feeding Operations.* Cincinnati, OH: US Environmental Protection Agency, National Risk Management Laboratory.

Hajnal, Zoltan, Nazita Lajevardi, and Lindsay Neilson. 2017. "Voter Identification and the Suppression of Minority Votes." *Journal of Politics* 79, no. 2: 363–64, 372–73.

Hall, William J., et al. 2015. "Implicit Racial/Ethnic Bias Among Health Care Professionals and Its Influence on Health Care Outcomes: A Systematic Review." *American Journal of Public Health* 105, no. 12 (December): 60–76.

Hamilton, Cynthia. 1993. "Environmental Consequences of Urban Growth and Blight." In *Toxic Struggles: The Theory and Practice of Environmental Justice,* ed. Richard Hofrichter. Philadelphia: New Society.

Han, Jeehoon, Bruce D. Meyer, and James X. Sullivan. 2020. *Real-Time Poverty Estimates during the COVID-19 Pandemic through November 2020.* Chicago and South Bend: University of Chicago and the University of Notre Dame.

Hartung, William D. 1994. *And Weapons for All.* New York: HarperCollins.

Hauerwas, Stanley. 1981. *A Community of Character: Toward a Constructive Christian Social Ethics.* Notre Dame: University of Notre Dame Press.

———. 1985. "The Gesture of a Truthful Story." *Theology Today* 42, no. 2: 181–89.

———. 1986. "Some Theological Reflections on Gutierrez's Use of 'Liberation' as a Theological Concept." *Modern Theology* 3, no. 1: 67–76.

———. 1991. *After Christendom? How the Church Is to Behave If Freedom, Justice, and a Christian Nation Are Bad Ideas.* Nashville: Abingdon.

Henderson, Errol Anthony. 1998. "Military Spending and Poverty." *Journal of Politics* 60, no. 2 (May): 503–20.

Heyward, Carter. 2004. "Jesus Christ." In *Handbook of U.S. Theologies of Liberation*, ed. by Miguel A. De La Torre. St. Louis: Chalice Press.

Himmelstein, Gracie, David Bates, and Li Zhou. 2022. "Examination of Stigmatizing Language in the Electronic Health Record." *JAMA Network Open* 5, no. 1: 1–14.

Hinkelammert, Franz J. 1986. *The Ideological Weapon of Death: A Theological Critique*. Translated by Phillip Berryman. Maryknoll, NY: Orbis Books.

———. 1995. *Cultura de la Esperanza y Sociedad sin Exclusión*. San José, Costa Rica: Departamento Ecuménico de Investigaciones.

———. 2001. "Globalization as Cover-Up." In *Globalization and Its Victims*. London: SCM Press.

Hodson, Gordon, John F. Dovidio, and Samuel L. Gaertner. 2009. "The Aversive Form of Racism." In *The Psychology of Prejudice and Discrimination: A Revised and Condensed Edition*, ed. Jean Lau Chin. Santa Barbara, CA: Praeger.

Hoffman, Kelly M., Sophie Tranwalter, Jordan R. Axt, and M. Norman Oliver. 2016. "Racial Bias in Pain Assessment and Treatment Recommendations, and False Beliefs about Biological Differences Between Blacks and Whites." *Proceedings of the National Academy of Sciences* 113, no. 16 (April 19): 4296–301.

Hope, David, and Jlian Limberg. 2020. *The Economic Consequences of Major Tax Cuts for the Rich: Working Paper 55*. London: London School of Economics and Political Science.

Hopkins, Dwight N. 2000. *Shoes That Fit Our Feet: Sources for a Constructive Black Theology*. Maryknoll, NY: Orbis Books.

Hoxby, Caroline M., and Christopher Avery. 2012. "The Missing 'One-Offs': The Hidden Supply of High-Achieving, Low Income Students." Washington, DC: National Bureau of Economic Research.

Huang, Ganlin, and Jonathan London. 2012. "Mapping Cumulative Environmental Effects, Social Vulnerability, and Health in the San Joaquin Valley, California." *American Journal of Public Health* 102, no. 5 (May): 830–32.

Hussar, Bill, Jijun Zhang, Sarah Hein, Ke Wang, Ashley Roberts, Jiashan Cui, Mary Smith, Farrah Bullock Mann, Amy Barmer, and Rita Dilig. 2020. *The Condition of Education 2020—NCES 2020-144*. Washington, DC: US Department of Education, National Center for Education Statistics.

"Improving Occupational Health in China." 2019. *The Lancet* 394 (August 10): 443.

Internal Revenue Service. 2022. *Internal Revenue Service Data Book 2021: Publication 55-B*. Washington, DC: Internal Revenue Service.

Jiang Xing. 2022. "Letter from China." *The Nation* 274, no. 8 (March 4): 23–25.

John Paul II. 1995. *The Gospel of Life*. New York: Random House.

Jones, Rachel K., Elizabeth Witwer, and Jenna Jerman. 2019. *Abortion Incidence and Service Availability in the United States*. New York: Guttmacher Institute.

Katznelson, Ira. 2005. *When Affirmative Action Was White: An Untold History of Racial Inequality in Twentieth-Century America*. New York: W.W. Norton & Company.

Kidwell, Clara Sue, Homer Noley, and George E. Tinker. 2001. *A Native American Theology*. Maryknoll, NY: Orbis Books.

King, Martin Luther, Jr. 1958. *Stride toward Freedom: The Montgomery Story*. New York: Harper.

———. 1963. *Strength to Love*. Philadelphia: Fortress Press.

———. 1964. *Why We Can't Wait?* New York: Mentor Book.

———. 1967. "Beyond Vietnam: A Time to Break Silence." Speech given at Riverside Church. New York, April 4.

———. 1986. "Pilgrimage to Nonviolence." In *A Testament of Hope: The Essential Writings of Martin Luther King Jr*. Edited by James Melvin Washington. New York: HarperCollins.

Koopman, Robert, et al. 2020. *World Trade Statistical Review 2020*. Geneva: World Trade Organization.

Kortsmit, Katherine, Michele G. Mandel, Jennifer A. Reeves, Elizabeth Clark, Pamela Pagano, Antoinette Nguyen, Emily E. Petersen, and Maura K. Whiteman. 2021. *Abortion Surveillance—United States, 2019*. Washington, DC: US Department of Health and Human Services.

Kozol, Jonathan. 1991. *Savage Inequalities: Children in America's Schools*. New York: Crown.

Kruse, Kevin M. 2015. *One Nation under God: How Corporate America Invented Christian America*. New York: Basic Books.

Kwok Pui-lan. 2000. *Introducing Asian Feminist Theology*. Cleveland: Pilgrim Press.

Labor Council for Latin American Advancement (LCLAA) and Public Citizen. 2004. *Another America Is Possible: The Impact of NAFTA on the U.S. Latino Community and Lessons for Future Trade Agreements*. Washington, DC: LCLAA and Public Citizen.

Lacan, Jacques. 1977. *Écrits: A Selection*. Translated by Alan Sheridan. New York: W. W. Norton.

Ladd, Helen F. 2012. "Education and Poverty: Confronting the Evidence." *Journal of Policy Analysis and Management* 31, no. 2: 203–27.

LaDuke, Winona. 1993. "A Society Based on Conquest Cannot Be Sustained: Native Peoples and the Environmental Crises." In *Toxic Struggles: The Theory and Practice of Environmental Justice*, ed. Richard Hofrichter. Philadelphia: New Society Publishers.

Lambert, Frank. 2008. *Religion in American Politics: A Short History*. Princeton, NJ: Princeton University Press.

Lane, Haley M., Rachel Morello-Frosch, Julian D. Marshall, and Joshua S. Apte. 2022. "Historical Redlining Is Associated with Present-Day Air Pollution Disparities in U.S. Cities." *Environmental Science & Technology Letters* 9: 345–50.

Lett, Elle, Emmanuella Ngozi Asabor, Theodore Corbin, and Dowin Boatright. 2021. "Racial Inequity in Fatal US Police Shootings, 2015–2020." *Journal of Epidemiology and Community Health* 75, no. 4 (April): 394–97.

Lindberg, Laura, John Santelli, and Sheila Desai. 2016. "Understanding the Decline in Adolescent Fertility in the United States, 2007–2012." *Journal of Adolescent Health* 59: 577–83.

Liu, Jiawen, Lara P. Clark, Matthew J. Bechle, Anjum Hajat, Sun-Young Kim, Allen L. Robinson, Lianne Sheppard, Adam A. Szpiro, and Julian D. Marshall. 2021. "Disparities in Air Pollution Exposure in the United States by Race/Ethnicity and Income, 1990–2010." *Environmental Health Perspective* 129, no. 12 (December): 1–14.

Locke, John. 1952 [1689]. *The Second Treatise of Government.* Edited by Thomas P. Peardon. Indianapolis: Bobbs-Merrill Educational Publishing.

Long, Mark C., and Nicole A. Bateman. 2020. "Long-Run Changes in Under-representation after Affirmative Action Bans in Public Universities." *Educational Evaluation and Policy Analysis* 42, no. 2 (June): 188–207.

López, Ann Aurelia. 2007. *The Farmworkers' Journal.* Berkeley: University of California Press.

Lundberg, Dielle J., et al. 2022. "Geographic and Temporal Patterns in Covid-19 Mortality by Race and Ethnicity in the United States from March 2020 to February 2022." *medRxiv* (July 21): 1–35.

Luther, Martin. 1967 [1525]. "Admonition to Peace: A Reply to the Twelve Articles of the Peasants in Swabia." *Luther's Works: The Christian in Society III, Vol. 46.* Edited by Robert C. Schultz. Philadelphia: Fortress Press.

Madison, James. 2001 [1787]. "Federalist Paper #10." In *The Federalist by Alexander Hamilton, John Jay, and James Madison,* ed. George W. Carey and James McClellan. Indianapolis: Liberty Fund.

Mahajan, Shiwani, et al. 2021. "Trends in Differences in Health Status and Health Care Access and Affordability by Race and Ethnicity in the United States, 1999–2018." *JAMA* 326, no. 7 (August 17): 637–48.

Malcolm X. 1968 [1964]. "The Leverett House Forum of March 18, 1964." In *The Speeches of Malcolm X at Harvard,* ed. Archie Epps. New York: William Morrow & Company.

Marin, Jennifer R., Jonathan Rodean, Matt Hall, et al. 2021. "Racial and Ethnic Differences in Emergency Department Diagnostic Imaging at US Children's Hospitals, 2016–2019." *JAMA Network Open* 4, no. 1 (January 29): 1–14.

Mateo-Sagasta, Javier, Sara Marjani, and Hugh Turral. 2017. *Water Pollution from Agriculture: A Global Review.* Rome: Food and Agriculture Organization of the United Nations.

Mathur, Vani A., Jennifer A. Richeson, Judith A. Paice, Michael Muzyka, and Joan Y. Chiao. 2014. "Racial Bias in Pain Perception and Response: Experimental Examination of Automatic and Deliberate Processes." *Journal of Pain* 15, no. 5 (May): 476–84.

McCann, Dennis P., and Charles R. Strain. 1985. *Polity and Praxis: A Program for American Practical Theology.* Minneapolis: Winston Press.

McConnell, D. R. 1995. *A Different Gospel: Biblical and Historical Insights into the Word of Faith Movement.* Peabody, MA: Hendrickson.

Mitchem, Stephanie Y. 2002. *Introducing Womanist Theology.* Maryknoll, NY: Orbis Books.

Mizelle, Richard M. 2021. "Diabetes, Race, and Amputations." *The Lancet* 397, no. 10281 (April 3): 1256–57.

Moltmann, Jürgen. 1998. "Political Theology and Theology of Liberation." In *Liberating the Future: God, Mammon, and Theology*, ed. Joerg Rieger. Minneapolis: Fortress Press.

Morgan, Edmund S. 1975. *American Slavery, American Freedom: The Ordeal of Colonial Virginia*. New York: W. W. Norton.

Morgan, Ivy, and Ary Amerikaner. 2018. *Funding Gaps: An Analysis of School Funding Equity across the U.S. and within Each State*. Washington, DC: Education Trust.

Morgan, Rachel E., and Jennifer L. Truman. 2020. *Criminal Victimization, 2019*. NCJ 255113. Washington, DC: US Department of Justice.

Nafiu, Olubukola O., Christian Mpody, Stephani S. Kim, Joshua C. Uffman, and Joseph D. Tobias. 2020. "Race, Postoperative Complications, and Death in Apparently Healthy Children." *Pediatrics* 146, no. 2 (August): 1–8.

Ndulue, Ngozi. 2020. *Enduring Injustice: The Persistence of Racial Discrimination in the U.S. Death Penalty*. Edited by Robert Dunham. Washington, DC: Death Penalty Information Center.

Niebuhr, H. Richard. 1963. *The Responsible Self: An Essay in Christian Moral Philosophy*. New York: Harper & Row.

Niebuhr, Reinhold. 1943. *The Nature and Destiny of Man: Human Destiny, Vol. II*. New York: Charles Scribner.

———. 1960. *Moral Man and Immoral Society: A Study in Ethics and Politics*. New York: Scribner.

No More Deaths. 2011. *A Culture of Cruelty: Abuse and Impunity in Short-Term U.S. Border Patrol Custody*. Tucson, AZ: No More Deaths.

Obermeyer, Ziad, Rebecca Nissan, Michael Stern, Stephanie Eanedd, Emily Joy Bembenneck, and Sendhil Mullainathan. 2021. *Algorithmic Bias Playbook*. Chicago: University of Chicago Center for Applied Artificial Intelligence.

OECD—Social Policy Division—Directorate of Employment, Labour and Social Affairs. 2011. *Child Poverty*. Paris: OECD Family Database.

Orfield, Gary, Erica Frankenberg, Jongyeon Ee, and Jennifer B. Ayscue. 2019. *Harming Our Common Future: America's Segregated Schools 65 Years after Brown*. Los Angeles: Regents of the University of California.

Ortega, Bob. 1998. *In Sam We Trust: The Untold Story of Sam Walton and How Wal-Mart Is Devouring America*. New York: Random House.

Owens, Ann. 2010. "Neighborhoods and Schools as Competing and Reinforcing Contexts for Educational Attainment." *Sociology of Education* 83, no. 4 (October): 287–311.

Parolin, Zachary, Sophie Collyer, and Megan A. Curran. 2022. "Absence of Monthly Child Tax Credit Leads to 3.7 Million More Children in Poverty in January 2022." *Poverty and Social Policy Brief* 6, no. 2 (February 17): 1–5.

Peterson, Dana M., and Catherine L. Mann. 2020. *Closing the Racial Inequality Gaps: The Economic Cost of Black Inequality in the U.S.* Internal Report. Citi Global Perspectives and Solutions.

Pettigrew, Stephen. 2021. "The Downstream Consequences of Long Waits: How Lines at Precinct Depress Future Turnout." *Electoral Studies* 71: 1–17.

Phillips, Kevin. 1990. *The Politics of Rich and Poor: Wealth and the American Electorate in the Reagan Aftermath.* New York: Random House.

Phillips, Richard, Matt Gardner, Alexandria Robins, and Michelle Surka. 2017. *Offshore Shell Game 2017: The Use of Offshore Tax Havens by Fortune 500 Companies.* Washington D.C.: Institute on Taxation and Economic Policy.

Phillips, Scott, and Justin Marceau. 2020. "Whom the State Kills." *Harvard Civil Rights—Civil Liberties Law Review* 55, no. 2 (Summer): 587–654.

Pimentel, David, and Marcia Pimentel. 2003. "Sustainability of Meat-Based and Plant-Based Diets and the Environment." *American Society for Clinical Nutrition* 78, no. 3: 660–63.

Pixley, George V. 1987. *On Exodus: A Liberation Perspective.* Translated by Robert R. Barr. Maryknoll, NY: Orbis Books.

Public Religion Research Institute. 2013. *Survey: Americans Divided between Principle and Practice on Affirmative Action, Divided on DOMA.* Washington, DC: Public Religion Research Institute.

Raboteau, Albert J. 1978. *Slave Religion: The "Invisible Institution" in the Antebellum South.* New York: Oxford University Press.

Ramsey, Paul. 1961. *Christian Ethics and the Sit-In.* New York: Association Press.

Rawls, John. 1971. *A Theory of Justice.* Cambridge, MA: Belknap Press of Harvard University Press.

Rees, Nicholas, Amy Wickham, and Yoonie Choi. 2019. *Silent Suffocation in Africa: Air Pollution Is a Growing Menace, Affecting the Poorest Children the Most.* New York: United Nations Children's Fund.

Reinbold, Brian, and Yi Wen. 2019. "Historical U.S. Trade Deficits." *Economic Synopses* no. 13: 1–2.

Rejón, Francisco Moreno. 1993. "Fundamental Moral Theory in the Theology of Liberation." In *Mysterium Liberationis: Fundamental Concepts of Liberation Theology,* ed. Ignacio Ellacuría and Jon Sobrino. Maryknoll, NY: Orbis Books.

Renzulli, Linda A., and Lorraine Evans. 2005. "School Choice, Charter Schools, and White Flight." *Social Problems* 52, no. 3: 398–418.

Ricoeur, Paul. 1976. *Interpretation Theory: Discourse and the Surplus of Meaning.* Fort Worth: Texas Christian University Press.

Roberts, Mary Louise. 2013. *What Soldiers Do: Sex and the American G.I. in World War II France.* Chicago: University of Chicago Press.

Rollin, Bernie. 2008. "The Ethics of Agriculture: The End of True Husbandry." In *The Future of Animal Farming: Renewing the Ancient Contract,* ed. Marian Stamp Dawkins and Roland Bonney. Oxford: Blackwell, 2008.

Ross, Martha, and Nicole Bateman. 2019. *Meet the Low-Wage Workforce.* Washington, DC: Metropolitan Policy Program at Brookings.

Rousseau, Jean-Jacques. 1964 [1755]. *The First and Second Discourses.* Edited by Roger D. Masters. Translated by Roger D. Masters and Judith R. Masters. New York: St. Martin's Press.

Russell, Roberta, and Bernard Toyler. 2019. *Operations and Supply Chain Management*. Hoboken, NJ: Wiley.

Sanders, Cheryl. 1995. *Empowerment Ethics for a Liberated People: A Path to African American Social Transformation*. Minneapolis: Fortress Press.

Sarkozy, Nicolas. 2010. *Opening Speech by Nicolas Sarkozy at the 40th World Economic Forum*. Davos, Switzerland, January 27.

Sawyer, Pamela J., et al. 2012. "Discrimination and the Stress Response: Psychological and Physiological Consequences of Anticipating Prejudice in Interethnic Interactions." *American Journal of Public Health* 102, no. 5 (May): 1020–26.

Schenck, Anna, et al. 2019. *America's Health Ranking*. Minnetonka, MN: United Health Foundation.

Schmidt, Peter. 2010. "A History of Legacy Preferences and Privilege." In *Affirmative Action for the Rich: Legacy Preference in College Admissions*, ed. Richard D. Kahlenberg. New York: Century Foundation Press.

Schneider, Eric C., Arnav Shah, Michelle M. Doty, Roosa Tikkanen, Katharine Fields, and Reginald D. Williams III. 2021. *Mirror, Mirror 2021: Reflecting Poorly: Health Care in the U.S. Compared to Other High-Income Countries*. New York: Commonwealth Fund.

Seager, Joni. 1993. "Creating a Culture of Destruction: Gender, Militarism, and the Environment." In *Toxic Struggles: The Theory and Practice of Environmental Justice*, ed. Richard Hofrichter. Philadelphia: New Society Publishers.

Segundo, Juan Luis. 1993. "Conversion and Reconciliation in the Perspective of Modern Liberation Theology." In *Signs of the Times: Theological Reflections*, trans. Robert R. Barr. Maryknoll, NY: Orbis Books.

Semega, Jessica, Melissa Kollar, Emily A. Shrider, and John F. Creamer. *Income, Poverty, and Health Insurance Coverage in the United States: 2019* (Washington, DC: US Census Bureau, 2020).

Shiva, Vandana. 1996. "Let Us Survive: Women, Ecology and Development." In *Women Healing Earth: Third World Women on Ecology, Feminism, and Religion*, ed. Rosemary Radford Ruether. Maryknoll, NY: Orbis Books.

Shute, Sara. 1981. "Sexist Language and Sexism." In *Sexist Language: A Modern Philosophical Analysis*, edited by Mary Vetterling-Braggin, 23–33. Totowa, NJ: Littlefield, Adams.

Singh, Amrit. 2013. *Globalizing Torture: CIA Secret Detention and Extraordinary Rendition*. New York: Open Society Foundation.

Skrepnek, Grant H., Joseph L. Mills Sr., and David G. Armstrong. 2015. "A Diabetic Emergency One Million Feet Long: Disparities and Burdens of Illness among Diabetic Foot Ulcer Cases within Emergency Departments in the United States, 2006–2010." *PLOS ONE* 10, no. 8 (August 6): 1–15.

Smith, Adam. 1976 [1776]. *An Inquiry into the Nature and Causes of the Wealth of Nations, Vol. I*. Edited by R. H. Campbell, A. S. Skinner, and W. B. Todd. Oxford: Clarendon Press.

Smith, Sharon G., Xinjian Zhang, Kathleen C. Basile, Melissa T. Merrick, Jing Wang, Marcie-jo Kresnow, and Jieru Chen. 2018. *The National Intimate Partner and Sexual Violence Survey: 2015 Data Brief—Updated Release.* Atlanta: Centers for Disease Control and Prevention.

Sobrino, Jon. 1978. *Christology at the Crossroads: A Latin American Approach.* Translated by John Drury. Maryknoll, NY: Orbis Books.

———. 1993. *Jesus the Liberator: A Historical-Theological Reading of Jesus of Nazareth.* Translated by P. Burns and F. McDonagh. Maryknoll, NY: Orbis Books.

Splan, Eric D., and Chad E. Forbes. 2022. "Fight or Flight: The Role of Context on Biased Intergroup Shooting Behaviors." *Journal of Experimental Psychology: General* 151, no. 2: 437–54.

Steinfeld, Henning, et al. 2006. *Livestock's Long Shadow: Environmental Issues and Options.* Rome: Food and Agriculture Organization of the United Nations.

Suh, Joo Yeoun, Jennifer Clark, and Jeff Hayes. 2018. "Basic Economic Security in the United States: How Much Income Do Working Adults Need in Each State?" Institute for Women's Policy Research Fact Sheet (October): 1–8.

Suitt, Thomas Howard. 2021. "High Suicide Rates among United States Service Members and Veterans of the Post-9/11 Wars." *20 Years of War: A Costs of War Research Series.* Boston: Watson Institute and Boston University (June 21): 1–35.

Sun, Michael, Tomasz Oliwa, Monica E. Peek, and Elizabeth L. Tung. 2022. "Negative Patient Descriptors: Documenting Racial Bias in the Electronic Health Record." *Health Affairs* 41, no. 2: 203–11.

Taub, Jennifer. 2020. *Big Dirty Money: Making White-Collar Criminals Pay.* New York: Penguin.

Taylor, Mark Lewis. 2001. *The Executed God: The Way of the Cross in Lockdown America.* Minneapolis: Fortress Press.

Tessum, Christopher W., et al. 2019. "Inequity in Consumption of Goods and Services Adds to Racial-Ethnic Disparities in Air Pollution Exposure." *Proceedings of the National Academy of Sciences of the United States* 116, no. 13 (March 26): 6001–6.

———. 2021. "$PM_{2.5}$ Polluters Disproportionately and Systemically Affect People of Color in the United States." *Science Advances* 7, no. 18 (April 28): 1–6.

Thandeka. 1999. *Learning to Be White: Money, Race, and God in America.* New York: Continuum.

Tillich, Paul. 1959. *Theology of Culture.* Oxford: Oxford University Press.

Tinker, George. 1994. "Spirituality, Native American Personhood, Sovereignty and Solidarity." In *Spirituality of the Third World: A Cry for Life,* ed. K. C. Abraham and B. Mbuy-Beya. Maryknoll, NY: Orbis Books.

———. "John Locke on Property." 2011. In *Beyond the Pale: Reading Ethics from the Margins,* edited by Stacey M. Floyd-Thomas and Miguel A. De La Torre, 49–60. Louisville: Westminster John Knox.

Towery, Britt. 2008. "Torture and We're Number 1?" *Christian Ethics Today: Journal of Christian Ethics* 71, no. 4 (Fall): 19–20.

Townes, Emilie. 1995. *In a Blaze of Glory: Womanist Spirituality as Social Witness*. Nashville: Abingdon Press.

Trimiew, Darryl M. 1993. *Voices of the Silenced: The Responsible Self in a Marginalized Community*. Cleveland: Pilgrim Press.

———. 2004. "Ethics." In *Handbook of U.S. Theologies of Liberation*, ed. Miguel A. De La Torre. St. Louis: Chalice Press.

Tucker, Jasmine. 2021. *The Wage Gap Has Robbed Women of Their Ability to Weather COVID-19*. Washington, DC: National Woman's Law Center.

Tutu, Desmond. 1991. "South Africa's Blacks: Aliens in Their Own Land." In *Ethics in the Present Tense: Readings from Christianity and Crisis 1966–1991*, ed. Leon Howell and Vivian Lindermayer. New York: Friendship Press.

UNICEF. 2022. *UNICEF 2021 Annual Report to the U.S. Department of State: Eliminating Female Genital Mutilation*. New York: United Nations Children's Fund.

United Nations Department of Public Information. 2013. *Sexual Violence: A Tool of War*. New York: Outreach Programme on the Rwanda Genocide and the United Nations.

United Nations Development Programme and the Oxford Poverty & Human Development Initiative. 2020. *Global Multidimensional Poverty Index 2020: Charting Pathways out of Multidimensional Poverty, Achieving the SDGs*. New York: United Nations Development Programme.

United Way ALICE Project. 2020. *On Uneven Ground: ALICE and Financial Hardship in the U.S.: 2020 National Report*. Cedar Knolls, NJ: United Way of Northern New Jersey.

US Department of Defense. 2012. Department of Defense Annual Report on Sexual Assault in the Military: Fiscal Year 2012. Washington, DC: Department of Defense.

US Department of Education. 2020. "Race and Ethnicity of Public School Teachers and Their Students." Washington, DC: Institute of Educational Sciences.

US Department of Health and Human Services. 2022. "Annual Update of the HHS Poverty Guidelines." *Federal Register* 87, no. 14 (January 21): 3315–16.

US Department of the Treasury. 2019. *Financial Report of the United States Government FY18*. Washington, DC: US Department of the Treasury.

US Energy Information Administration. 2011. *Rising Asian Demand Drives Global Coal Consumption Growth*. Washington, DC: US Energy Information Administration.

———. 2020. *Country Analysis Executive Summary: China*. Washington, DC: US Energy Information Administration.

US House of Representatives. 2021. *Baby Foods Are Tainted with Dangerous Levels of Arsenic, Lead, Cadmium, and Mercury*. Washington, DC: Subcommittee on Economic and Consumer Policy Committee on Oversight and Reform.

Veblen, Thorstein. 1953. *The Theory of the Leisure Class*. New York: New American Library.

Violence Policy Center. 2019. *When Men Murder Women*. Washington, DC: Violence Policy Center.

Von Rad, Gerhard. 1962. *Old Testament Theology: A Theology of Israel's Historical Traditions, Vol. I.* Translated by D. M. G. Stalker. New York: Harper & Row.

Vyas, Darshali A., Leo G. Eisenstein, and David S. Jones. 2020. "Hidden in Plain Sight—Reconsidering the Use of Race Correction in Clinical Algorithms." *New England Journal of Medicine* 383, no. 9 (August 27): 874–82.

Walker, Alice. 1981. *Living by the Word.* San Diego: Harcourt Brace & Company.

Wallace, Maeve E., Donna Hoyert, Corrine Williams, and Pauline Mendola. 2016. "Pregnancy-Associated Homicide and Suicide in 37 US States with Enhanced Pregnancy Surveillance." *American Journal of Obstetrics and Gynecology* 215, no. 3 (September): 364 e1–e10.

Warren, Karen. 1987. "Feminism and Ecology: Making Connections." *Environmental Ethics* 9 (Spring): 3–20.

Warrior, Robert. 1989. "Canaanites, Cowboys and Indians: Deliverance, Conquest, and Liberation Theology Today." *Christianity and Crisis* 49: 261–65.

Waytz, Adam, Kelly Marie Hoffman, and Sophie Trawalter. 2014. "A Superhumanization in Whites' Perceptions of Blacks." *Social Psychological and Personality Science* (October 8): 1–8.

West, Cornel. 2009. *Brother West: Living and Loving Out Loud.* Carson, CA: Smiley-Books.

Wezeman, Siemon T., and Aude Fleurant. 2018. "Military Spending and Armaments, 2018." In *SIPRI Yearbook 2019: Armaments, Disarmament and International Security.* Solna, Sweden: Oxford University Press.

Wheaton, Laura, and Danielle Kwon. 2022. "Effect of the Reevaluated Thrifty Food Plan and Emergency Allotments on Supplemental Nutrition Assistance Program Benefits and Poverty." Urban Institute (August): 1–27.

Wiehe, Meg, Emanuel Nieves, Jeremie Greer, and David Newville. 2018. "Race, Wealth, and Taxes: How the Tax Cuts and Jobs Act Supercharges the Racial Wealth Divide." Institute on Taxation and Economic Policy (October): 1–12.

Williams, Delores S. 1991. "Black Women's Surrogacy Experience and the Christian Notion of Redemption." In *After Patriarchy: Feminist Transformation of World Religions,* ed. Paula M. Cooey et al. Maryknoll, NY: Orbis Books.

———. 1993. *Sisters in the Wilderness: The Challenge of Womanist God-Talk.* Maryknoll, NY: Orbis Books.

Wilson, William Julius. 1987. *The Truly Disadvantaged: The Inner City, the Underclass, and Public Policy.* Chicago: University of Chicago Press.

———. 1999. *The Bridge over the Racial Divide: Rising Inequality and Coalition Politics.* Berkeley: University of California Press.

Winant, Howard. 2004. *The New Politics of Race: Globalism, Difference, Justice.* Minneapolis: University of Minnesota Press.

Wolfensohn, James D. 2001. *The Challenge of Globalization: The Role of the World Bank.* Speech given to the Bundestag at Berlin, Germany. April 2.

Woodson, Carter G. 2006. *The Mis-Education of the Negro.* San Diego, CA: Book Tree.

World Health Organization (WHO). 2021. *Violence Against Women Prevalence Estimates, 2018: Global, Regional and National Prevalence Estimates for Intimate Partner Violence Against Women and Global and Regional Prevalence Estimates for Non-Partner Sexual Violence Against Women.* Geneva: World Health Organization.

Wright, Erik Olin. 1985. *Classes.* London: Verso.

Xiao Wu, et al. 2020. *Exposure to Air Pollution and COVID-19 Mortality in the United States: A Nationwide Cross-Section Study.* Boston: Harvard Department of Biostatistics, Chan School of Public Health.

Yang, Seung A. 2004. "Asian-American." In *Handbook on U.S. Theologies of Liberation,* ed. Miguel A. De La Torre. St. Louis: Chalice Press.

Yang, Y. Tony, Brian Chen, and Charles L. Bennett. 2018. "Offshore Pharmaceutical Trails: Evidence, Economics, and Ethics." *Mayo Clinic Proceedings: Innovations, Quality & Outcomes* 2, no. 3 (September): 226–28.

Yildirmaz, Ahu, Christopher Ryan, and Jeff Nezaj. 2019. *2019 State of the Workforce Report: Pay, Promotion, and Retention.* Roseland, NJ: ADP Research Institute.

Yip, Fuyuen Y., Jeffrey N. Pearcy, Paul L. Garbe, and Benedict I. Truman. 2011. "Unhealthy Air Quality—United States, 2006–2009." In *CDC Health Disparities and Inequalities Report—United States, 2011.* Atlanta: Centers for Disease Control and Prevention.

Zahnd, Whitney E., et al. 2019. "Spatial Accessibility to Mammography Services in the Lower Mississippi Delta Region States." *Journal of Rural Health* 35, no. 4: 550–59.

Index